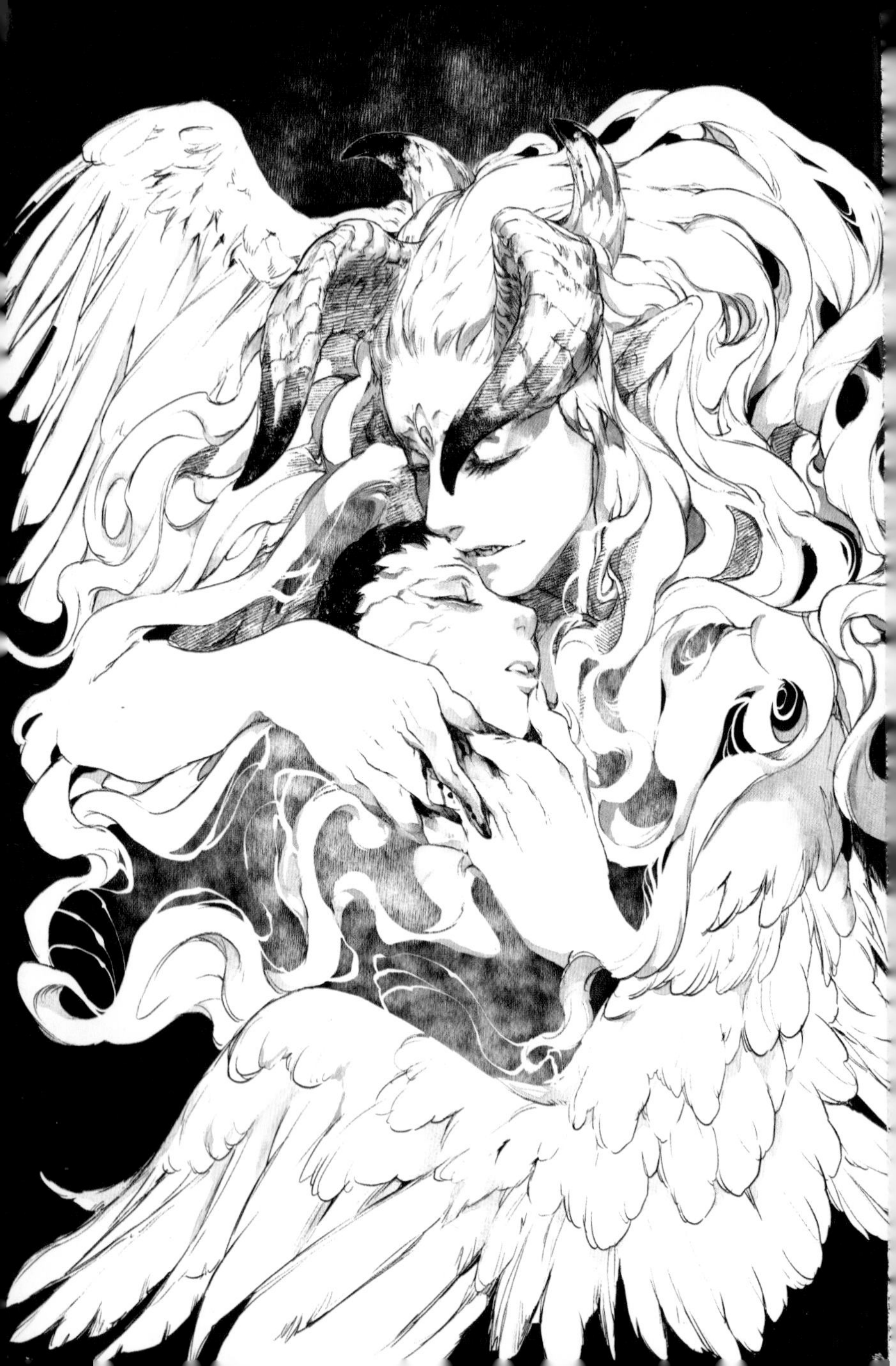

Contents

THERE ARE A LOT OF DEMON-SUMMONING BOOKS HIDING ON DUSTY BACK SHELVES.

MOST ARE FAKE, OF COURSE. THE IDEA ITSELF IS DUMB, AFTER ALL.

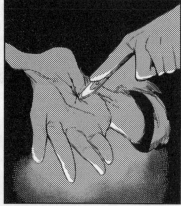

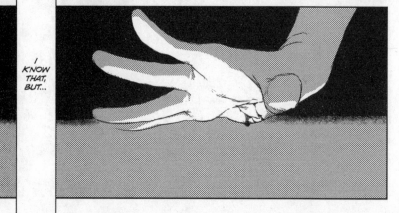

I KNOW THAT, BUT...

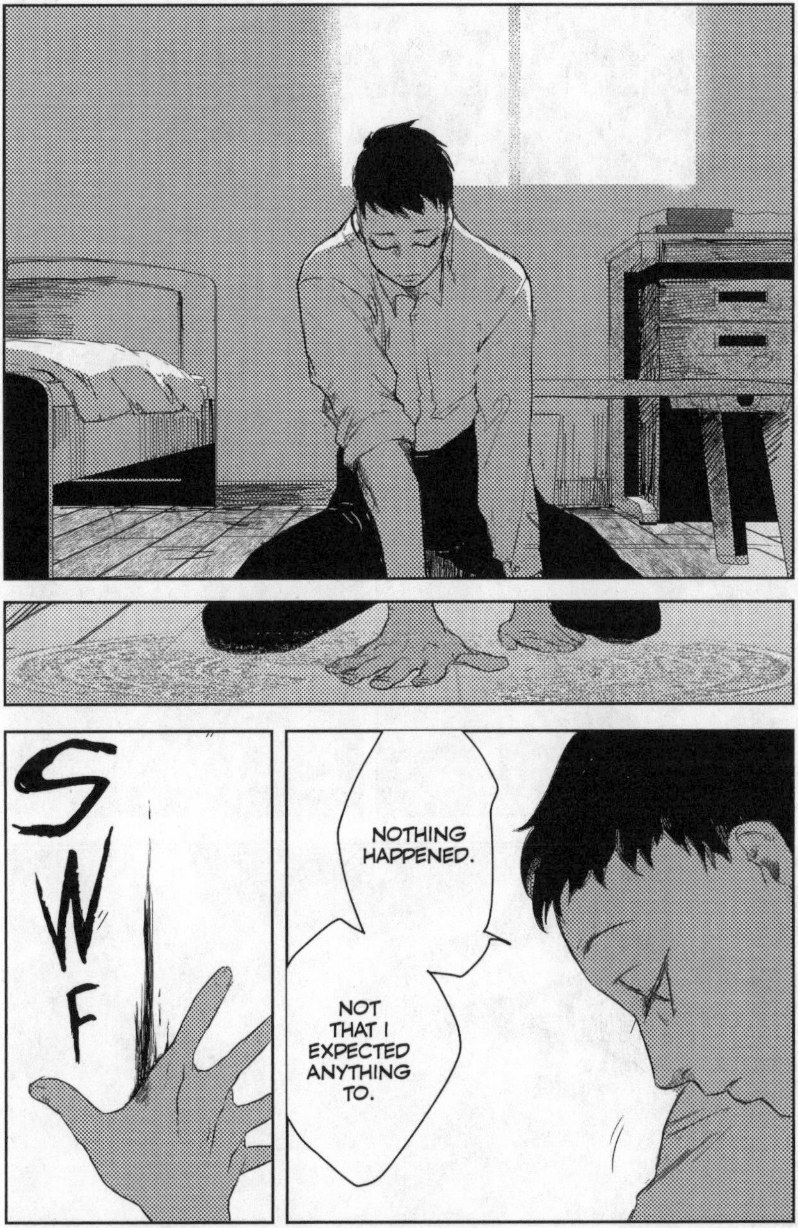
NOTHING HAPPENED.
NOT THAT I EXPECTED ANYTHING TO.
SWF

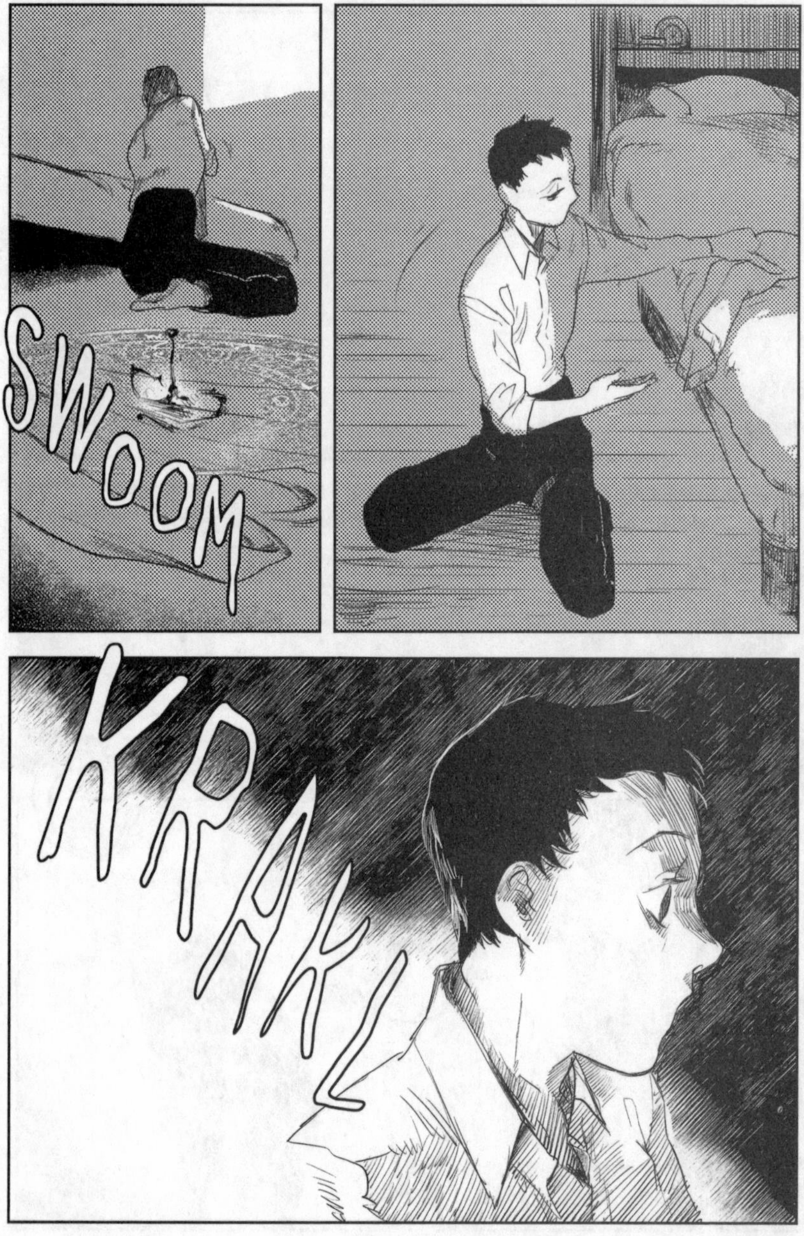
SWOOM
KRAKL

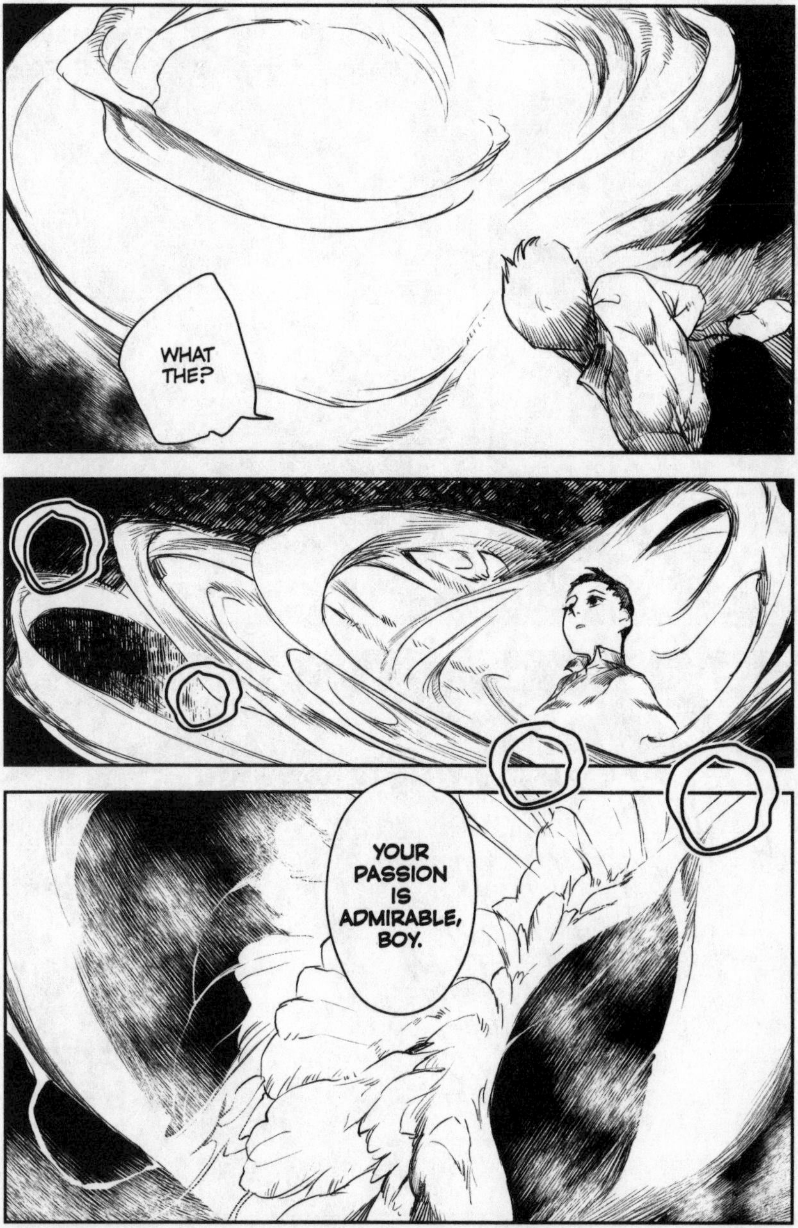
WHAT THE?
YOUR PASSION IS ADMIRABLE, BOY.

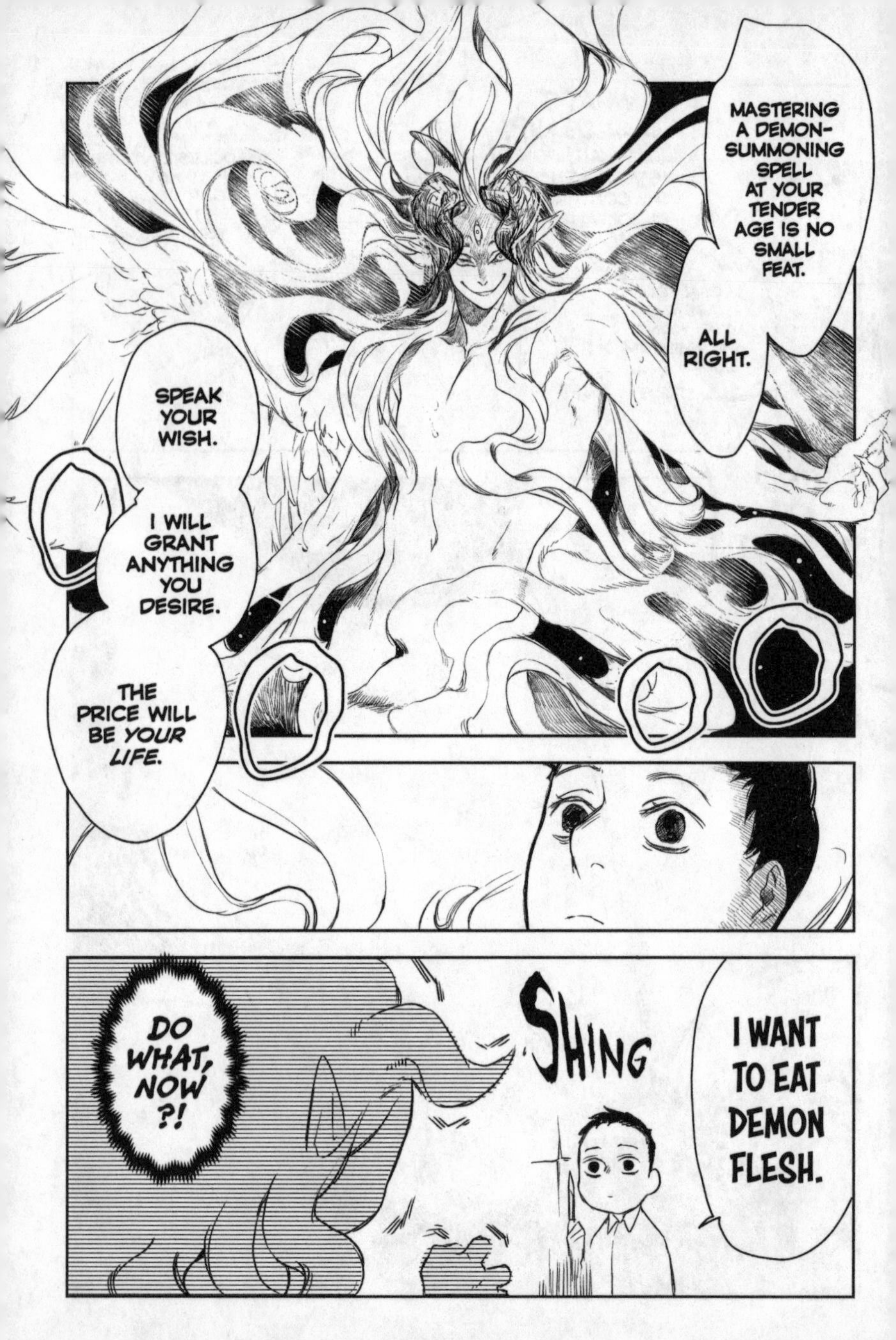
MASTERING A DEMON-SUMMONING SPELL AT YOUR TENDER AGE IS NO SMALL FEAT.
ALL RIGHT.
SPEAK YOUR WISH.
I WILL GRANT ANYTHING YOU DESIRE.
THE PRICE WILL BE *YOUR LIFE*.
I WANT TO EAT DEMON FLESH.
SHING
DO WHAT, NOW ?!

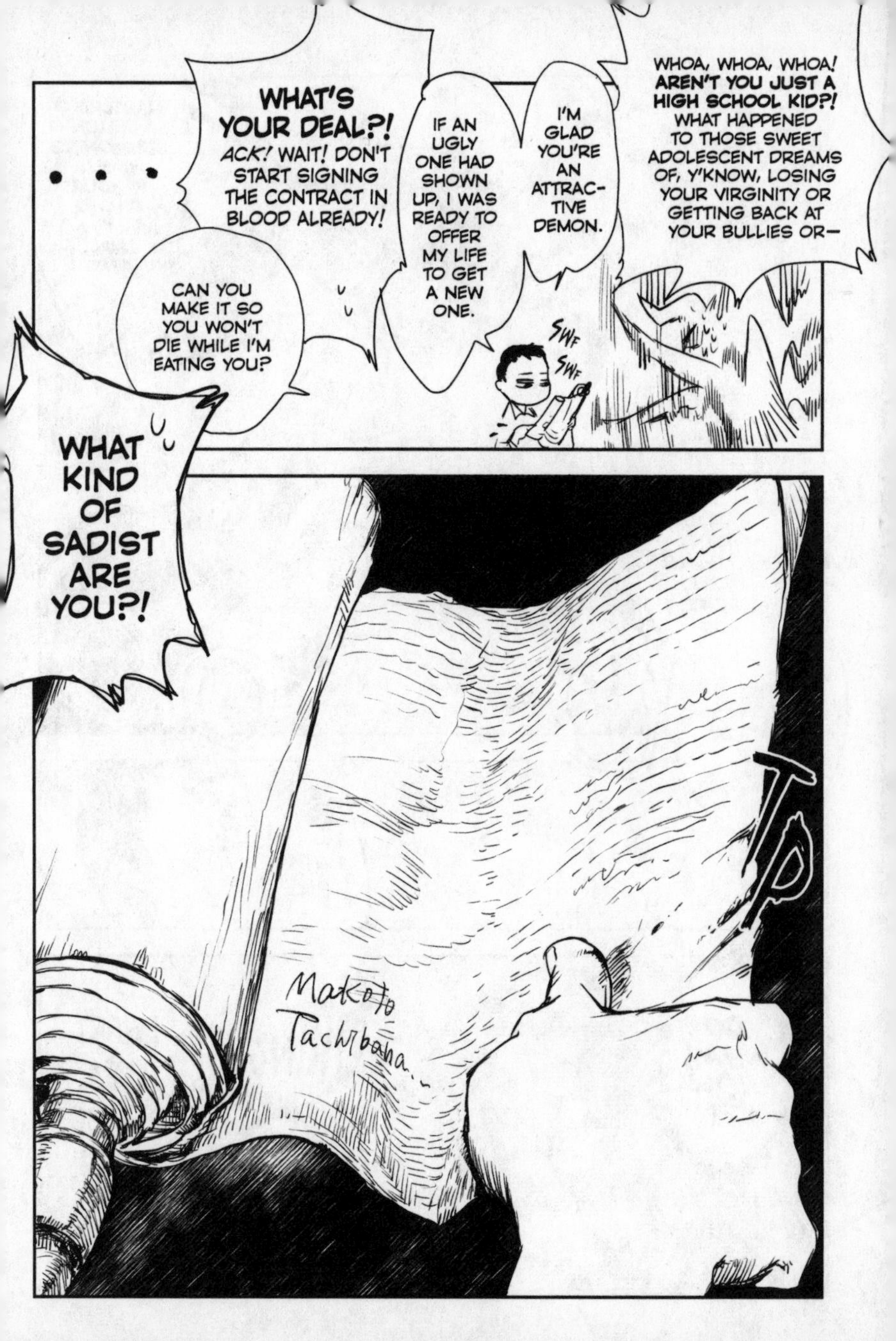
WHOA, WHOA, WHOA! **AREN'T YOU JUST A HIGH SCHOOL KID?!** WHAT HAPPENED TO THOSE SWEET ADOLESCENT DREAMS OF, Y'KNOW, LOSING YOUR VIRGINITY OR GETTING BACK AT YOUR BULLIES OR—
I'M GLAD YOU'RE AN ATTRACTIVE DEMON.
IF AN UGLY ONE HAD SHOWN UP, I WAS READY TO OFFER MY LIFE TO GET A NEW ONE.
WHAT'S YOUR DEAL?! *ACK!* WAIT! DON'T START SIGNING THE CONTRACT IN BLOOD ALREADY!
SWF SWF
• • •
CAN YOU MAKE IT SO YOU WON'T DIE WHILE I'M EATING YOU?
WHAT KIND OF SADIST ARE YOU?!
Makoto Tachibana

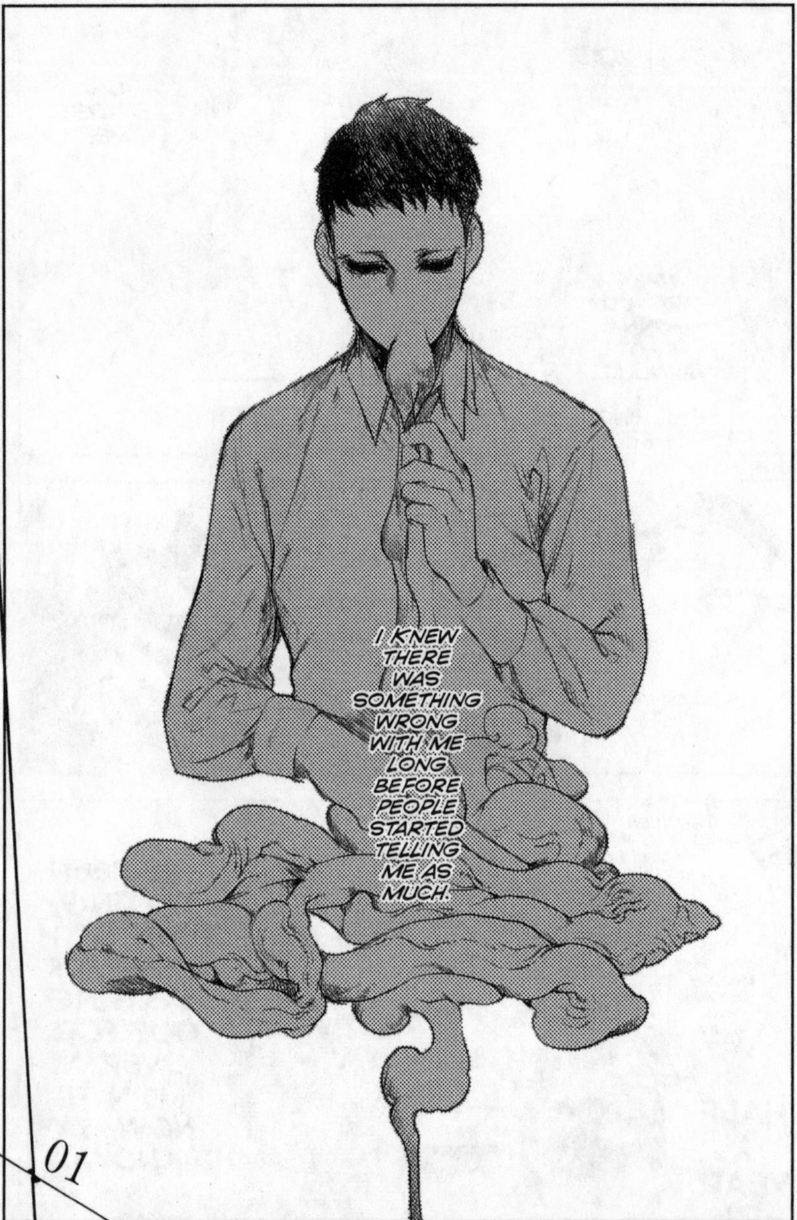
I KNEW THERE WAS SOMETHING WRONG WITH ME LONG BEFORE PEOPLE STARTED TELLING ME AS MUCH.

01

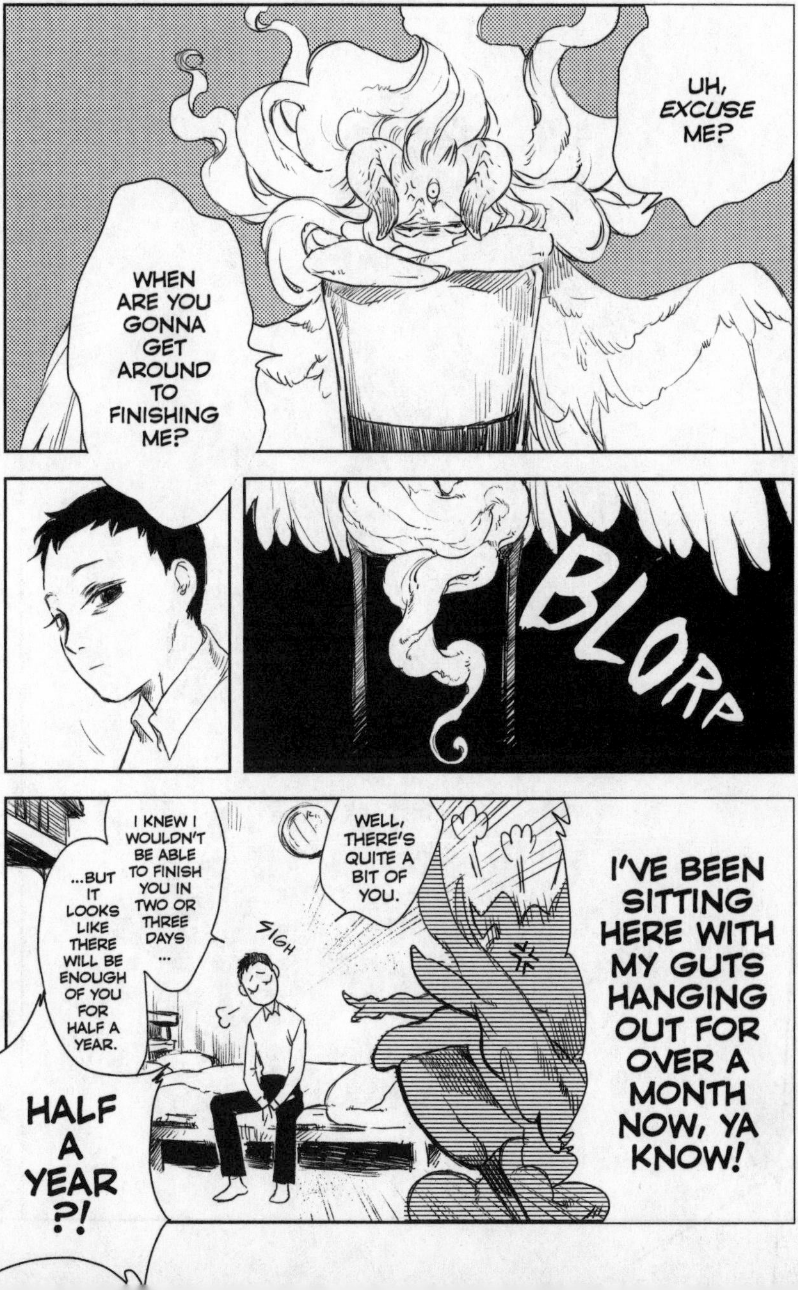
UH, EXCUSE ME?
WHEN ARE YOU GONNA GET AROUND TO FINISHING ME?
BLORP
I'VE BEEN SITTING HERE WITH MY GUTS HANGING OUT FOR OVER A MONTH NOW, YA KNOW!
WELL, THERE'S QUITE A BIT OF YOU.
SIGH
I KNEW I WOULDN'T BE ABLE TO FINISH YOU IN TWO OR THREE DAYS...
...BUT IT LOOKS LIKE THERE WILL BE ENOUGH OF YOU FOR HALF A YEAR.
HALF A YEAR?!

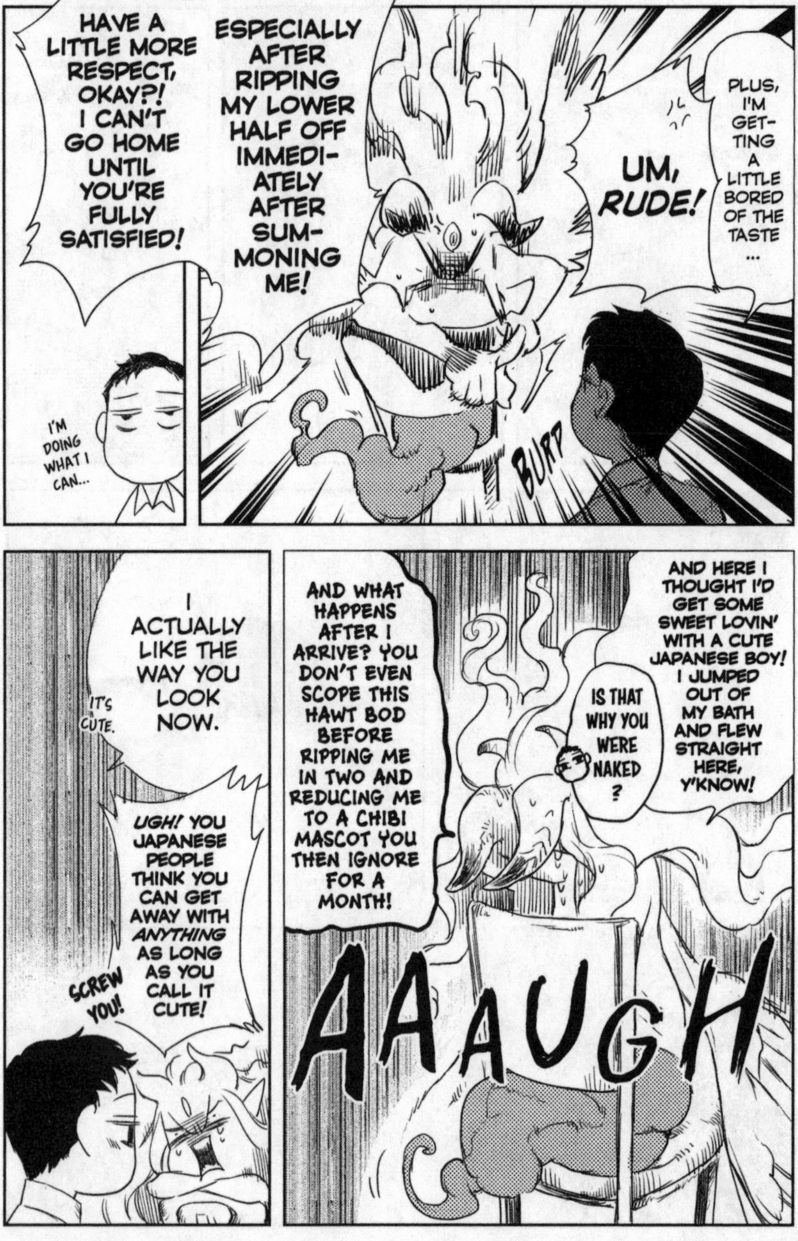
PLUS, I'M GETTING A LITTLE BORED OF THE TASTE ...
UM, RUDE!
ESPECIALLY AFTER RIPPING MY LOWER HALF OFF IMMEDIATELY AFTER SUMMONING ME!
HAVE A LITTLE MORE RESPECT, OKAY?! I CAN'T GO HOME UNTIL YOU'RE FULLY SATISFIED!
BURP
I'M DOING WHAT I CAN...
AND HERE I THOUGHT I'D GET SOME SWEET LOVIN' WITH A CUTE JAPANESE BOY! I JUMPED OUT OF MY BATH AND FLEW STRAIGHT HERE, Y'KNOW!
IS THAT WHY YOU WERE NAKED ?
AND WHAT HAPPENS AFTER I ARRIVE? YOU DON'T EVEN SCOPE THIS HAWT BOD BEFORE RIPPING ME IN TWO AND REDUCING ME TO A CHIBI MASCOT YOU THEN IGNORE FOR A MONTH!
AAAUGH
I ACTUALLY LIKE THE WAY YOU LOOK NOW.
IT'S CUTE.
UGH! YOU JAPANESE PEOPLE THINK YOU CAN GET AWAY WITH ANYTHING AS LONG AS YOU CALL IT CUTE!
SCREW YOU!

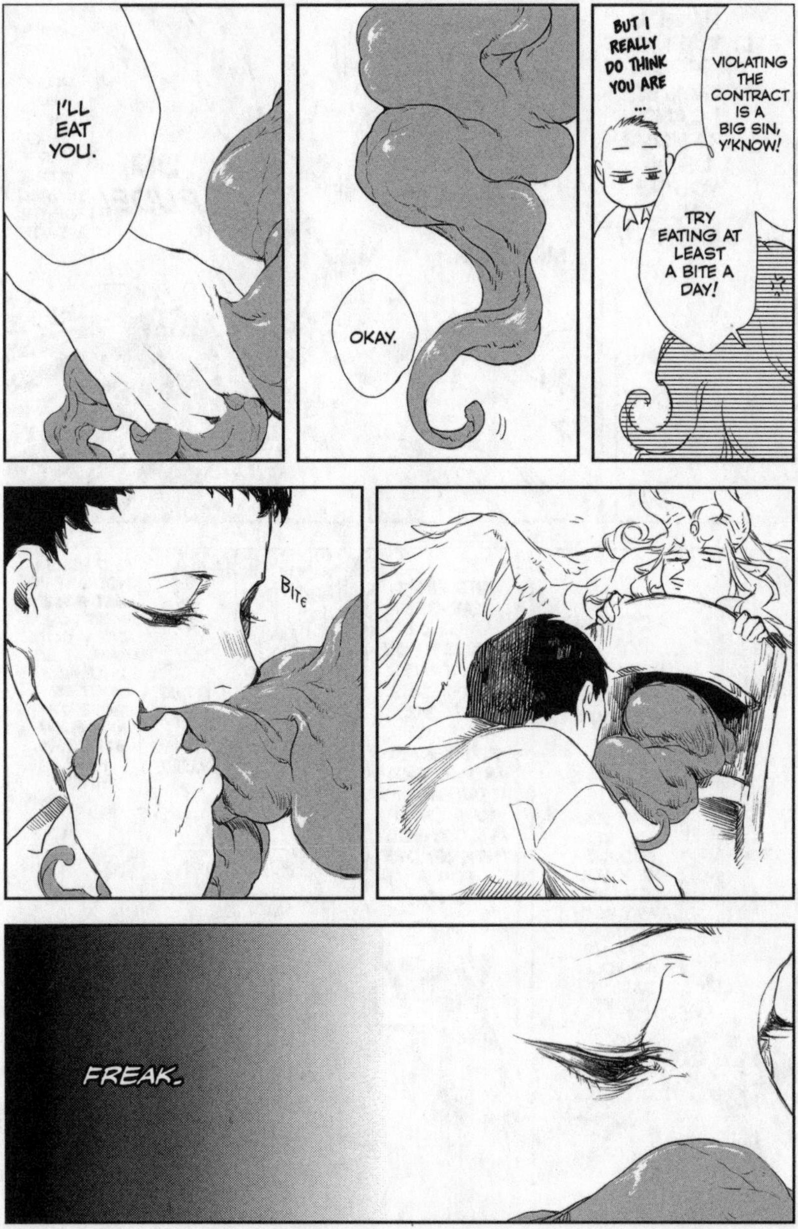
VIOLATING THE CONTRACT IS A BIG SIN, Y'KNOW!
BUT I REALLY DO THINK YOU ARE ...
TRY EATING AT LEAST A BITE A DAY!
OKAY.
I'LL EAT YOU.
BITE
FREAK.

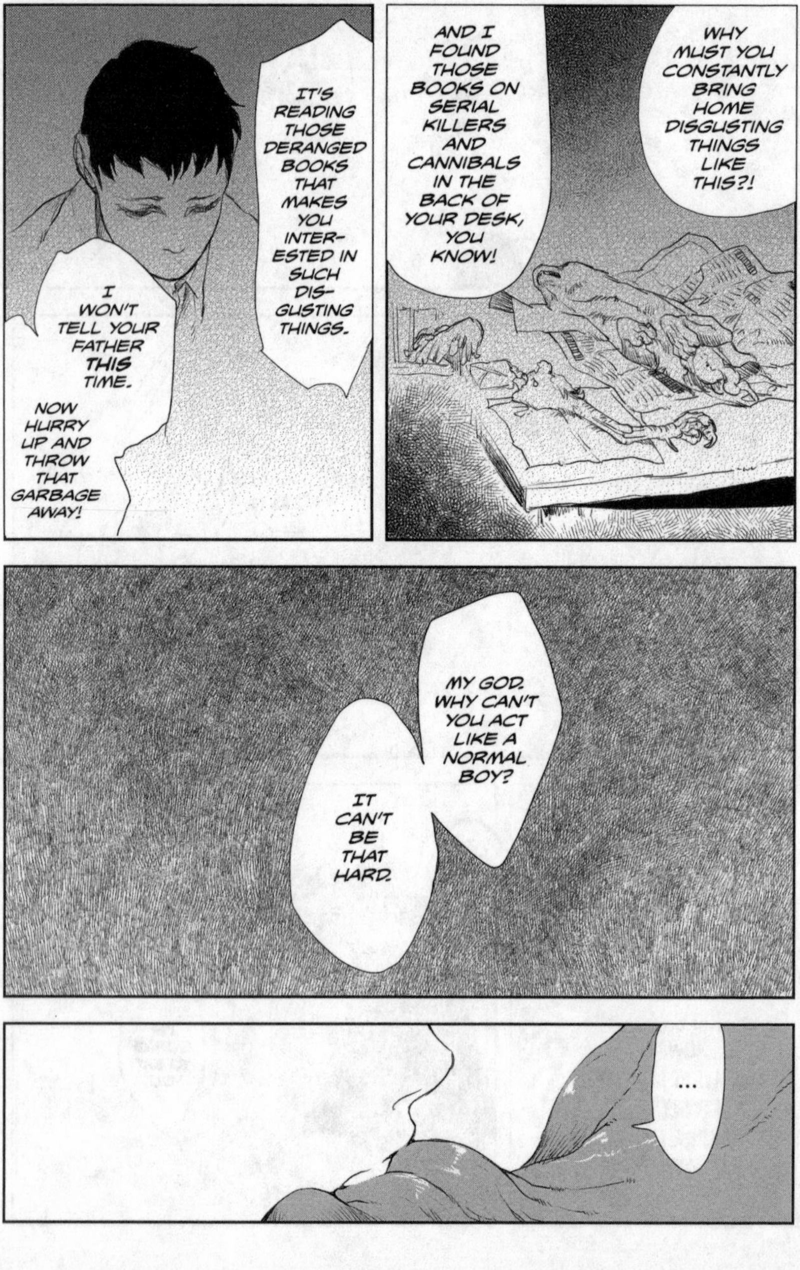
WHY MUST YOU CONSTANTLY BRING HOME DISGUSTING THINGS LIKE THIS?!
AND I FOUND THOSE BOOKS ON SERIAL KILLERS AND CANNIBALS IN THE BACK OF YOUR DESK, YOU KNOW!
IT'S READING THOSE DERANGED BOOKS THAT MAKES YOU INTER-ESTED IN SUCH DIS-GUSTING THINGS.
I WON'T TELL YOUR FATHER THIS TIME.
NOW HURRY UP AND THROW THAT GARBAGE AWAY!
MY GOD. WHY CAN'T YOU ACT LIKE A NORMAL BOY?
IT CAN'T BE THAT HARD.
...

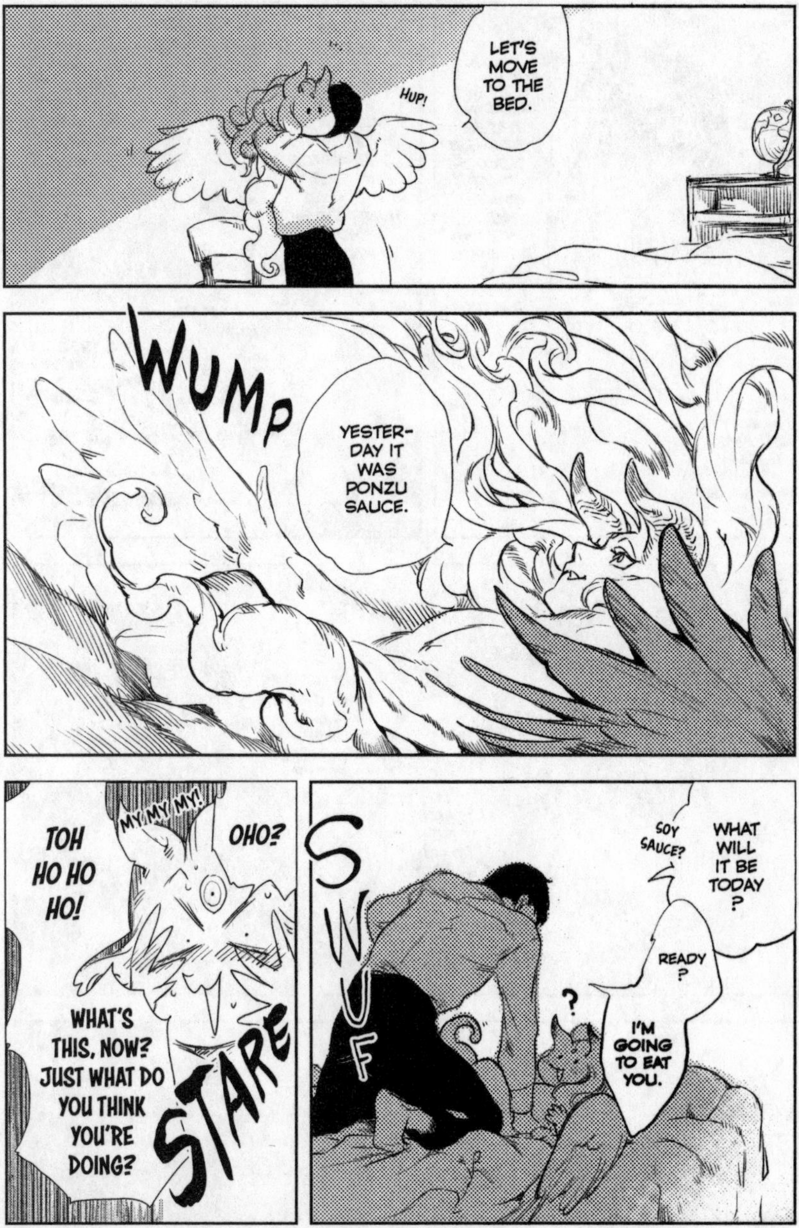
LET'S MOVE TO THE BED.
HUP!
WUMP
YESTER-DAY IT WAS PONZU SAUCE.
WHAT WILL IT BE TODAY?
SOY SAUCE?
READY?
I'M GOING TO EAT YOU.
?
SWUF
OHO?
MY MY MY!
TOH HO HO HO!
STARE
WHAT'S THIS, NOW? JUST WHAT DO YOU THINK YOU'RE DOING?

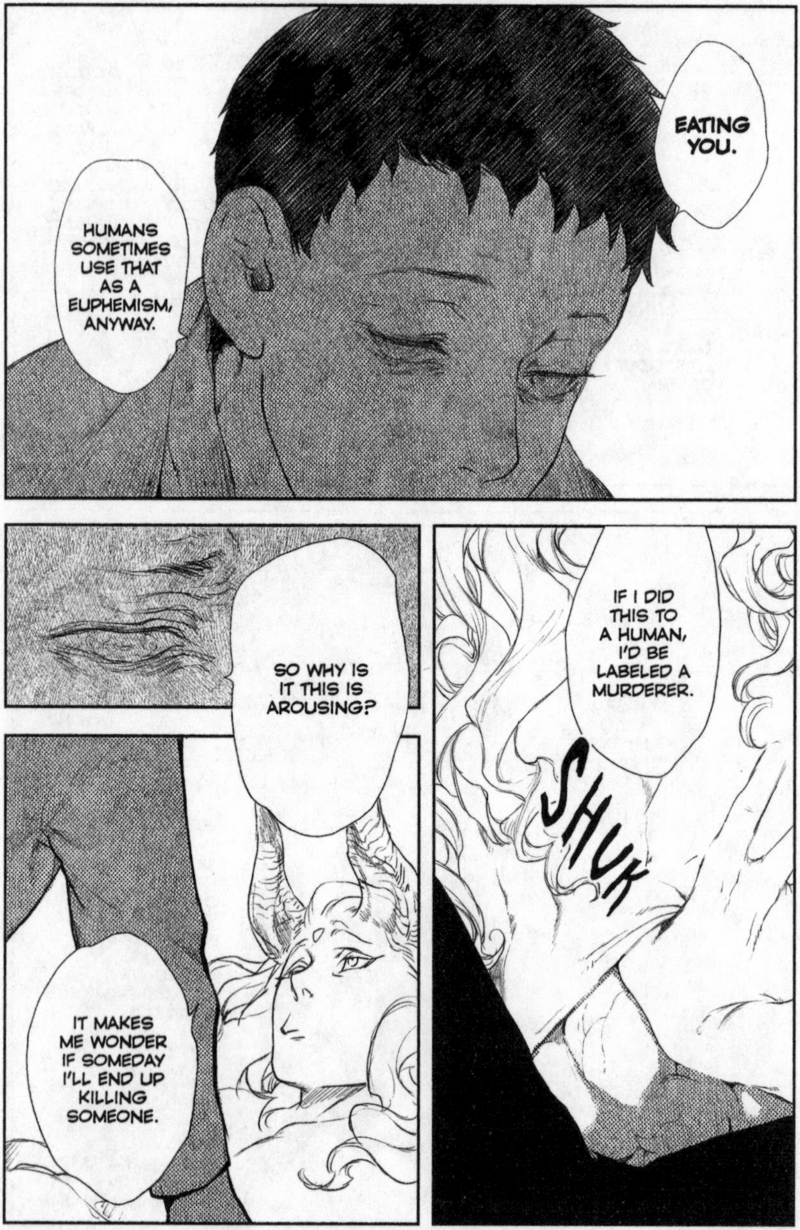
EATING YOU.
HUMANS SOMETIMES USE THAT AS A EUPHEMISM, ANYWAY.
IF I DID THIS TO A HUMAN, I'D BE LABELED A MURDERER.
SHUK
SO WHY IS IT THIS IS AROUSING?
IT MAKES ME WONDER IF SOMEDAY I'LL END UP KILLING SOMEONE.

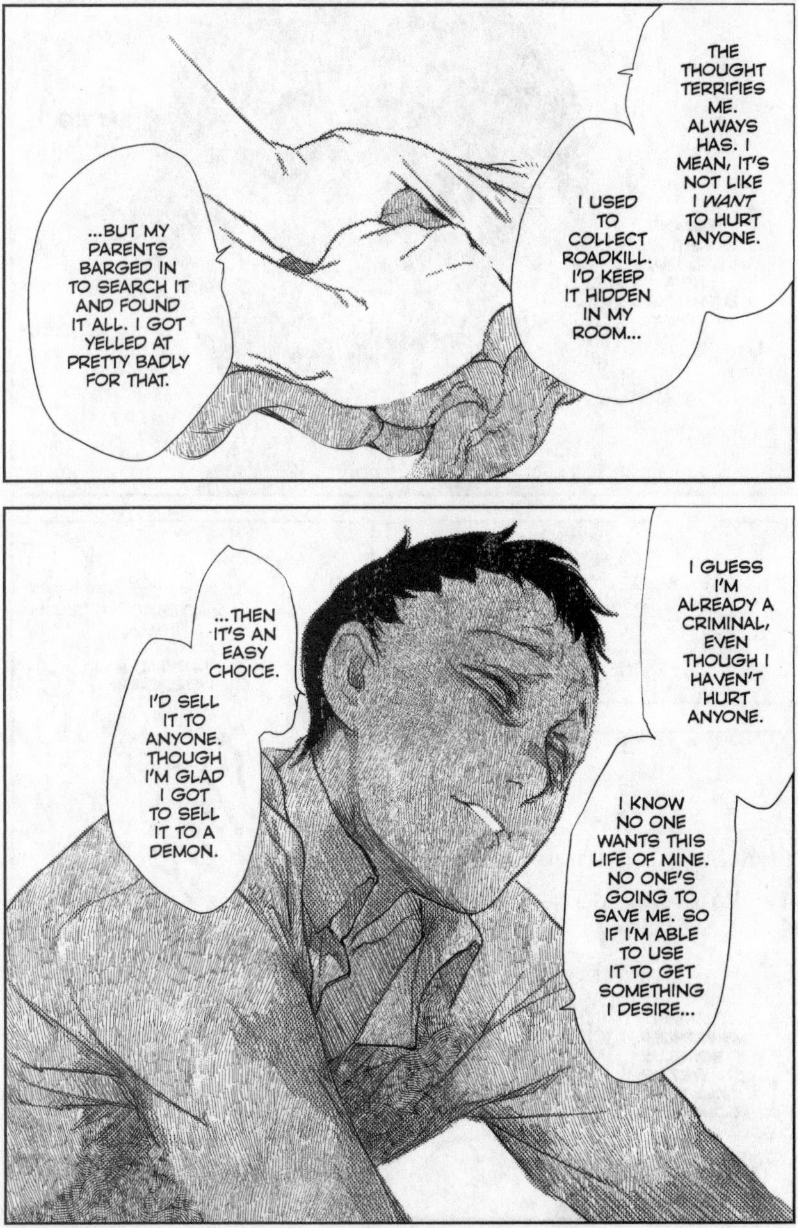
THE THOUGHT TERRIFIES ME. ALWAYS HAS. I MEAN, IT'S NOT LIKE I *WANT* TO HURT ANYONE.
I USED TO COLLECT ROADKILL. I'D KEEP IT HIDDEN IN MY ROOM...
...BUT MY PARENTS BARGED IN TO SEARCH IT AND FOUND IT ALL. I GOT YELLED AT PRETTY BADLY FOR THAT.
I GUESS I'M ALREADY A CRIMINAL, EVEN THOUGH I HAVEN'T HURT ANYONE.
I KNOW NO ONE WANTS THIS LIFE OF MINE. NO ONE'S GOING TO SAVE ME. SO IF I'M ABLE TO USE IT TO GET SOMETHING I DESIRE...
...THEN IT'S AN EASY CHOICE.
I'D SELL IT TO ANYONE. THOUGH I'M GLAD I GOT TO SELL IT TO A DEMON.

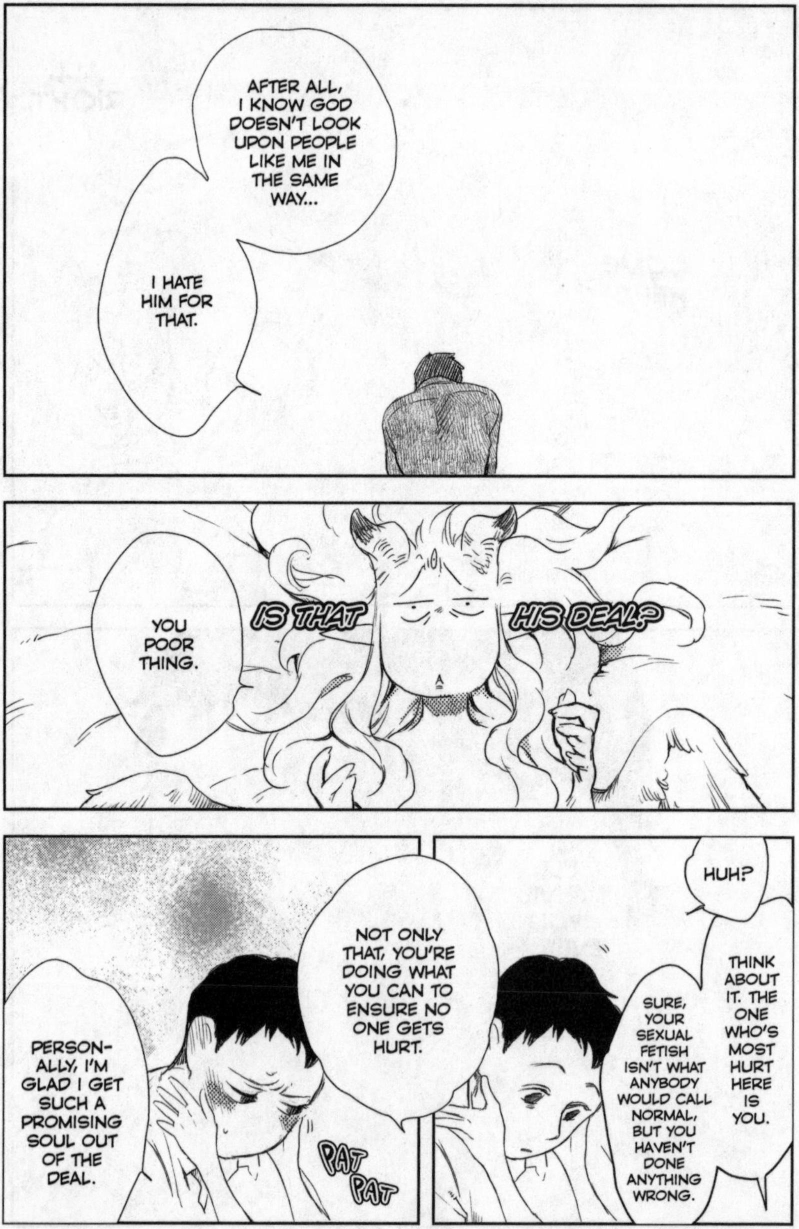
AFTER ALL, I KNOW GOD DOESN'T LOOK UPON PEOPLE LIKE ME IN THE SAME WAY...
I HATE HIM FOR THAT.
IS THAT HIS DEAL?
YOU POOR THING.
HUH?
THINK ABOUT IT. THE ONE WHO'S MOST HURT HERE IS YOU.
SURE, YOUR SEXUAL FETISH ISN'T WHAT ANYBODY WOULD CALL NORMAL, BUT YOU HAVEN'T DONE ANYTHING WRONG.
NOT ONLY THAT, YOU'RE DOING WHAT YOU CAN TO ENSURE NO ONE GETS HURT.
PAT PAT
PERSON-ALLY, I'M GLAD I GET SUCH A PROMISING SOUL OUT OF THE DEAL.

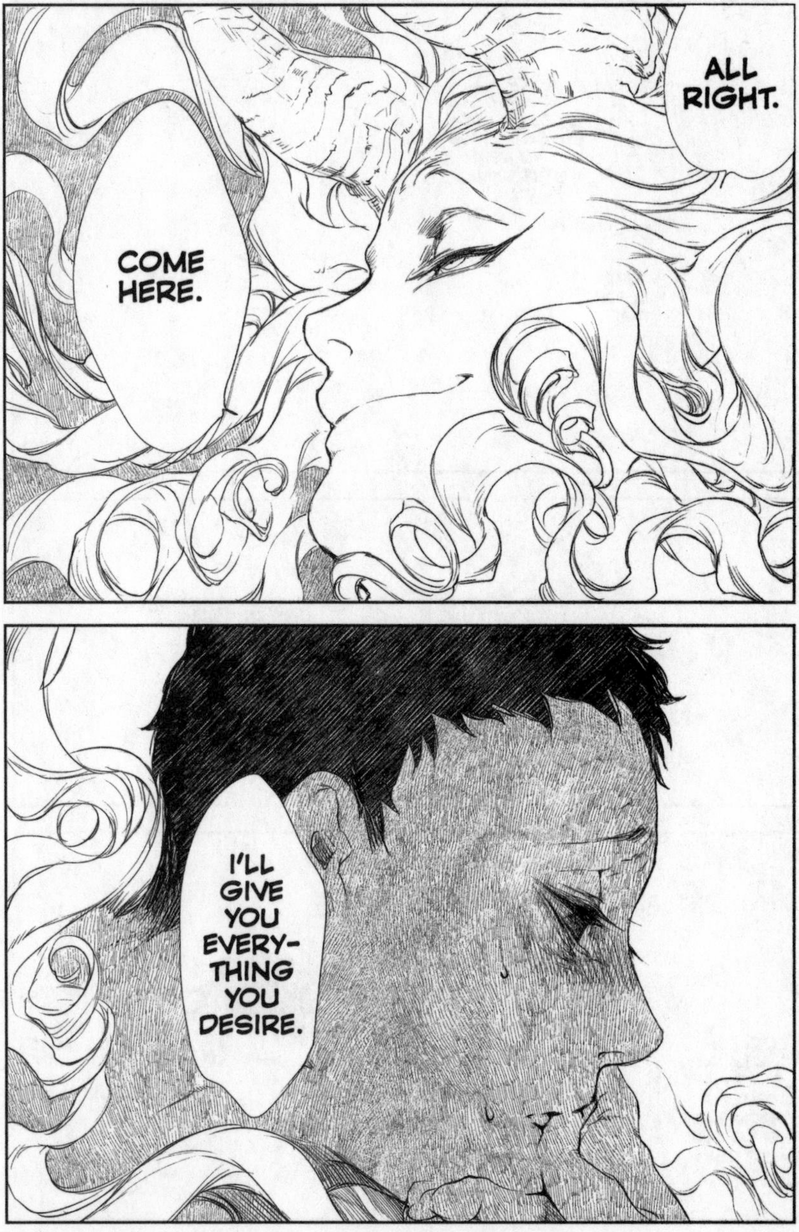
ALL RIGHT.
COME HERE.
I'LL GIVE YOU EVERY-THING YOU DESIRE.

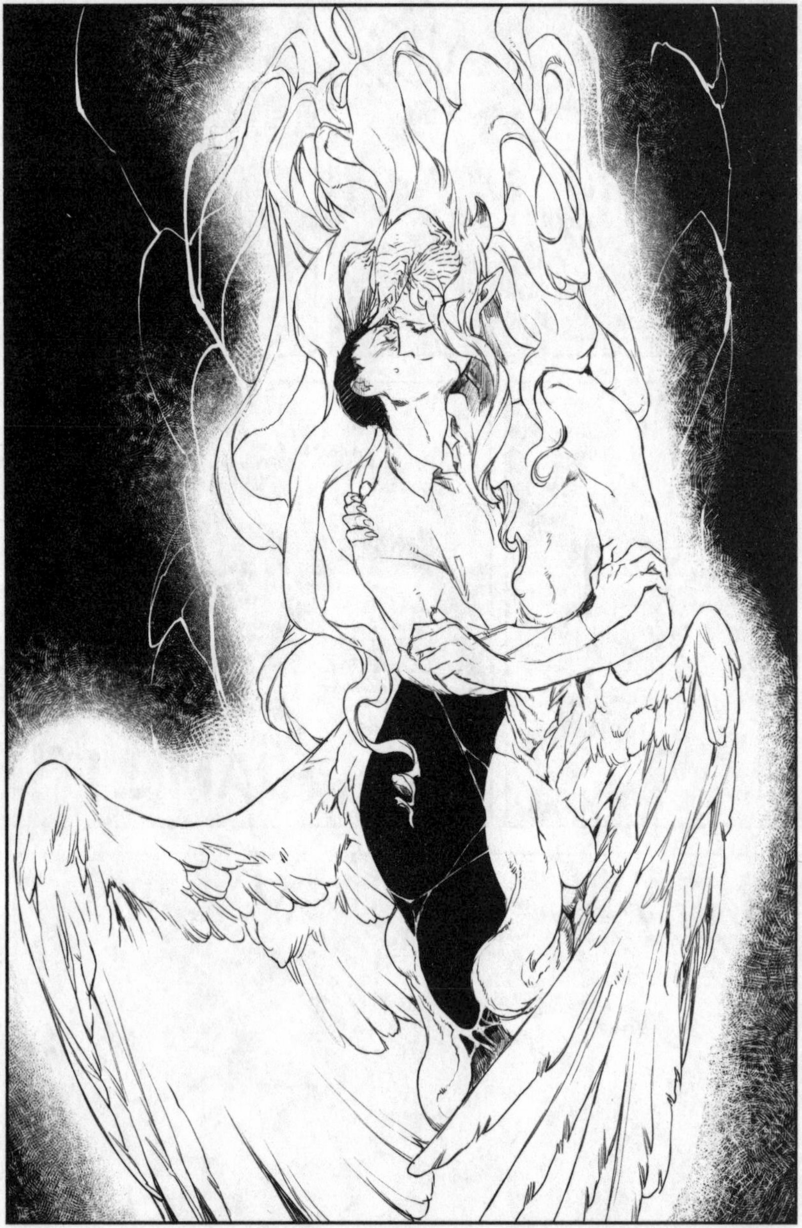

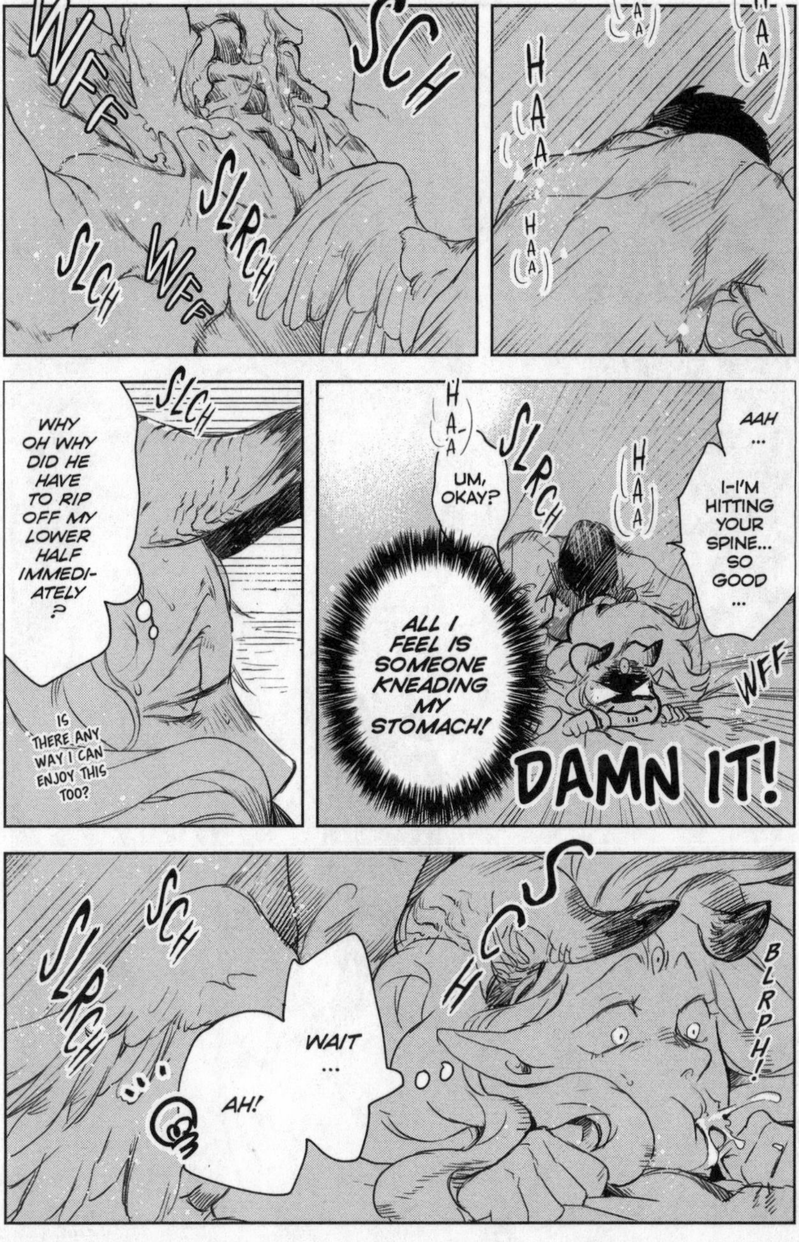
HAA
HAA
HAA
HAA
SCH
WFF
SLRCH
WFF
SLCH
AAH ...
I-I'M HITTING YOUR SPINE... SO GOOD ...
HAA
SLRCH
HAA
UM, OKAY?
ALL I FEEL IS SOMEONE KNEADING MY STOMACH!
WFF
DAMN IT!
SLCH
WHY OH WHY DID HE HAVE TO RIP OFF MY LOWER HALF IMMEDIATELY?
IS THERE ANY WAY I CAN ENJOY THIS TOO?
BLRPH!
SCHS
WAIT ...
AH!
SCH
SLRCH

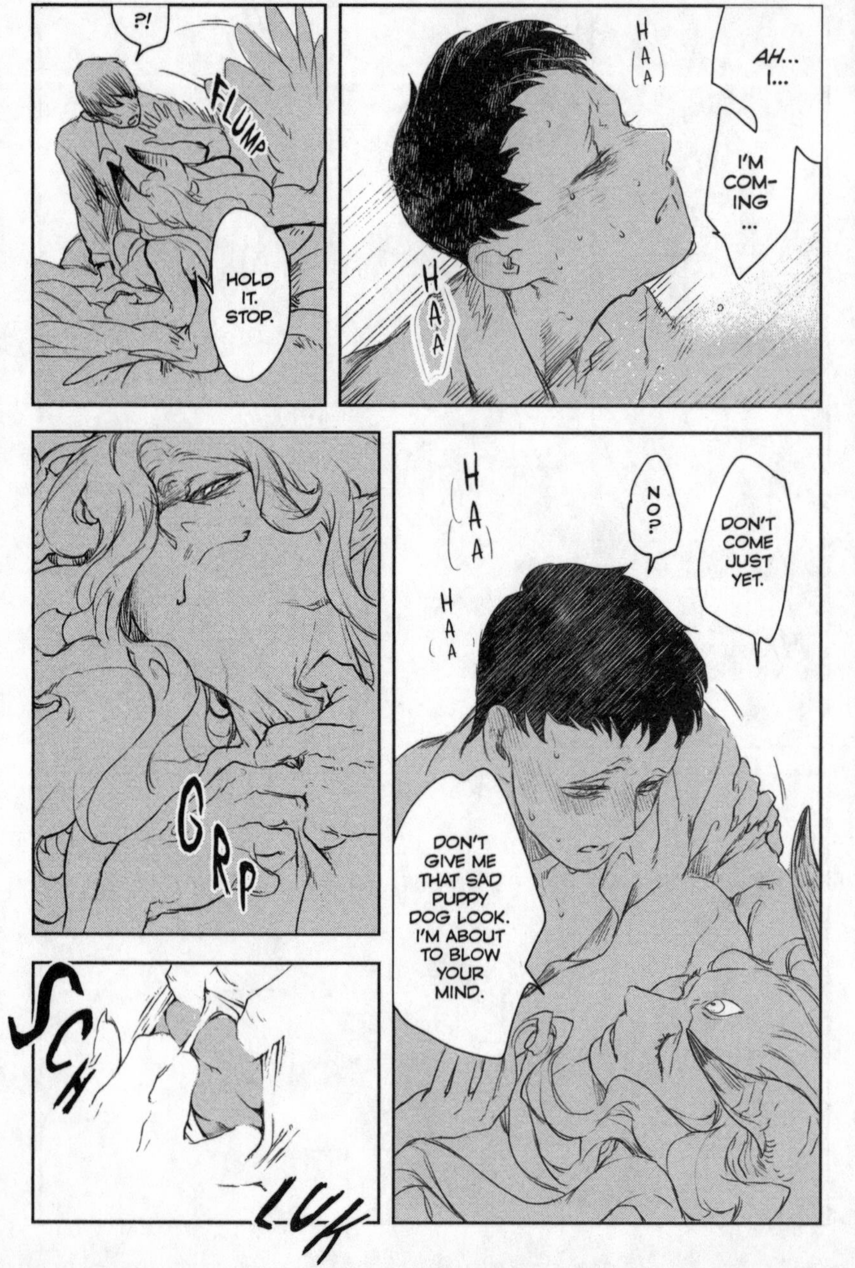
HAA
HAA
AH... I...
I'M COMING...
?!
FLUMP
HOLD IT. STOP.
DON'T COME JUST YET.
NO?
HAA
HAA
DON'T GIVE ME THAT SAD PUPPY DOG LOOK. I'M ABOUT TO BLOW YOUR MIND.
GRP
SCH
LUK

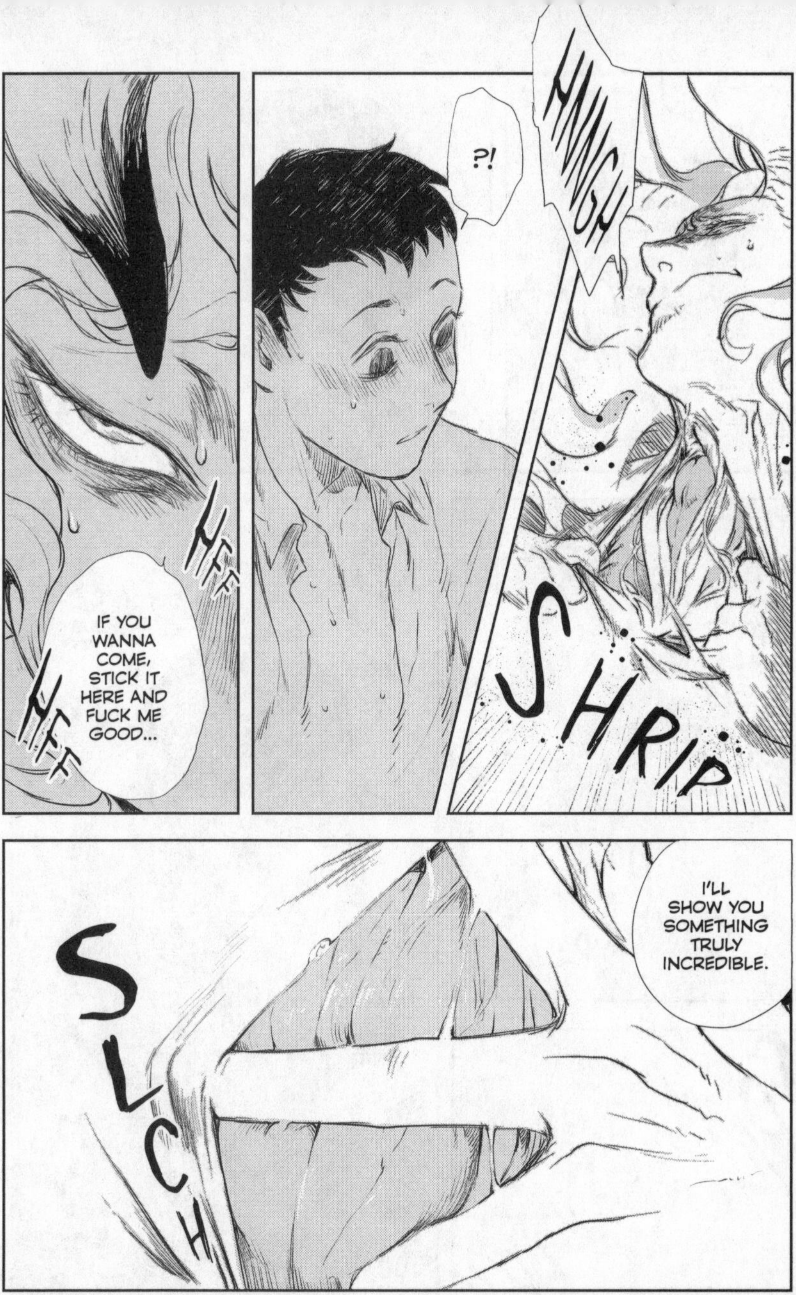
HNNGH
SHRIP
?!
HFF
HFF
IF YOU WANNA COME, STICK IT HERE AND FUCK ME GOOD...
I'LL SHOW YOU SOMETHING TRULY INCREDIBLE.
SLCH

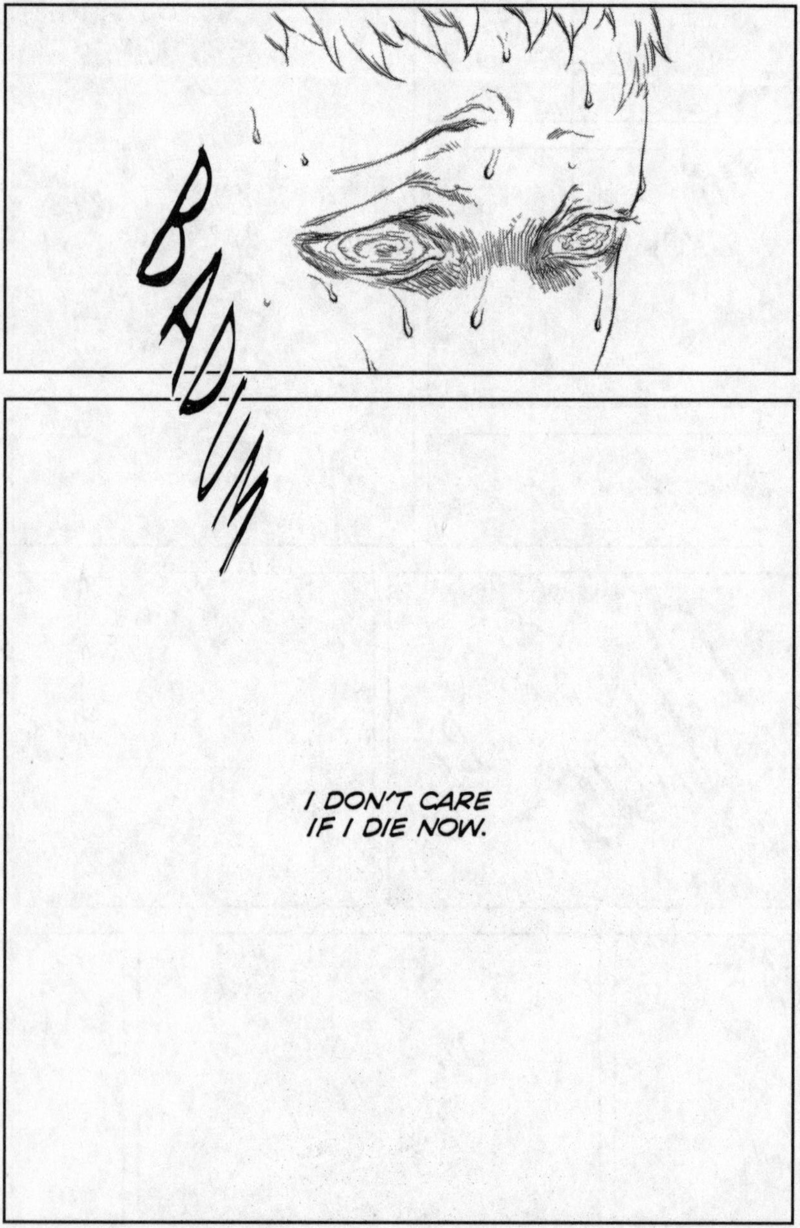
BADUM
I DON'T CARE
IF I DIE NOW.

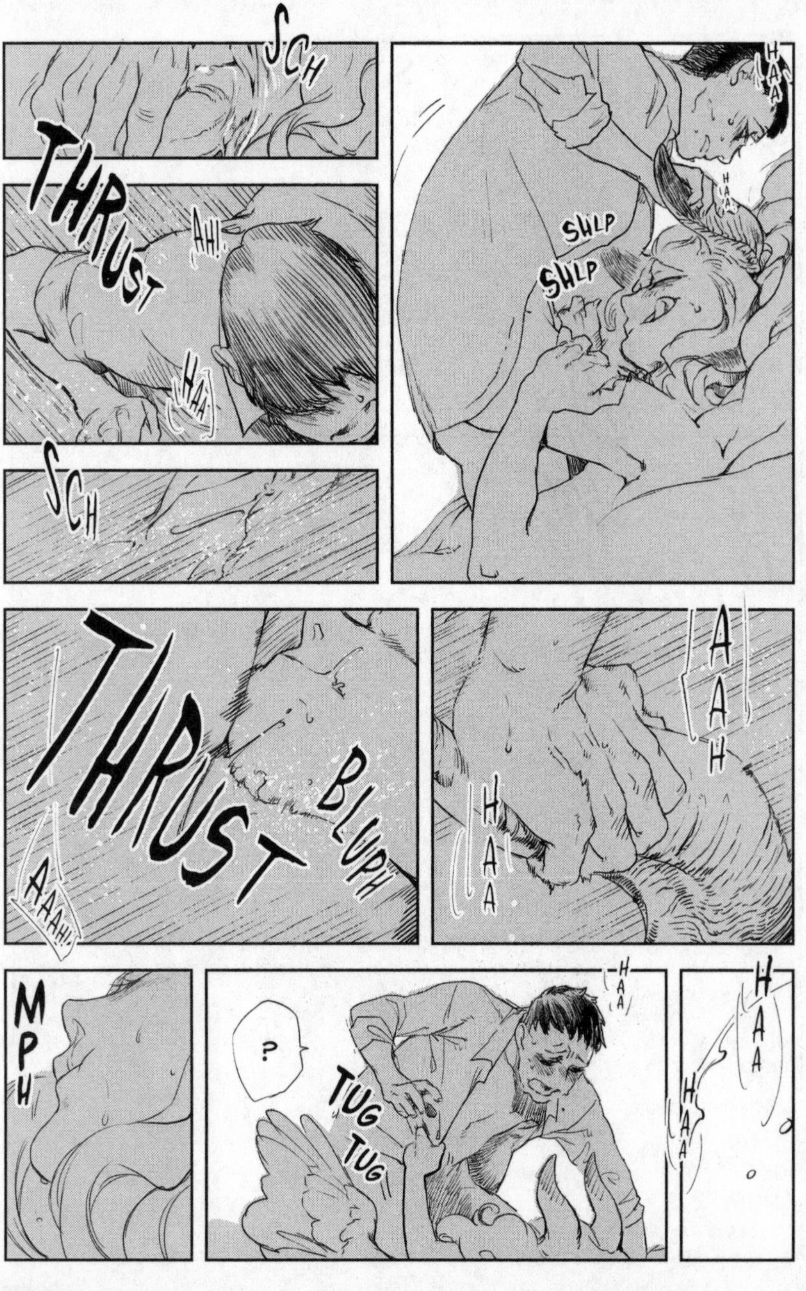
HAA
HAA
SHLP
SHLP
SCH
THRUST
AH!
HAA
SCH
AAAH
HAA
THRUST
BLUPH
AAAAH!
HAA
HAA
HAA
?
TUG
TUG
MPH

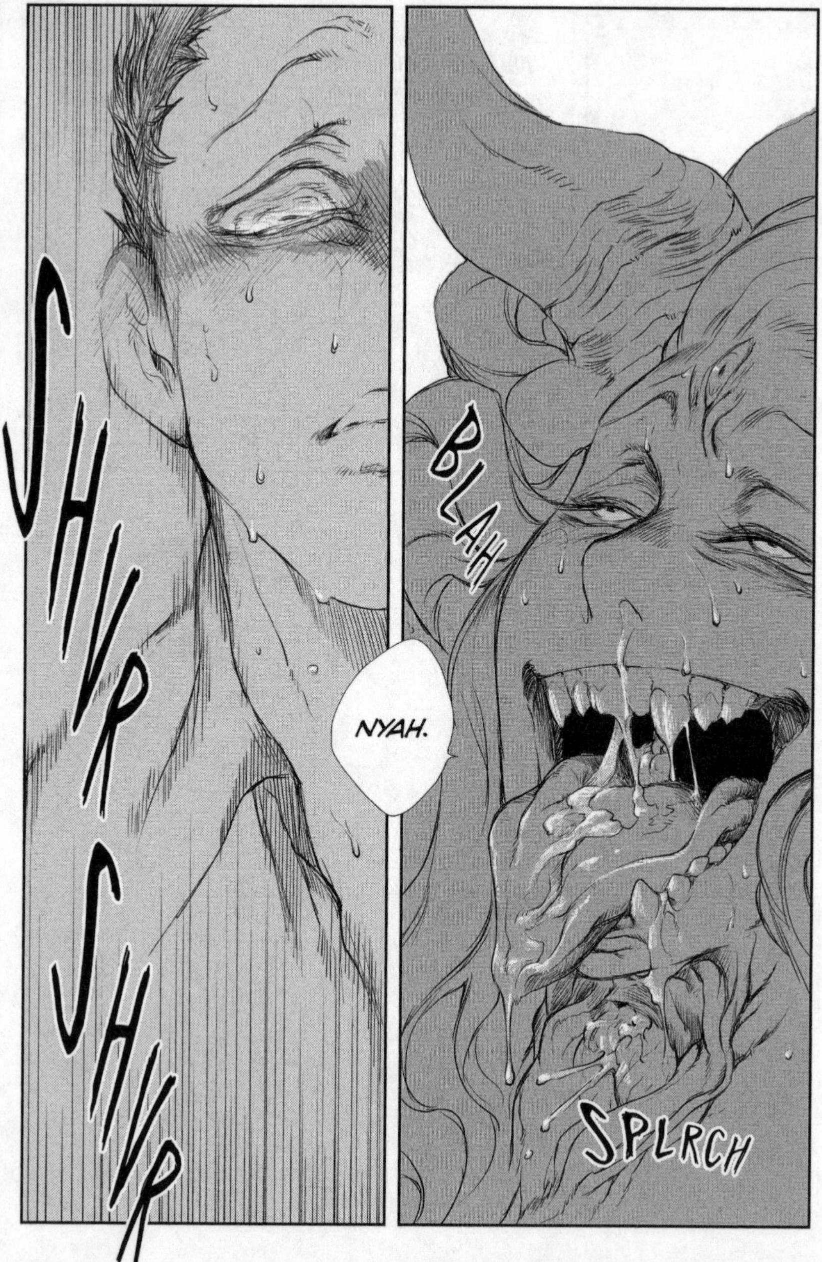
BLAH
NYAH.
SPLRCH
SHIVR SHIVR

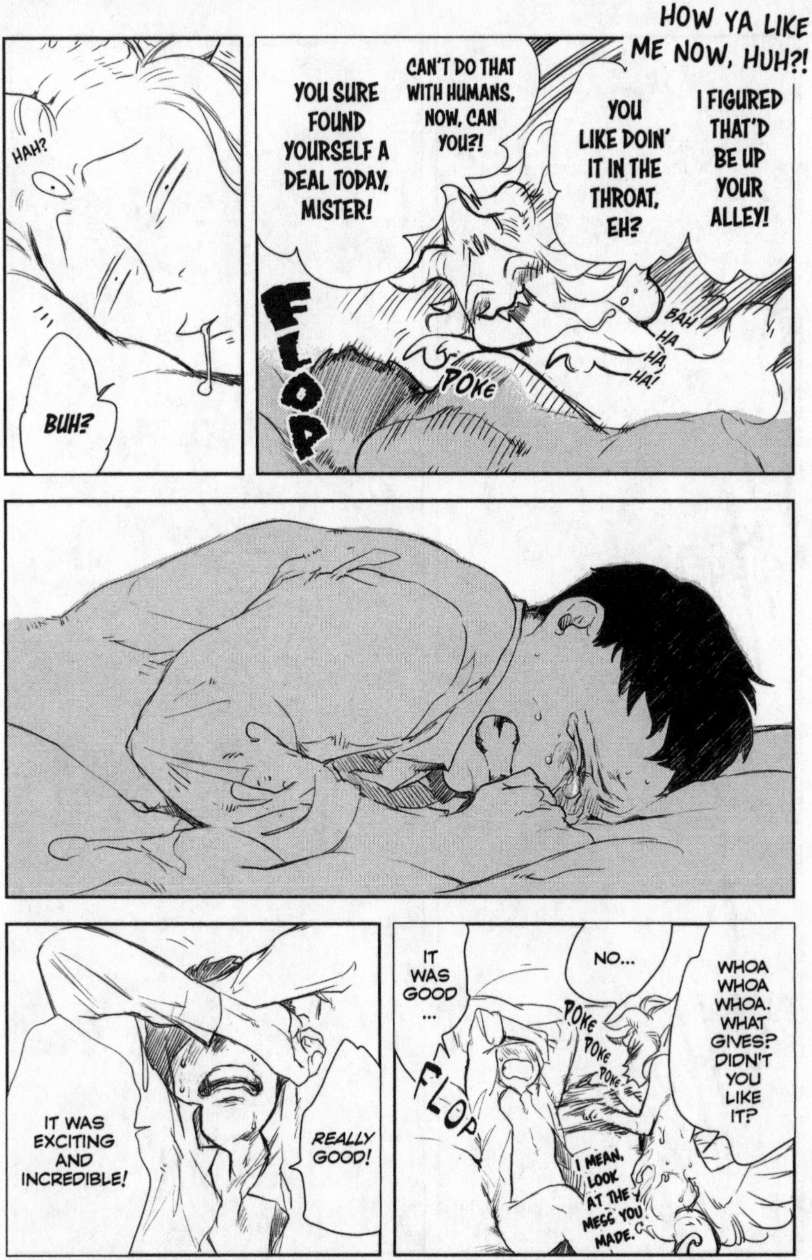
HOW YA LIKE ME NOW, HUH?!
I FIGURED THAT'D BE UP YOUR ALLEY!
YOU LIKE DOIN' IT IN THE THROAT, EH?
CAN'T DO THAT WITH HUMANS, NOW, CAN YOU?!
YOU SURE FOUND YOURSELF A DEAL TODAY, MISTER!
BAH HA HA, HA!
POKE
FLOP
HAH?
BUH?
WHOA WHOA WHOA. WHAT GIVES? DIDN'T YOU LIKE IT?
NO...
POKE POKE POKE
I MEAN, LOOK AT THE MESS YOU MADE.
IT WAS GOOD ...
FLOP
REALLY GOOD!
IT WAS EXCITING AND INCREDIBLE!

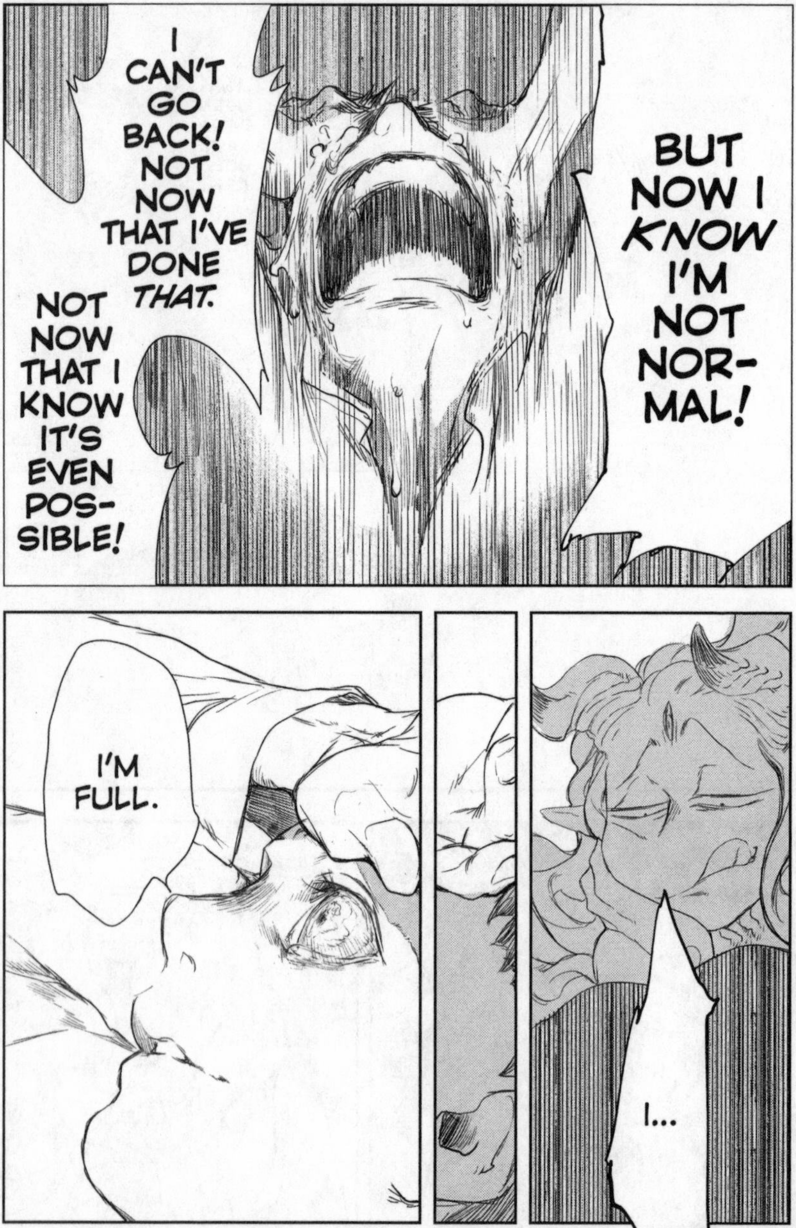
BUT NOW I KNOW I'M NOT NOR-MAL!
I CAN'T GO BACK! NOT NOW THAT I'VE DONE THAT.
NOT NOW THAT I KNOW IT'S EVEN POS-SIBLE!
I...
I'M FULL.

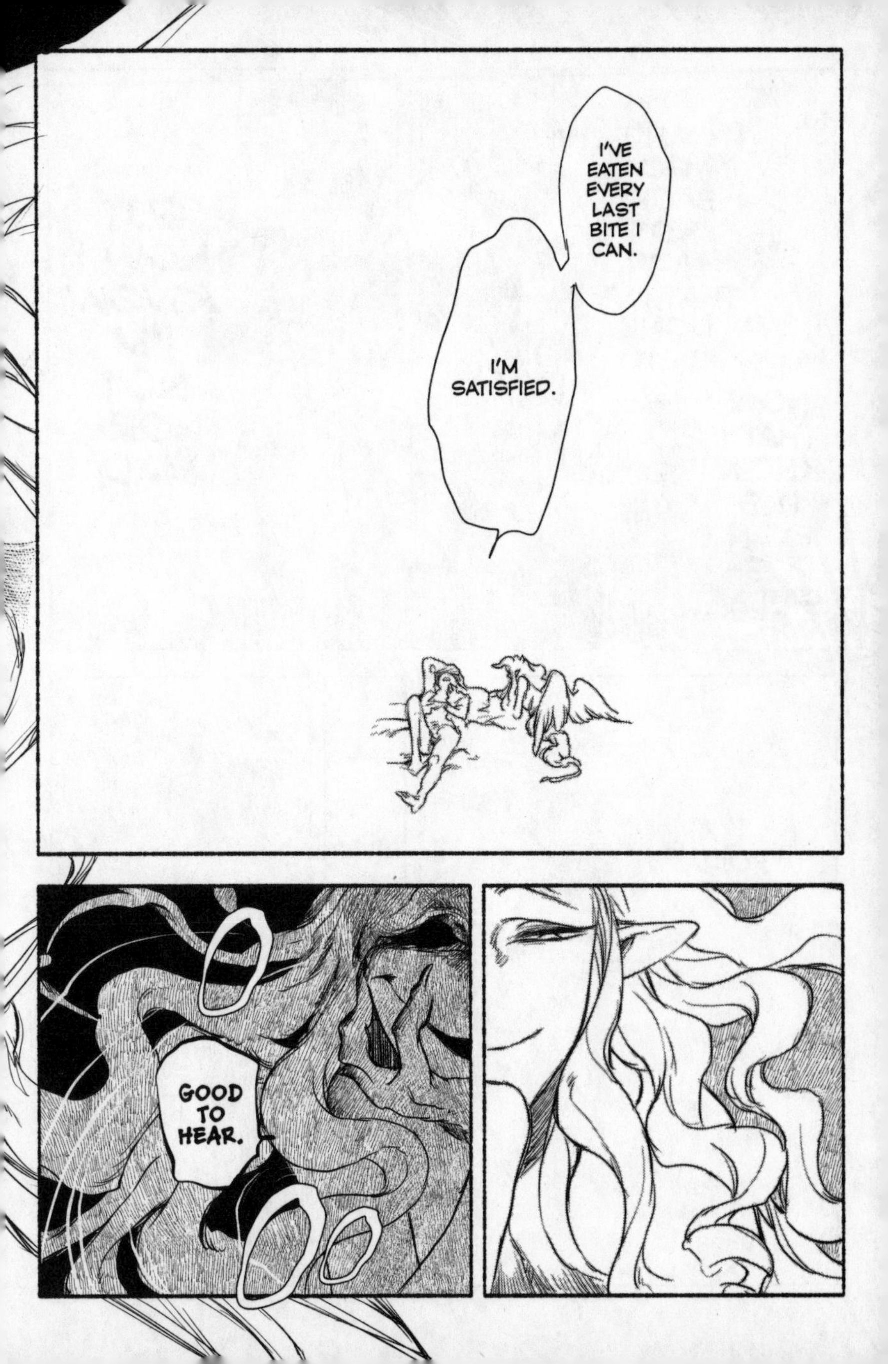
I'VE EATEN EVERY LAST BITE I CAN.
I'M SATISFIED.
GOOD TO HEAR.

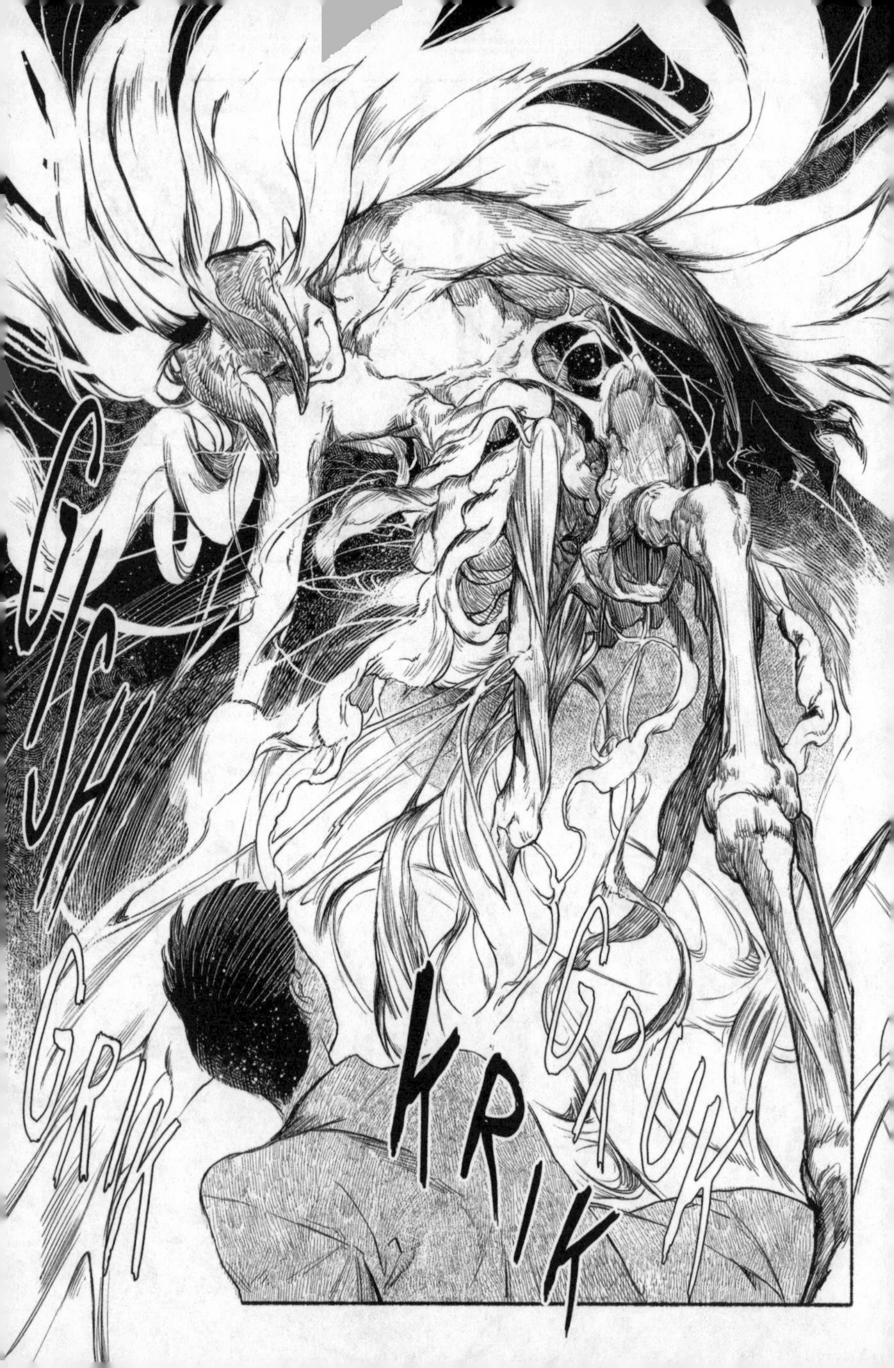
GRUK
KRIK
GRIK

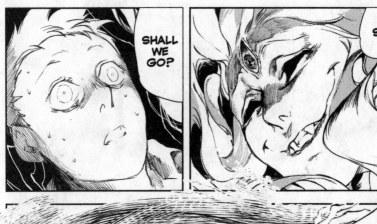

SHALL WE GO?

SO.

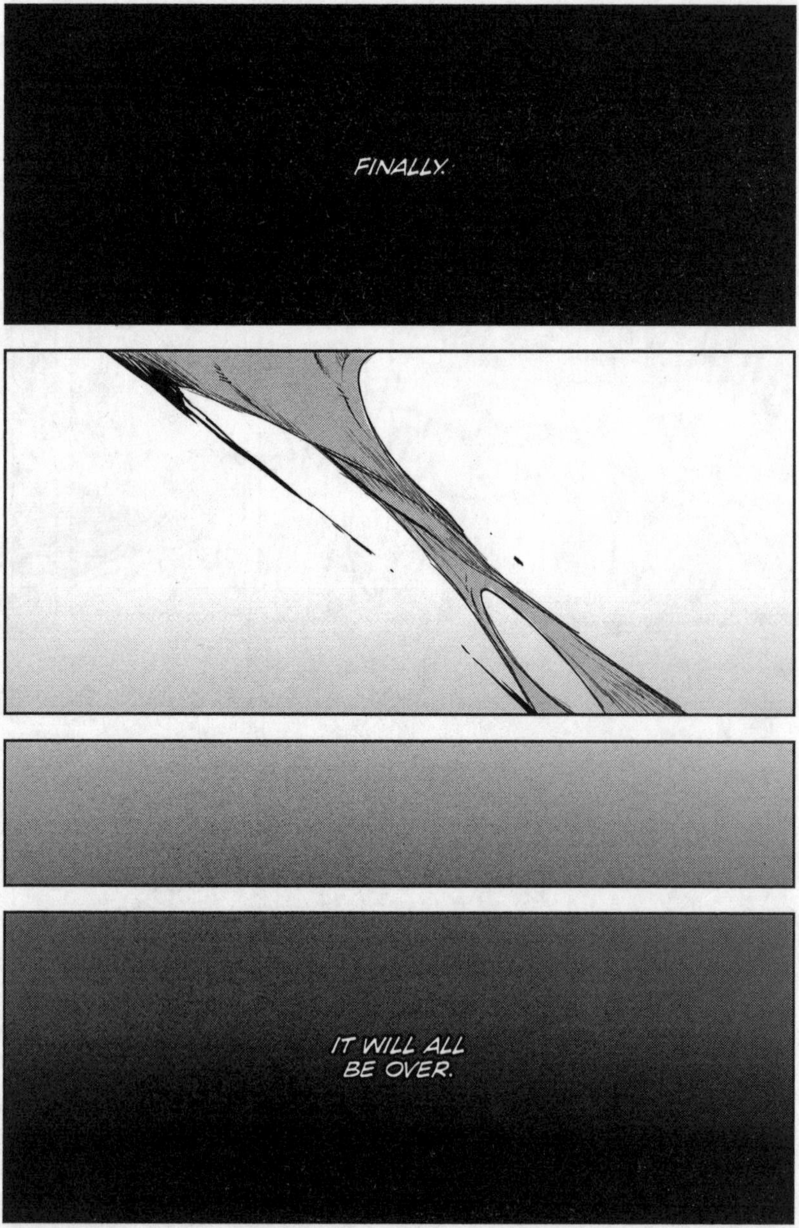
FINALLY.
IT WILL ALL BE OVER.

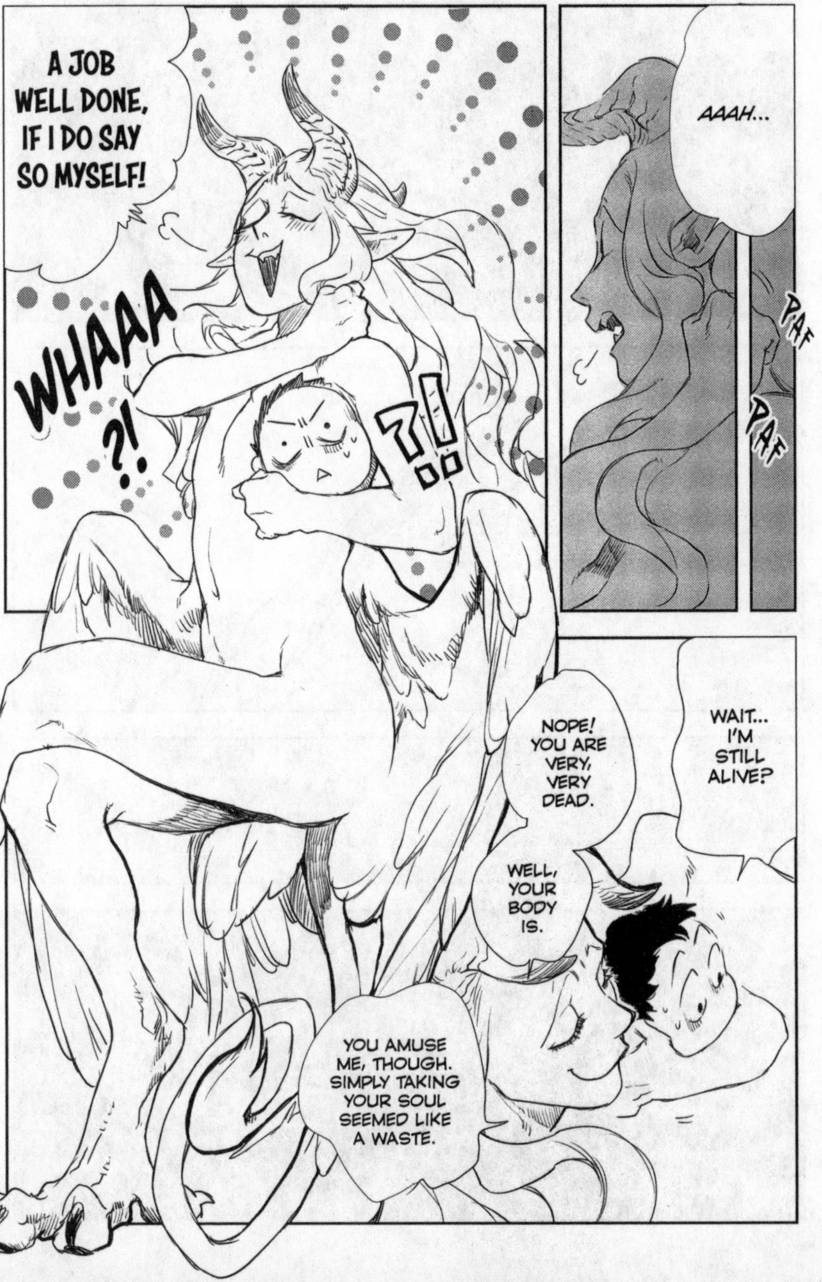
AAAH...
PAF
PAF
A JOB WELL DONE, IF I DO SAY SO MYSELF!
WHAAA ?!
?!
WAIT... I'M STILL ALIVE?
NOPE! YOU ARE VERY, VERY DEAD.
WELL, YOUR BODY IS.
YOU AMUSE ME, THOUGH. SIMPLY TAKING YOUR SOUL SEEMED LIKE A WASTE.

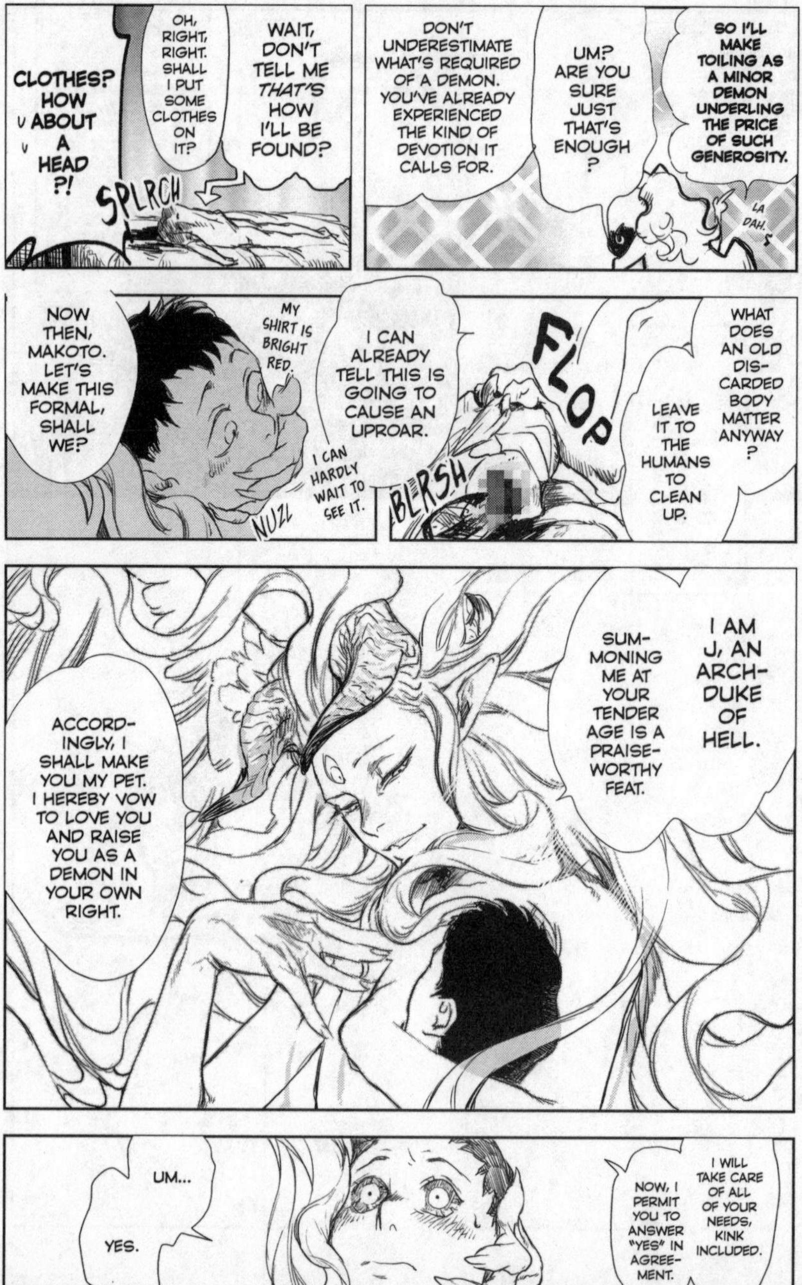

SO I'LL MAKE TOILING AS A MINOR DEMON UNDERLING THE PRICE OF SUCH GENEROSITY.
LA DAH.
UM? ARE YOU SURE JUST THAT'S ENOUGH?
DON'T UNDERESTIMATE WHAT'S REQUIRED OF A DEMON. YOU'VE ALREADY EXPERIENCED THE KIND OF DEVOTION IT CALLS FOR.
WAIT, DON'T TELL ME *THAT'S* HOW I'LL BE FOUND?
OH, RIGHT, RIGHT. SHALL I PUT SOME CLOTHES ON IT?
CLOTHES? HOW ABOUT A HEAD?!
SPLRCH
WHAT DOES AN OLD DISCARDED BODY MATTER ANYWAY?
LEAVE IT TO THE HUMANS TO CLEAN UP.
FLOP
BLRSH
I CAN ALREADY TELL THIS IS GOING TO CAUSE AN UPROAR.
MY SHIRT IS BRIGHT RED.
I CAN HARDLY WAIT TO SEE IT.
NOW THEN, MAKOTO. LET'S MAKE THIS FORMAL, SHALL WE?
NUZL
I AM J, AN ARCHDUKE OF HELL.
SUMMONING ME AT YOUR TENDER AGE IS A PRAISEWORTHY FEAT.
ACCORDINGLY, I SHALL MAKE YOU MY PET. I HEREBY VOW TO LOVE YOU AND RAISE YOU AS A DEMON IN YOUR OWN RIGHT.
I WILL TAKE CARE OF ALL OF YOUR NEEDS, KINK INCLUDED.
NOW, I PERMIT YOU TO ANSWER "YES" IN AGREEMENT.
UM...
YES.

THE CASE OF THE BOY WITH THE MISSING HEAD MADE HEADLINES ACROSS THE NATION, GOING DOWN AS ONE OF THE MOST BIZARRE MURDERS OF THE ERA.

GIVEN THE VARIOUS BOOK'S DISCOVERED IN HIS ROOM, RUMORS FLEW THAT HE'D BEEN INVOLVED IN SOME SHADY CULT BUSINESS...

...BUT TO MAKOTO, IT NO LONGER MATTERED.

HE'D JUST BEEN REBORN AS A DEMON.

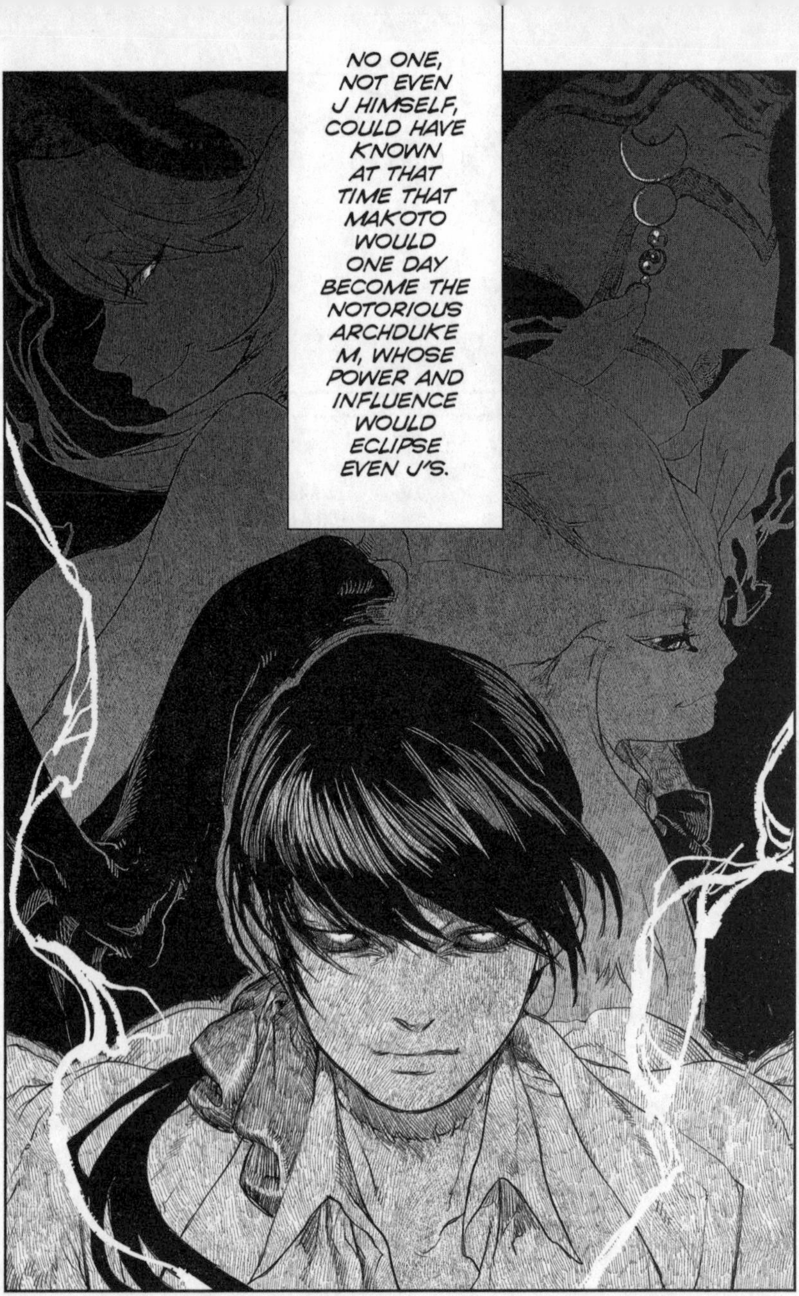
NO ONE, NOT EVEN J HIMSELF, COULD HAVE KNOWN AT THAT TIME THAT MAKOTO WOULD ONE DAY BECOME THE NOTORIOUS ARCHDUKE M, WHOSE POWER AND INFLUENCE WOULD ECLIPSE EVEN J'S.

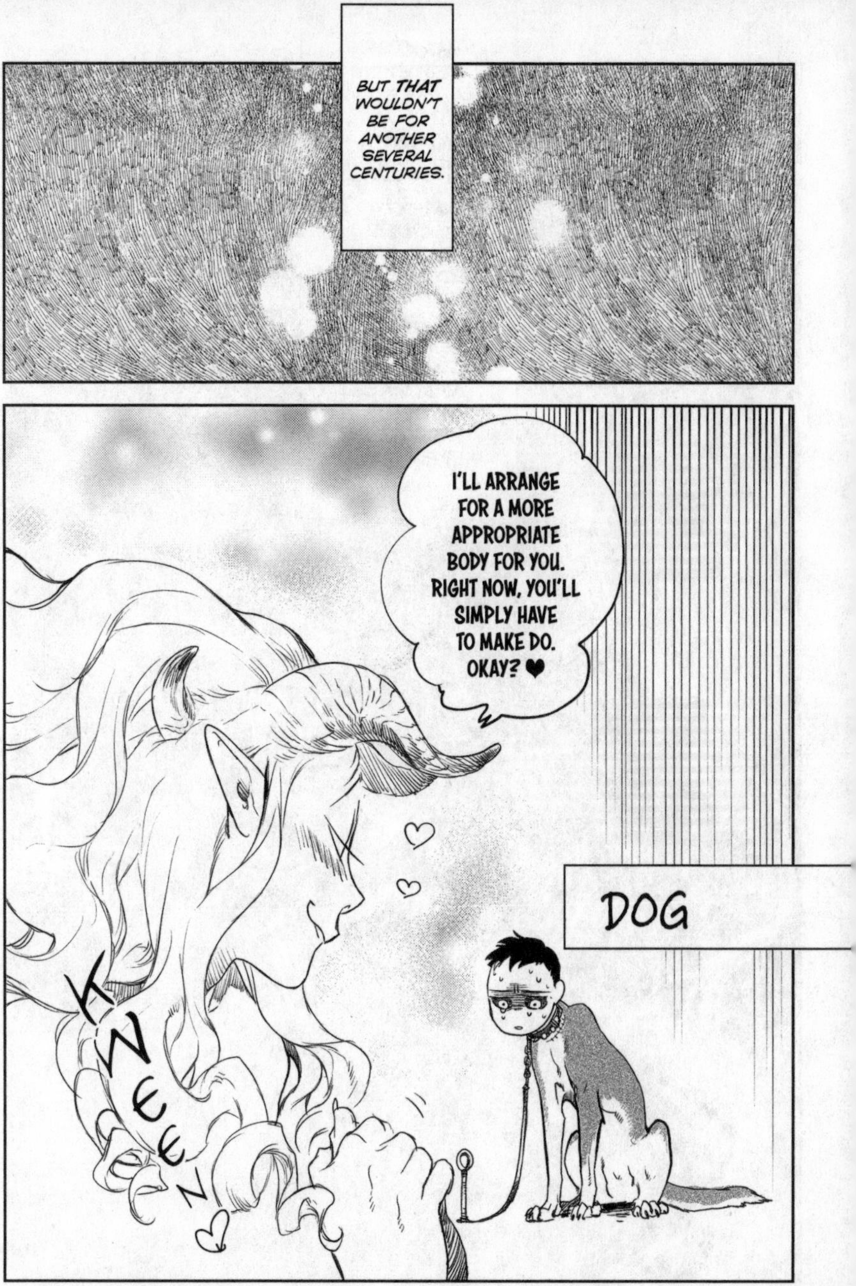
BUT THAT WOULDN'T BE FOR ANOTHER SEVERAL CENTURIES.
I'LL ARRANGE FOR A MORE APPROPRIATE BODY FOR YOU. RIGHT NOW, YOU'LL SIMPLY HAVE TO MAKE DO. OKAY? ❤
KWEEEN
DOG

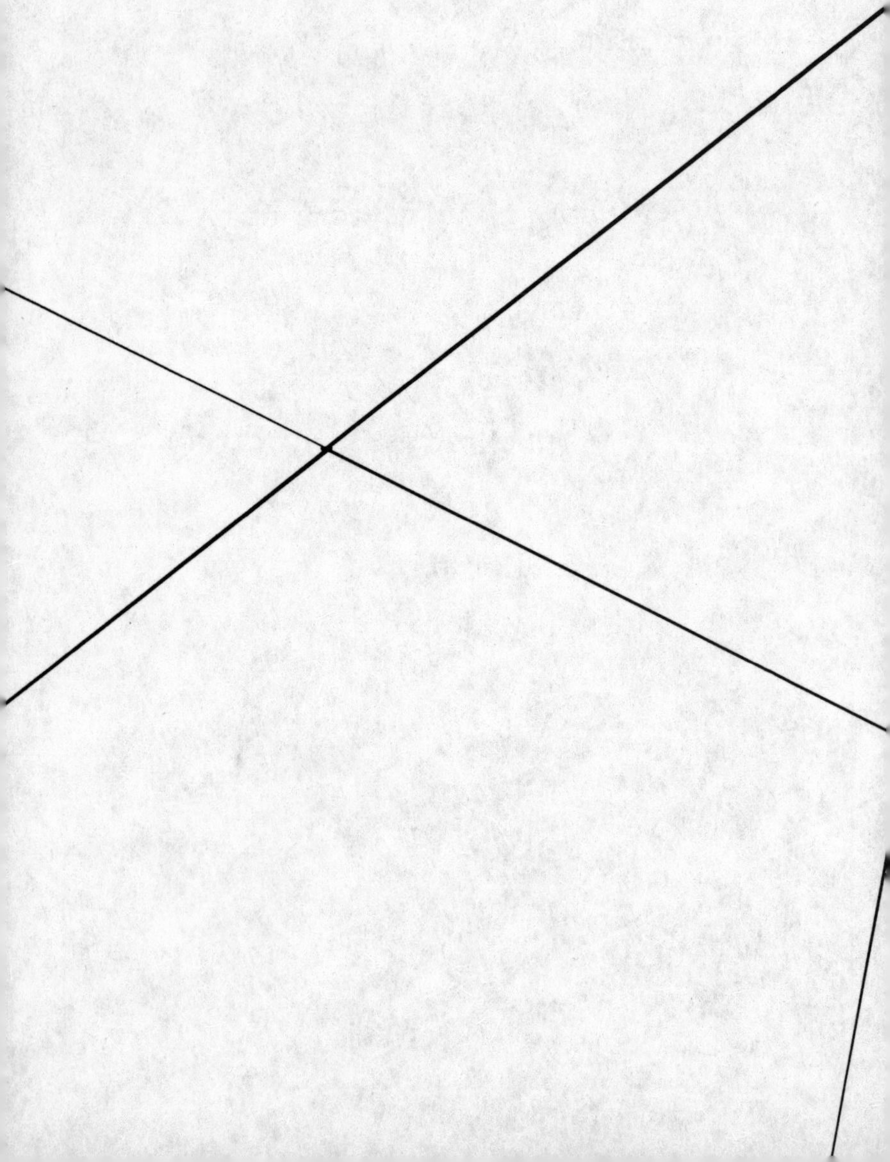

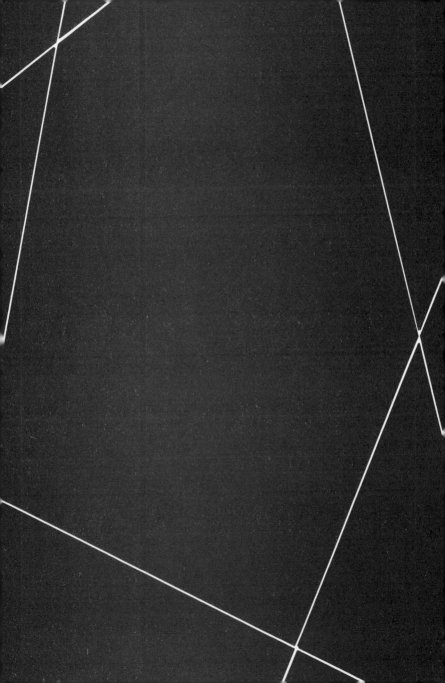

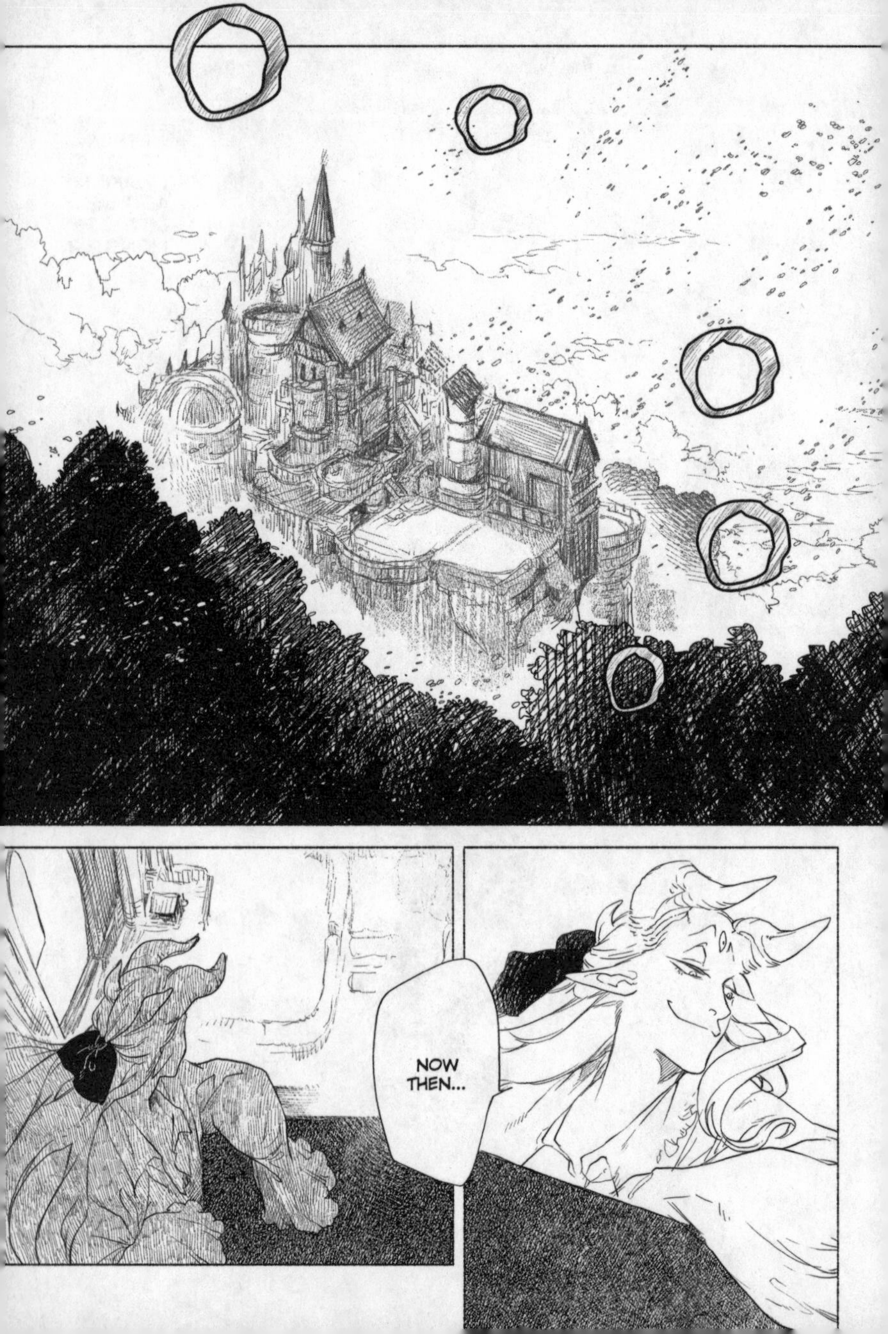
NOW THEN...

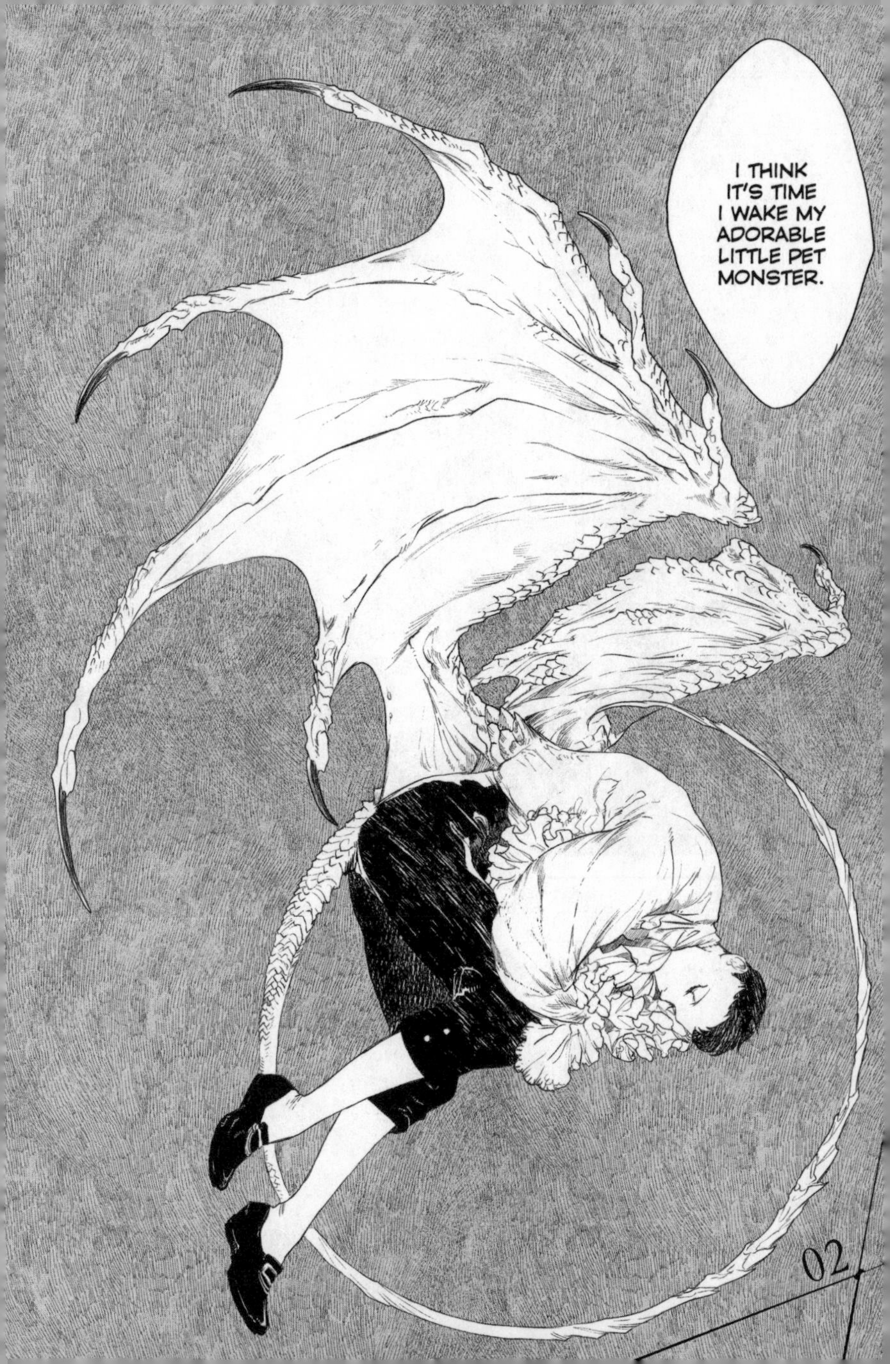
I THINK IT'S TIME I WAKE MY ADORABLE LITTLE PET MONSTER.
02

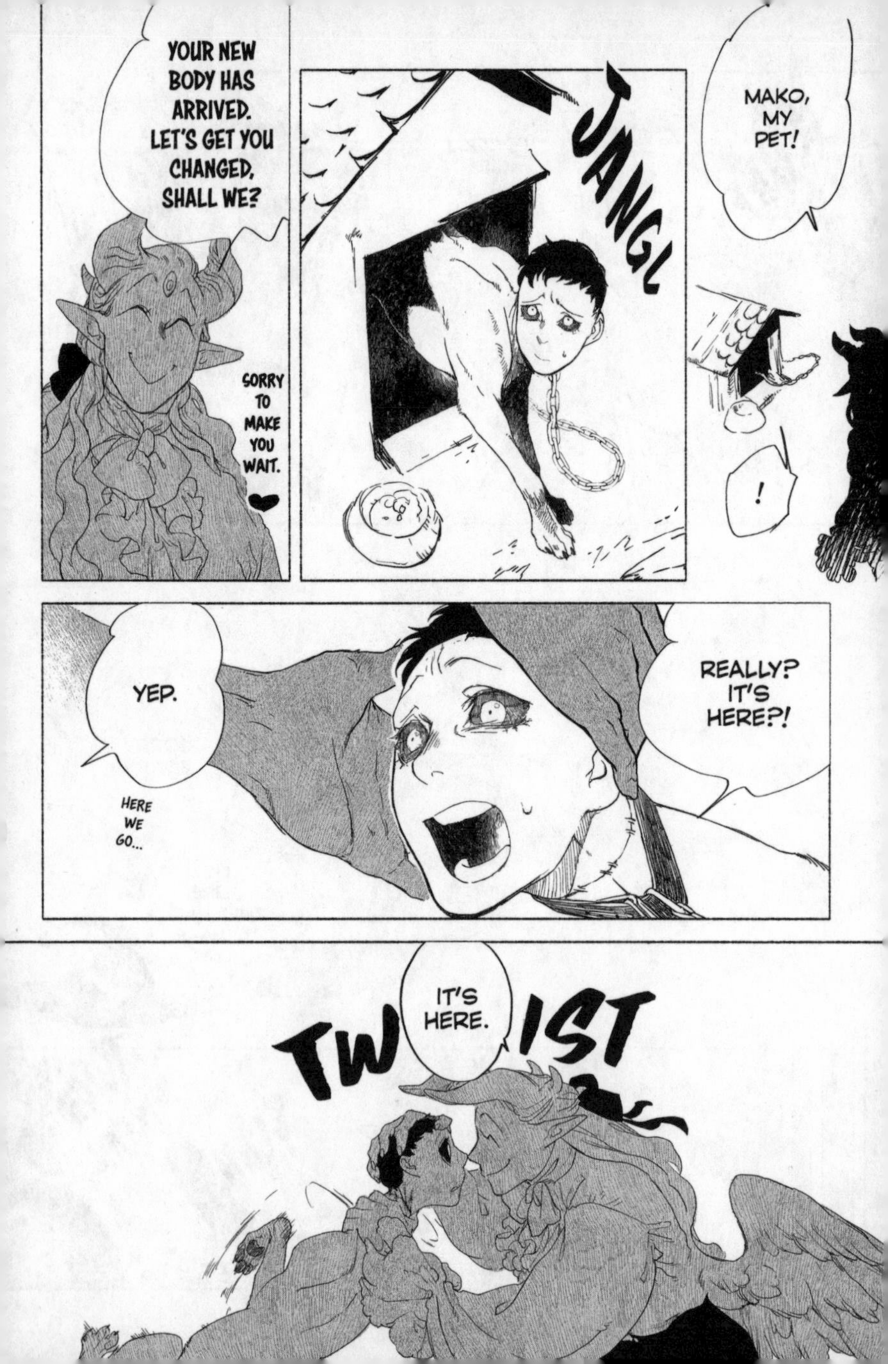
MAKO, MY PET!
!
JANGL
YOUR NEW BODY HAS ARRIVED. LET'S GET YOU CHANGED, SHALL WE?
SORRY TO MAKE YOU WAIT. ❤
REALLY? IT'S HERE?!
YEP.
HERE WE GO...
IT'S HERE.
TWIST

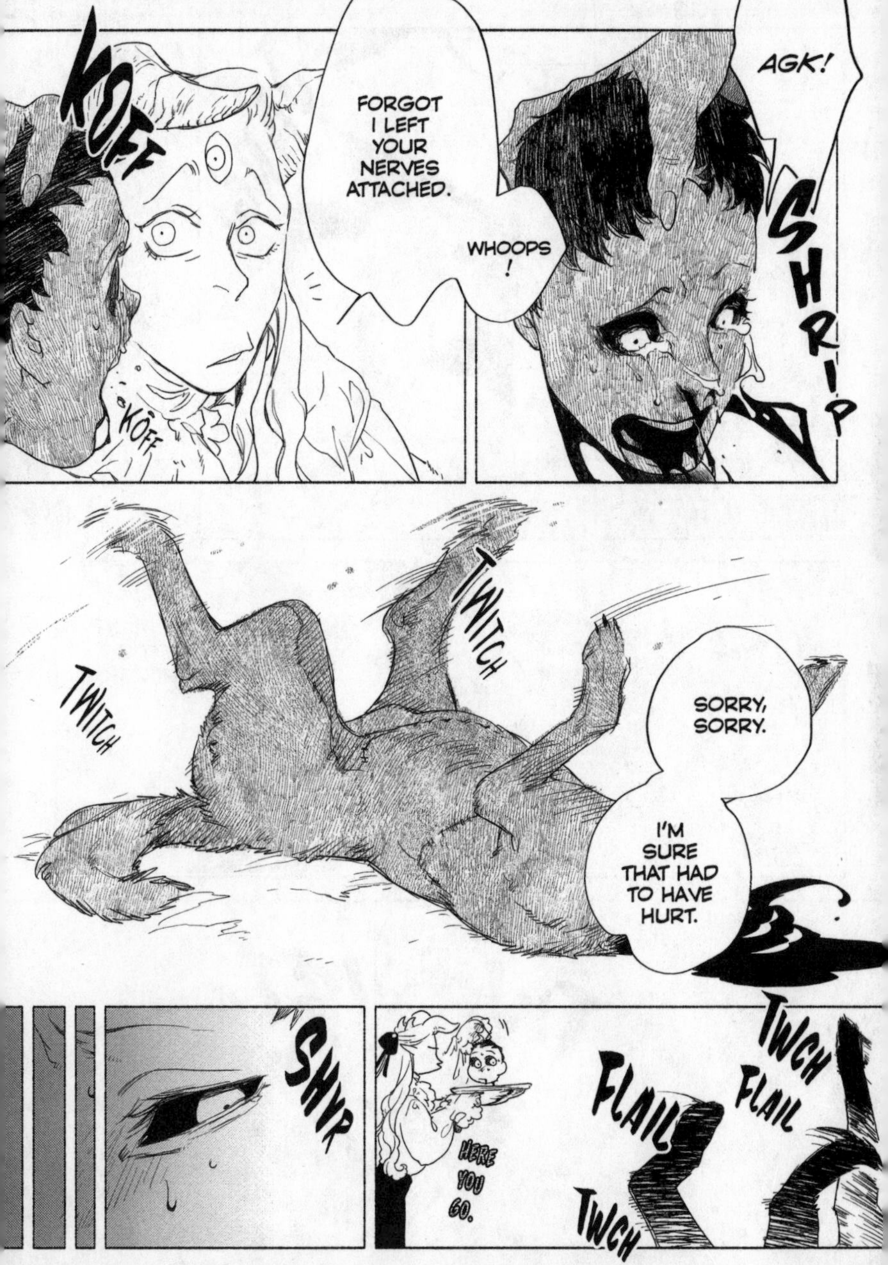
AGK!
SHRIP
WHOOPS!
FORGOT I LEFT YOUR NERVES ATTACHED.
KÖFF
KÖFF
TWITCH
SORRY, SORRY.
I'M SURE THAT HAD TO HAVE HURT.
TWITCH
TWCH
FLAIL
FLAIL
TWCH
HERE YOU GO.
SHVR

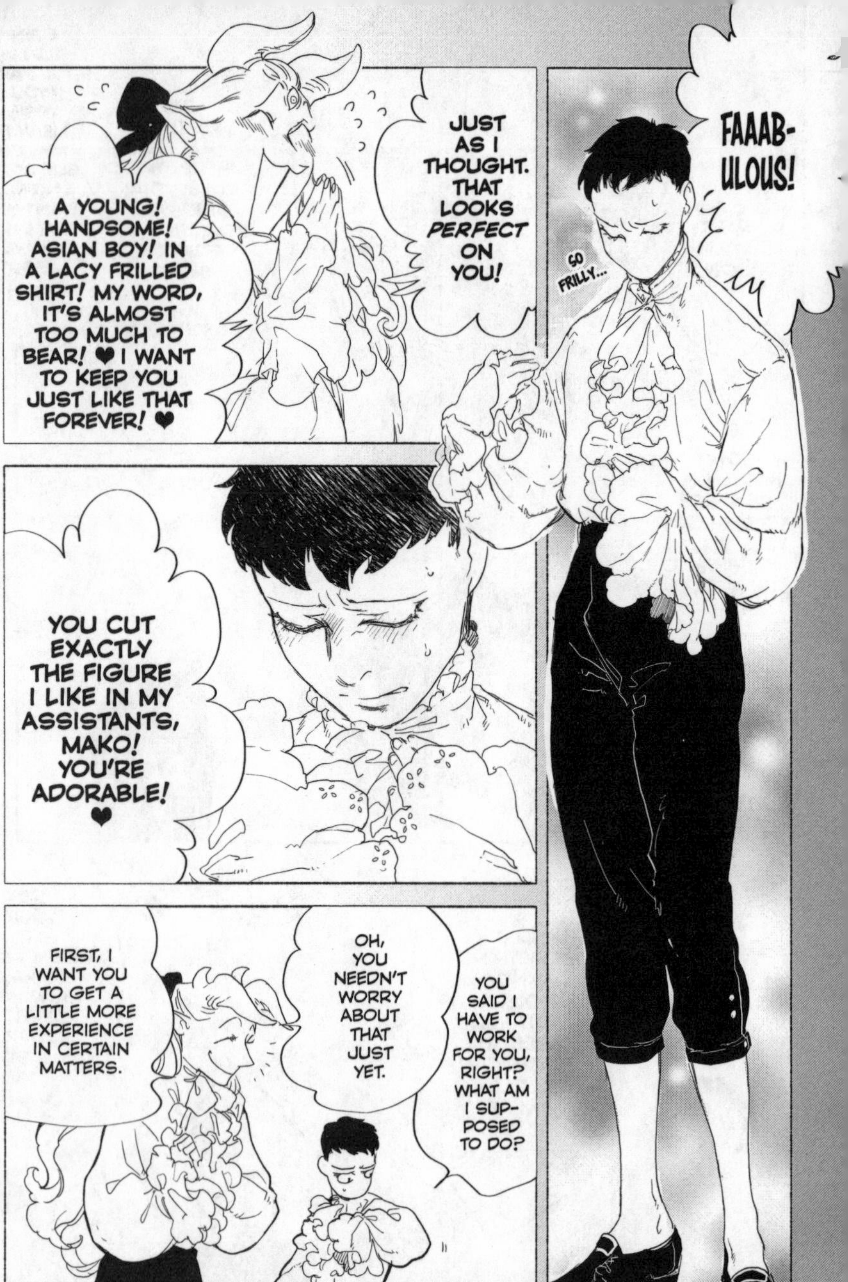
FAAAB-ULOUS!
SO FRILLY...
JUST AS I THOUGHT. THAT LOOKS *PERFECT* ON YOU!
A YOUNG! HANDSOME! ASIAN BOY! IN A LACY FRILLED SHIRT! MY WORD, IT'S ALMOST TOO MUCH TO BEAR! ❤ I WANT TO KEEP YOU JUST LIKE THAT FOREVER! ❤
YOU CUT EXACTLY THE FIGURE I LIKE IN MY ASSISTANTS, MAKO! YOU'RE ADORABLE! ❤
YOU SAID I HAVE TO WORK FOR YOU, RIGHT? WHAT AM I SUP-POSED TO DO?
OH, YOU NEEDN'T WORRY ABOUT THAT JUST YET.
FIRST, I WANT YOU TO GET A LITTLE MORE EXPERIENCE IN CERTAIN MATTERS.

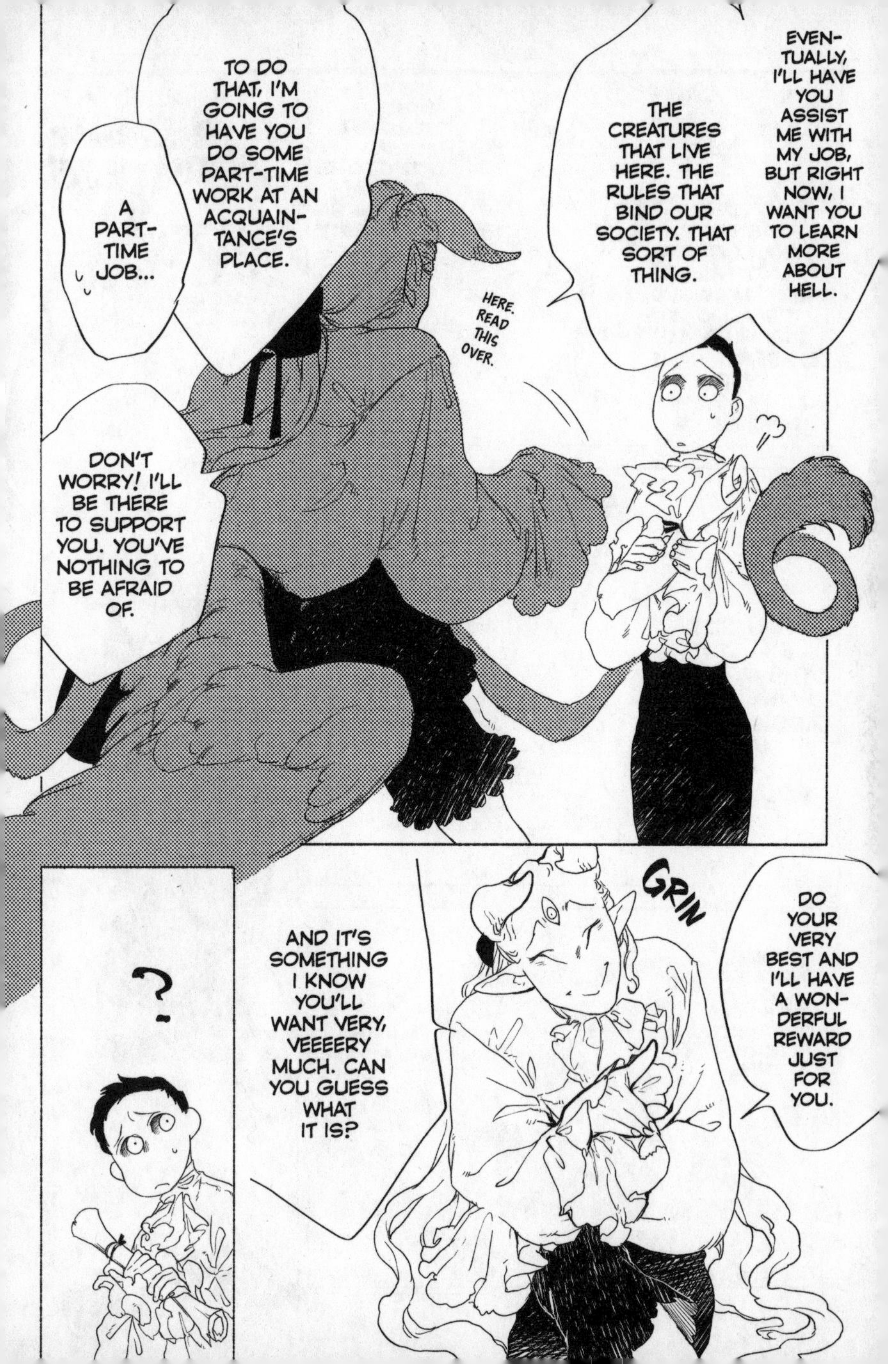
EVEN-TUALLY, I'LL HAVE YOU ASSIST ME WITH MY JOB, BUT RIGHT NOW, I WANT YOU TO LEARN MORE ABOUT HELL.
THE CREATURES THAT LIVE HERE. THE RULES THAT BIND OUR SOCIETY. THAT SORT OF THING.
HERE. READ THIS OVER.
TO DO THAT, I'M GOING TO HAVE YOU DO SOME PART-TIME WORK AT AN ACQUAIN-TANCE'S PLACE.
A PART-TIME JOB...
DON'T WORRY! I'LL BE THERE TO SUPPORT YOU. YOU'VE NOTHING TO BE AFRAID OF.
GRIN
DO YOUR VERY BEST AND I'LL HAVE A WON-DERFUL REWARD JUST FOR YOU.
AND IT'S SOMETHING I KNOW YOU'LL WANT VERY, VEEEERY MUCH. CAN YOU GUESS WHAT IT IS?
?

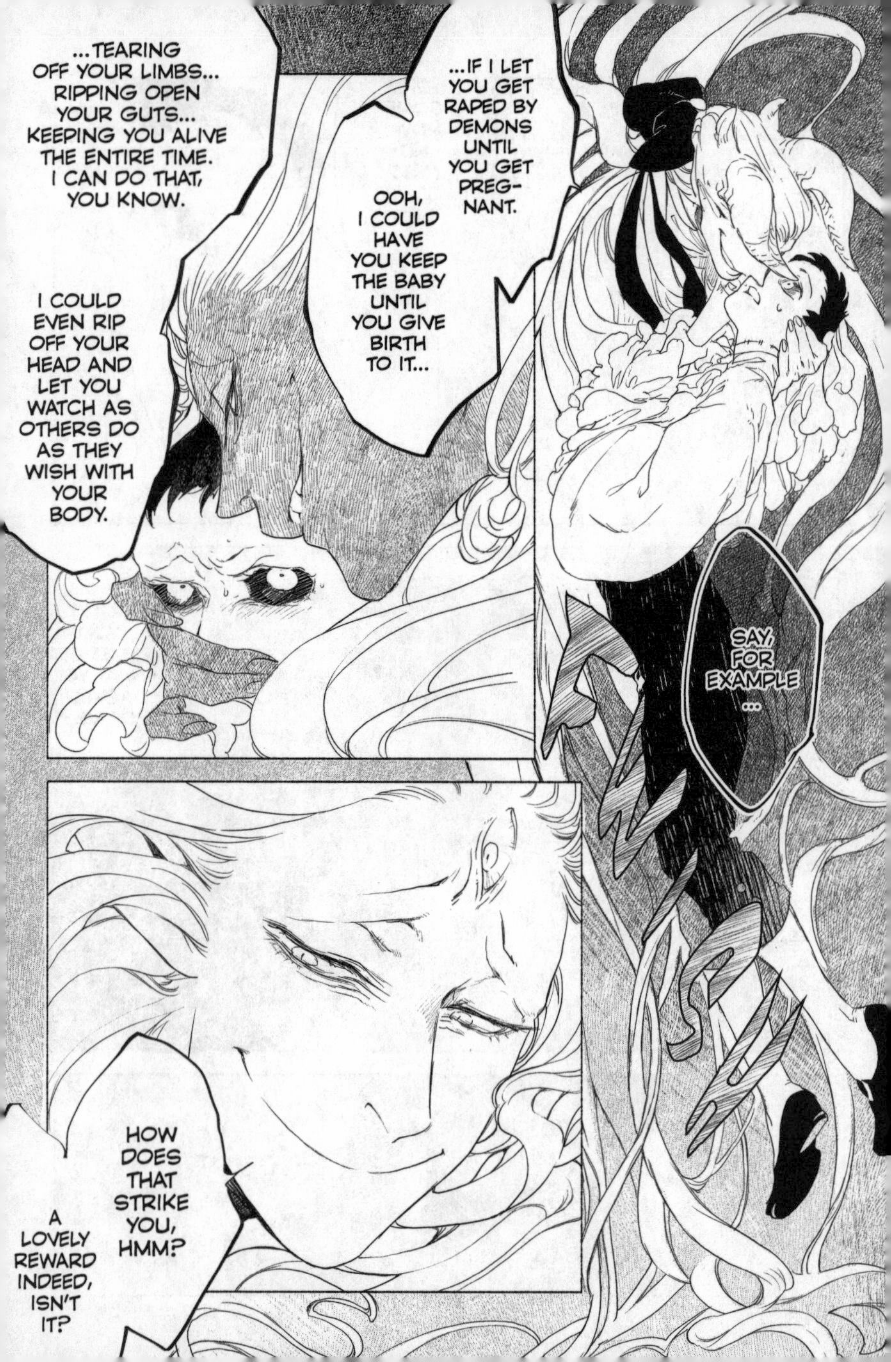
SAY, FOR EXAMPLE...
...IF I LET YOU GET RAPED BY DEMONS UNTIL YOU GET PREGNANT.
OOH, I COULD HAVE YOU KEEP THE BABY UNTIL YOU GIVE BIRTH TO IT...
...TEARING OFF YOUR LIMBS... RIPPING OPEN YOUR GUTS... KEEPING YOU ALIVE THE ENTIRE TIME. I CAN DO THAT, YOU KNOW.
I COULD EVEN RIP OFF YOUR HEAD AND LET YOU WATCH AS OTHERS DO AS THEY WISH WITH YOUR BODY.
HOW DOES THAT STRIKE YOU, HMM?
A LOVELY REWARD INDEED, ISN'T IT?

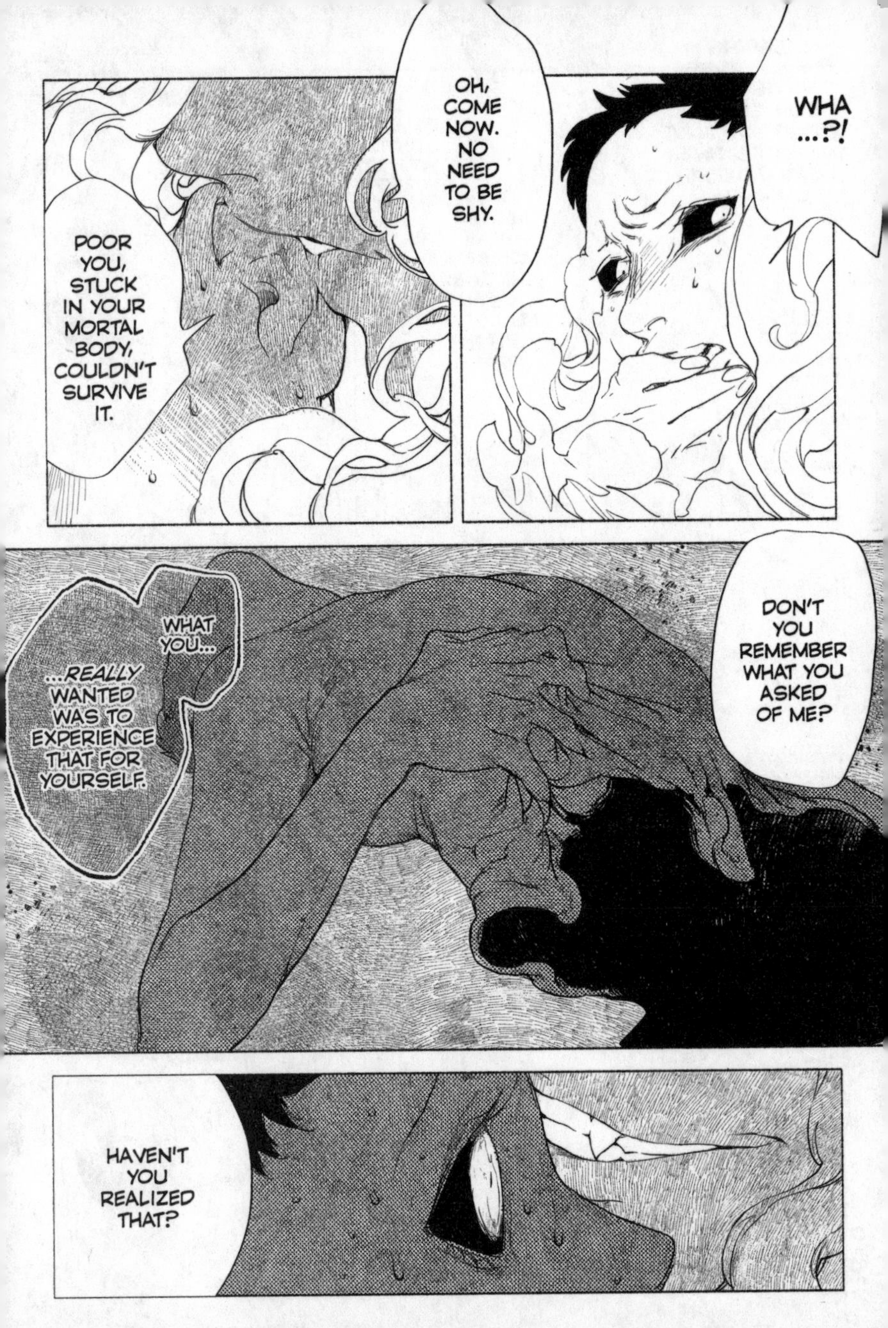
WHA ...?!
OH, COME NOW. NO NEED TO BE SHY.
POOR YOU, STUCK IN YOUR MORTAL BODY, COULDN'T SURVIVE IT.
DON'T YOU REMEMBER WHAT YOU ASKED OF ME?
WHAT YOU...
...*REALLY* WANTED WAS TO EXPERIENCE THAT FOR YOURSELF.
HAVEN'T YOU REALIZED THAT?

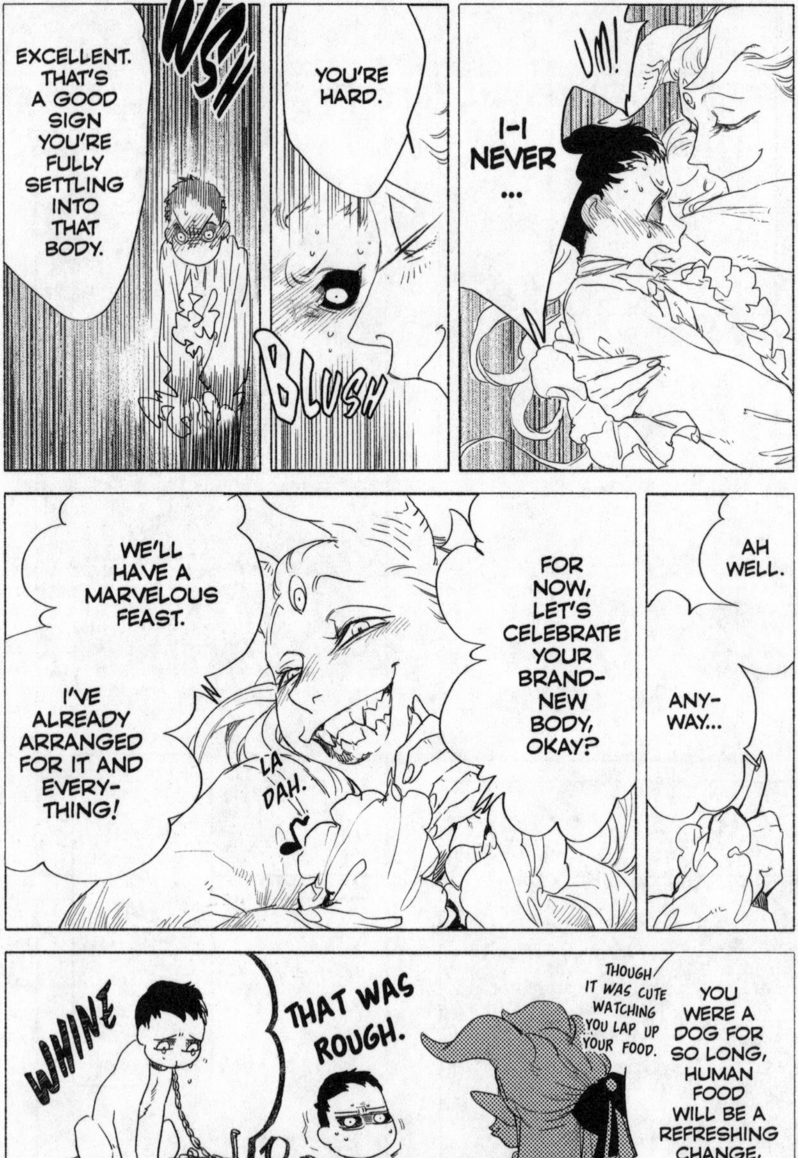
UM!
I-I NEVER ...
YOU'RE HARD.
BLUSH
WSH
EXCELLENT. THAT'S A GOOD SIGN YOU'RE FULLY SETTLING INTO THAT BODY.
AH WELL.
ANY-WAY...
FOR NOW, LET'S CELEBRATE YOUR BRAND-NEW BODY, OKAY?
WE'LL HAVE A MARVELOUS FEAST.
LA DAH.
I'VE ALREADY ARRANGED FOR IT AND EVERY-THING!
YOU WERE A DOG FOR SO LONG, HUMAN FOOD WILL BE A REFRESHING CHANGE, I'M SURE.
THOUGH IT WAS CUTE WATCHING YOU LAP UP YOUR FOOD.
THAT WAS ROUGH.
WHINE
MAKO

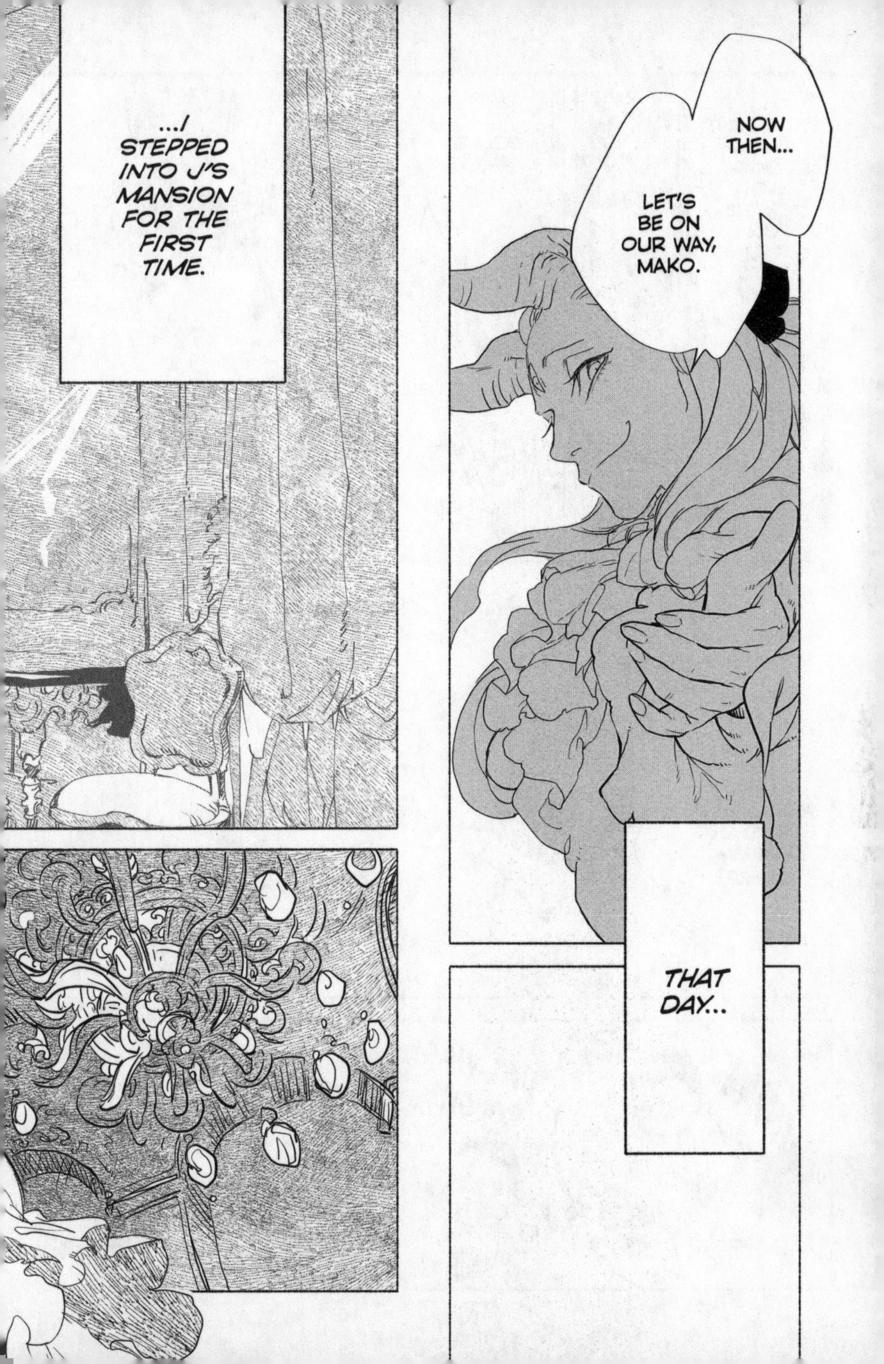
NOW THEN... LET'S BE ON OUR WAY, MAKO.
THAT DAY...
...I STEPPED INTO J'S MANSION FOR THE FIRST TIME.

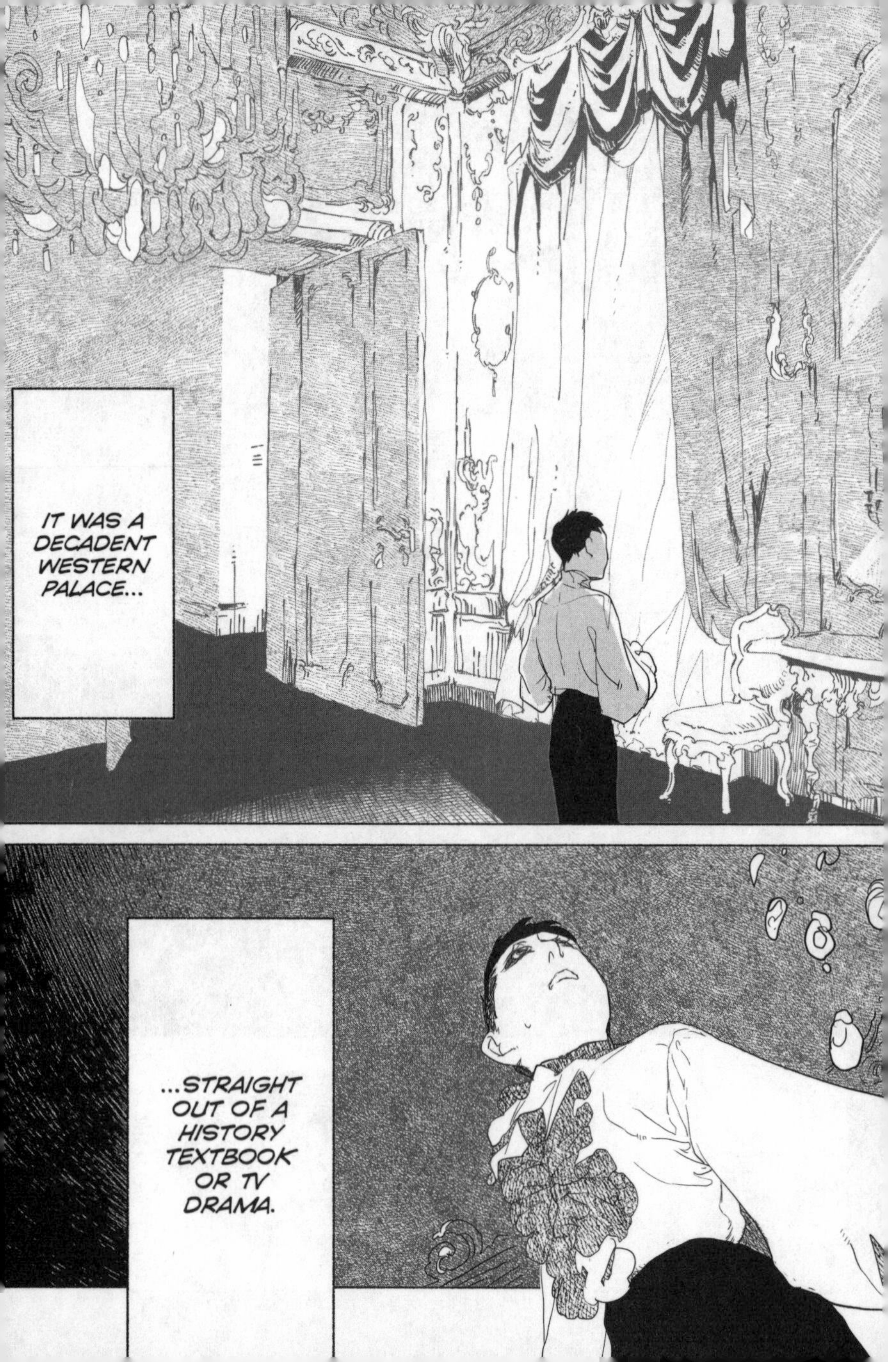
IT WAS A DECADENT WESTERN PALACE...
...STRAIGHT OUT OF A HISTORY TEXTBOOK OR TV DRAMA.

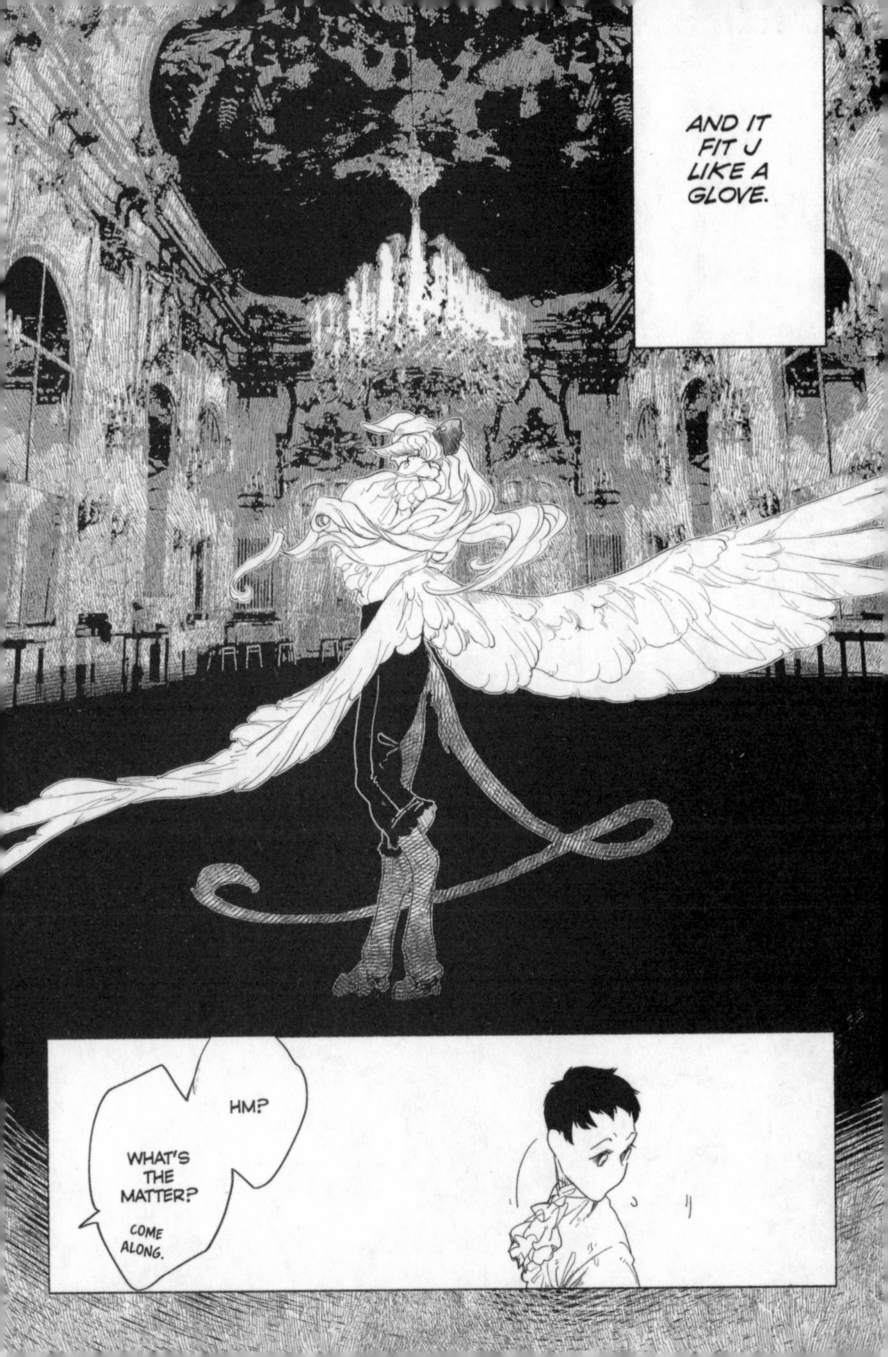
AND IT FIT J LIKE A GLOVE.
HM?
WHAT'S THE MATTER?
COME ALONG.

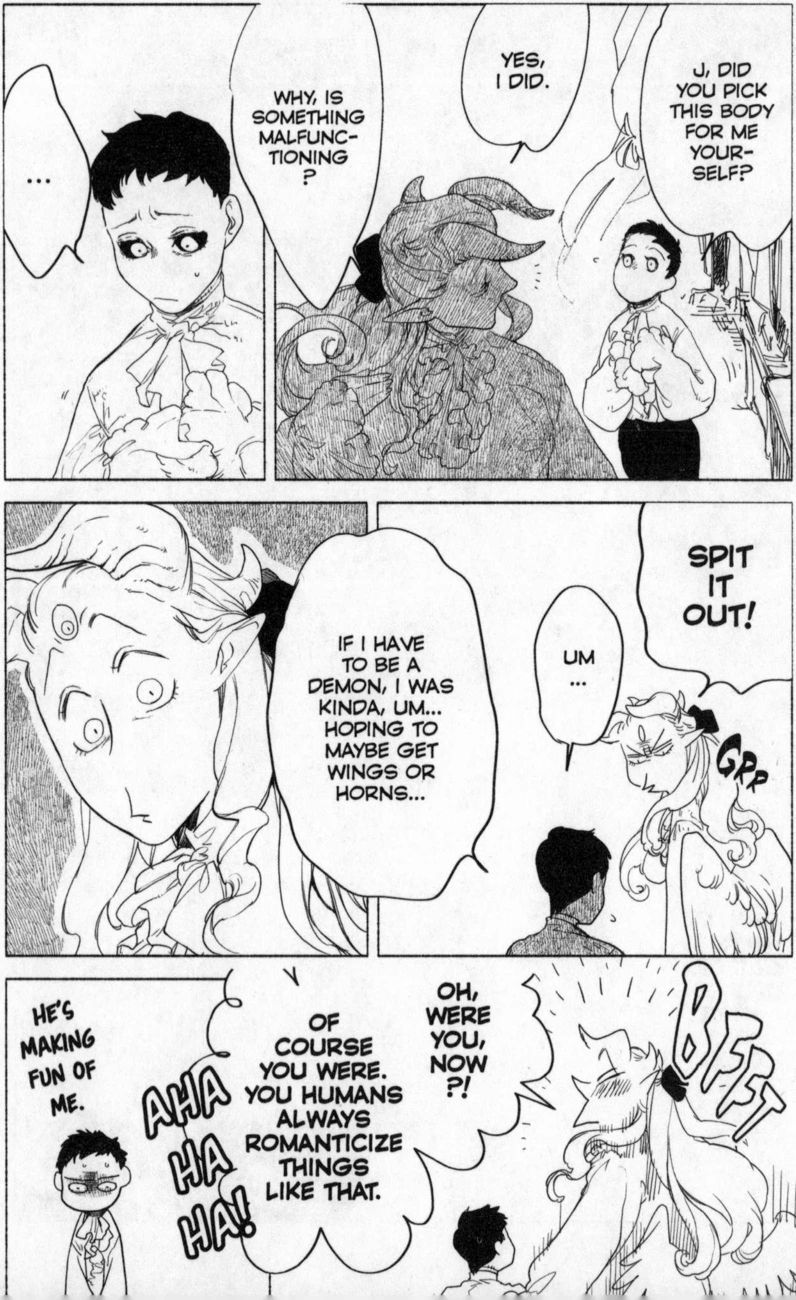
J, DID YOU PICK THIS BODY FOR ME YOURSELF?
YES, I DID.
WHY, IS SOMETHING MALFUNCTIONING?
...
SPIT IT OUT!
UM ...
GRR
IF I HAVE TO BE A DEMON, I WAS KINDA, UM... HOPING TO MAYBE GET WINGS OR HORNS...
BFFT
OH, WERE YOU, NOW?!
OF COURSE YOU WERE. YOU HUMANS ALWAYS ROMANTICIZE THINGS LIKE THAT.
AHA HA HA!
HE'S MAKING FUN OF ME.

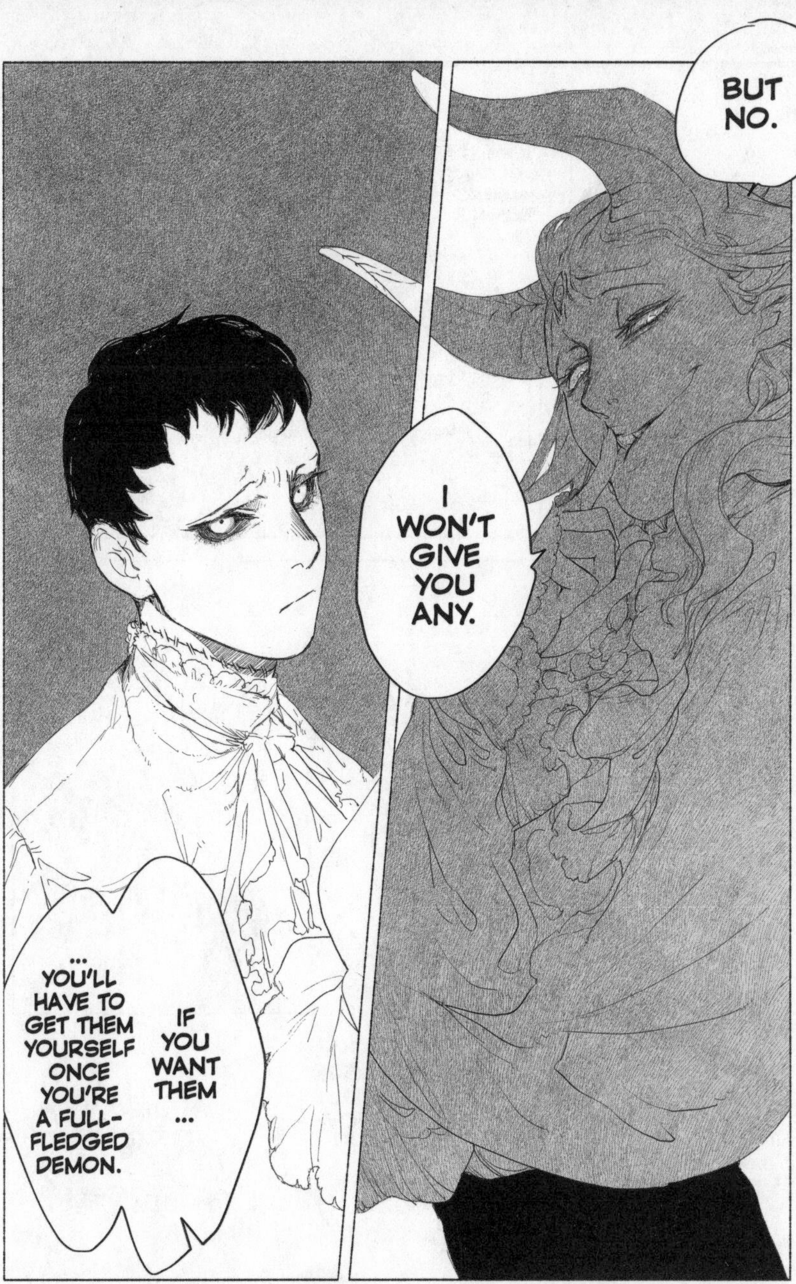
BUT NO.
I WON'T GIVE YOU ANY.
IF YOU WANT THEM ...
... YOU'LL HAVE TO GET THEM YOURSELF ONCE YOU'RE A FULL-FLEDGED DEMON.

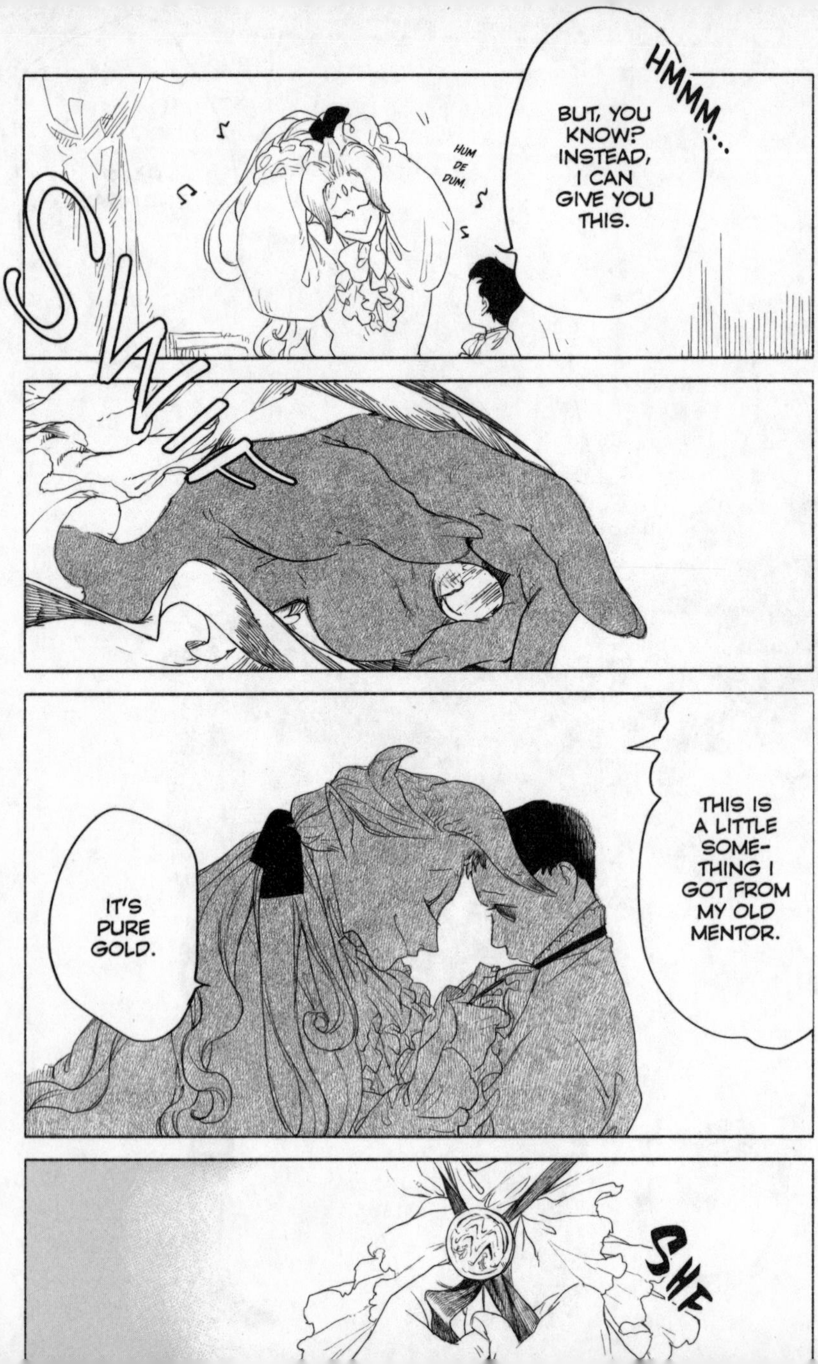
HMMM...
BUT, YOU KNOW? INSTEAD, I CAN GIVE YOU THIS.
HUM DE DUM.
SNIF
THIS IS A LITTLE SOME-THING I GOT FROM MY OLD MENTOR.
IT'S PURE GOLD.
SHF

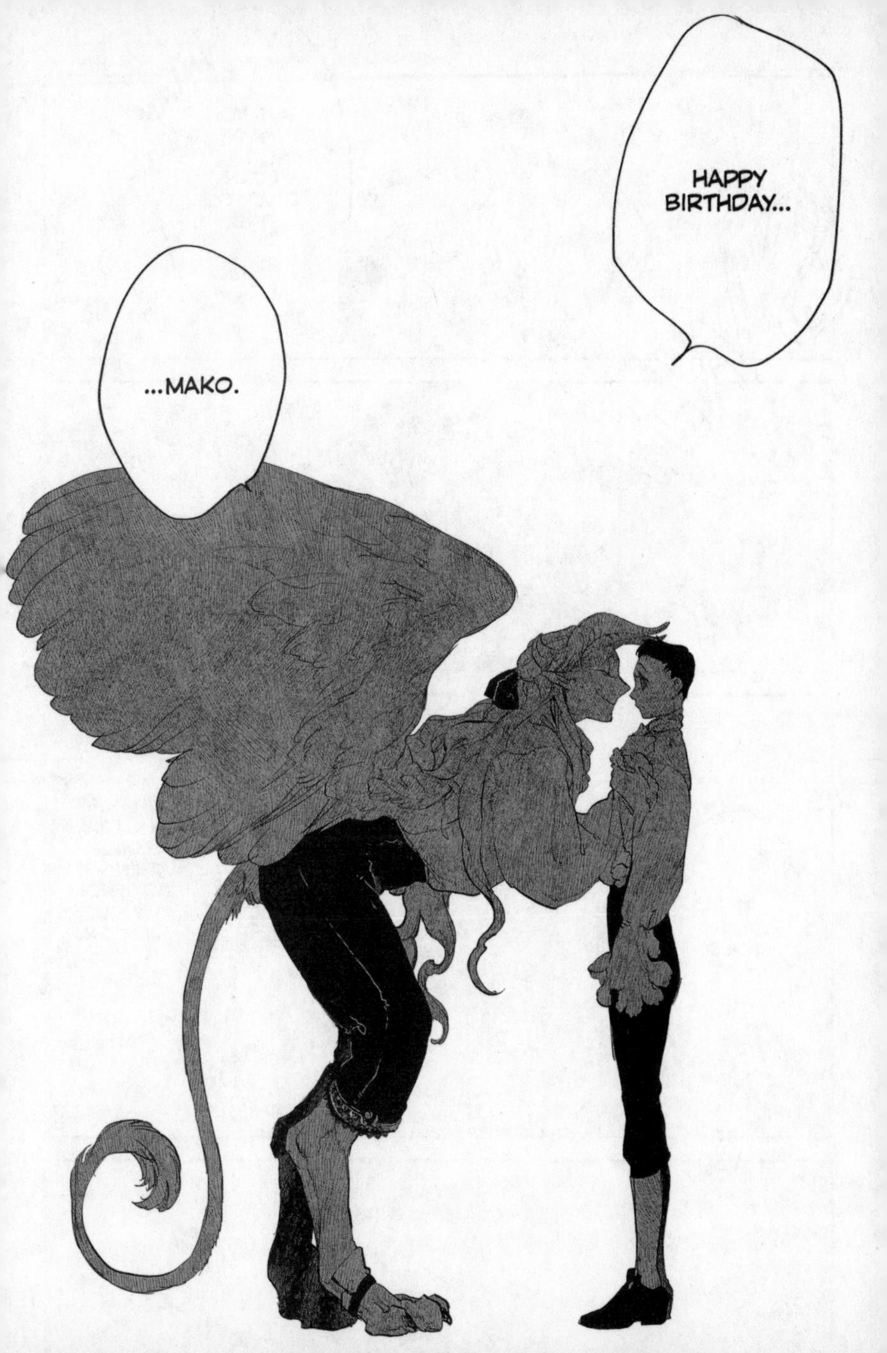
HAPPY BIRTHDAY...
...MAKO.

NOW THE REGRETS SINK IN.

I'D THOUGHT THAT ONCE I GOT MY WISH MY LIFE WOULD FINALLY BE OVER.

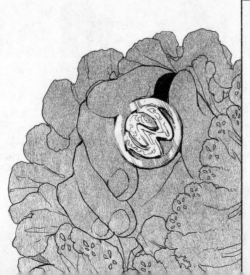

I NEVER EXPECTED I'D HAVE TO START A NEW ONE.

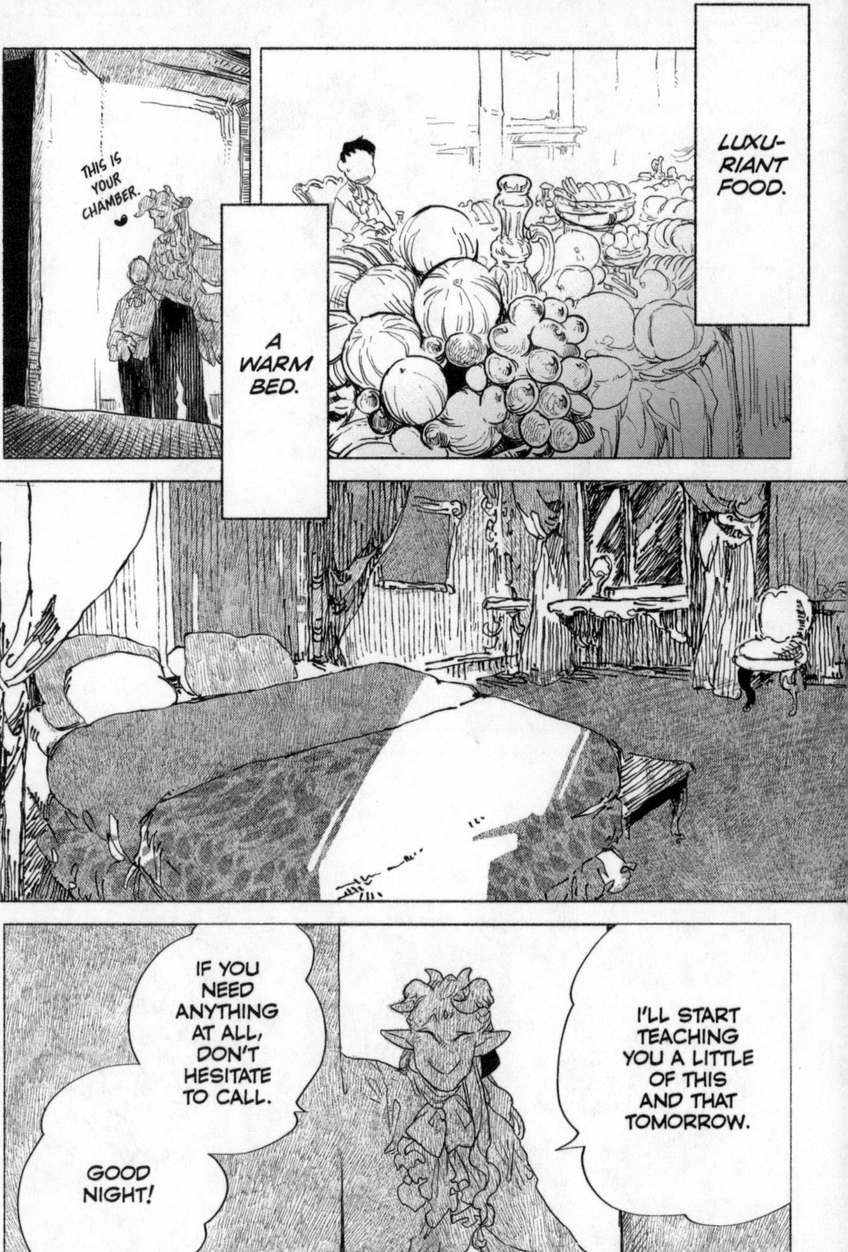
LUXU-
RIANT
FOOD.
A
WARM
BED.
THIS IS
YOUR
CHAMBER.
I'LL START
TEACHING
YOU A LITTLE
OF THIS
AND THAT
TOMORROW.
IF YOU
NEED
ANYTHING
AT ALL,
DON'T
HESITATE
TO CALL.
GOOD
NIGHT!

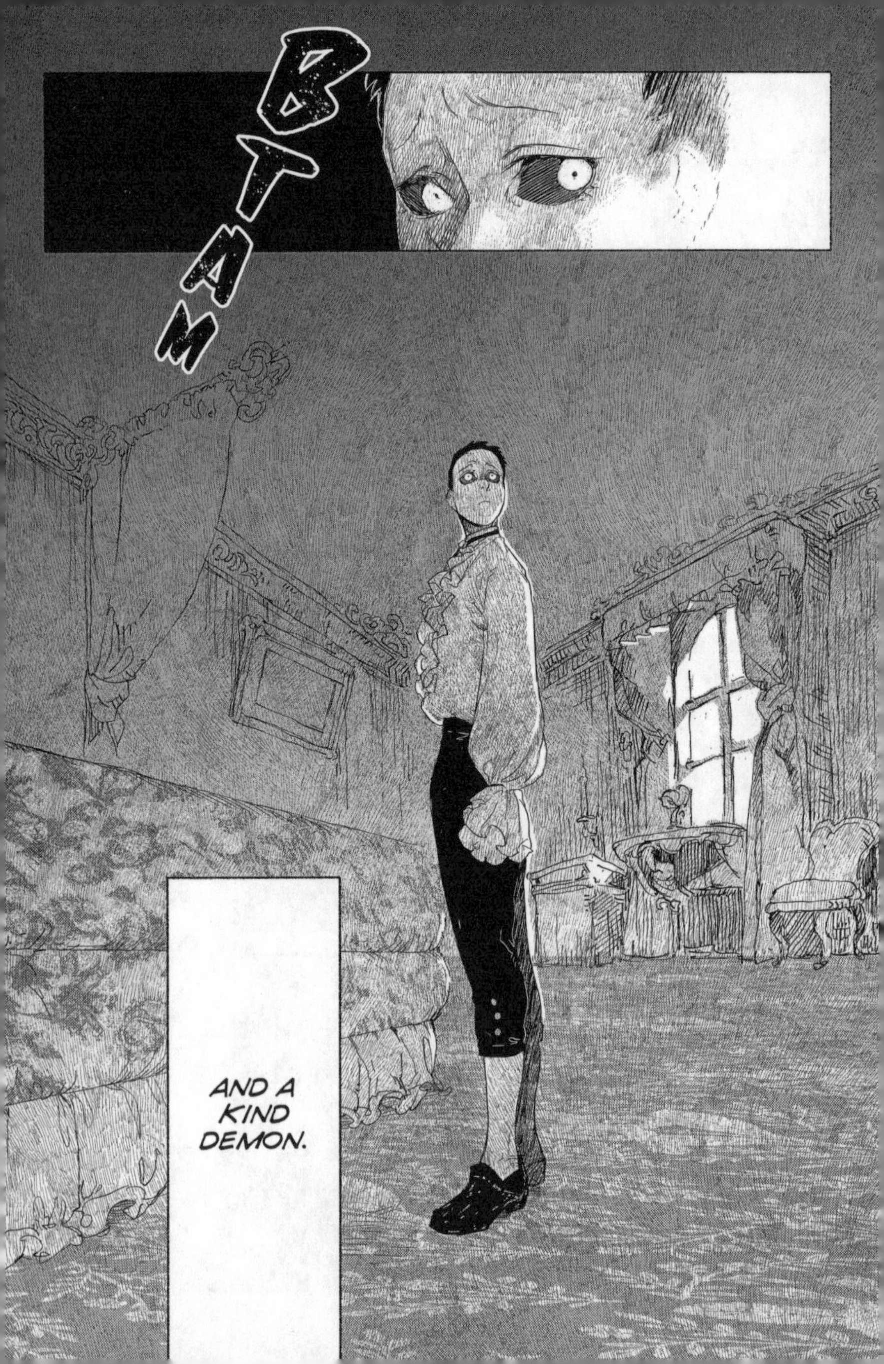
BTAM
AND A KIND DEMON.

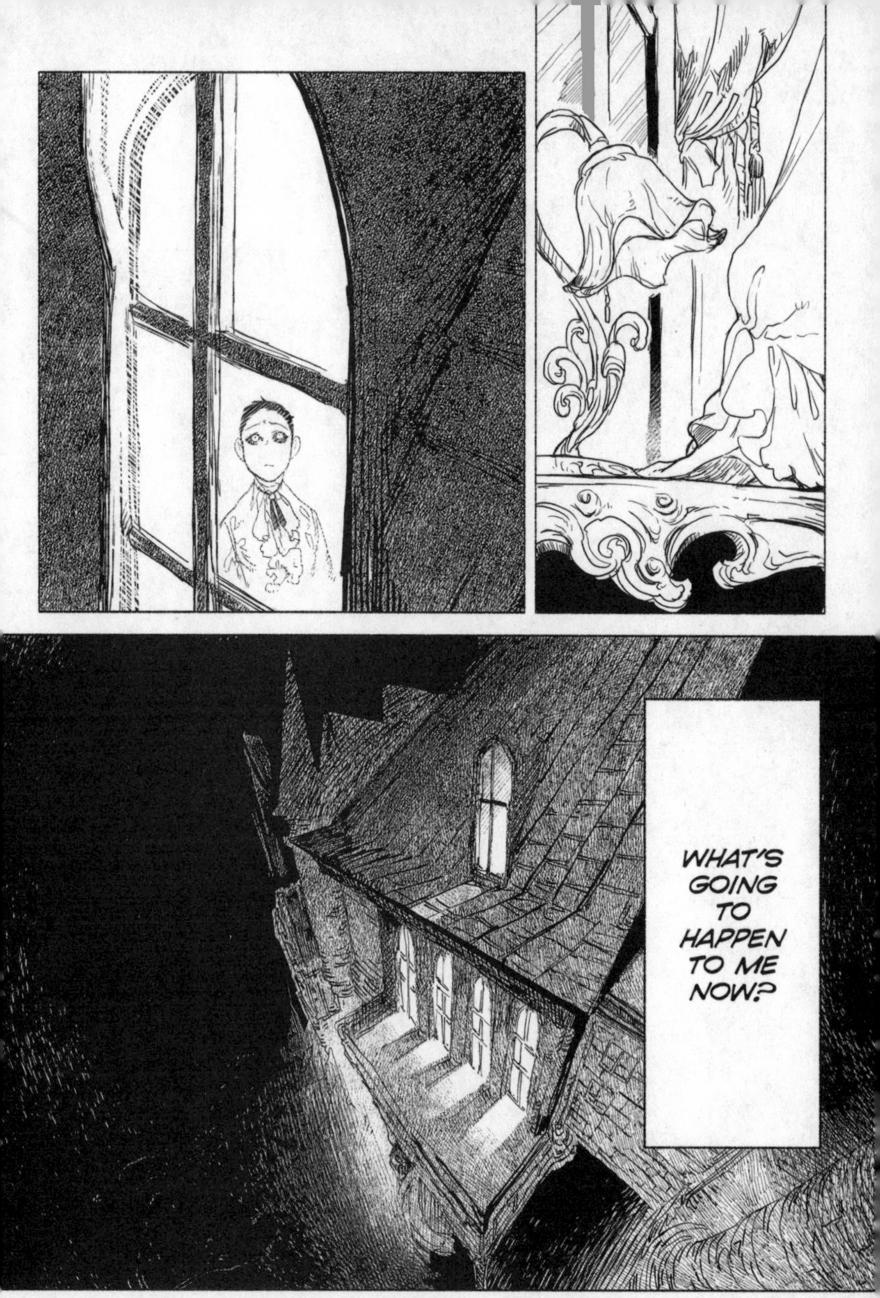
WHAT'S GOING TO HAPPEN TO ME NOW?

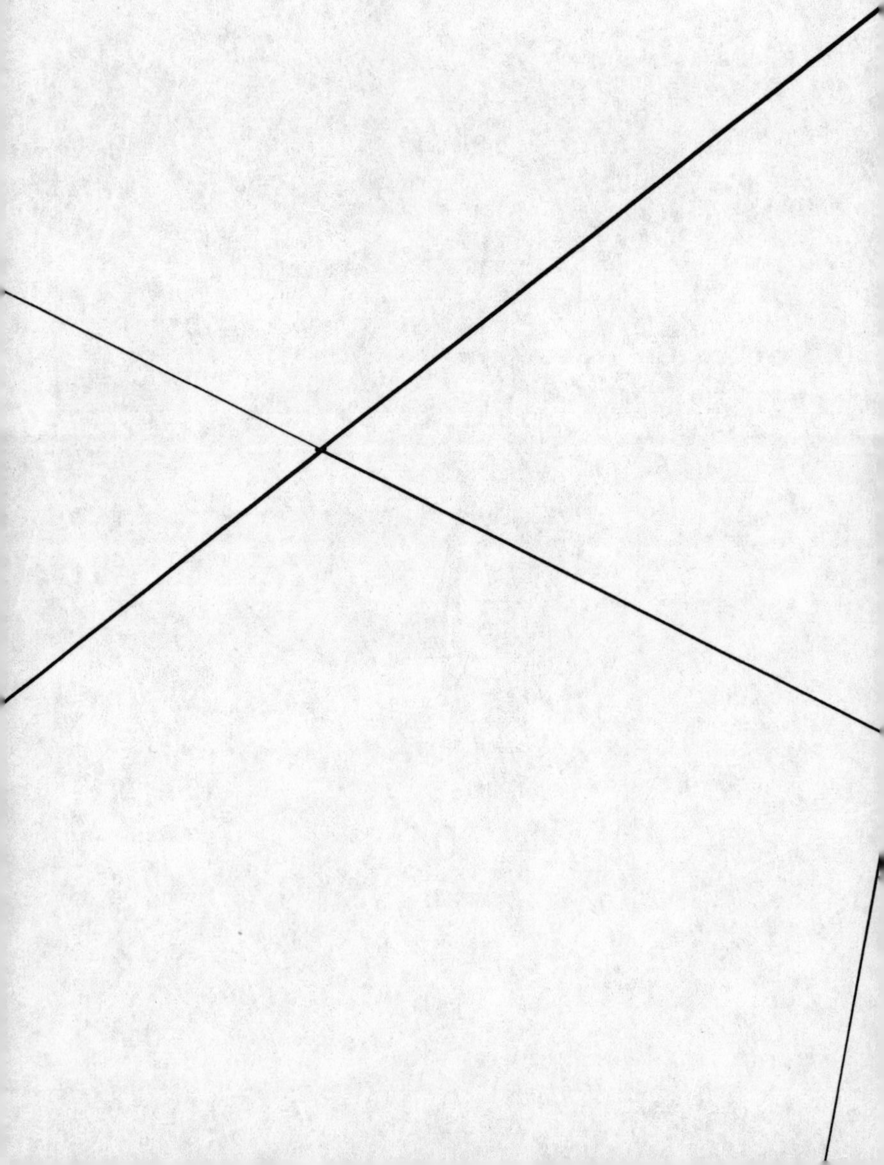

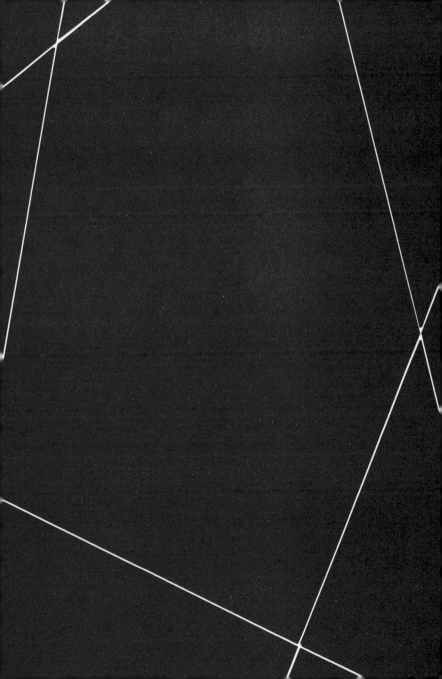

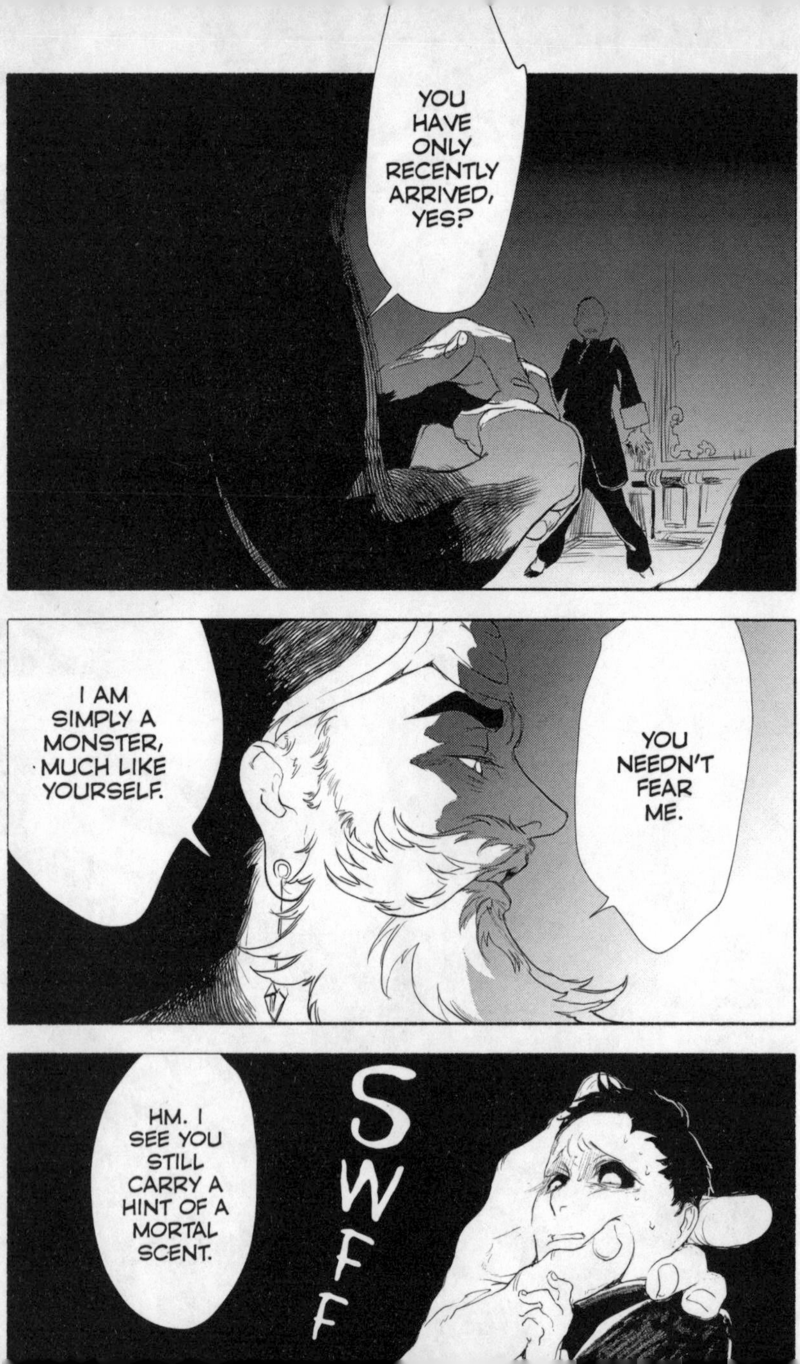
YOU HAVE ONLY RECENTLY ARRIVED, YES?
YOU NEEDN'T FEAR ME.
I AM SIMPLY A MONSTER, MUCH LIKE YOURSELF.
SWFF
HM. I SEE YOU STILL CARRY A HINT OF A MORTAL SCENT.

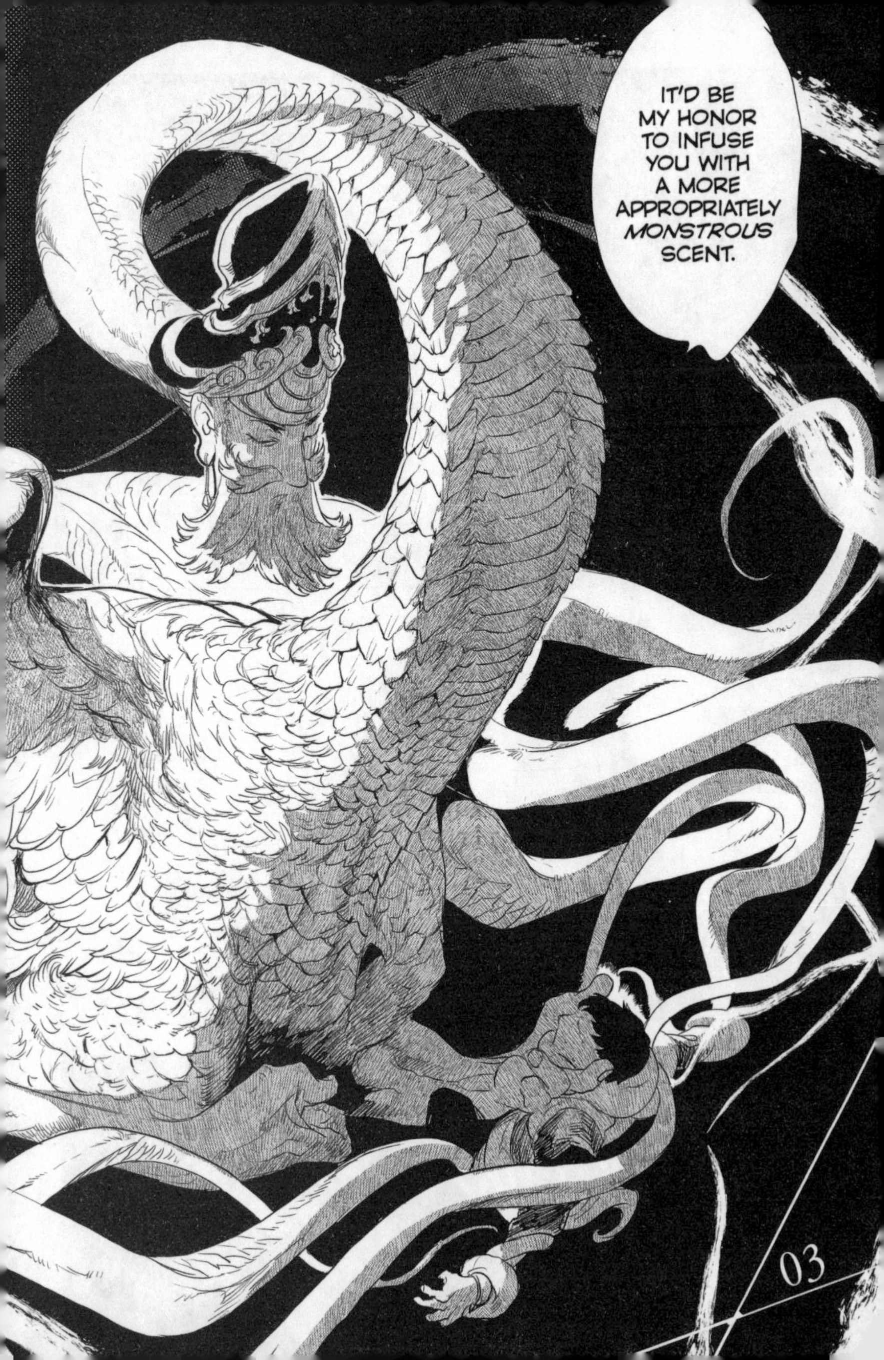
IT'D BE MY HONOR TO INFUSE YOU WITH A MORE APPROPRIATELY *MONSTROUS* SCENT.
03

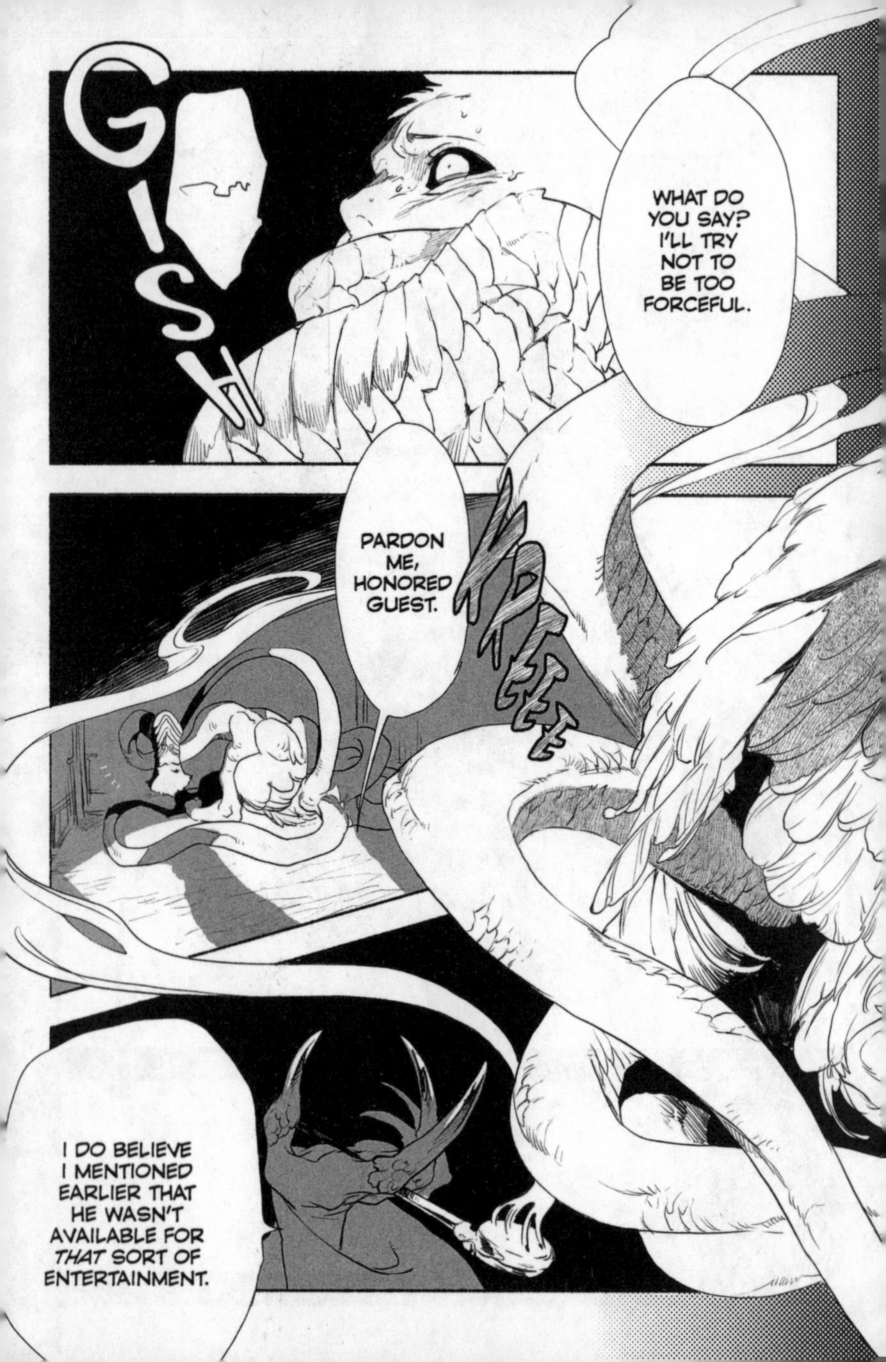
WHAT DO YOU SAY? I'LL TRY NOT TO BE TOO FORCEFUL.
GISH
PARDON ME, HONORED GUEST.
I DO BELIEVE I MENTIONED EARLIER THAT HE WASN'T AVAILABLE FOR *THAT* SORT OF ENTERTAINMENT.

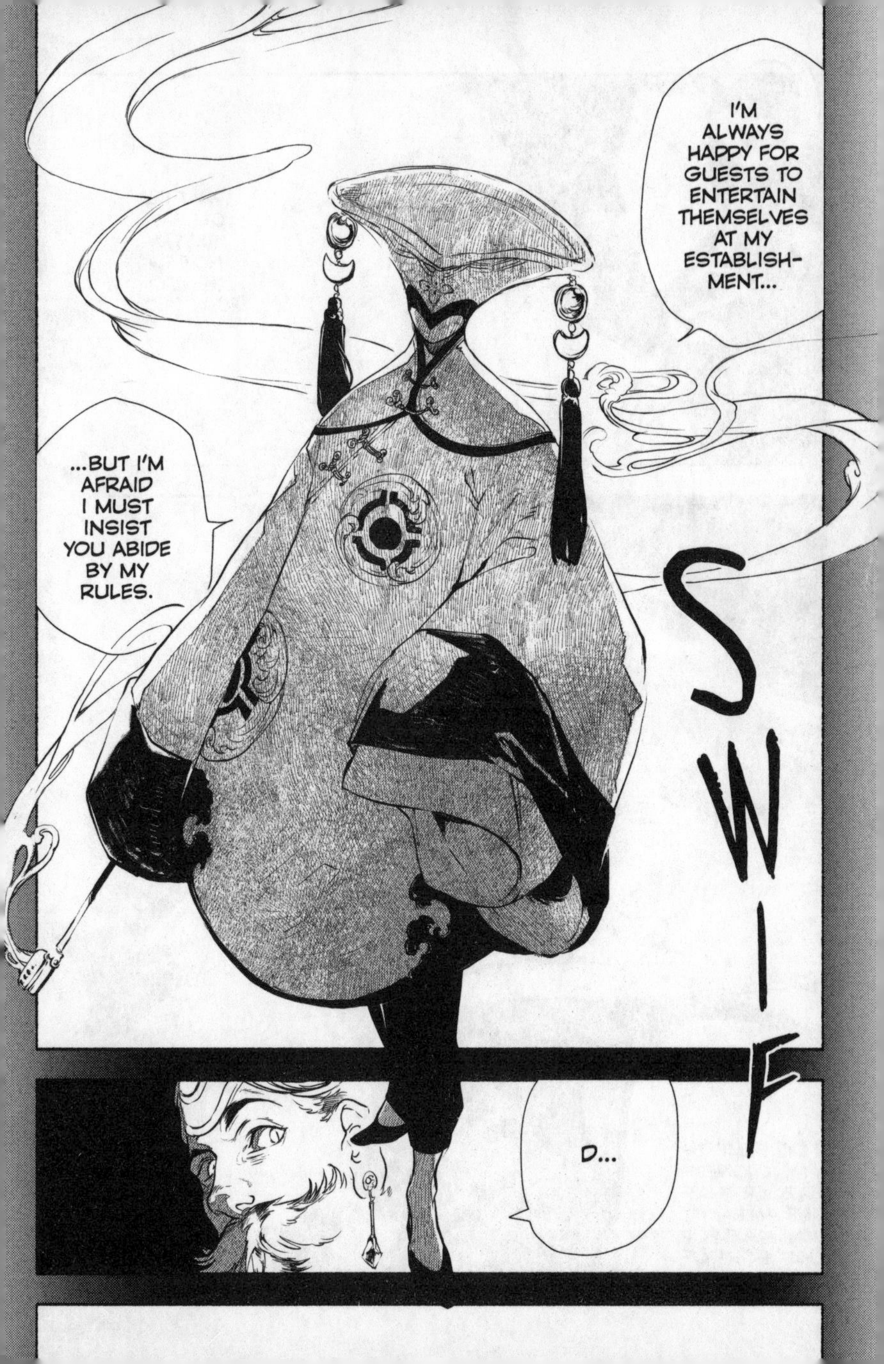
I'M ALWAYS HAPPY FOR GUESTS TO ENTERTAIN THEMSELVES AT MY ESTABLISH-MENT...
...BUT I'M AFRAID I MUST INSIST YOU ABIDE BY MY RULES.
SWIF
D...

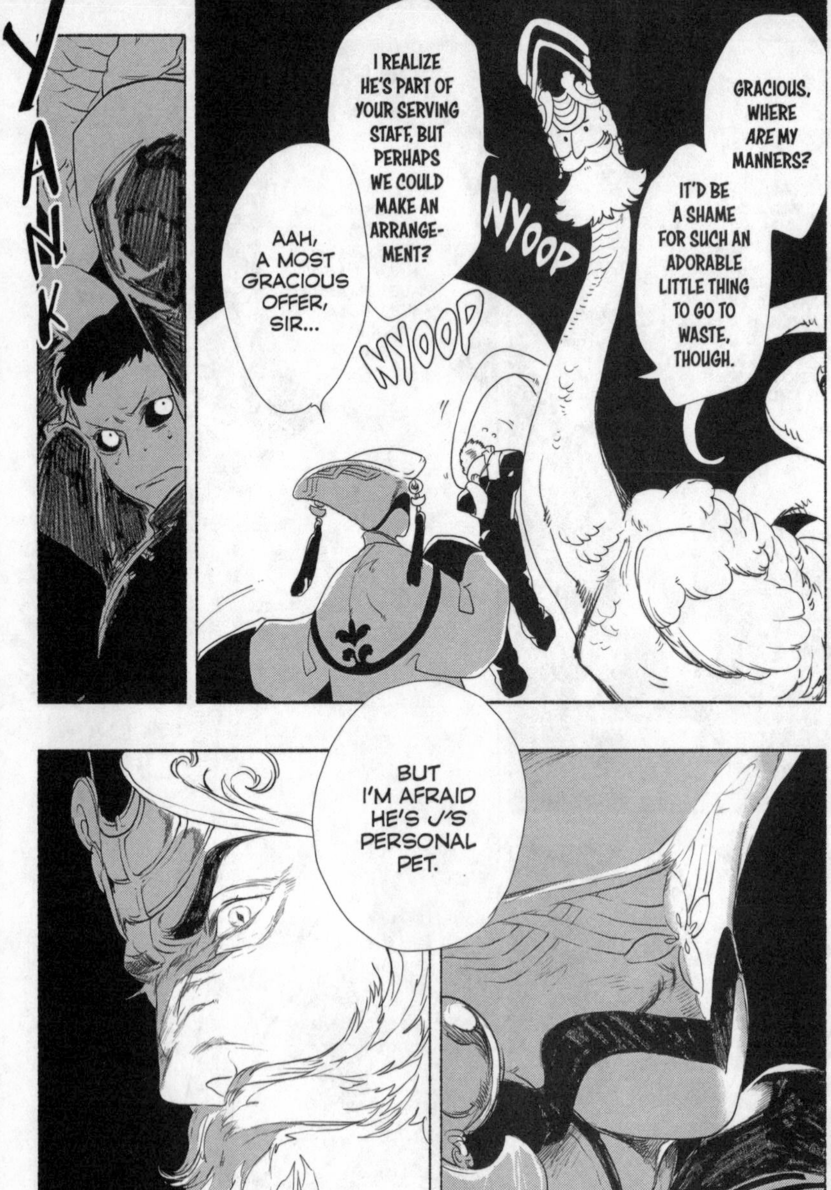
GRACIOUS, WHERE *ARE* MY MANNERS?
IT'D BE A SHAME FOR SUCH AN ADORABLE LITTLE THING TO GO TO WASTE, THOUGH.
I REALIZE HE'S PART OF YOUR SERVING STAFF, BUT PERHAPS WE COULD MAKE AN ARRANGE-MENT?
NYOOP
AAH, A MOST GRACIOUS OFFER, SIR...
NYOOP
YANK
BUT I'M AFRAID HE'S J'S PERSONAL PET.

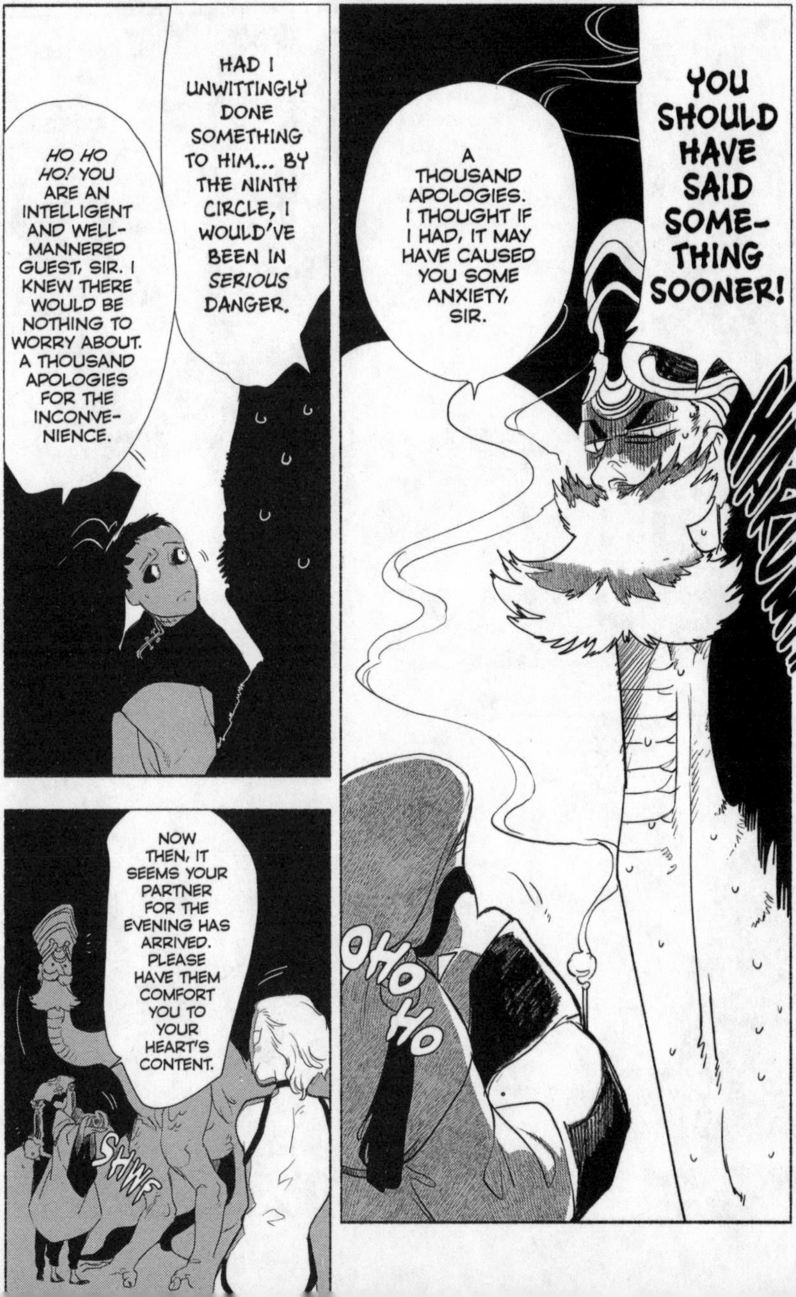
YOU SHOULD HAVE SAID SOME-THING SOONER!
HARRUMPH
A THOUSAND APOLOGIES. I THOUGHT IF I HAD, IT MAY HAVE CAUSED YOU SOME ANXIETY, SIR.
HO HO HO HO
HAD I UNWITTINGLY DONE SOMETHING TO HIM... BY THE NINTH CIRCLE, I WOULD'VE BEEN IN *SERIOUS* DANGER.
HO HO HO! YOU ARE AN INTELLIGENT AND WELL-MANNERED GUEST, SIR. I KNEW THERE WOULD BE NOTHING TO WORRY ABOUT. A THOUSAND APOLOGIES FOR THE INCONVENIENCE.
NOW THEN, IT SEEMS YOUR PARTNER FOR THE EVENING HAS ARRIVED. PLEASE HAVE THEM COMFORT YOU TO YOUR HEART'S CONTENT.
SHWF

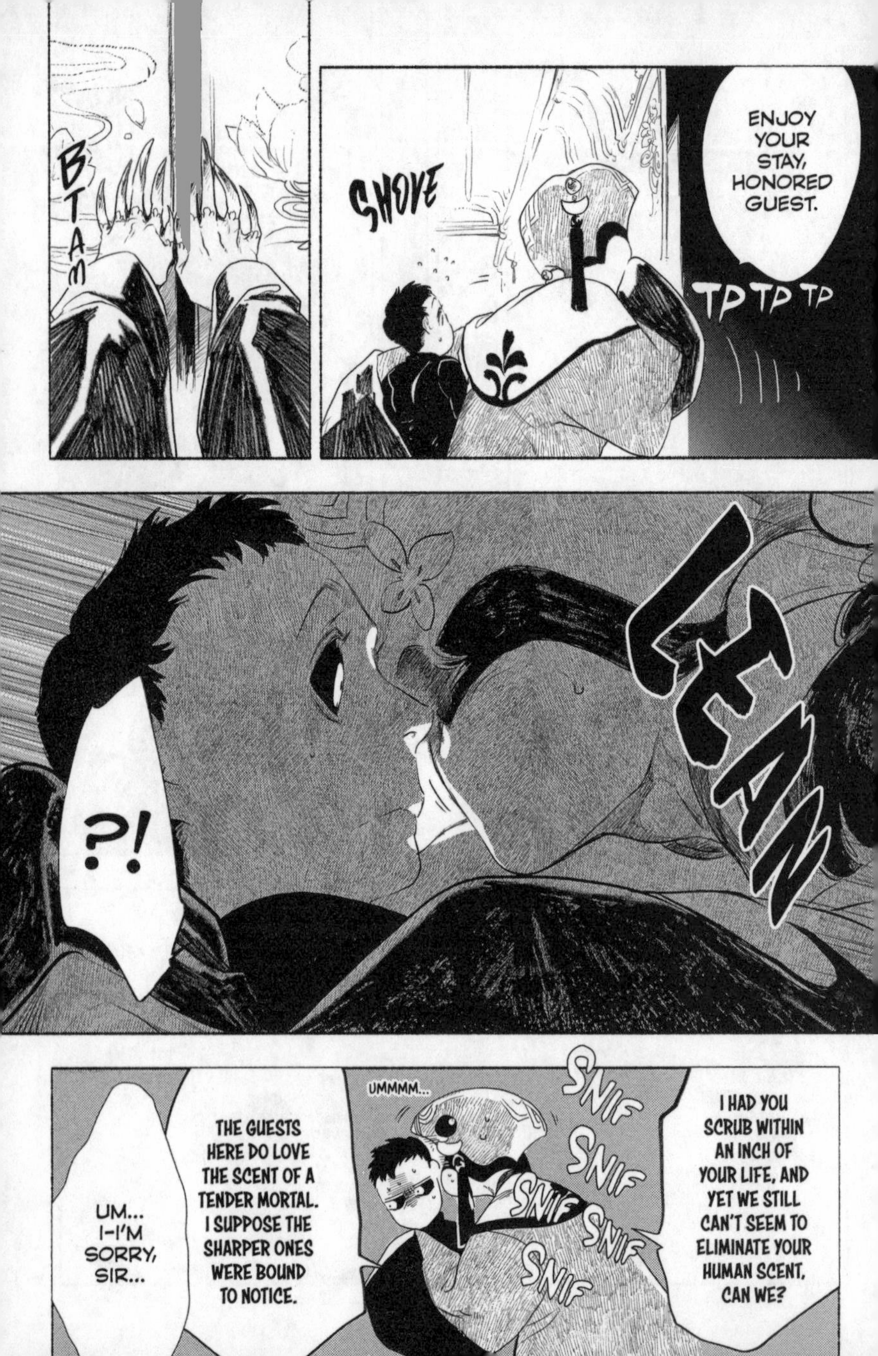
ENJOY YOUR STAY, HONORED GUEST.
TP TP TP
SHOVE
BTAM
LEAN
?!
I HAD YOU SCRUB WITHIN AN INCH OF YOUR LIFE, AND YET WE STILL CAN'T SEEM TO ELIMINATE YOUR HUMAN SCENT, CAN WE?
SNIF SNIF SNIF SNIF SNIF
UMMMM...
THE GUESTS HERE DO LOVE THE SCENT OF A TENDER MORTAL. I SUPPOSE THE SHARPER ONES WERE BOUND TO NOTICE.
UM... I-I'M SORRY, SIR...

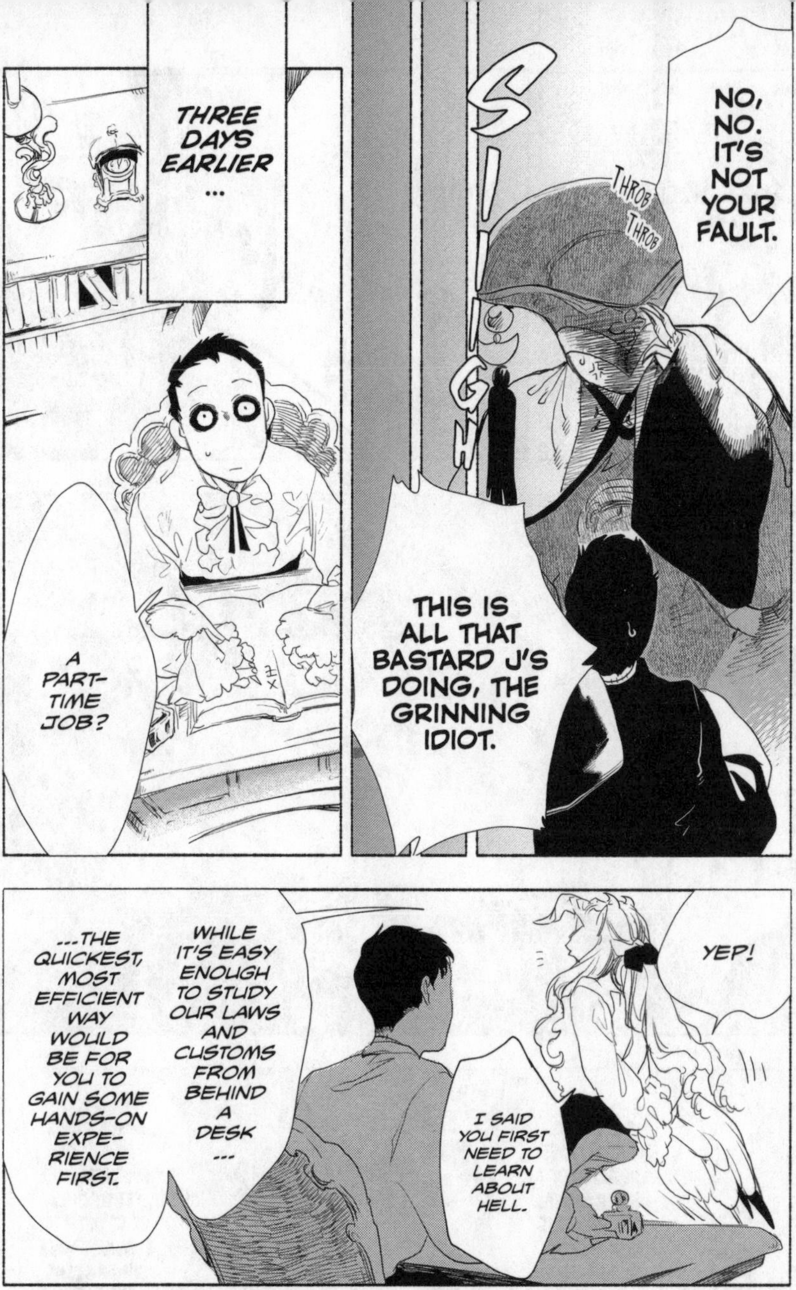
NO, NO. IT'S NOT YOUR FAULT.
THROB THROB
THIS IS ALL THAT BASTARD J'S DOING, THE GRINNING IDIOT.
THREE DAYS EARLIER ...
A PART-TIME JOB?
YEP!
I SAID YOU FIRST NEED TO LEARN ABOUT HELL.
WHILE IT'S EASY ENOUGH TO STUDY OUR LAWS AND CUSTOMS FROM BEHIND A DESK ...
...THE QUICKEST, MOST EFFICIENT WAY WOULD BE FOR YOU TO GAIN SOME HANDS-ON EXPE-RIENCE FIRST.

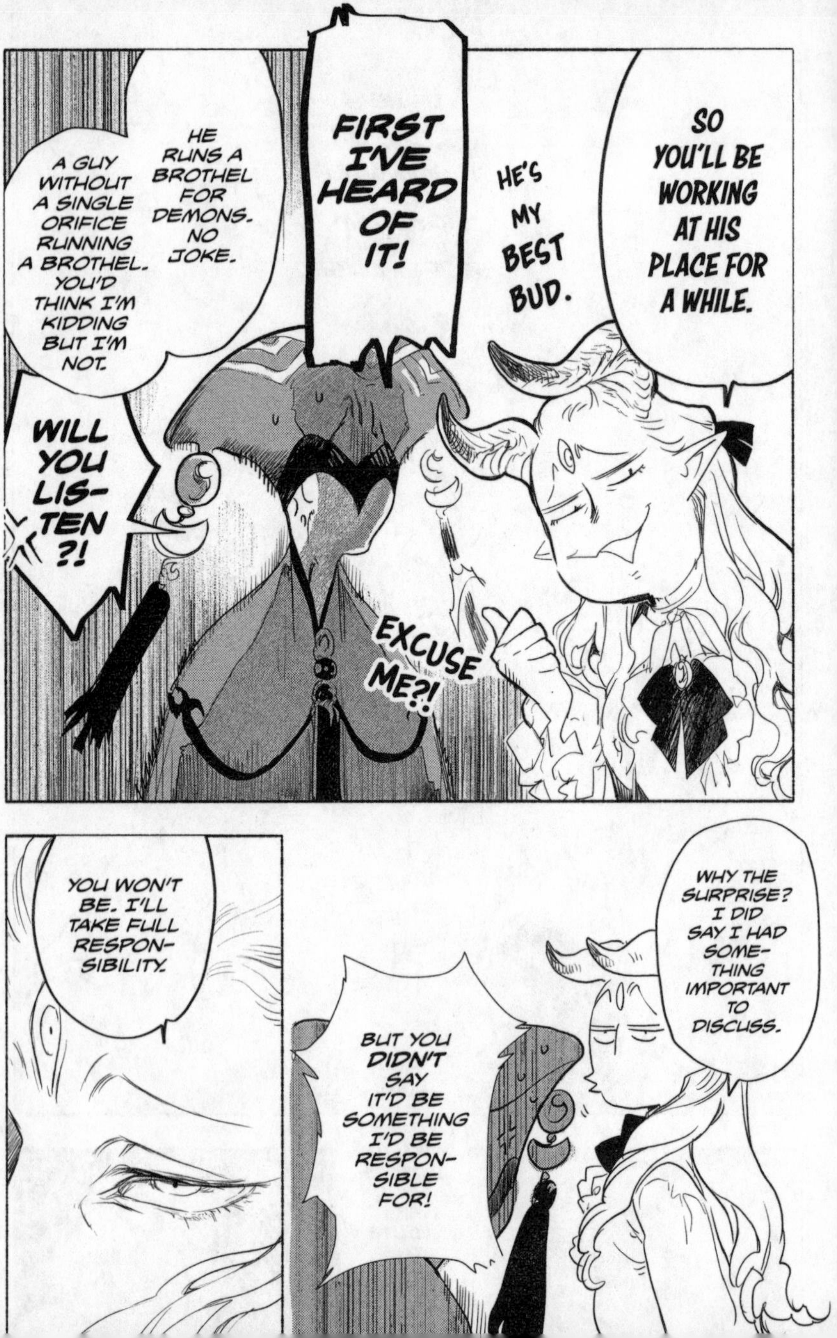
SO YOU'LL BE WORKING AT HIS PLACE FOR A WHILE.
HE'S MY BEST BUD.
FIRST I'VE HEARD OF IT!
HE RUNS A BROTHEL FOR DEMONS. NO JOKE.
A GUY WITHOUT A SINGLE ORIFICE RUNNING A BROTHEL. YOU'D THINK I'M KIDDING BUT I'M NOT.
WILL YOU LIS-TEN?!
EXCUSE ME?!
WHY THE SURPRISE? I DID SAY I HAD SOME-THING IMPORTANT TO DISCUSS.
BUT YOU DIDN'T SAY IT'D BE SOMETHING I'D BE RESPON-SIBLE FOR!
YOU WON'T BE. I'LL TAKE FULL RESPON-SIBILITY.

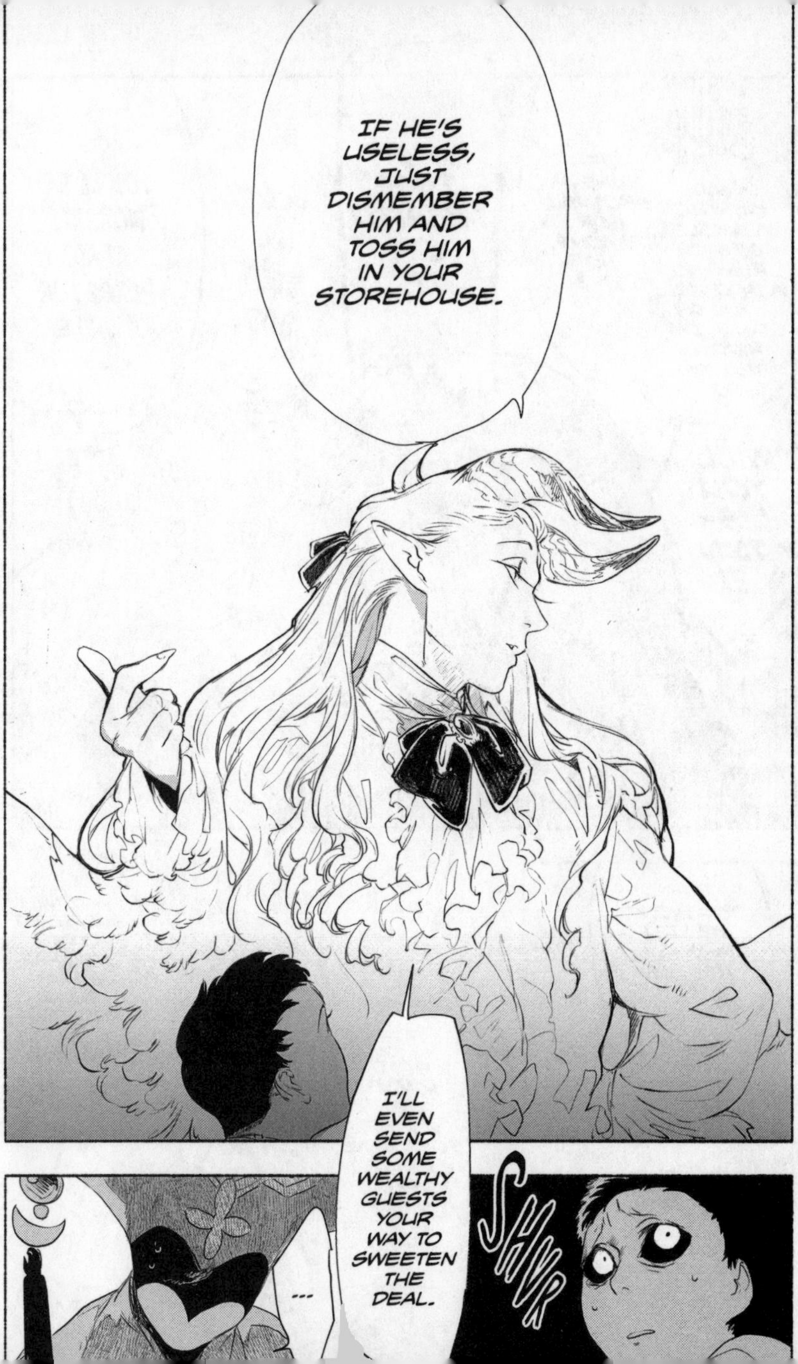
IF HE'S USELESS, JUST DISMEMBER HIM AND TOSS HIM IN YOUR STOREHOUSE.
I'LL EVEN SEND SOME WEALTHY GUESTS YOUR WAY TO SWEETEN THE DEAL.
SHWR
...

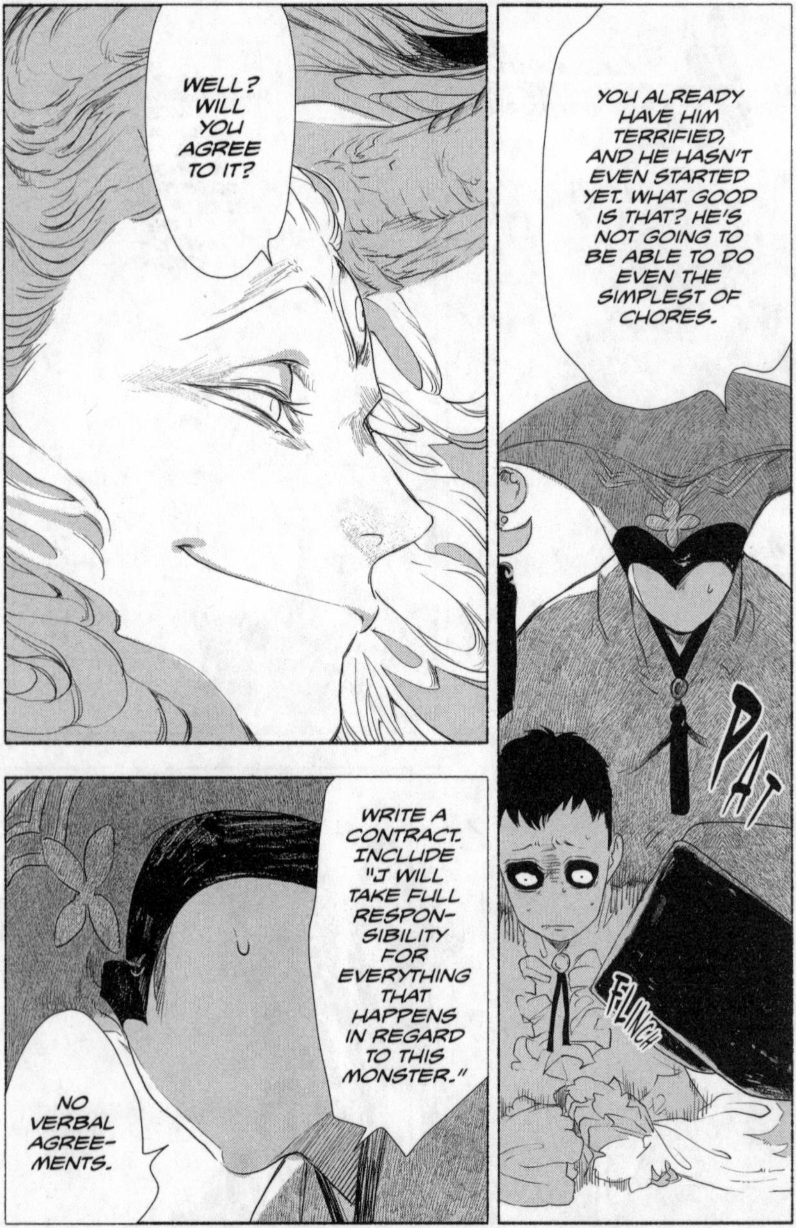
YOU ALREADY HAVE HIM TERRIFIED, AND HE HASN'T EVEN STARTED YET. WHAT GOOD IS THAT? HE'S NOT GOING TO BE ABLE TO DO EVEN THE SIMPLEST OF CHORES.
PAT
FLINCH
WELL? WILL YOU AGREE TO IT?
WRITE A CONTRACT. INCLUDE "I WILL TAKE FULL RESPON-SIBILITY FOR EVERYTHING THAT HAPPENS IN REGARD TO THIS MONSTER."
NO VERBAL AGREE-MENTS.

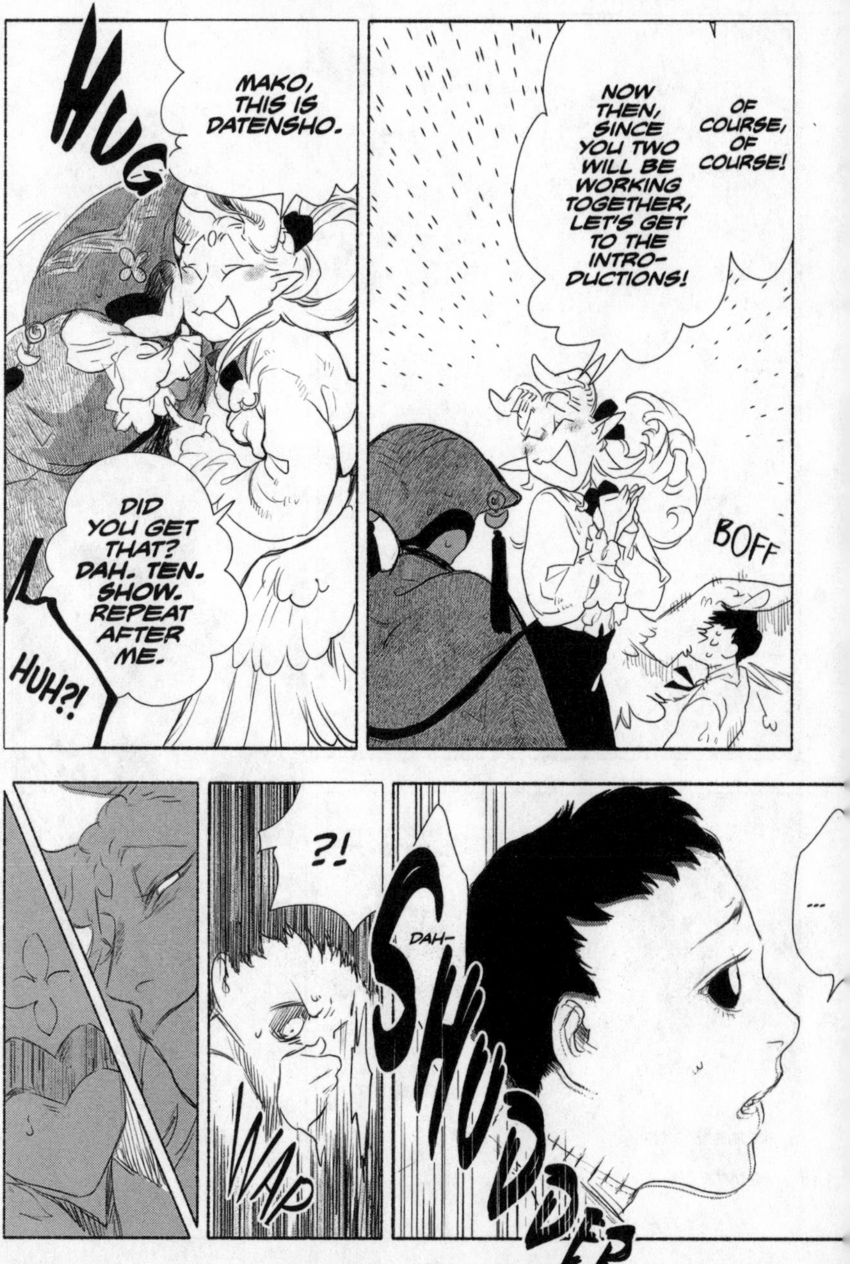
OF COURSE, OF COURSE!
NOW THEN, SINCE YOU TWO WILL BE WORKING TOGETHER, LET'S GET TO THE INTRO-DUCTIONS!
BOFF
MAKO, THIS IS DATENSHO.
HUG
DID YOU GET THAT? DAH- TEN- SHOW- REPEAT AFTER ME.
HUH?!
...
DAH-
SHUDDER
?!
WAP

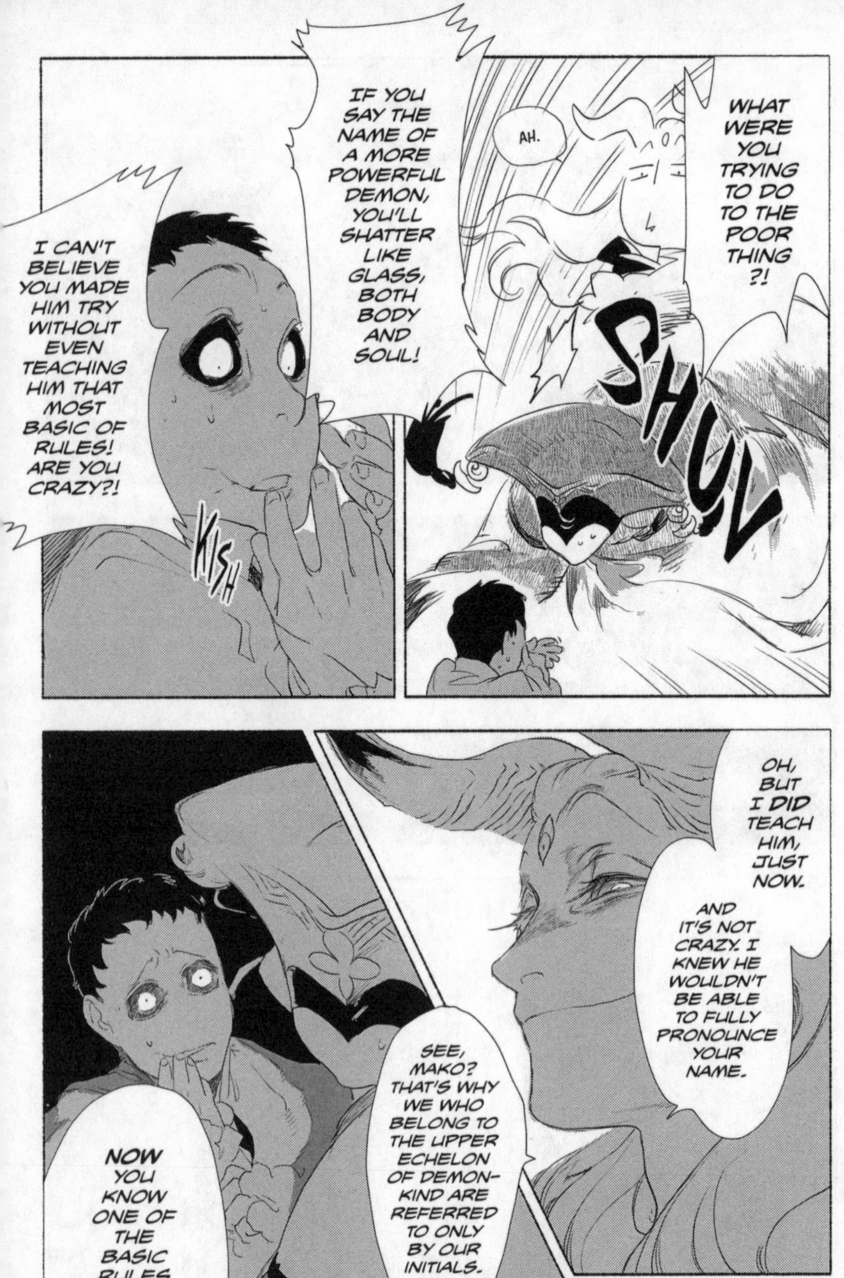
WHAT WERE YOU TRYING TO DO TO THE POOR THING?!
AH.
SHUVV
IF YOU SAY THE NAME OF A MORE POWERFUL DEMON, YOU'LL SHATTER LIKE GLASS, BOTH BODY AND SOUL!
I CAN'T BELIEVE YOU MADE HIM TRY WITHOUT EVEN TEACHING HIM THAT MOST BASIC OF RULES! ARE YOU CRAZY?!
KISH
OH, BUT I DID TEACH HIM, JUST NOW.
AND IT'S NOT CRAZY. I KNEW HE WOULDN'T BE ABLE TO FULLY PRONOUNCE YOUR NAME.
SEE, MAKO? THAT'S WHY WE WHO BELONG TO THE UPPER ECHELON OF DEMON-KIND ARE REFERRED TO ONLY BY OUR INITIALS.
NOW YOU KNOW ONE OF THE BASIC RULES OF HELL.

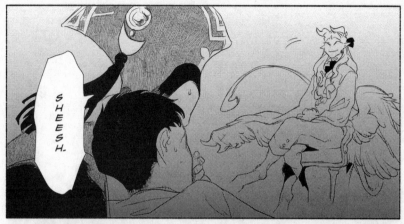

SHEESH.

WHAT A PIECE OF WORK. YOU CERTAINLY PICKED ONE OUTRAGEOUS DEMON TO SELL YOUR SOUL TO...

...DIDN'T YOU?

OH, DEAR. YOU POOR THING, DID THAT FRIGHTEN YOU TO TEARS?

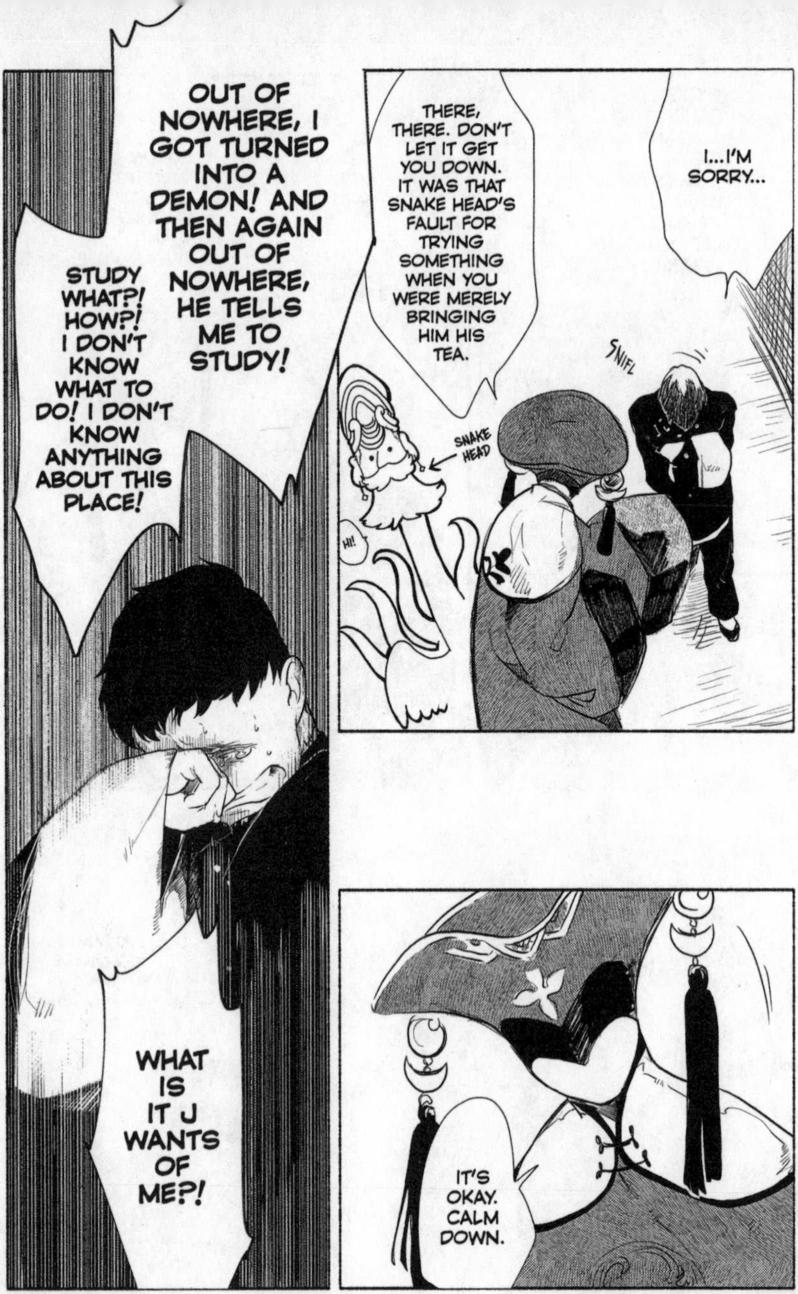
I...I'M SORRY...
THERE, THERE. DON'T LET IT GET YOU DOWN. IT WAS THAT SNAKE HEAD'S FAULT FOR TRYING SOMETHING WHEN YOU WERE MERELY BRINGING HIM HIS TEA.
SNIFL
SNAKE HEAD
HI!
IT'S OKAY. CALM DOWN.
OUT OF NOWHERE, I GOT TURNED INTO A DEMON! AND THEN AGAIN OUT OF NOWHERE, HE TELLS ME TO STUDY!
STUDY WHAT?! HOW?! I DON'T KNOW WHAT TO DO! I DON'T KNOW ANYTHING ABOUT THIS PLACE!
WHAT IS IT J WANTS OF ME?!

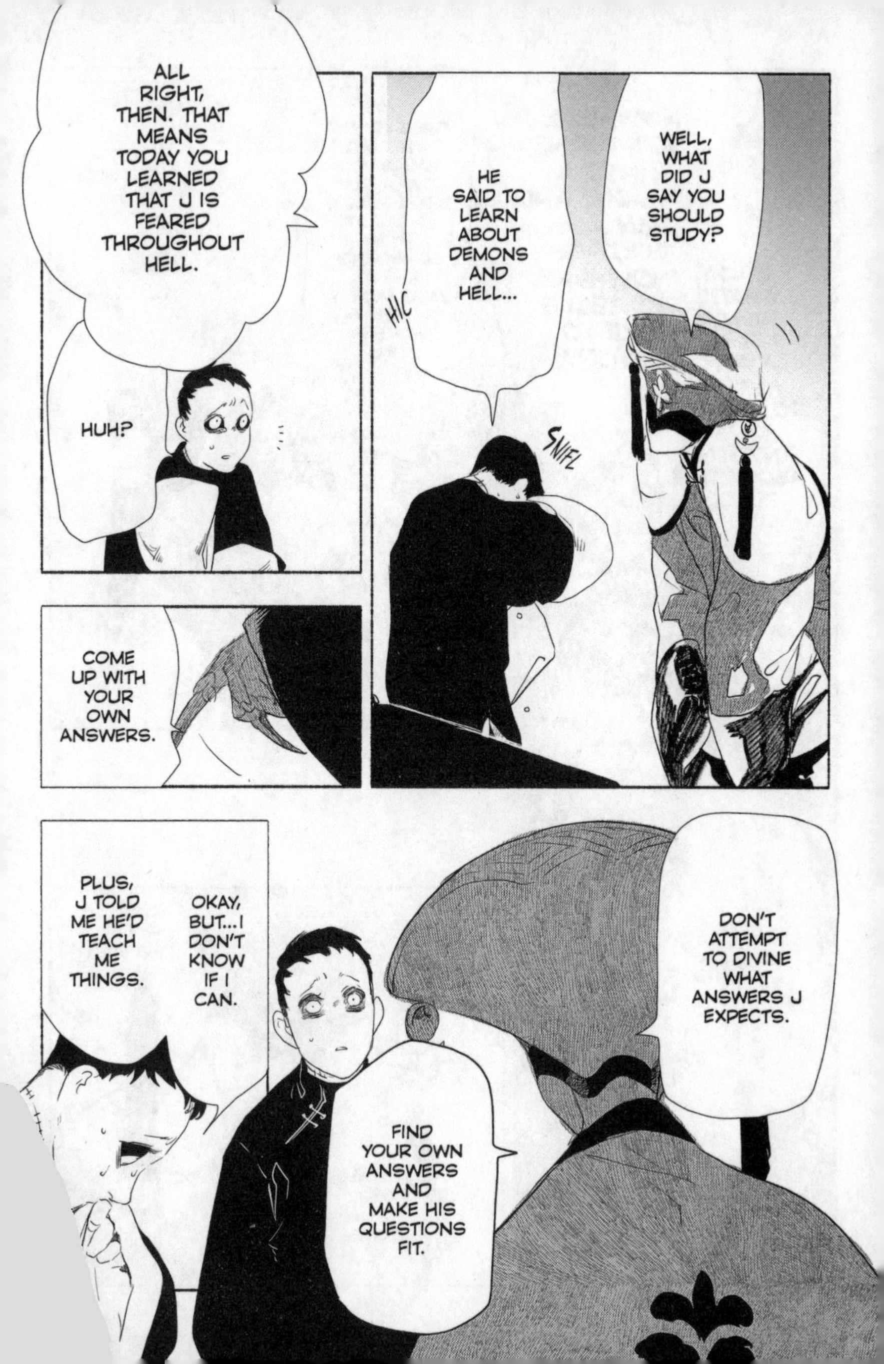
WELL, WHAT DID J SAY YOU SHOULD STUDY?
HE SAID TO LEARN ABOUT DEMONS AND HELL...
HIC
SNIFL
ALL RIGHT, THEN. THAT MEANS TODAY YOU LEARNED THAT J IS FEARED THROUGHOUT HELL.
HUH?
COME UP WITH YOUR OWN ANSWERS.
DON'T ATTEMPT TO DIVINE WHAT ANSWERS J EXPECTS.
FIND YOUR OWN ANSWERS AND MAKE HIS QUESTIONS FIT.
OKAY, BUT...I DON'T KNOW IF I CAN.
PLUS, J TOLD ME HE'D TEACH ME THINGS.

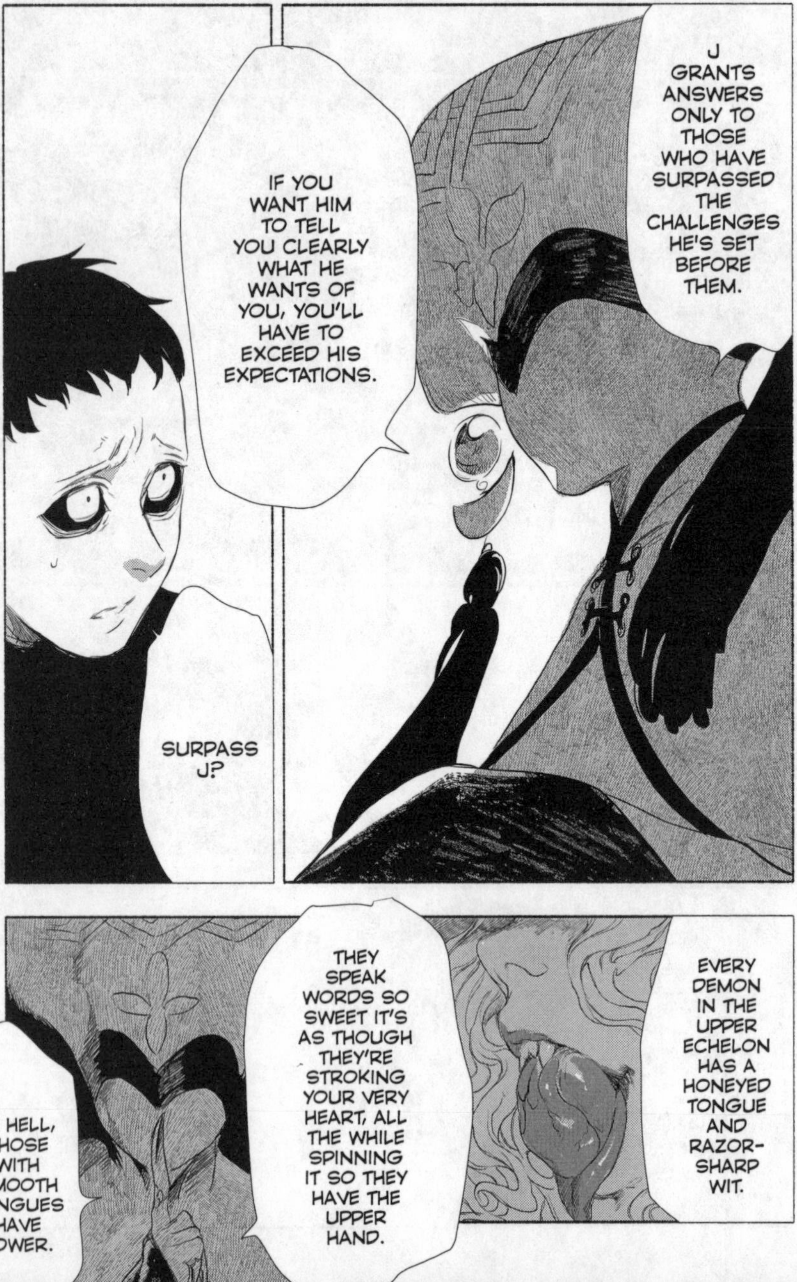
J GRANTS ANSWERS ONLY TO THOSE WHO HAVE SURPASSED THE CHALLENGES HE'S SET BEFORE THEM.
IF YOU WANT HIM TO TELL YOU CLEARLY WHAT HE WANTS OF YOU, YOU'LL HAVE TO EXCEED HIS EXPECTATIONS.
SURPASS J?
EVERY DEMON IN THE UPPER ECHELON HAS A HONEYED TONGUE AND RAZOR-SHARP WIT.
THEY SPEAK WORDS SO SWEET IT'S AS THOUGH THEY'RE STROKING YOUR VERY HEART, ALL THE WHILE SPINNING IT SO THEY HAVE THE UPPER HAND.
IN HELL, THOSE WITH SMOOTH TONGUES HAVE POWER.

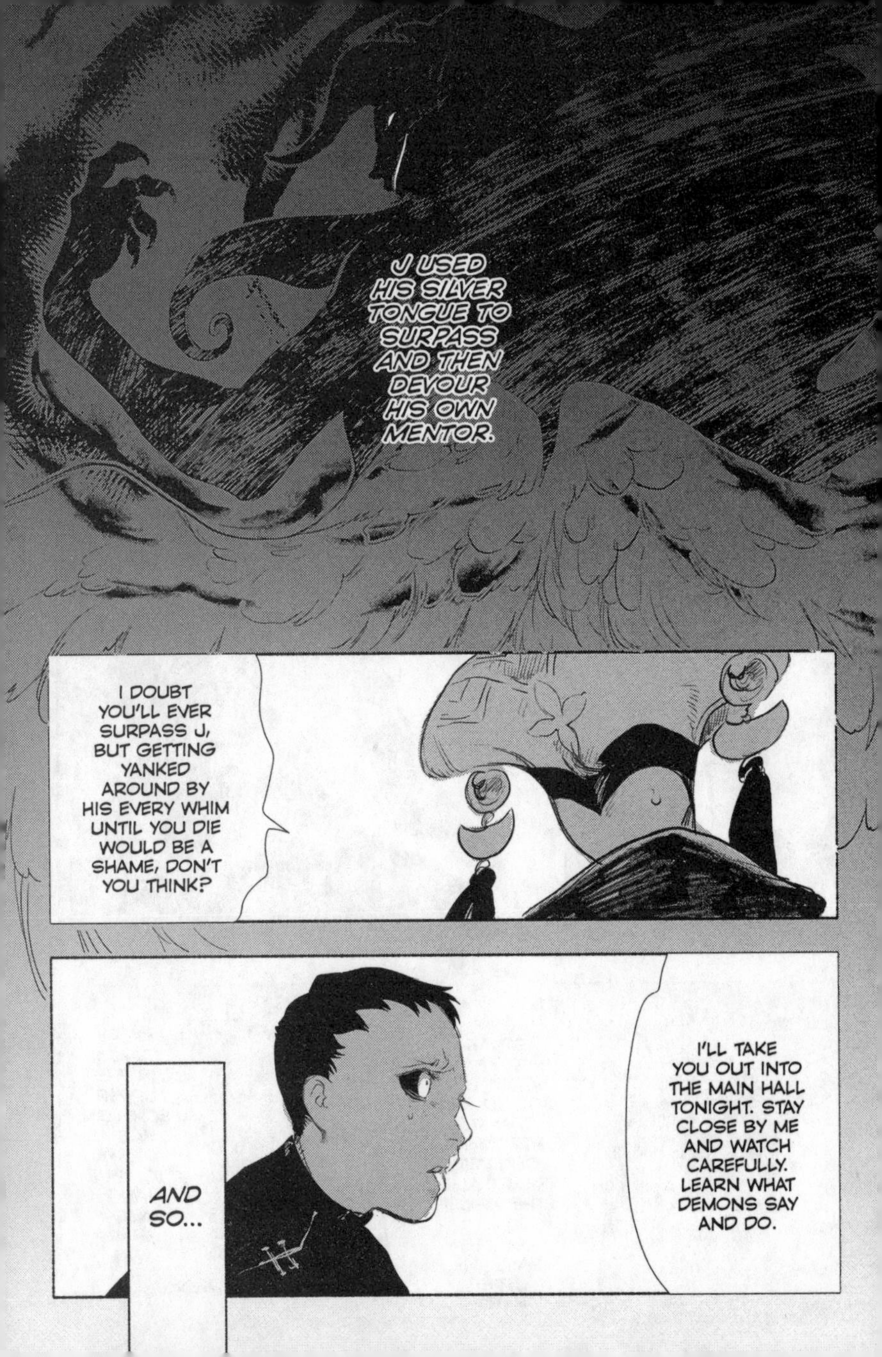
J USED HIS SILVER TONGUE TO SURPASS AND THEN DEVOUR HIS OWN MENTOR.
I DOUBT YOU'LL EVER SURPASS J, BUT GETTING YANKED AROUND BY HIS EVERY WHIM UNTIL YOU DIE WOULD BE A SHAME, DON'T YOU THINK?
I'LL TAKE YOU OUT INTO THE MAIN HALL TONIGHT. STAY CLOSE BY ME AND WATCH CAREFULLY. LEARN WHAT DEMONS SAY AND DO.
AND SO...

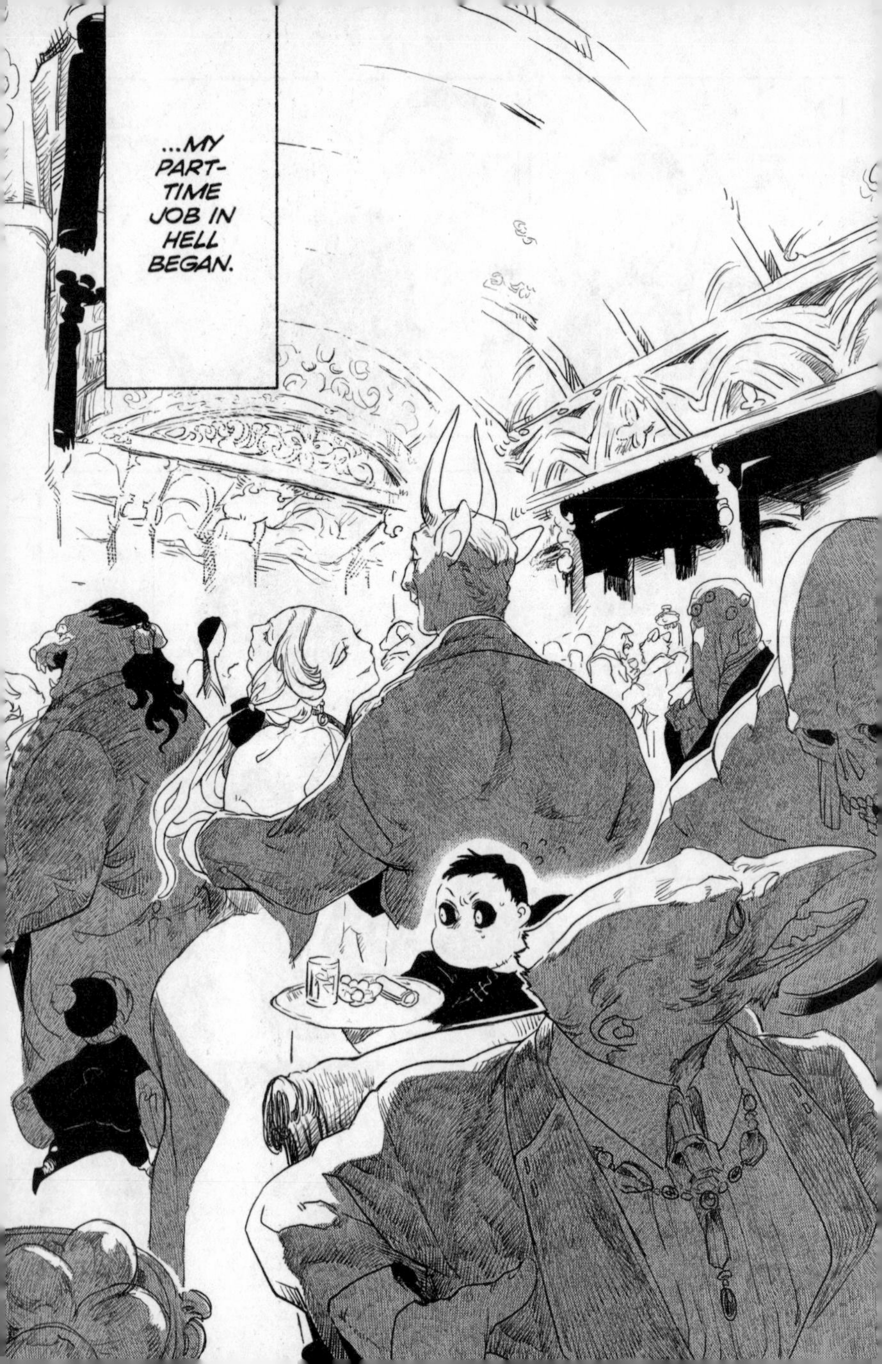
...MY PART-TIME JOB IN HELL BEGAN.

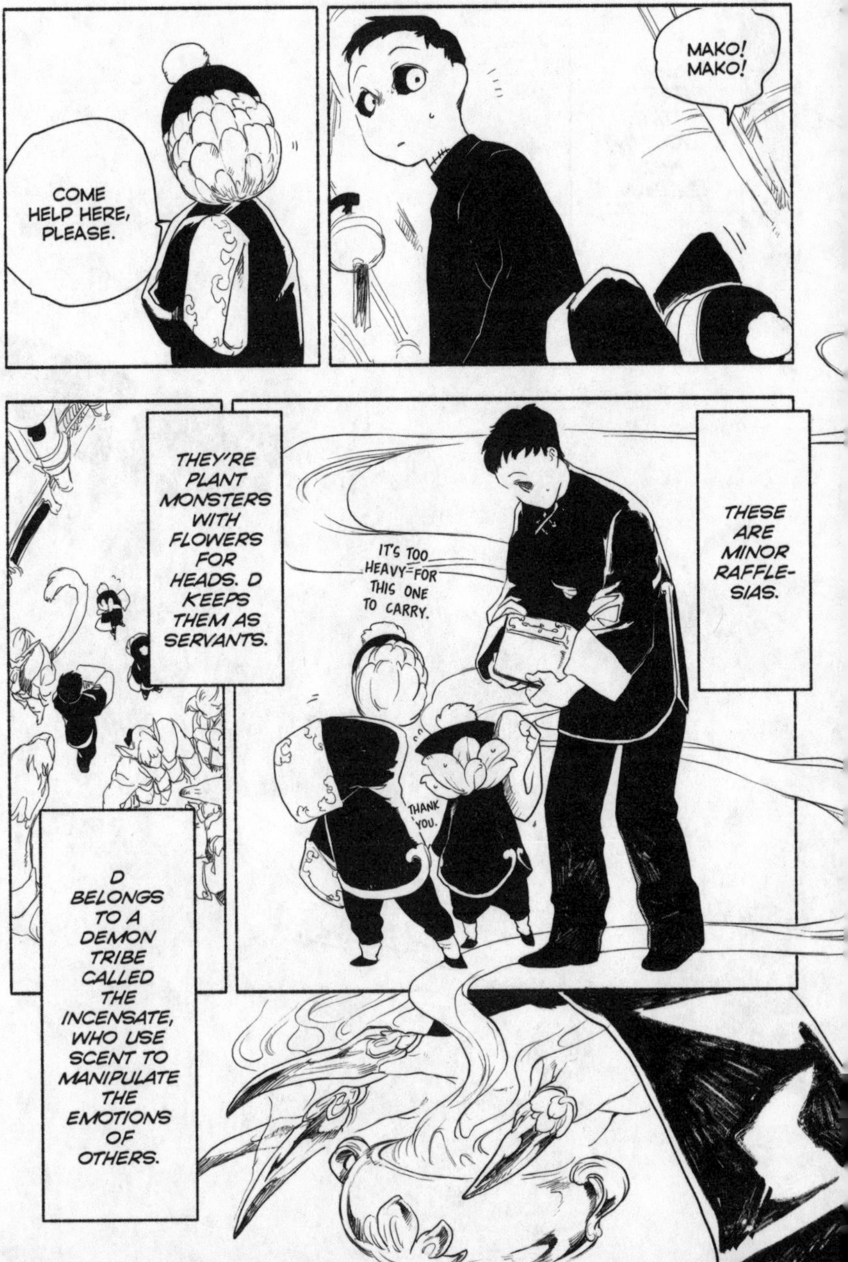
MAKO! MAKO!
COME HELP HERE, PLEASE.
THESE ARE MINOR RAFFLESIAS.
IT'S TOO HEAVY FOR THIS ONE TO CARRY.
THANK YOU.
THEY'RE PLANT MONSTERS WITH FLOWERS FOR HEADS. D KEEPS THEM AS SERVANTS.
D BELONGS TO A DEMON TRIBE CALLED THE INCENSATE, WHO USE SCENT TO MANIPULATE THE EMOTIONS OF OTHERS.

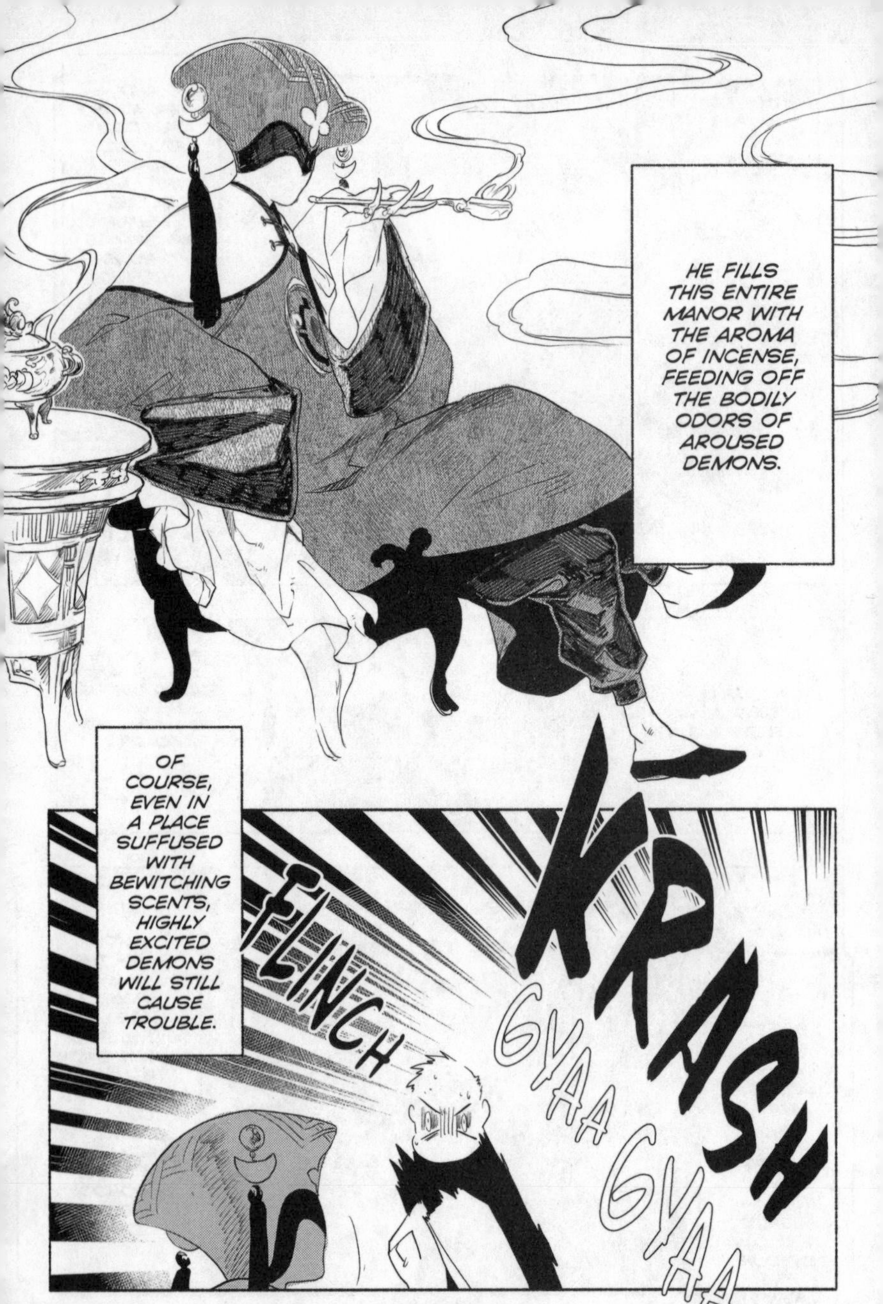
HE FILLS THIS ENTIRE MANOR WITH THE AROMA OF INCENSE, FEEDING OFF THE BODILY ODORS OF AROUSED DEMONS.
OF COURSE, EVEN IN A PLACE SUFFUSED WITH BEWITCHING SCENTS, HIGHLY EXCITED DEMONS WILL STILL CAUSE TROUBLE.
KRASH
GYAA GYAA
GYAA GYAA
FLINCH

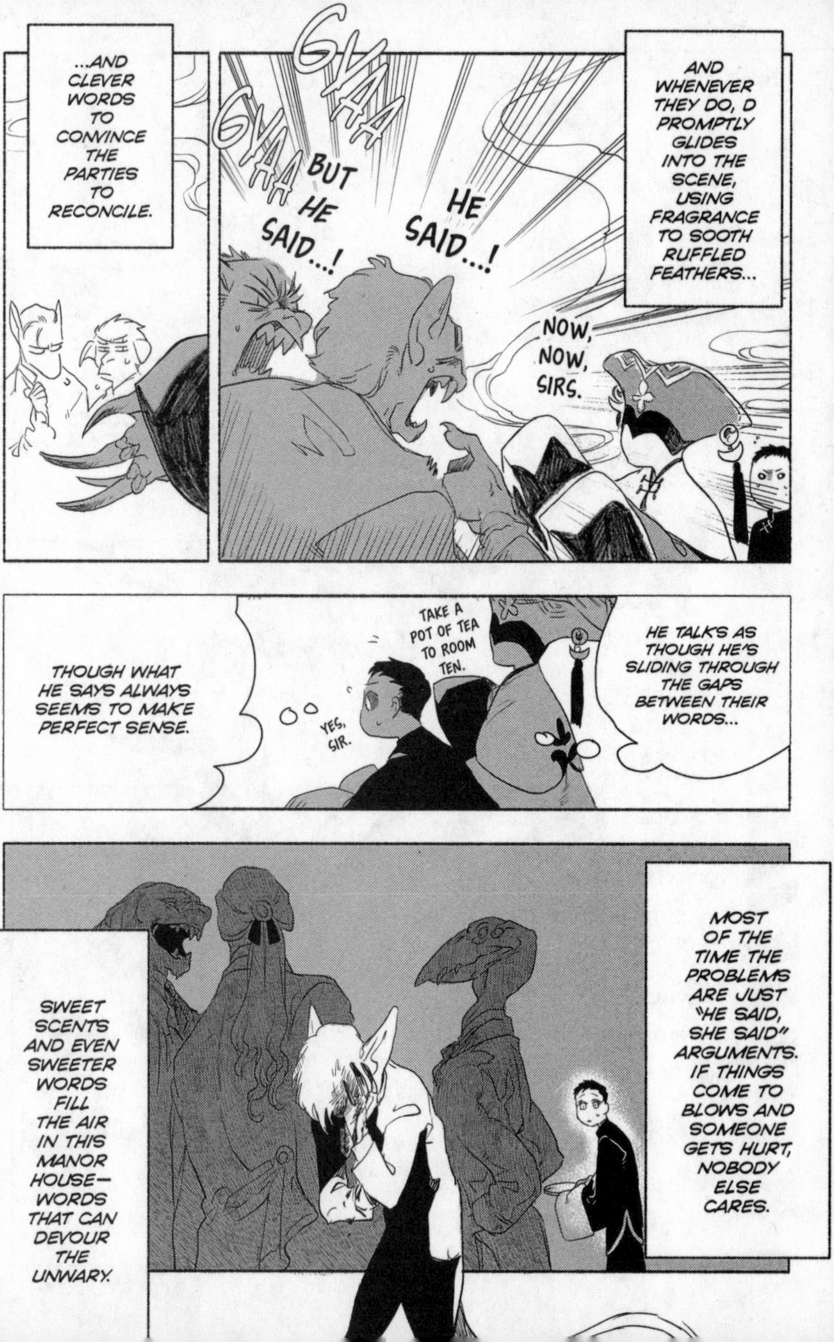
AND WHENEVER THEY DO, D PROMPTLY GLIDES INTO THE SCENE, USING FRAGRANCE TO SOOTH RUFFLED FEATHERS...
GYAA GYAA
HE SAID...!
BUT HE SAID...!
NOW, NOW, SIRS.
...AND CLEVER WORDS TO CONVINCE THE PARTIES TO RECONCILE.
HE TALK'S AS THOUGH HE'S SLIDING THROUGH THE GAPS BETWEEN THEIR WORDS...
TAKE A POT OF TEA TO ROOM TEN.
YES, SIR.
THOUGH WHAT HE SAYS ALWAYS SEEMS TO MAKE PERFECT SENSE.
MOST OF THE TIME THE PROBLEMS ARE JUST "HE SAID, SHE SAID" ARGUMENTS. IF THINGS COME TO BLOWS AND SOMEONE GETS HURT, NOBODY ELSE CARES.
SWEET SCENTS AND EVEN SWEETER WORDS FILL THE AIR IN THIS MANOR HOUSE— WORDS THAT CAN DEVOUR THE UNWARY.

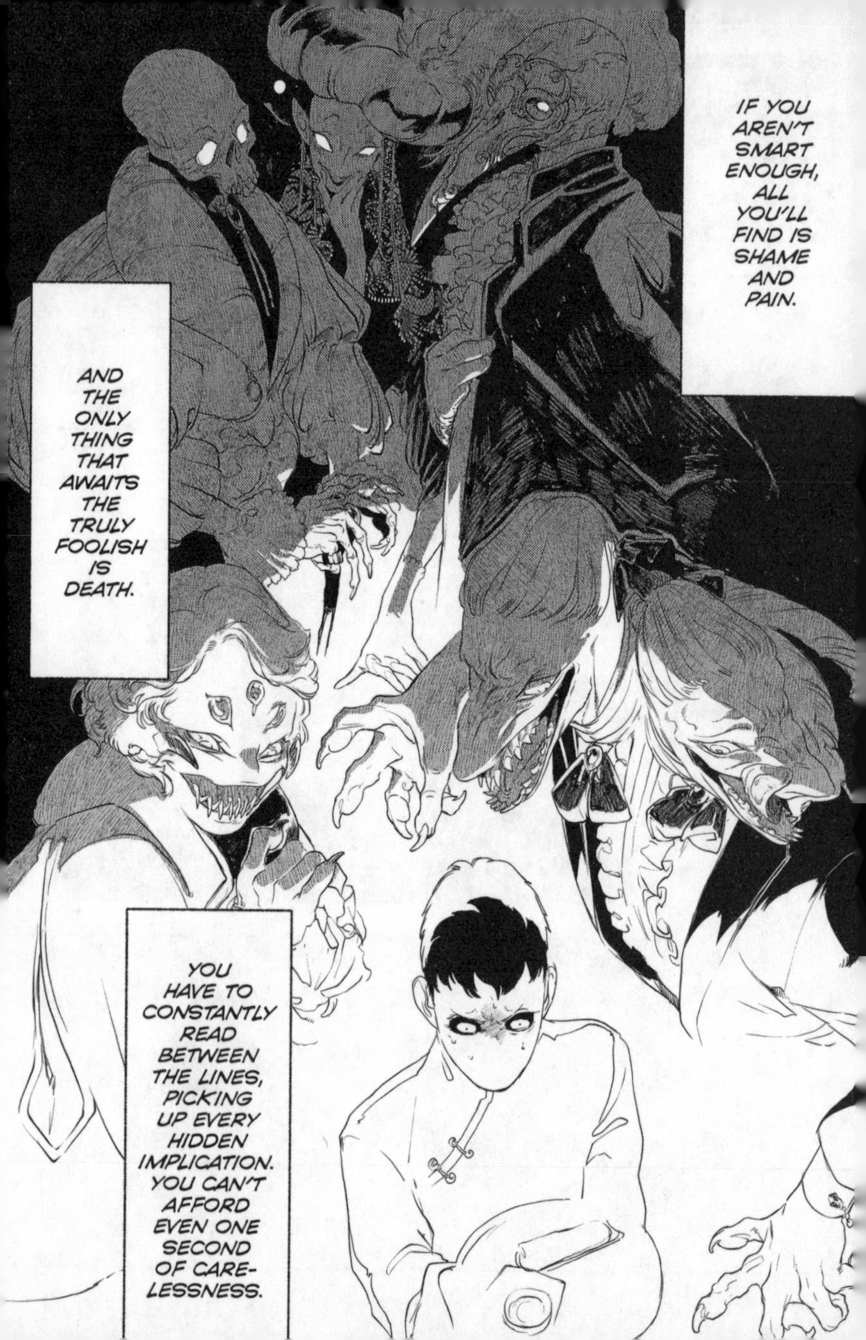
IF YOU AREN'T SMART ENOUGH, ALL YOU'LL FIND IS SHAME AND PAIN.
AND THE ONLY THING THAT AWAITS THE TRULY FOOLISH IS DEATH.
YOU HAVE TO CONSTANTLY READ BETWEEN THE LINES, PICKING UP EVERY HIDDEN IMPLICATION. YOU CAN'T AFFORD EVEN ONE SECOND OF CARE-LESSNESS.

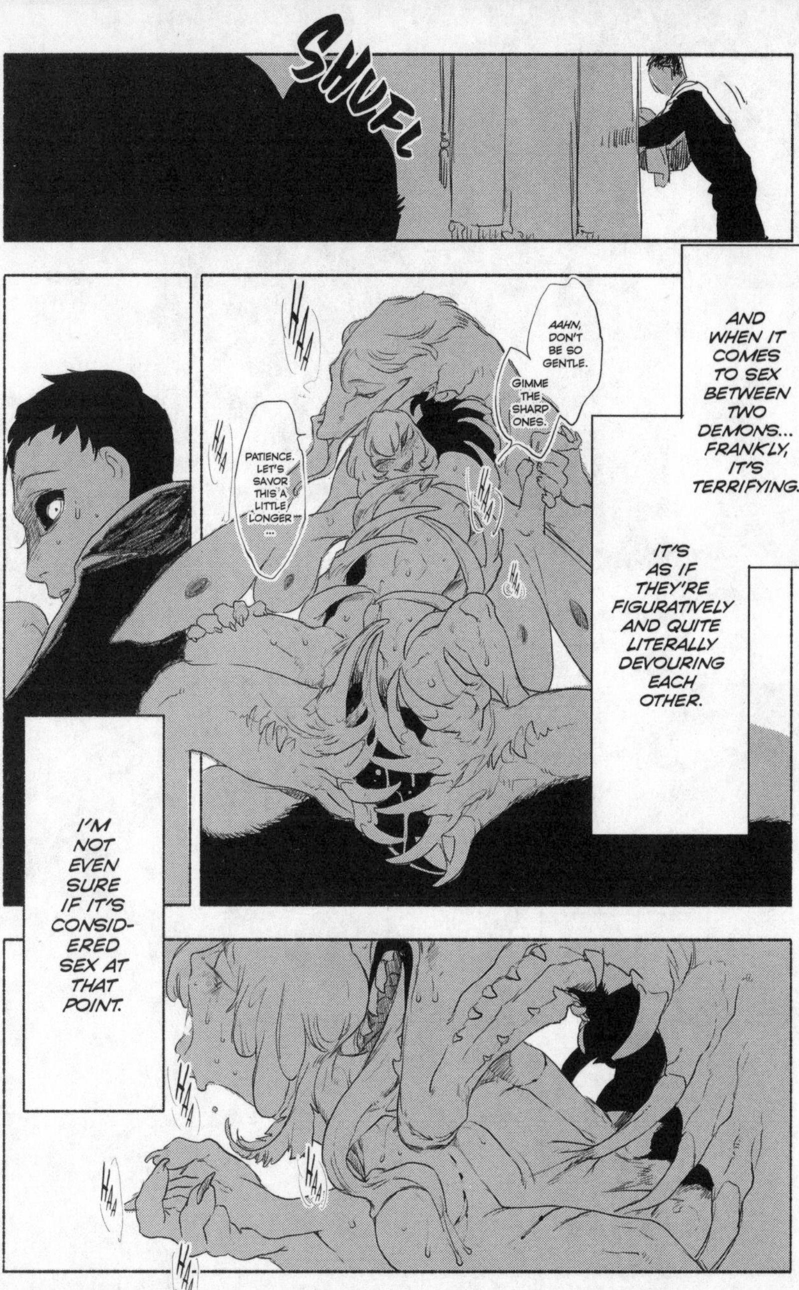
SHUFL
AND WHEN IT COMES TO SEX BETWEEN TWO DEMONS... FRANKLY, IT'S TERRIFYING.
AAHN, DON'T BE SO GENTLE.
GIMME THE SHARP ONES.
PATIENCE. LET'S SAVOR THIS A LITTLE LONGER...
HAA
HAA
HAA
IT'S AS IF THEY'RE FIGURATIVELY AND QUITE LITERALLY DEVOURING EACH OTHER.
I'M NOT EVEN SURE IF IT'S CONSIDERED SEX AT THAT POINT.
HAA
HAA
HAA
HAA

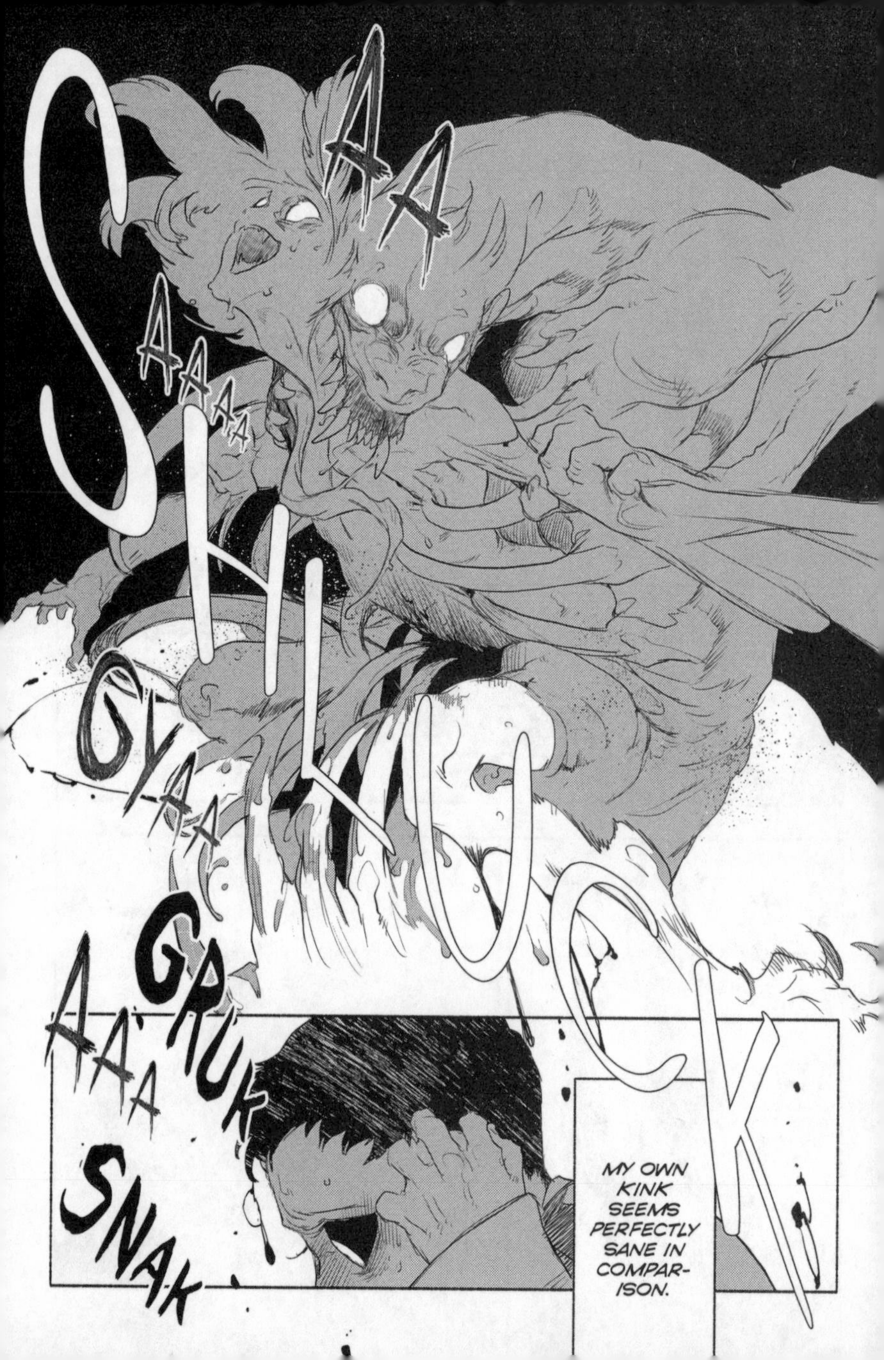
AAA
SAAAAA
SHLUCK
GYAAA
MY OWN KINK SEEMS PERFECTLY SANE IN COMPARISON.
GRUK
AAAA
SNAK

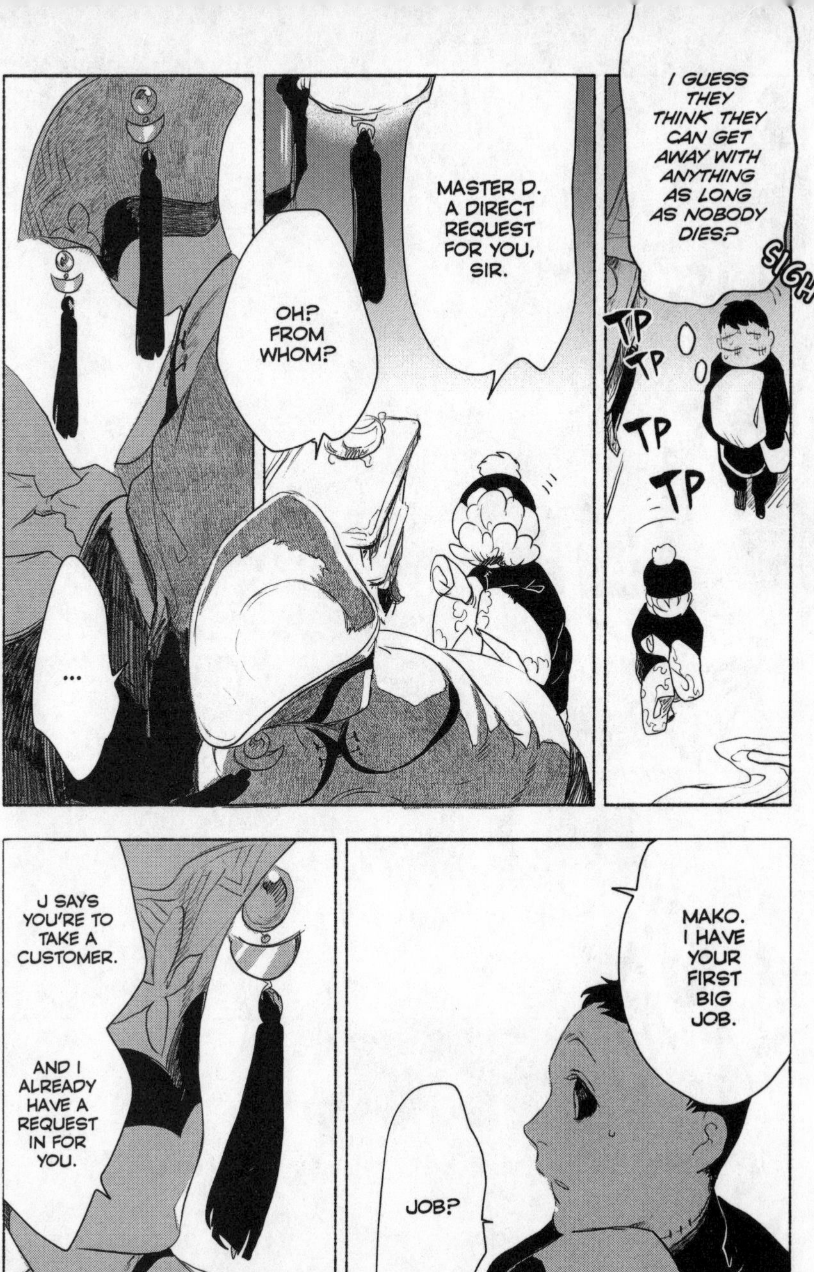
I GUESS THEY THINK THEY CAN GET AWAY WITH ANYTHING AS LONG AS NOBODY DIES?
SIGH
TP TP
TP
TP
MASTER D. A DIRECT REQUEST FOR YOU, SIR.
OH? FROM WHOM?
...
MAKO. I HAVE YOUR FIRST BIG JOB.
JOB?
J SAYS YOU'RE TO TAKE A CUSTOMER.
AND I ALREADY HAVE A REQUEST IN FOR YOU.

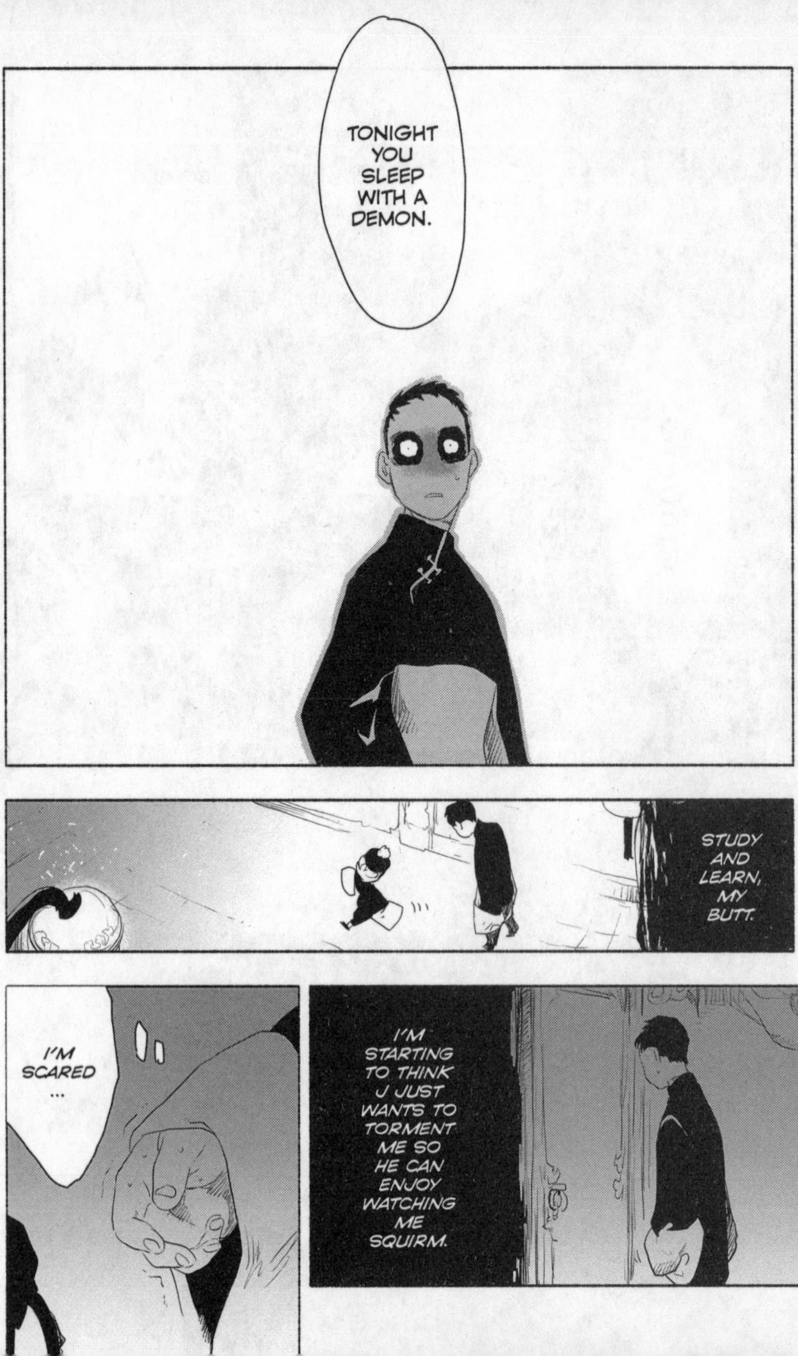
TONIGHT YOU SLEEP WITH A DEMON.
STUDY AND LEARN, MY BUTT.
I'M STARTING TO THINK J JUST WANTS TO TORMENT ME SO HE CAN ENJOY WATCHING ME SQUIRM.
I'M SCARED ...

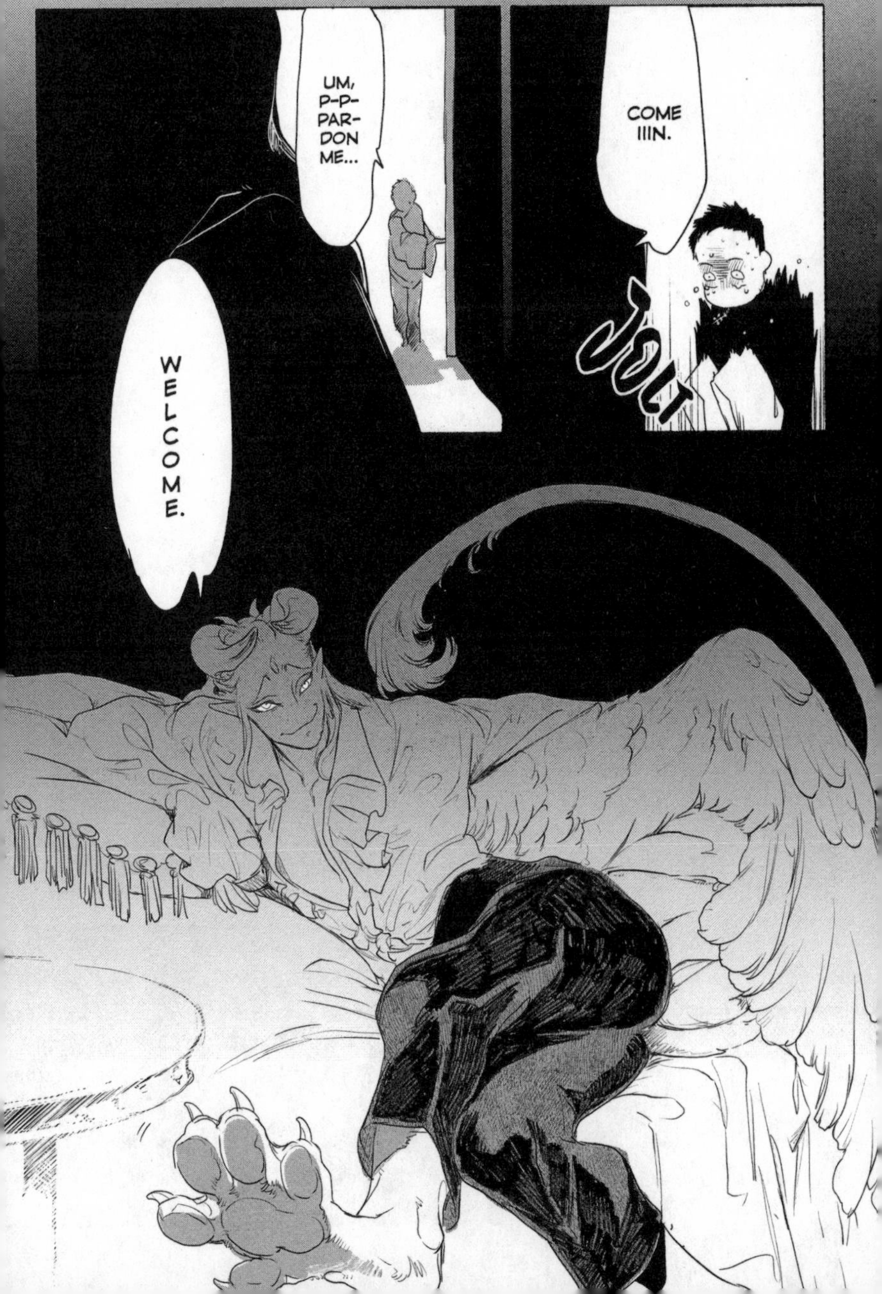
COME IIIN.
JOLT
UM, P-P-PARDON ME...
WELCOME.

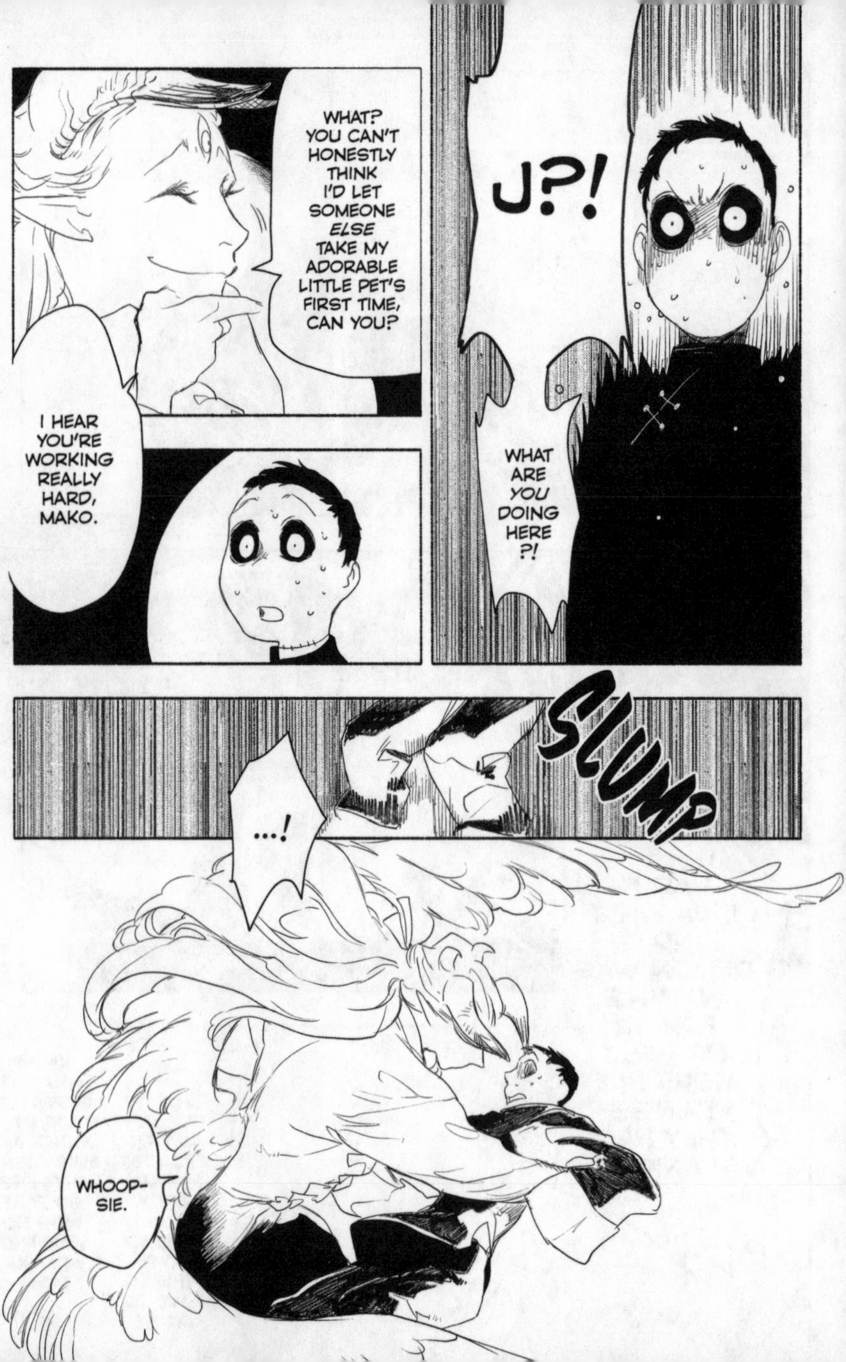
J?!
WHAT ARE *YOU* DOING HERE?!
WHAT? YOU CAN'T HONESTLY THINK I'D LET SOMEONE *ELSE* TAKE MY ADORABLE LITTLE PET'S FIRST TIME, CAN YOU?
I HEAR YOU'RE WORKING REALLY HARD, MAKO.
SLUMP
...!
WHOOP-SIE.

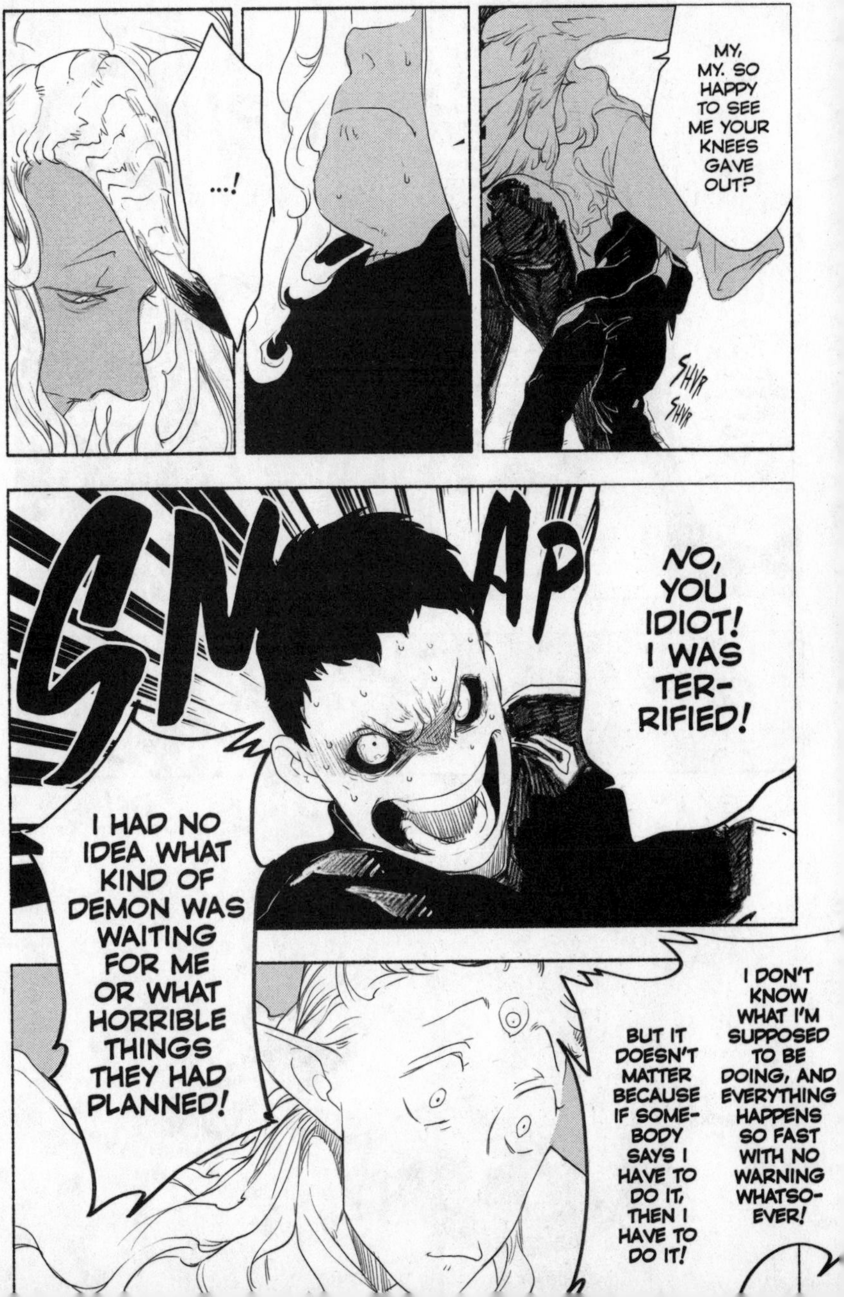
MY, MY. SO HAPPY TO SEE ME YOUR KNEES GAVE OUT?
SHVR SHVR
...!
SMAP
NO, YOU IDIOT! I WAS TER-RIFIED!
I HAD NO IDEA WHAT KIND OF DEMON WAS WAITING FOR ME OR WHAT HORRIBLE THINGS THEY HAD PLANNED!
I DON'T KNOW WHAT I'M SUPPOSED TO BE DOING, AND EVERYTHING HAPPENS SO FAST WITH NO WARNING WHATSO-EVER!
BUT IT DOESN'T MATTER BECAUSE IF SOME-BODY SAYS I HAVE TO DO IT, THEN I HAVE TO DO IT!

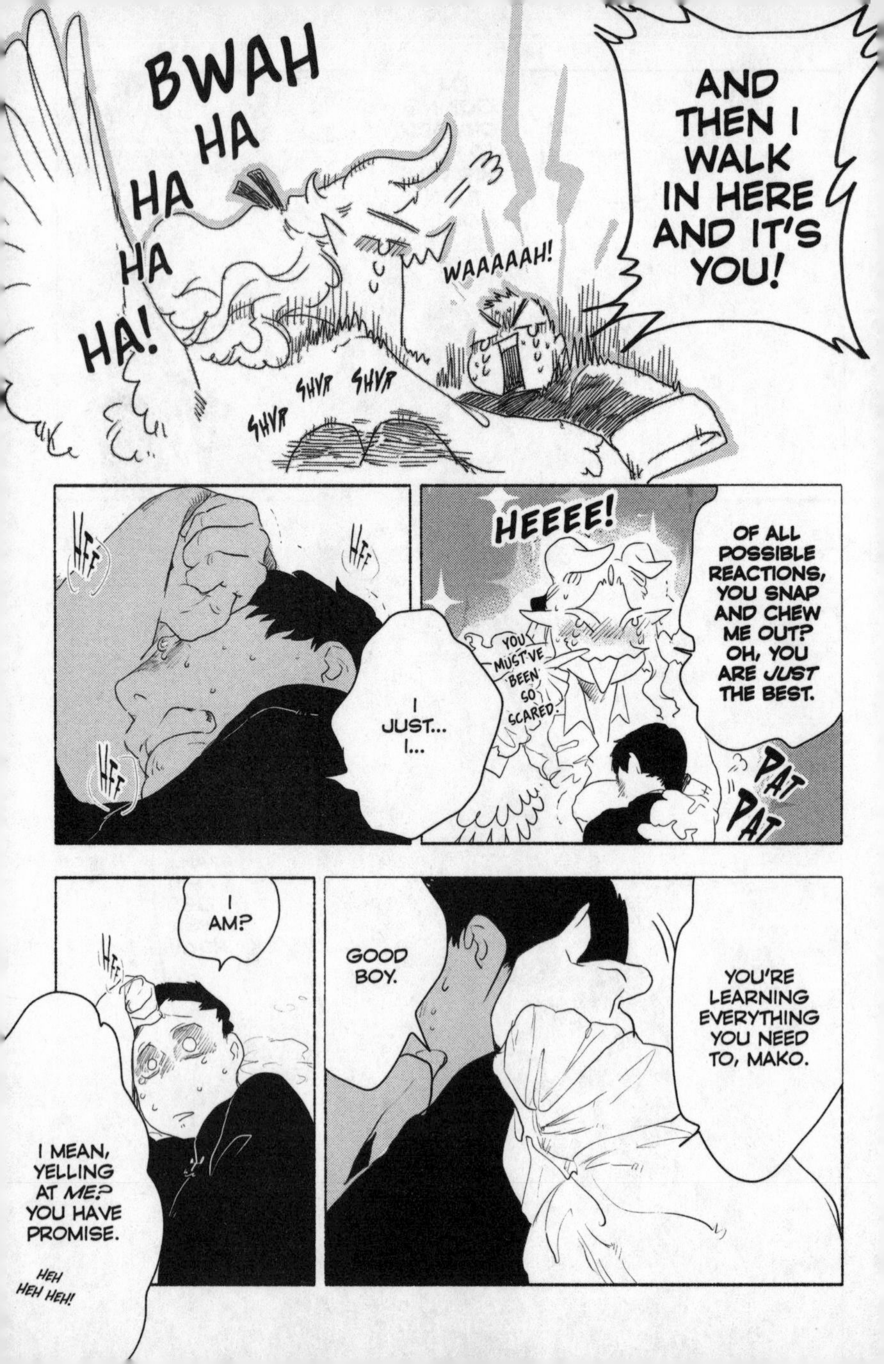
AND THEN I WALK IN HERE AND IT'S YOU!
WAAAAAH!
BWAH HA HA HA HA!
SHVR SHVR SHVR
HEEEE!
OF ALL POSSIBLE REACTIONS, YOU SNAP AND CHEW ME OUT? OH, YOU ARE *JUST* THE BEST.
YOU MUST'VE BEEN SO SCARED.
PAT PAT
HFF
HFF
I JUST... I...
HFF
YOU'RE LEARNING EVERYTHING YOU NEED TO, MAKO.
GOOD BOY.
I AM?
HFF
I MEAN, YELLING AT *ME*? YOU HAVE PROMISE.
HEH HEH HEH!

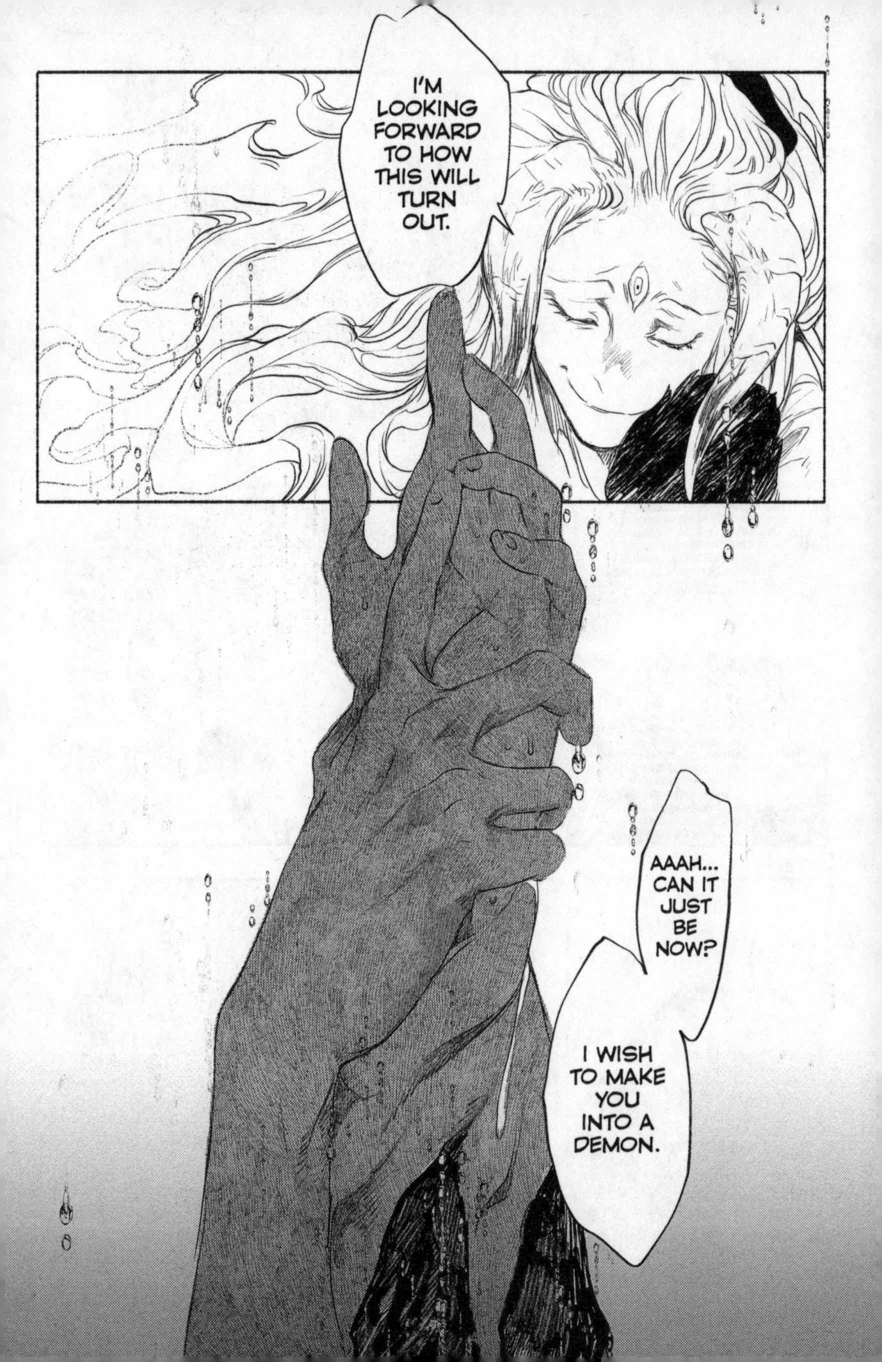
I'M LOOKING FORWARD TO HOW THIS WILL TURN OUT.
AAAH... CAN IT JUST BE NOW?
I WISH TO MAKE YOU INTO A DEMON.

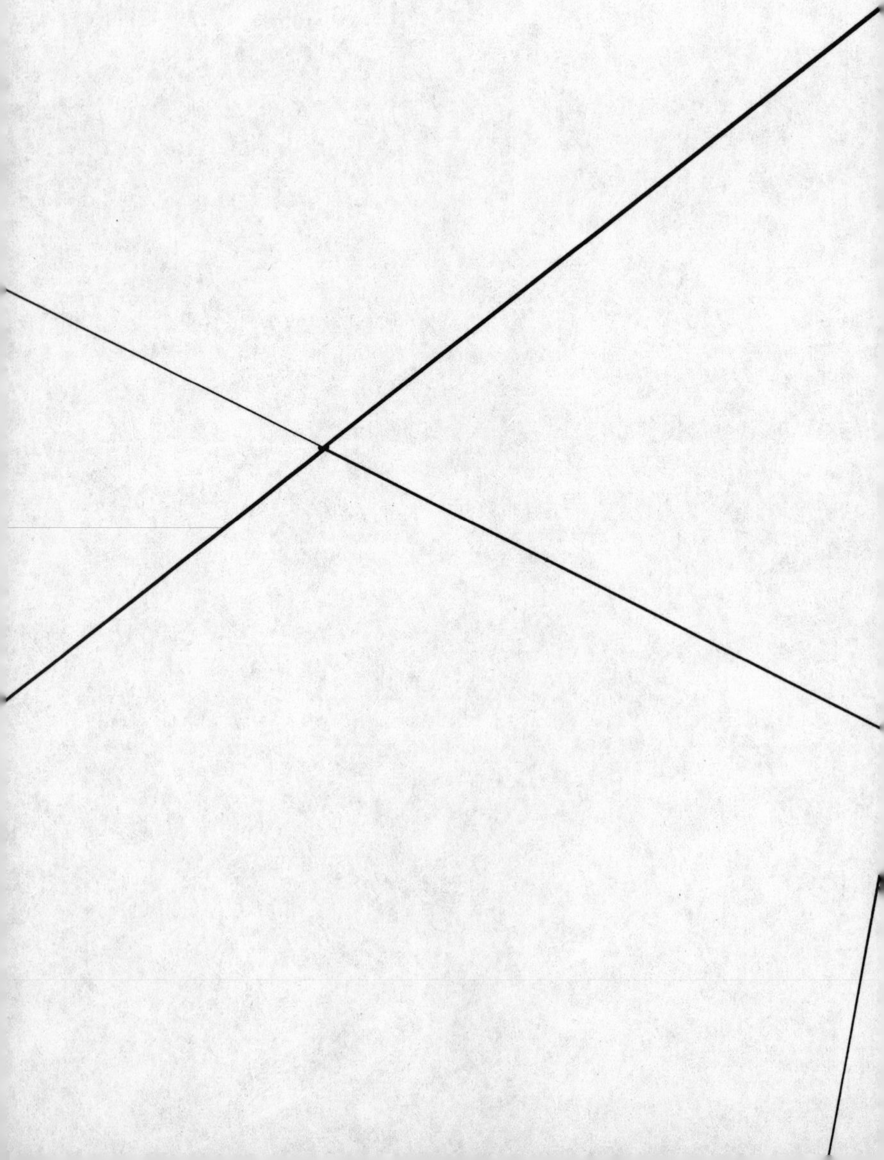

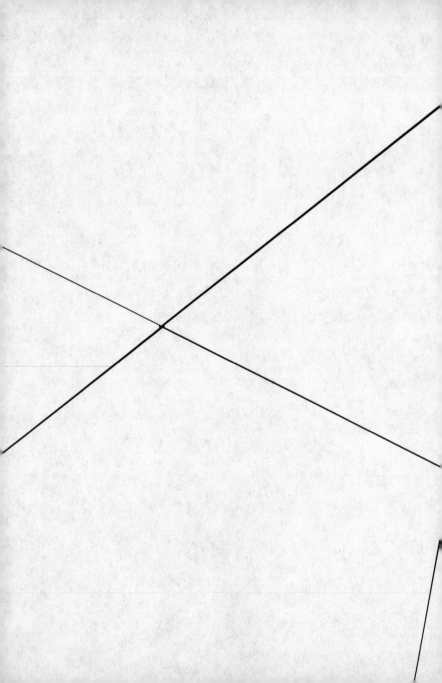

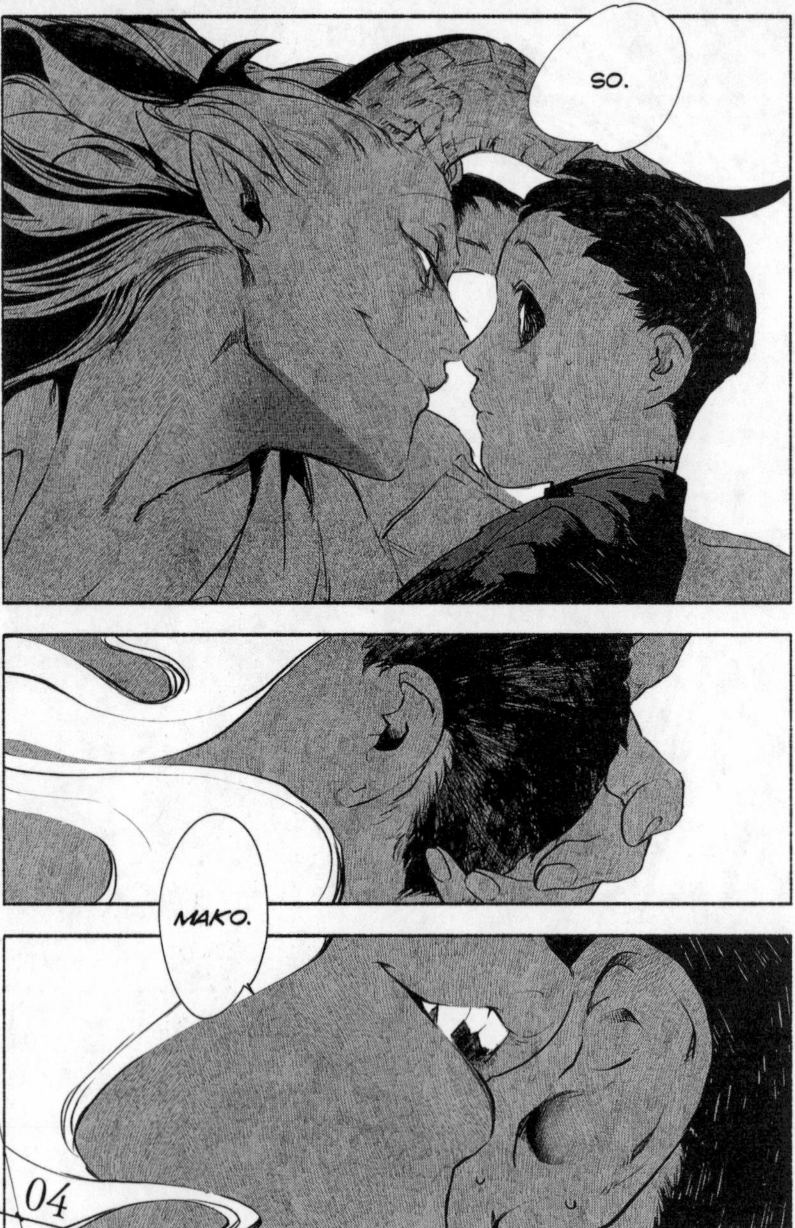
SO.
MAKO.

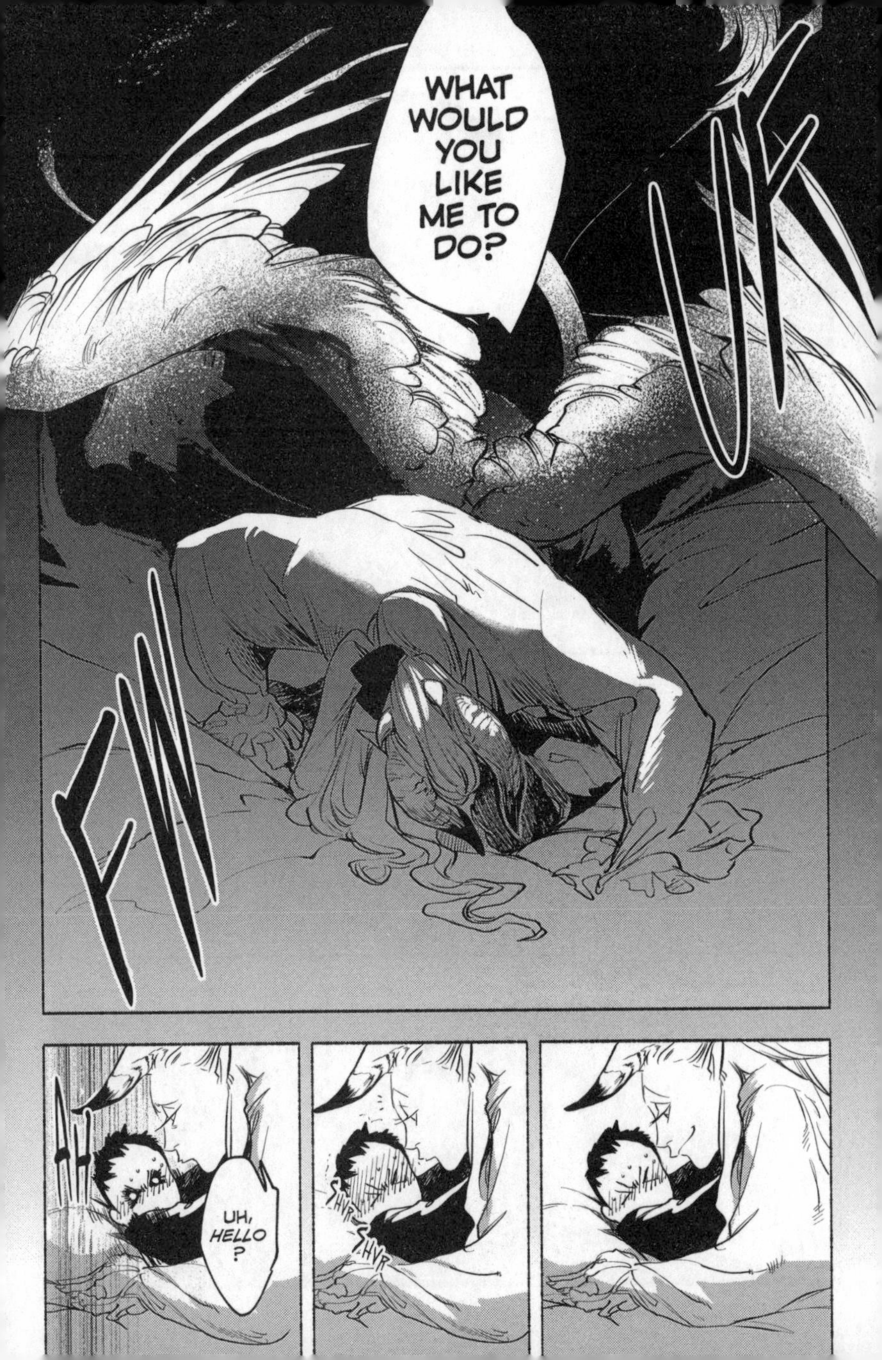
WHAT WOULD YOU LIKE ME TO DO?
UF
FW
SHVR
SHVR
AH
UH, HELLO?

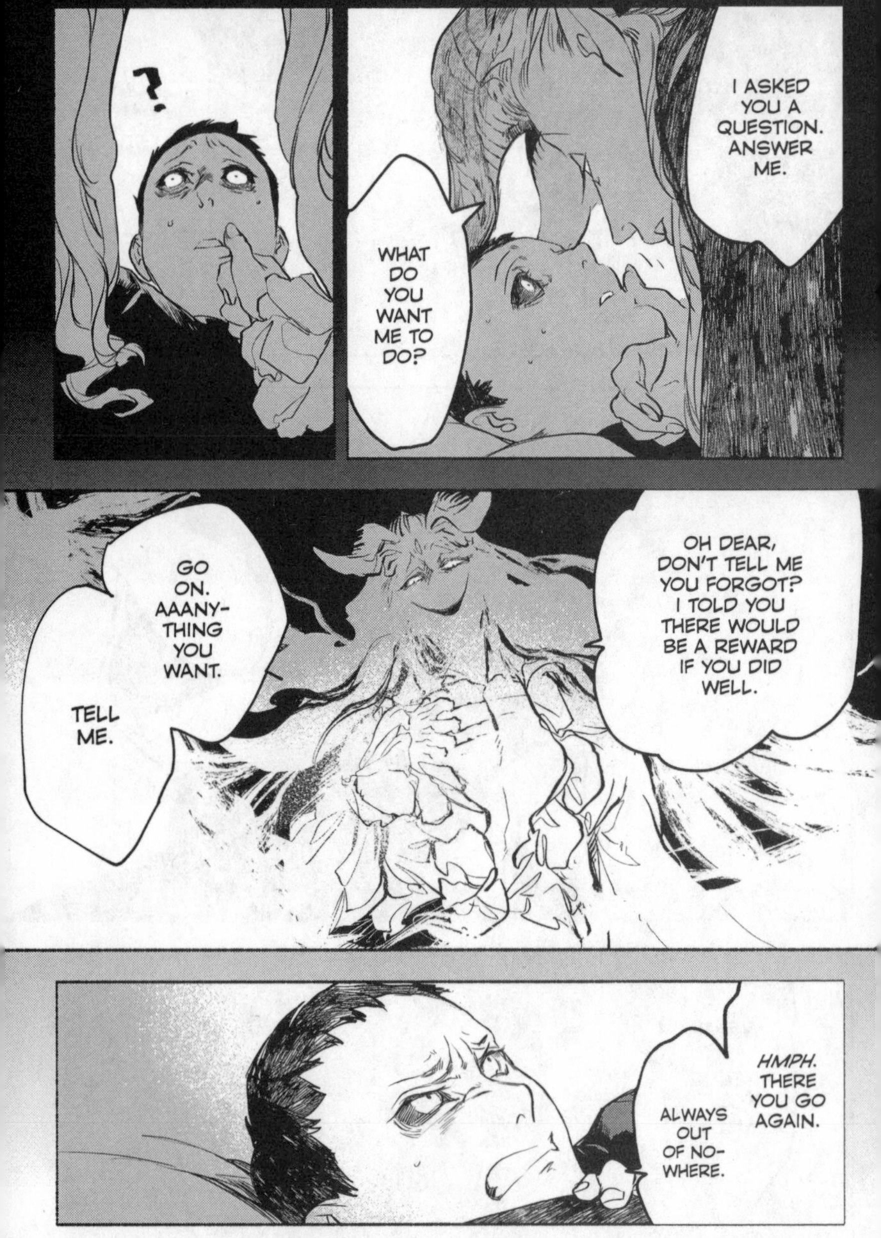
I ASKED YOU A QUESTION. ANSWER ME.
WHAT DO YOU WANT ME TO DO?
?
OH DEAR, DON'T TELL ME YOU FORGOT? I TOLD YOU THERE WOULD BE A REWARD IF YOU DID WELL.
GO ON. AAANY-THING YOU WANT.
TELL ME.
HMPH. THERE YOU GO AGAIN.
ALWAYS OUT OF NO-WHERE.

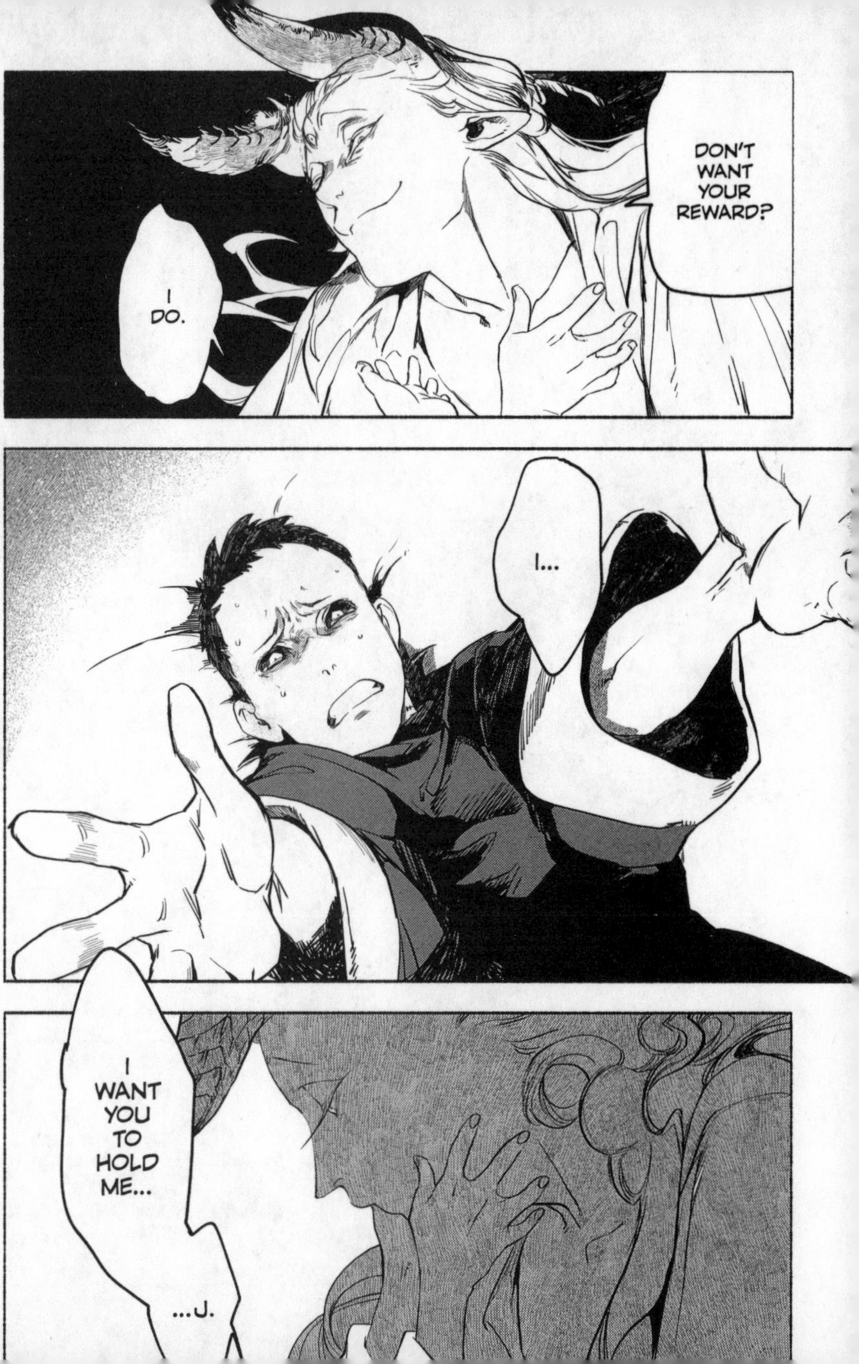
DON'T WANT YOUR REWARD?
I DO.
I...
I WANT YOU TO HOLD ME...
...J.

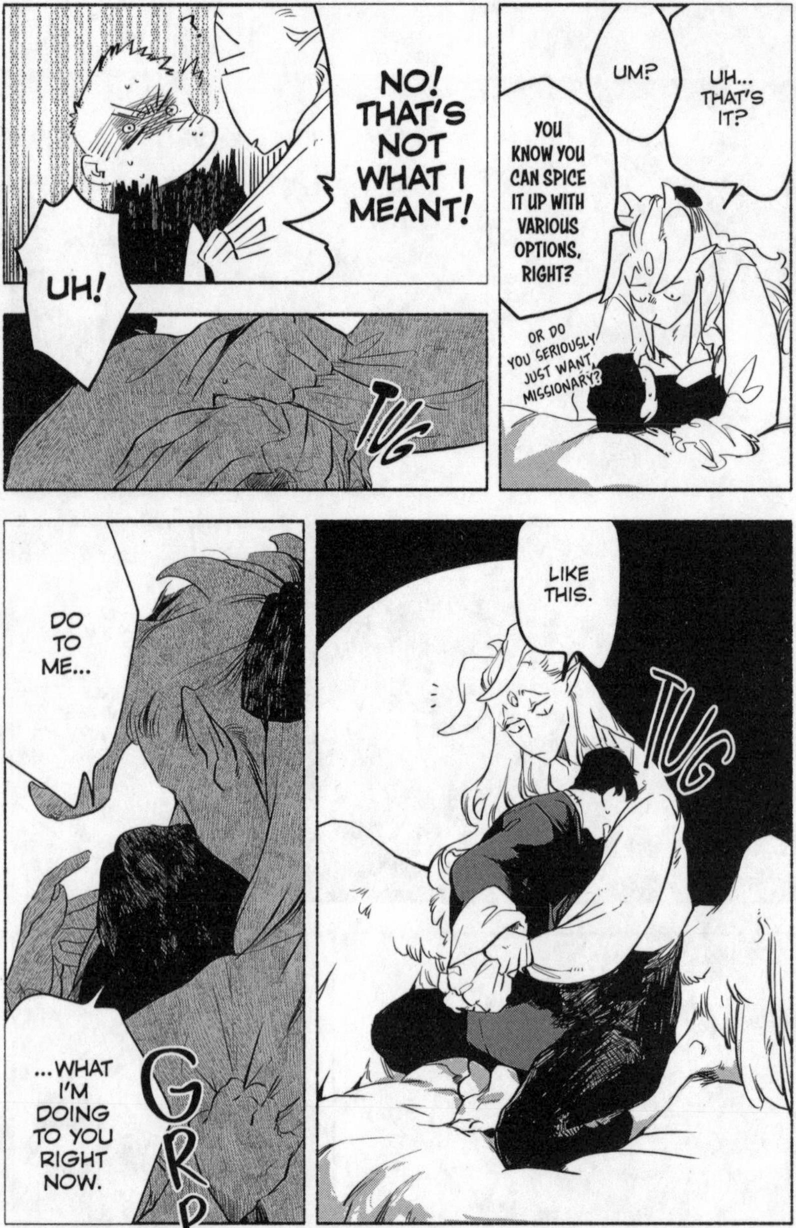
UH... THAT'S IT?
UM?
YOU KNOW YOU CAN SPICE IT UP WITH VARIOUS OPTIONS, RIGHT?
OR DO YOU SERIOUSLY JUST WANT MISSIONARY?
?
NO! THAT'S NOT WHAT I MEANT!
UH!
TUG
LIKE THIS.
TUG
DO TO ME...
...WHAT I'M DOING TO YOU RIGHT NOW.
GRP

YOU GET TURNED INTO A MONSTER WITHOUT YOUR PERMISSION...

...

THEN TOSSED INTO A BROTHEL IN HELL WITH NO CLUE AS TO WHAT'S HAPPENING...

...BUT YOU DESPERATELY DO WHAT YOU CAN, AND THIS IS THE REWARD YOU WANT?

I DON'T KNOW.

BUT RIGHT NOW, THIS IS THE ONLY THING I CAN THINK OF.

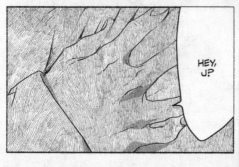

HEY, J?

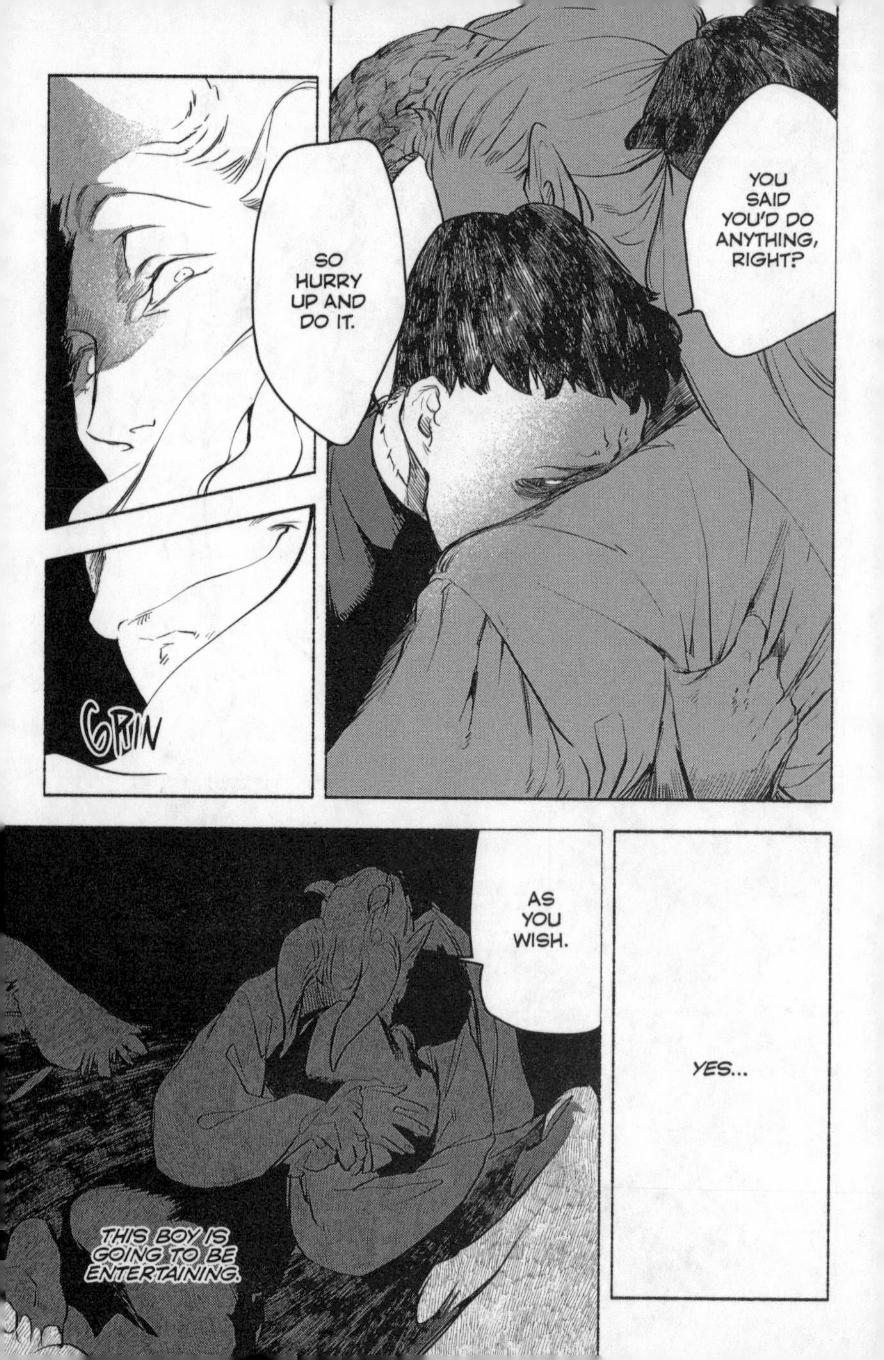
YOU SAID YOU'D DO ANYTHING, RIGHT?
SO HURRY UP AND DO IT.
GRIN
YES...
AS YOU WISH.
THIS BOY IS GOING TO BE ENTERTAINING.

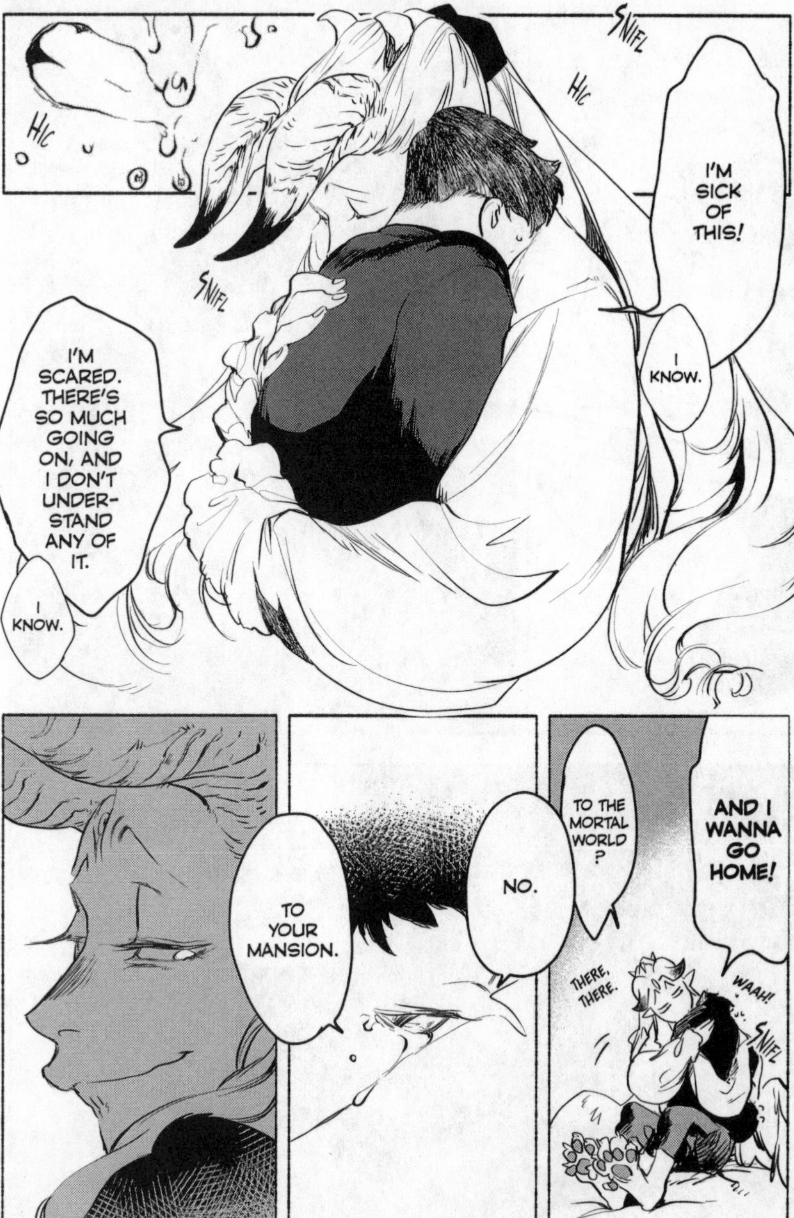
SNIFL
HIC
I'M SICK OF THIS!
I KNOW.
HIC
SNIFL
I'M SCARED. THERE'S SO MUCH GOING ON, AND I DON'T UNDER-STAND ANY OF IT.
I KNOW.
AND I WANNA GO HOME!
TO THE MORTAL WORLD?
THERE, THERE.
WAAH!
SNIFL
NO.
TO YOUR MANSION.

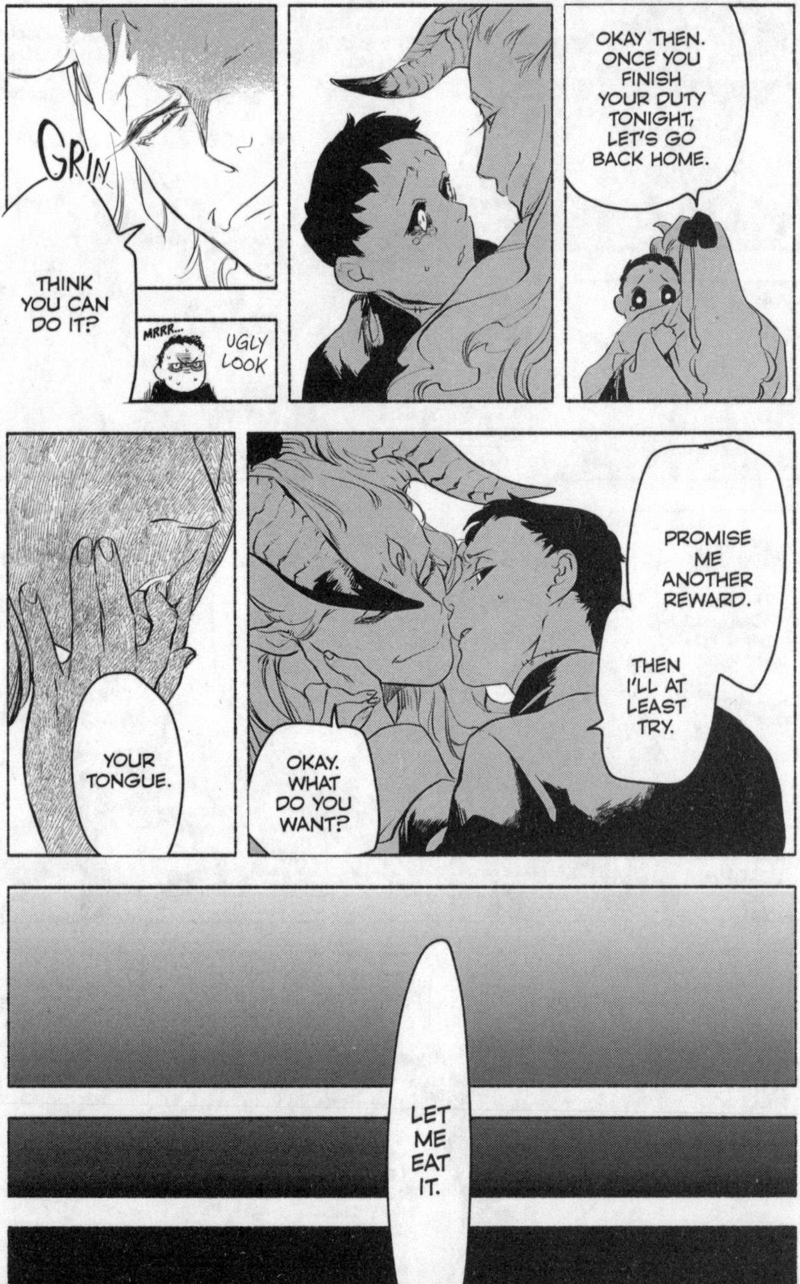
OKAY THEN. ONCE YOU FINISH YOUR DUTY TONIGHT, LET'S GO BACK HOME.
GRIN
THINK YOU CAN DO IT?
MRRR...
UGLY LOOK
PROMISE ME ANOTHER REWARD.
THEN I'LL AT LEAST TRY.
OKAY. WHAT DO YOU WANT?
YOUR TONGUE.
LET ME EAT IT.

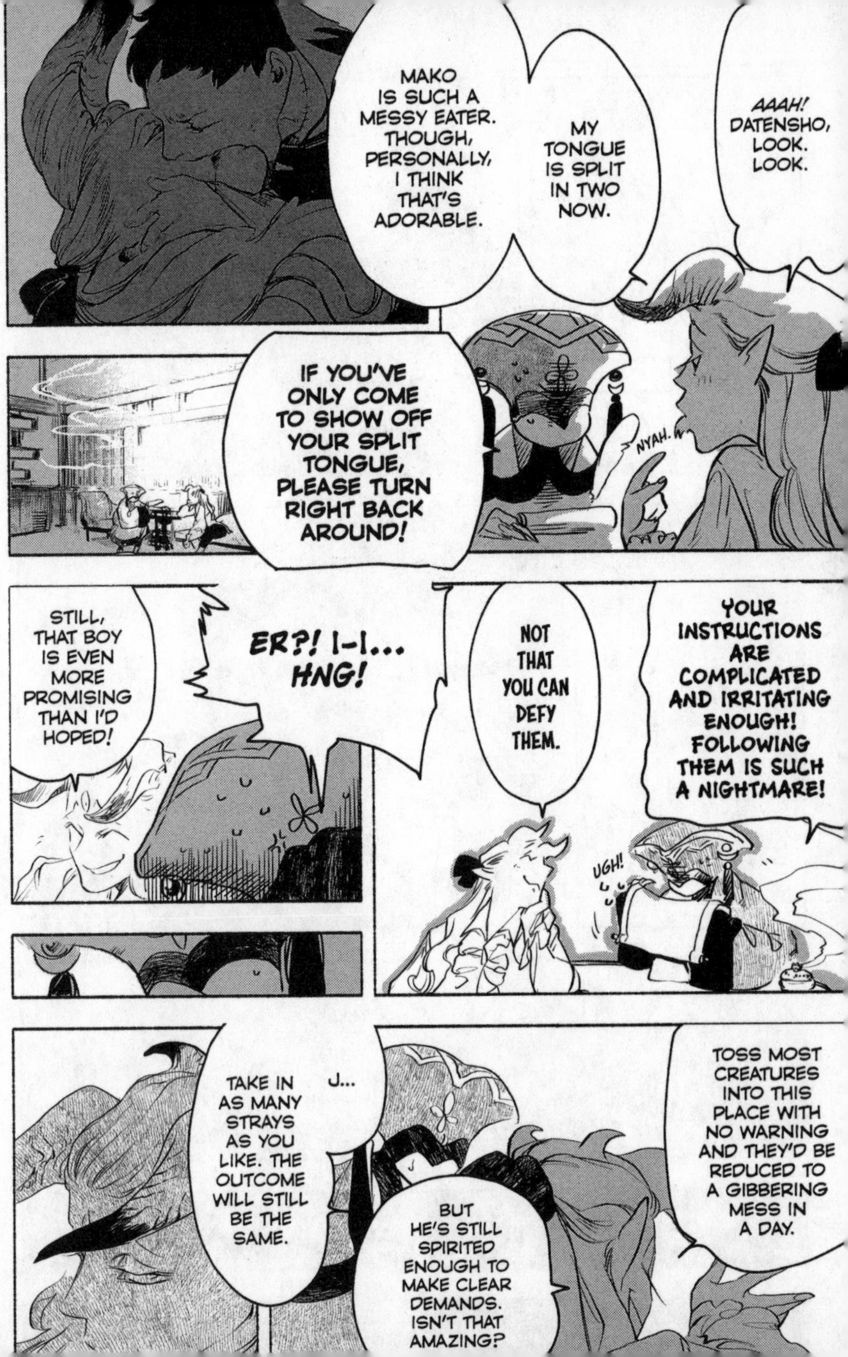
AAAH! DATENSHO, LOOK. LOOK.
MY TONGUE IS SPLIT IN TWO NOW.
MAKO IS SUCH A MESSY EATER. THOUGH, PERSONALLY, I THINK THAT'S ADORABLE.
NYAH.
IF YOU'VE ONLY COME TO SHOW OFF YOUR SPLIT TONGUE, PLEASE TURN RIGHT BACK AROUND!
YOUR INSTRUCTIONS ARE COMPLICATED AND IRRITATING ENOUGH! FOLLOWING THEM IS SUCH A NIGHTMARE!
UGH!
NOT THAT YOU CAN DEFY THEM.
ER?! I-I... HNG!
STILL, THAT BOY IS EVEN MORE PROMISING THAN I'D HOPED!
TOSS MOST CREATURES INTO THIS PLACE WITH NO WARNING AND THEY'D BE REDUCED TO A GIBBERING MESS IN A DAY.
BUT HE'S STILL SPIRITED ENOUGH TO MAKE CLEAR DEMANDS. ISN'T THAT AMAZING?
J...
TAKE IN AS MANY STRAYS AS YOU LIKE. THE OUTCOME WILL STILL BE THE SAME.

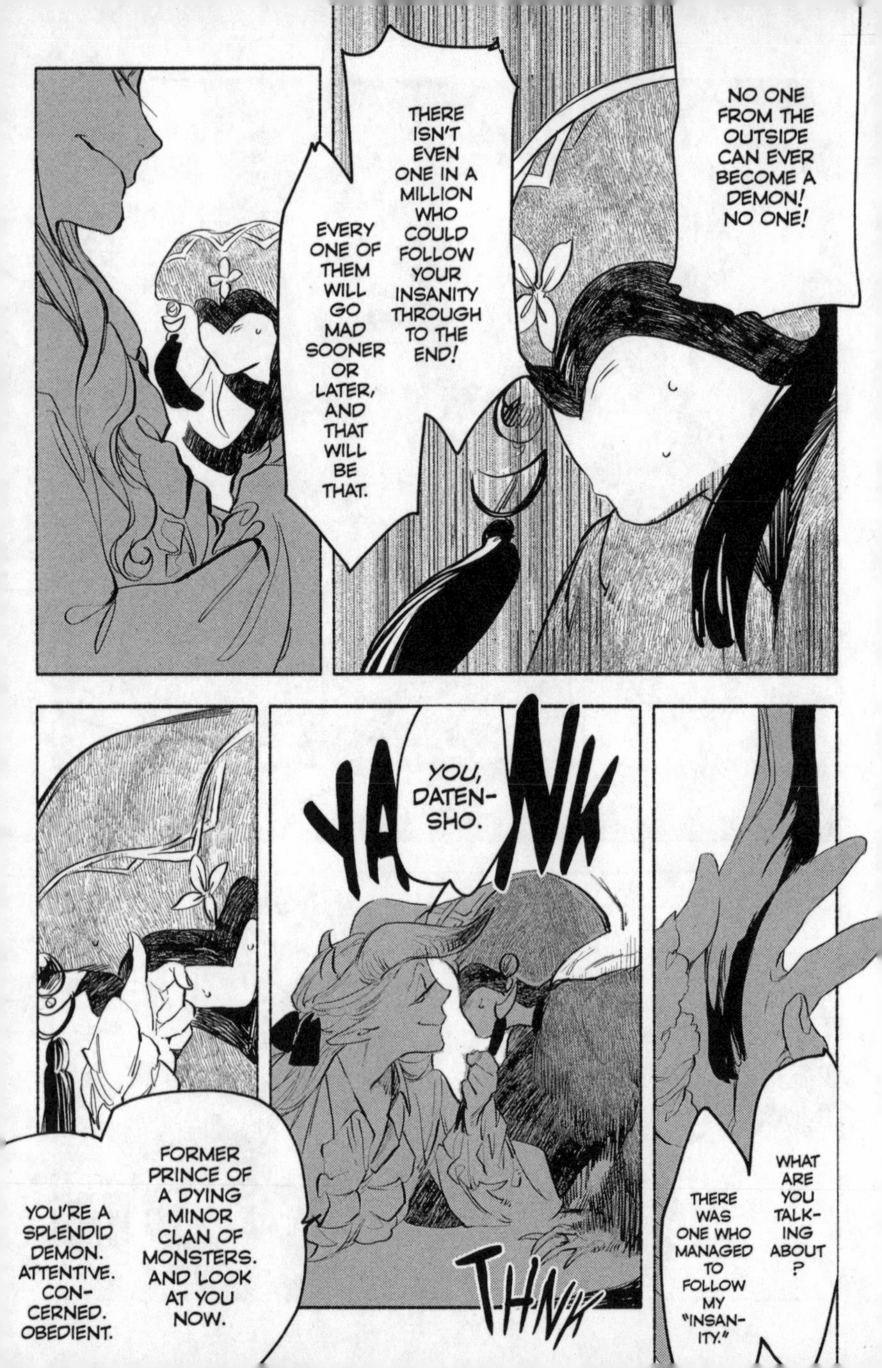
NO ONE FROM THE OUTSIDE CAN EVER BECOME A DEMON! NO ONE!
THERE ISN'T EVEN ONE IN A MILLION WHO COULD FOLLOW YOUR INSANITY THROUGH TO THE END!
EVERY ONE OF THEM WILL GO MAD SOONER OR LATER, AND THAT WILL BE THAT.
WHAT ARE YOU TALKING ABOUT?
THERE WAS ONE WHO MANAGED TO FOLLOW MY "INSANITY."
YANK
YOU, DATEN-SHO.
THNK
FORMER PRINCE OF A DYING MINOR CLAN OF MONSTERS. AND LOOK AT YOU NOW.
YOU'RE A SPLENDID DEMON. ATTENTIVE. CON-CERNED. OBEDIENT.

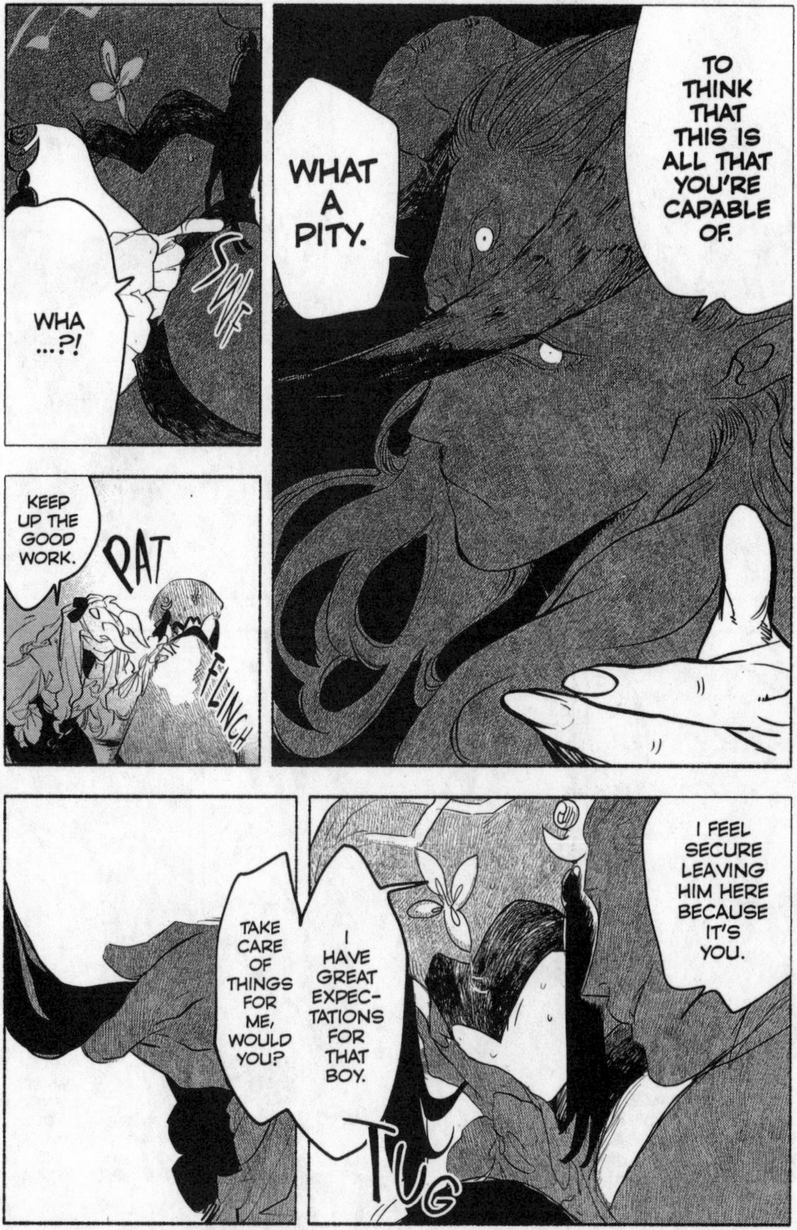
TO THINK THAT THIS IS ALL THAT YOU'RE CAPABLE OF.
WHAT A PITY.
WHA ...?!
KEEP UP THE GOOD WORK.
PAT
FLINCH
I FEEL SECURE LEAVING HIM HERE BECAUSE IT'S YOU.
I HAVE GREAT EXPECTATIONS FOR THAT BOY.
TAKE CARE OF THINGS FOR ME, WOULD YOU?
TUG

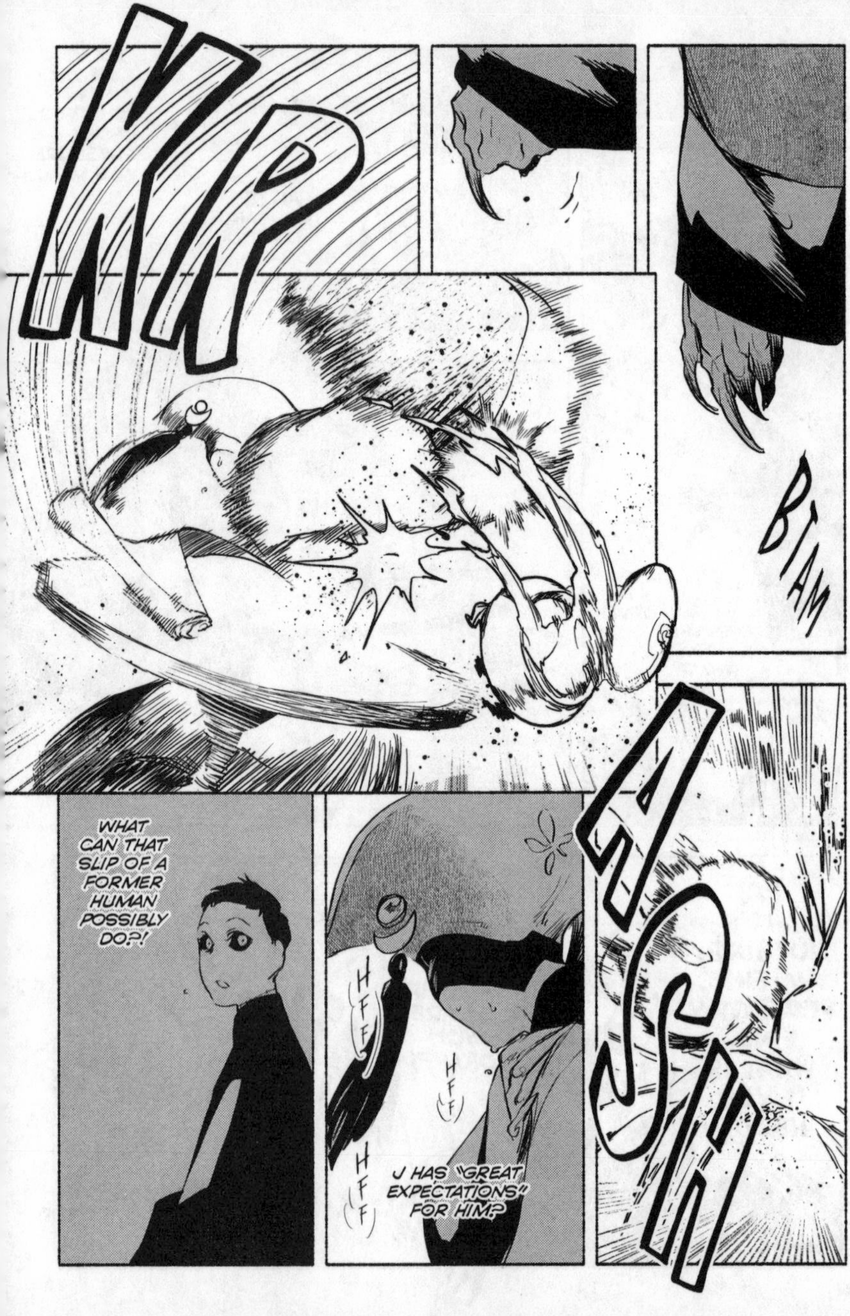
BTAM
WHP
ASH
HFF
HFF
HFF
J HAS "GREAT EXPECTATIONS" FOR HIM?
WHAT CAN THAT SLIP OF A FORMER HUMAN POSSIBLY DO?!

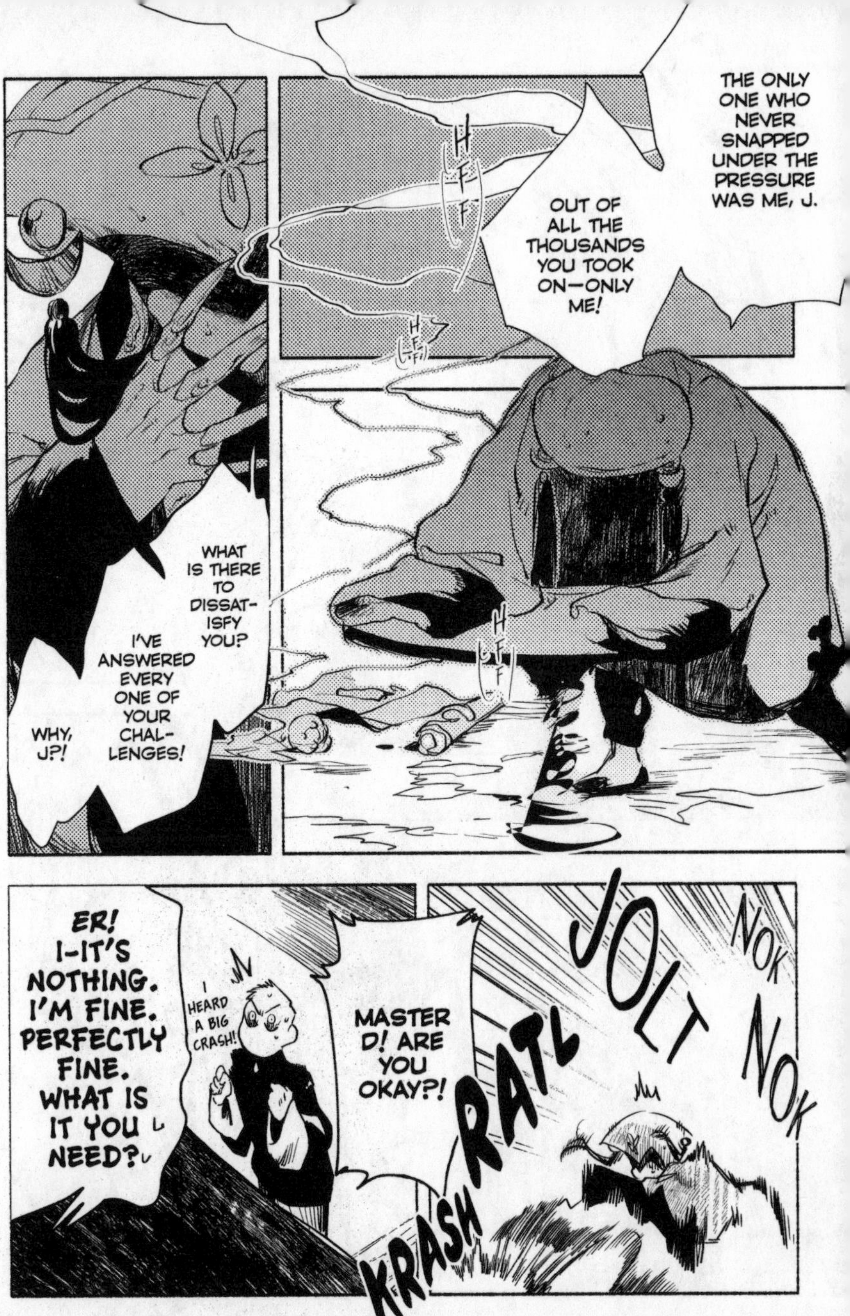
THE ONLY ONE WHO NEVER SNAPPED UNDER THE PRESSURE WAS ME, J.
OUT OF ALL THE THOUSANDS YOU TOOK ON—ONLY ME!
HFF
HFF
HFF
WHAT IS THERE TO DISSATISFY YOU?
I'VE ANSWERED EVERY ONE OF YOUR CHALLENGES!
WHY, J?!
NOK NOK
JOLT
RATL
KRASH
MASTER D! ARE YOU OKAY?!
I HEARD A BIG CRASH!
ER! I-IT'S NOTHING. I'M FINE. PERFECTLY FINE. WHAT IS IT YOU NEED?

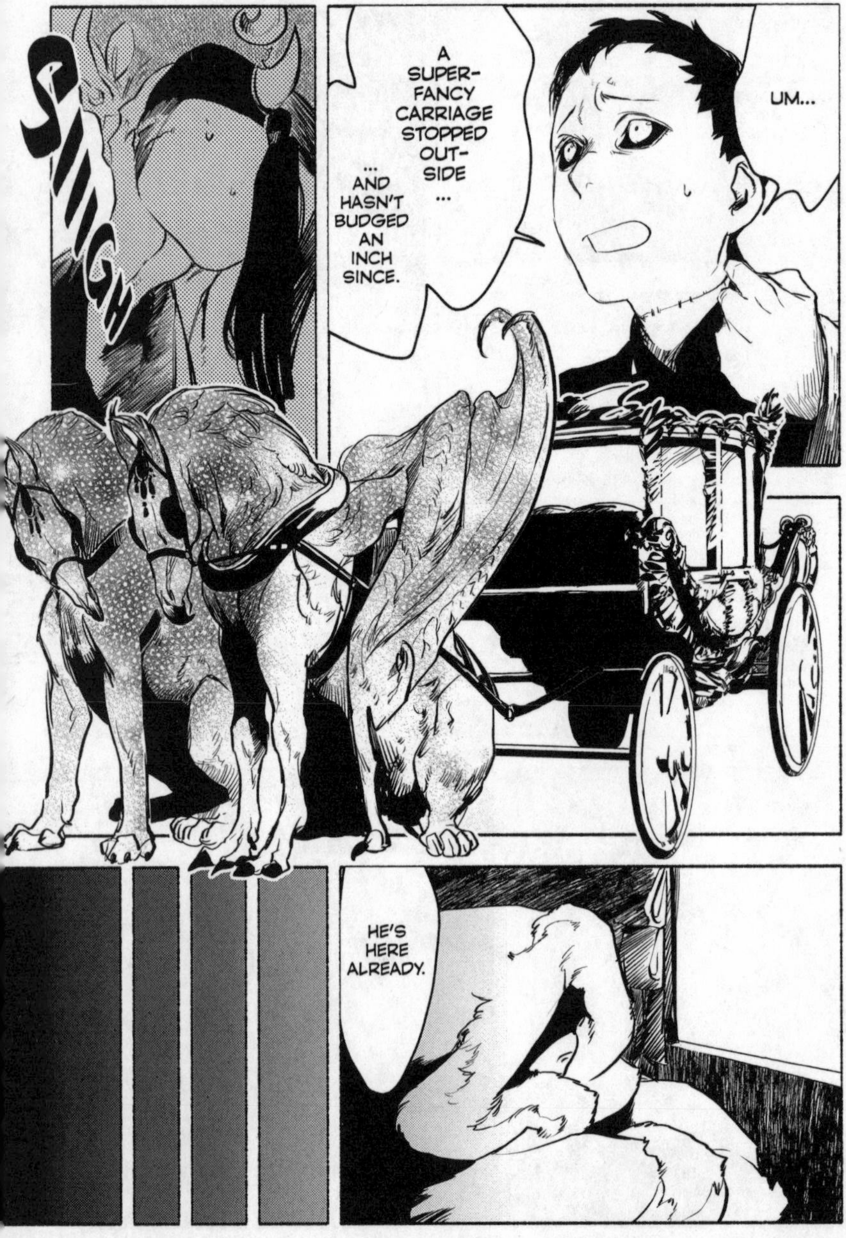
UM...
A SUPER-FANCY CARRIAGE STOPPED OUTSIDE...
...AND HASN'T BUDGED AN INCH SINCE.
SIIIGH
HE'S HERE ALREADY.

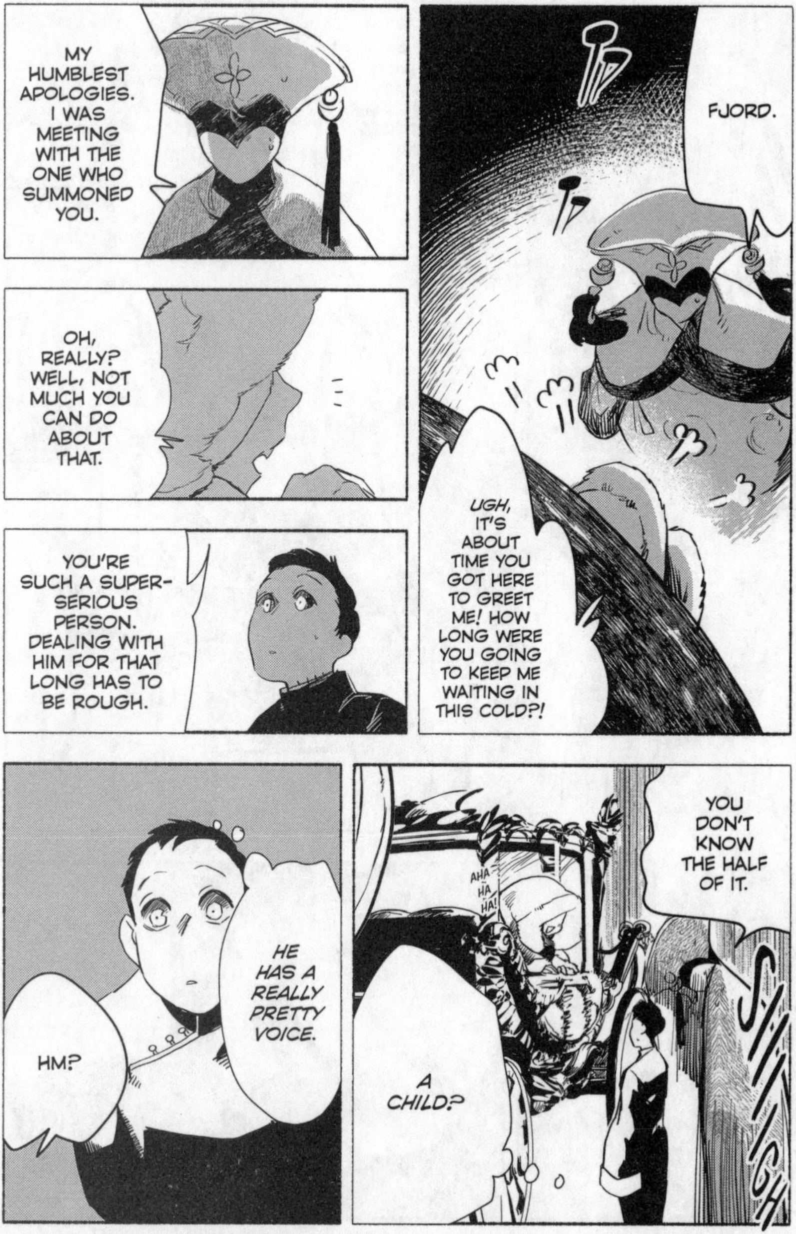
FJORD.
UGH, IT'S ABOUT TIME YOU GOT HERE TO GREET ME! HOW LONG WERE YOU GOING TO KEEP ME WAITING IN THIS COLD?!
MY HUMBLEST APOLOGIES. I WAS MEETING WITH THE ONE WHO SUMMONED YOU.
OH, REALLY? WELL, NOT MUCH YOU CAN DO ABOUT THAT.
YOU'RE SUCH A SUPER-SERIOUS PERSON. DEALING WITH HIM FOR THAT LONG HAS TO BE ROUGH.
YOU DON'T KNOW THE HALF OF IT.
S-SIGH
AHA HA HA!
A CHILD?
HE HAS A REALLY PRETTY VOICE.
HM?

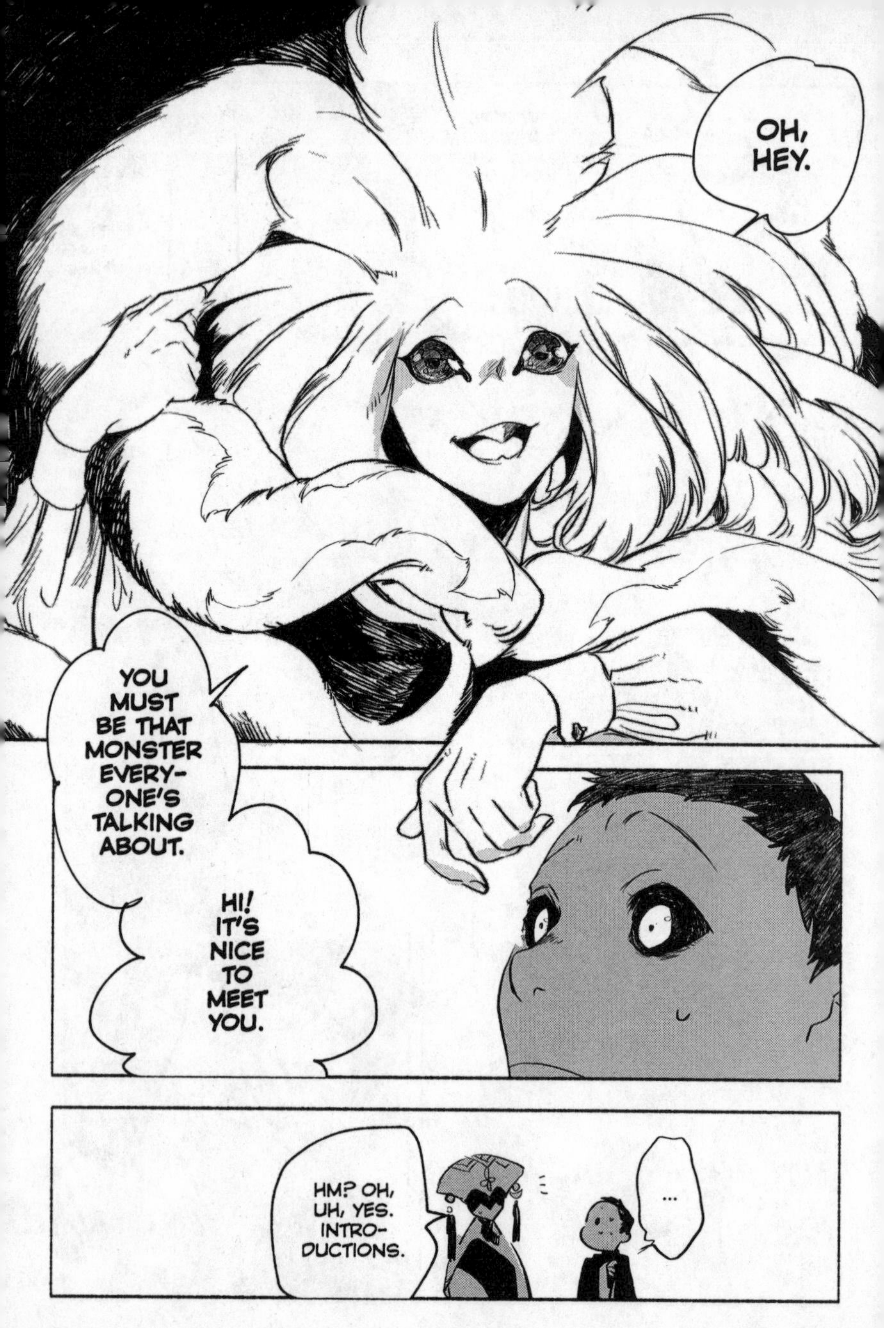
OH, HEY.
YOU MUST BE THAT MONSTER EVERY-ONE'S TALKING ABOUT.
HI! IT'S NICE TO MEET YOU.
...
HM? OH, UH, YES. INTRO-DUCTIONS.

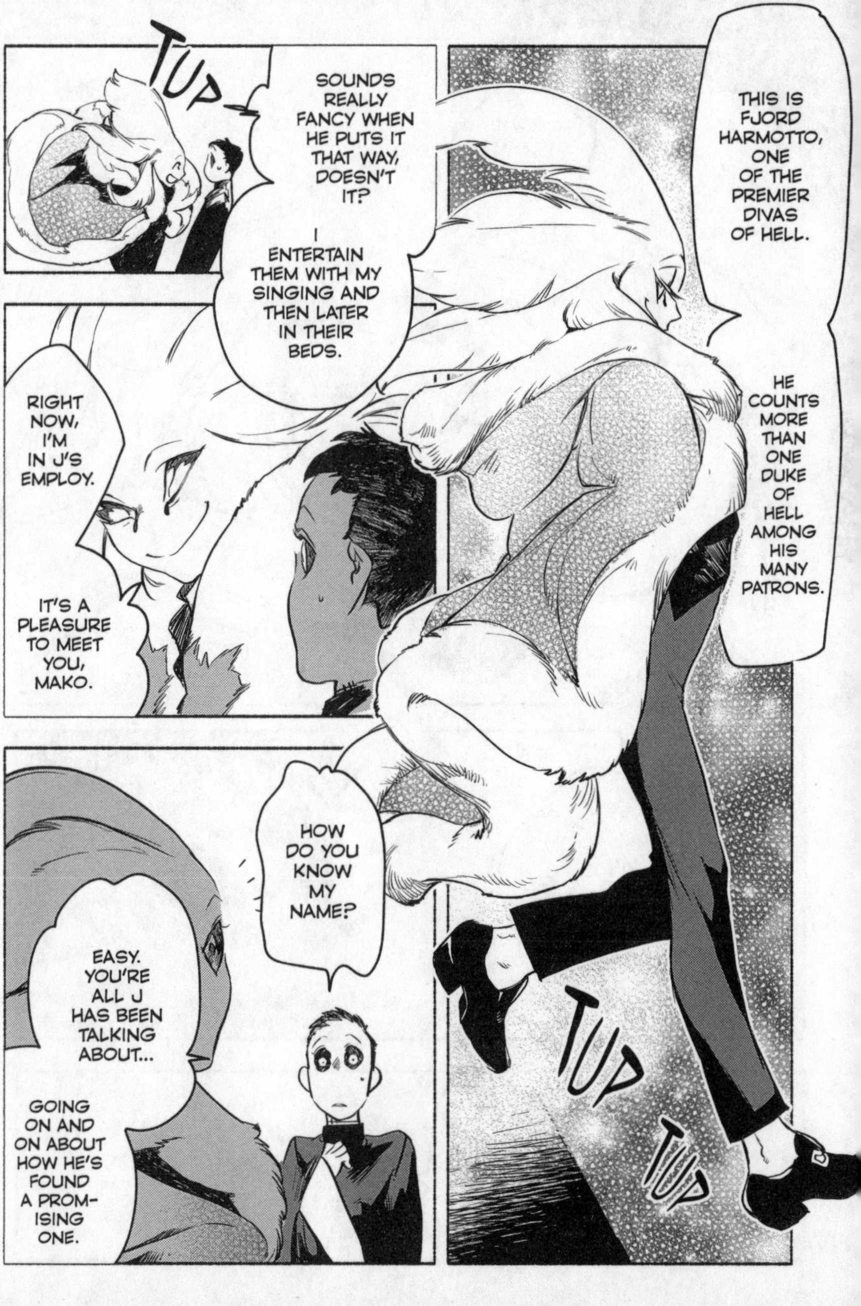
THIS IS FJORD HARMOTTO, ONE OF THE PREMIER DIVAS OF HELL.
HE COUNTS MORE THAN ONE DUKE OF HELL AMONG HIS MANY PATRONS.
TUP
TUP
TUP-
SOUNDS REALLY FANCY WHEN HE PUTS IT THAT WAY, DOESN'T IT?
I ENTERTAIN THEM WITH MY SINGING AND THEN LATER IN THEIR BEDS.
RIGHT NOW, I'M IN J'S EMPLOY.
IT'S A PLEASURE TO MEET YOU, MAKO.
HOW DO YOU KNOW MY NAME?
EASY. YOU'RE ALL J HAS BEEN TALKING ABOUT...
GOING ON AND ON ABOUT HOW HE'S FOUND A PROM-ISING ONE.

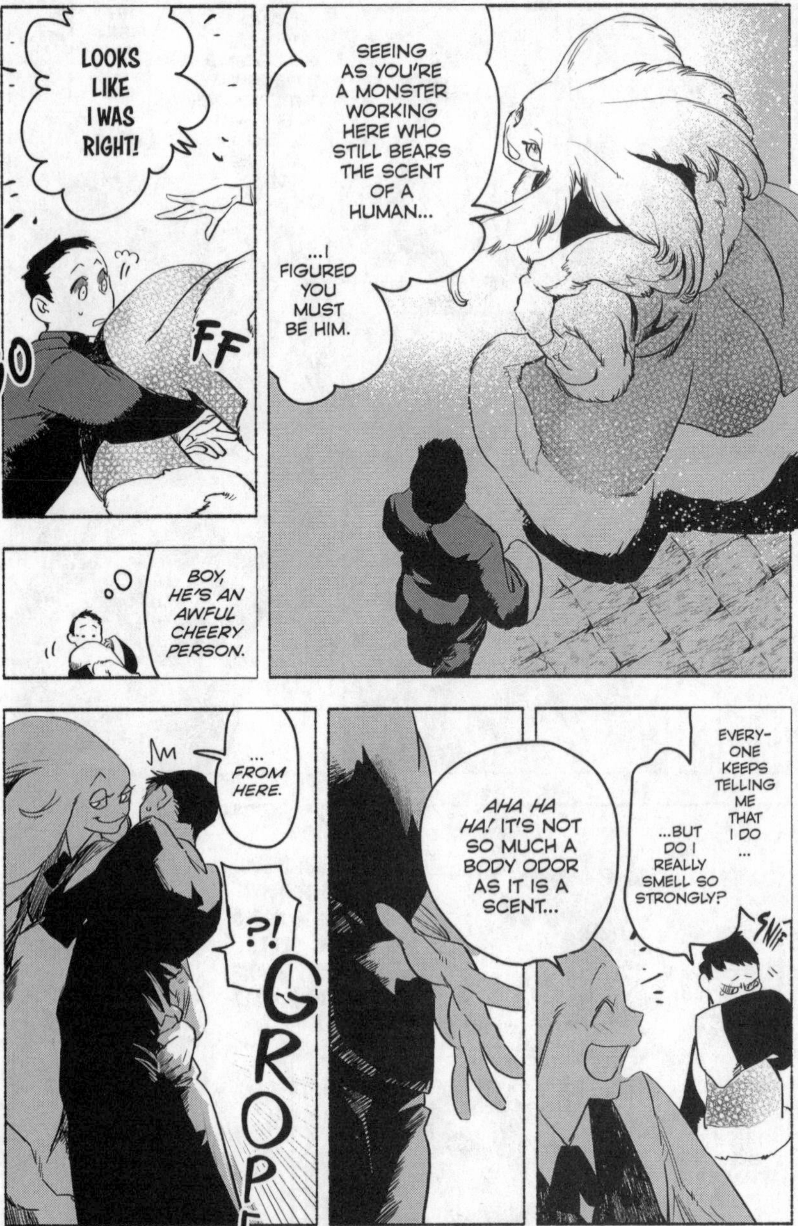
SEEING AS YOU'RE A MONSTER WORKING HERE WHO STILL BEARS THE SCENT OF A HUMAN...
...I FIGURED YOU MUST BE HIM.
LOOKS LIKE I WAS RIGHT!
BOFF
BOY, HE'S AN AWFUL CHEERY PERSON.
EVERY-ONE KEEPS TELLING ME THAT I DO ...
...BUT DO I REALLY SMELL SO STRONGLY?
SNIF
AHA HA HA! IT'S NOT SO MUCH A BODY ODOR AS IT IS A SCENT...
... FROM HERE.
?!
GROPE

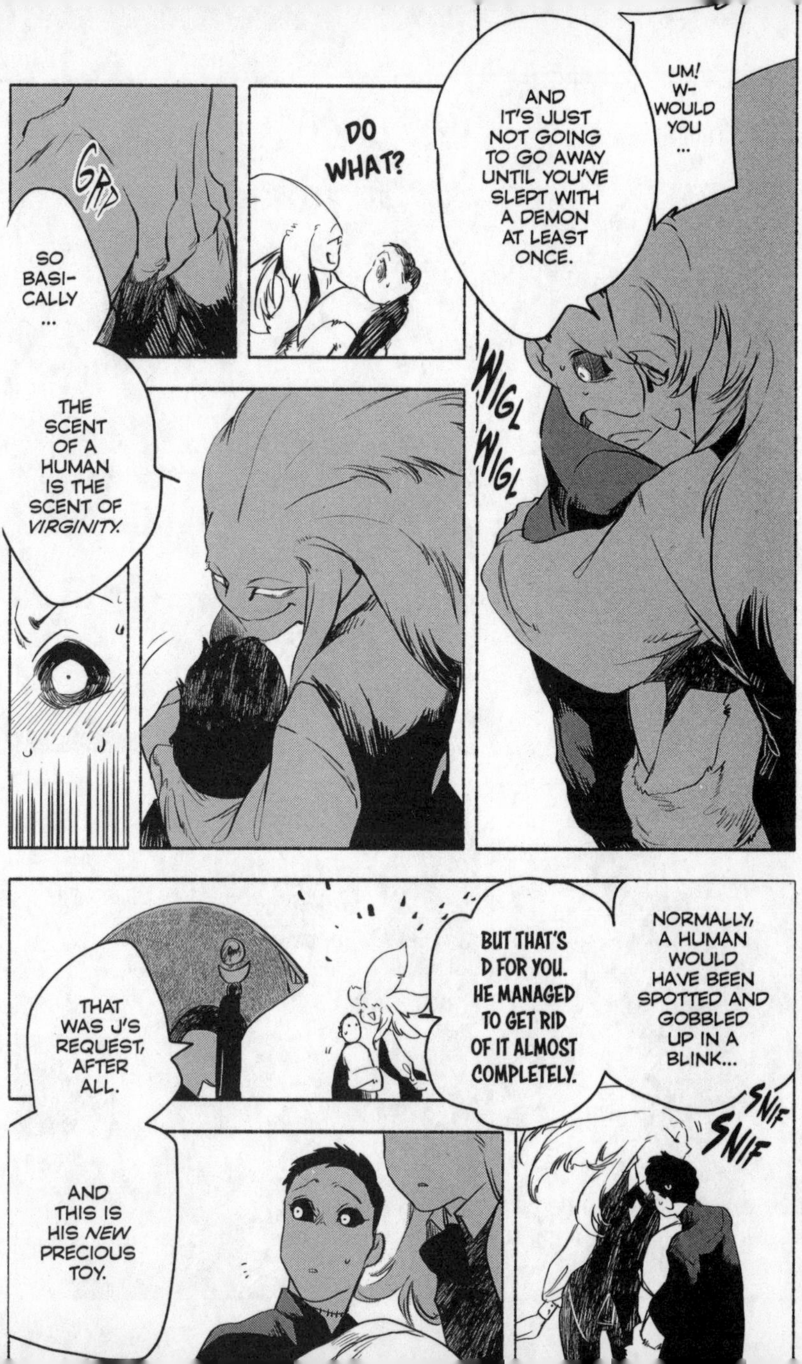
UM! W-WOULD YOU ...
AND IT'S JUST NOT GOING TO GO AWAY UNTIL YOU'VE SLEPT WITH A DEMON AT LEAST ONCE.
WIGL WIGL
DO WHAT?
GRP
SO BASI-CALLY ...
THE SCENT OF A HUMAN IS THE SCENT OF *VIRGINITY.*
NORMALLY, A HUMAN WOULD HAVE BEEN SPOTTED AND GOBBLED UP IN A BLINK...
BUT THAT'S D FOR YOU. HE MANAGED TO GET RID OF IT ALMOST COMPLETELY.
THAT WAS J'S REQUEST, AFTER ALL.
SNIF SNIF
AND THIS IS HIS *NEW* PRECIOUS TOY.

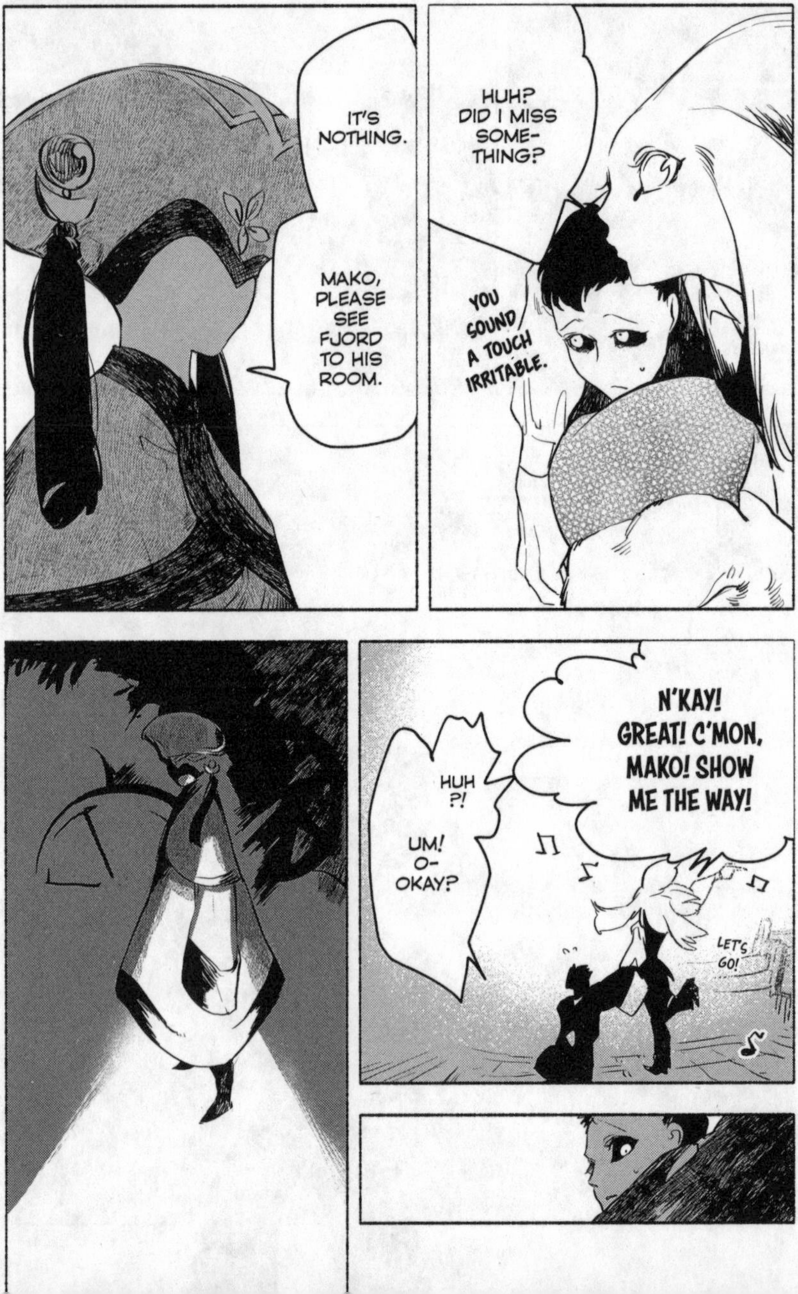
HUH? DID I MISS SOME-THING?
YOU SOUND A TOUCH IRRITABLE.
IT'S NOTHING.
MAKO, PLEASE SEE FJORD TO HIS ROOM.
N'KAY! GREAT! C'MON, MAKO! SHOW ME THE WAY!
HUH?!
UM! O-OKAY?
LET'S GO!

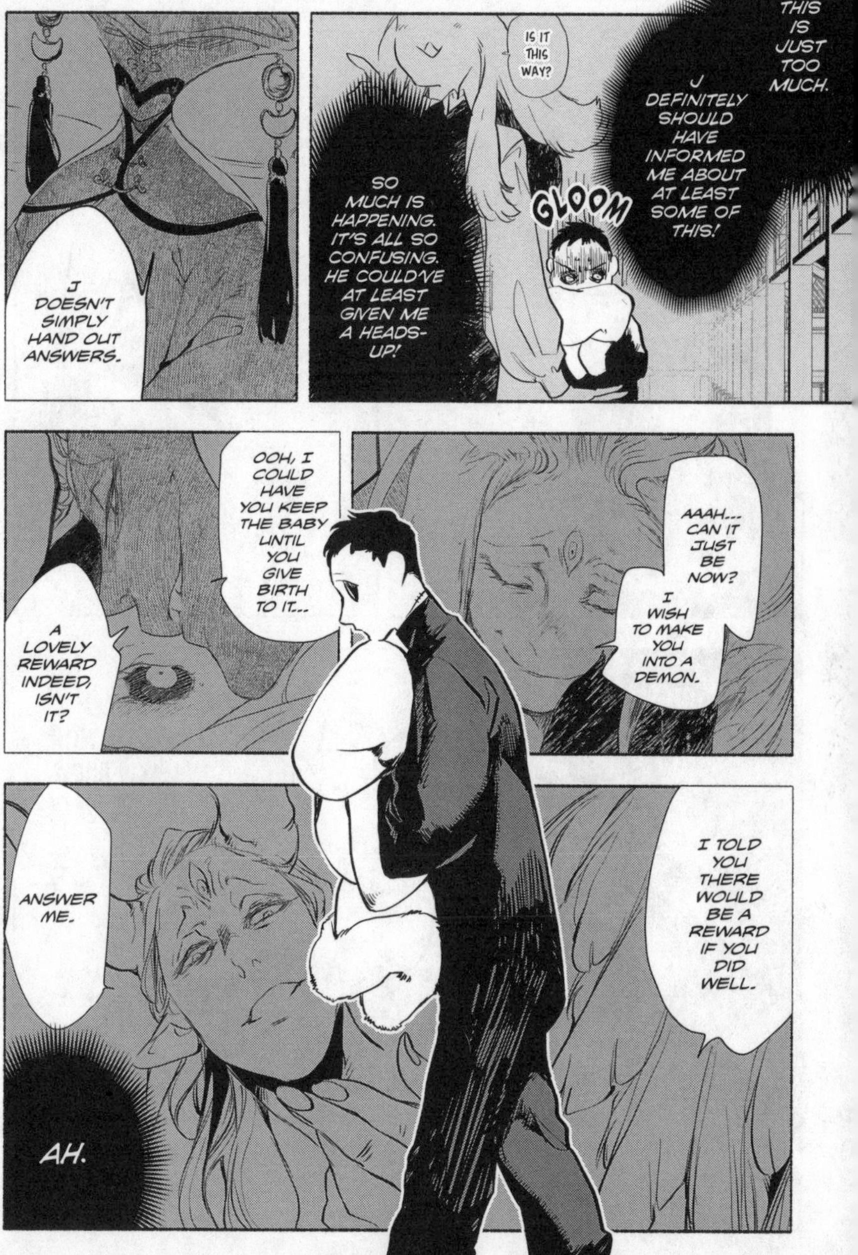
THIS IS JUST TOO MUCH.
J DEFINITELY SHOULD HAVE INFORMED ME ABOUT AT LEAST SOME OF THIS!
IS IT THIS WAY?
GLOOM
SO MUCH IS HAPPENING. IT'S ALL SO CONFUSING. HE COULD'VE AT LEAST GIVEN ME A HEADS-UP!
J DOESN'T SIMPLY HAND OUT ANSWERS.
AAAH... CAN IT JUST BE NOW?
I WISH TO MAKE YOU INTO A DEMON.
OOH, I COULD HAVE YOU KEEP THE BABY UNTIL YOU GIVE BIRTH TO IT...
A LOVELY REWARD INDEED, ISN'T IT?
I TOLD YOU THERE WOULD BE A REWARD IF YOU DID WELL.
ANSWER ME.
AH.

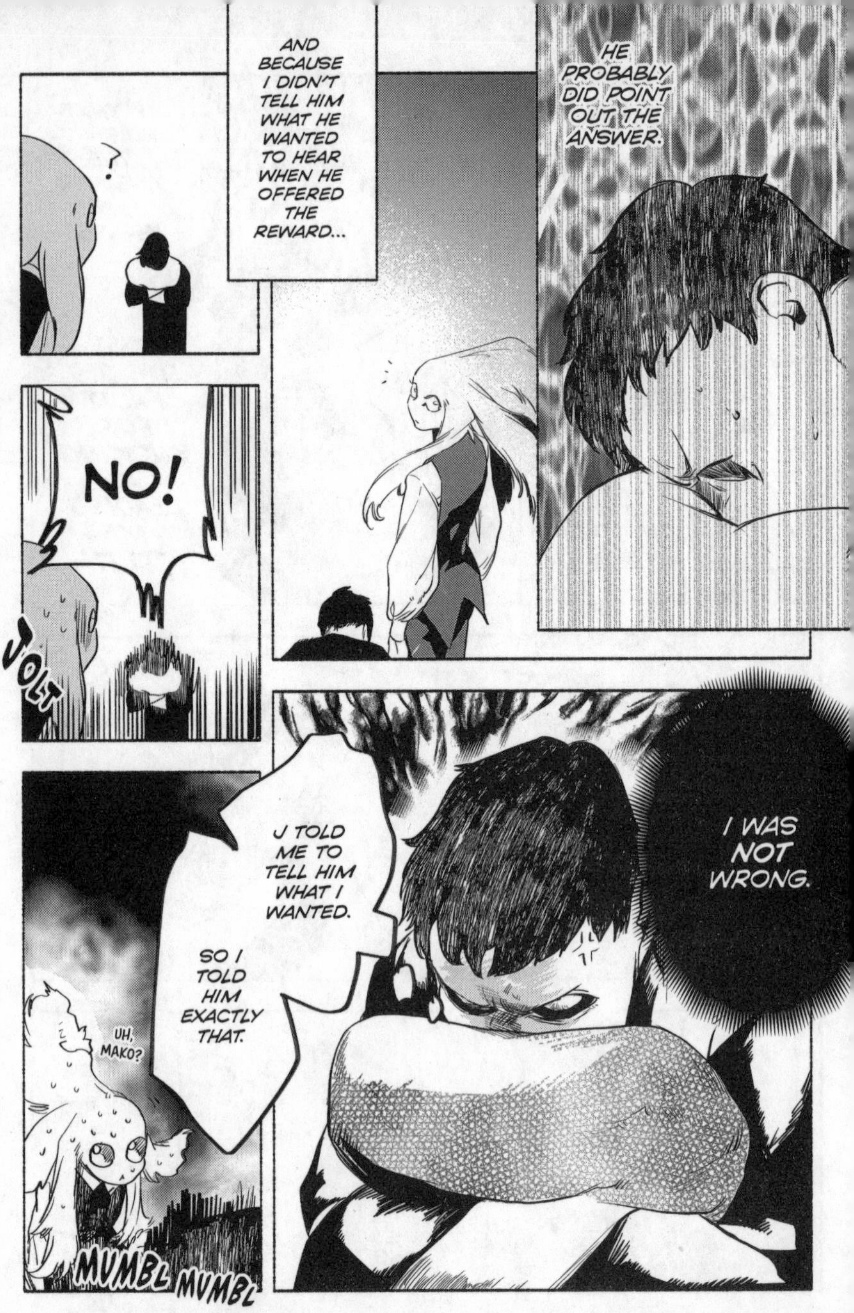
HE PROBABLY DID POINT OUT THE ANSWER.
AND BECAUSE I DIDN'T TELL HIM WHAT HE WANTED TO HEAR WHEN HE OFFERED THE REWARD...
?
NO!
JOLT
I WAS NOT WRONG.
J TOLD ME TO TELL HIM WHAT I WANTED.
SO I TOLD HIM EXACTLY THAT.
UH, MAKO?
MUMBL MUMBL

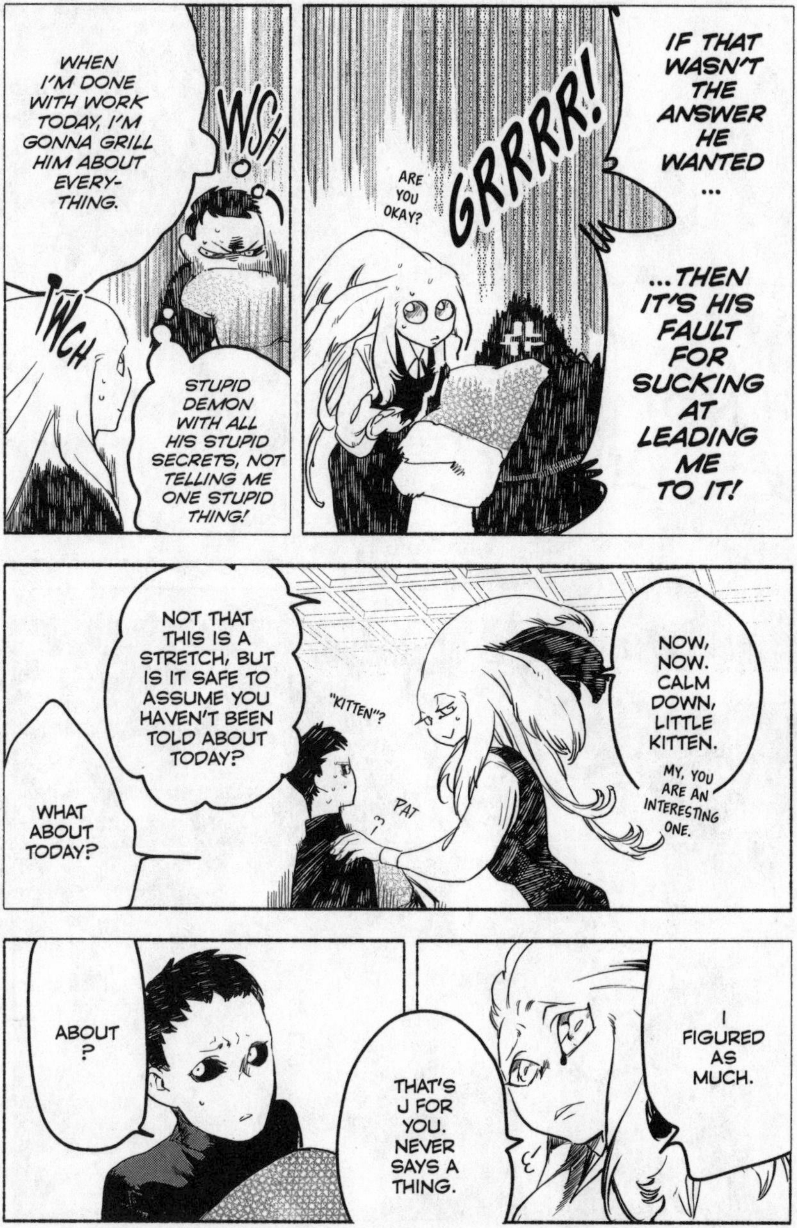
IF THAT WASN'T THE ANSWER HE WANTED ...
...THEN IT'S HIS FAULT FOR SUCKING AT LEADING ME TO IT!
GRRRR!
ARE YOU OKAY?
WHEN I'M DONE WITH WORK TODAY, I'M GONNA GRILL HIM ABOUT EVERY-THING.
WSH
TWCH
STUPID DEMON WITH ALL HIS STUPID SECRETS, NOT TELLING ME ONE STUPID THING!
NOW, NOW. CALM DOWN, LITTLE KITTEN.
MY, YOU ARE AN INTERESTING ONE.
"KITTEN"?
PAT
NOT THAT THIS IS A STRETCH, BUT IS IT SAFE TO ASSUME YOU HAVEN'T BEEN TOLD ABOUT TODAY?
WHAT ABOUT TODAY?
I FIGURED AS MUCH.
THAT'S J FOR YOU. NEVER SAYS A THING.
ABOUT ?

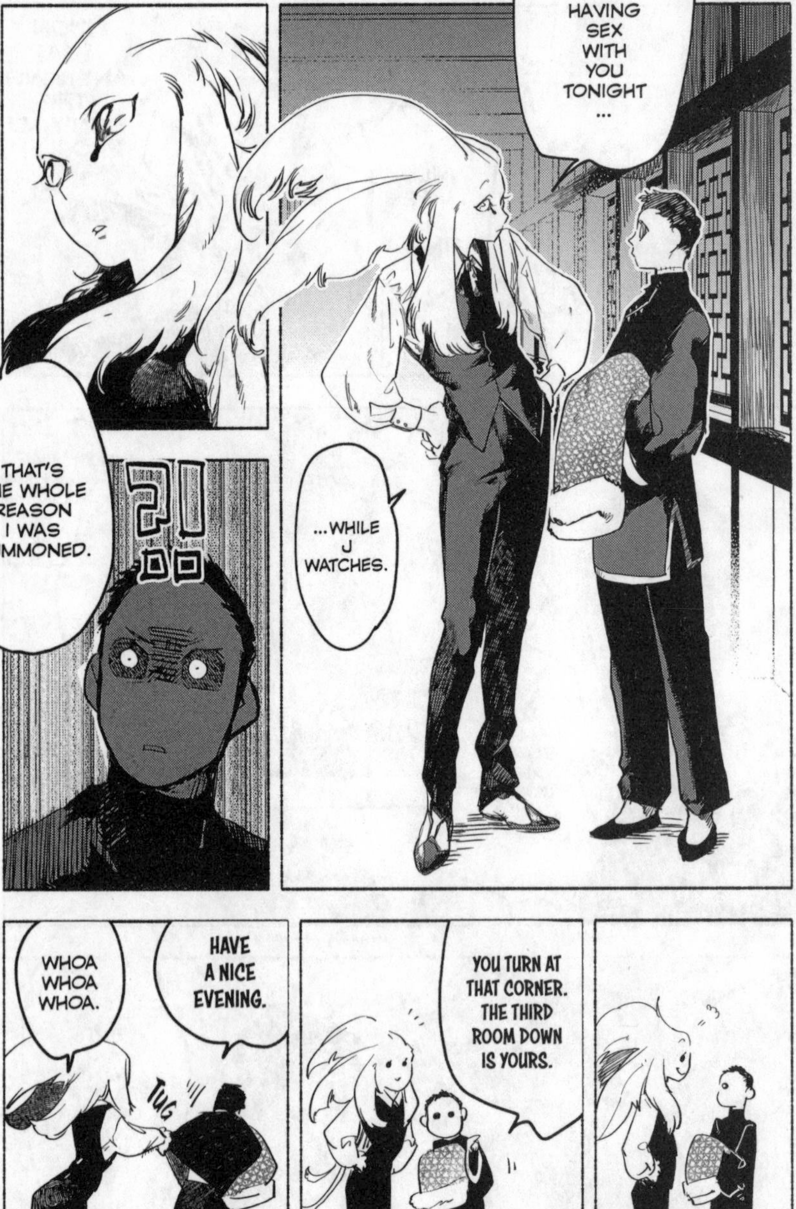

I'M HAVING SEX WITH YOU TONIGHT ...
...WHILE J WATCHES.
THAT'S THE WHOLE REASON I WAS SUMMONED.
YOU TURN AT THAT CORNER. THE THIRD ROOM DOWN IS YOURS.
HAVE A NICE EVENING.
WHOA WHOA WHOA.
TUG

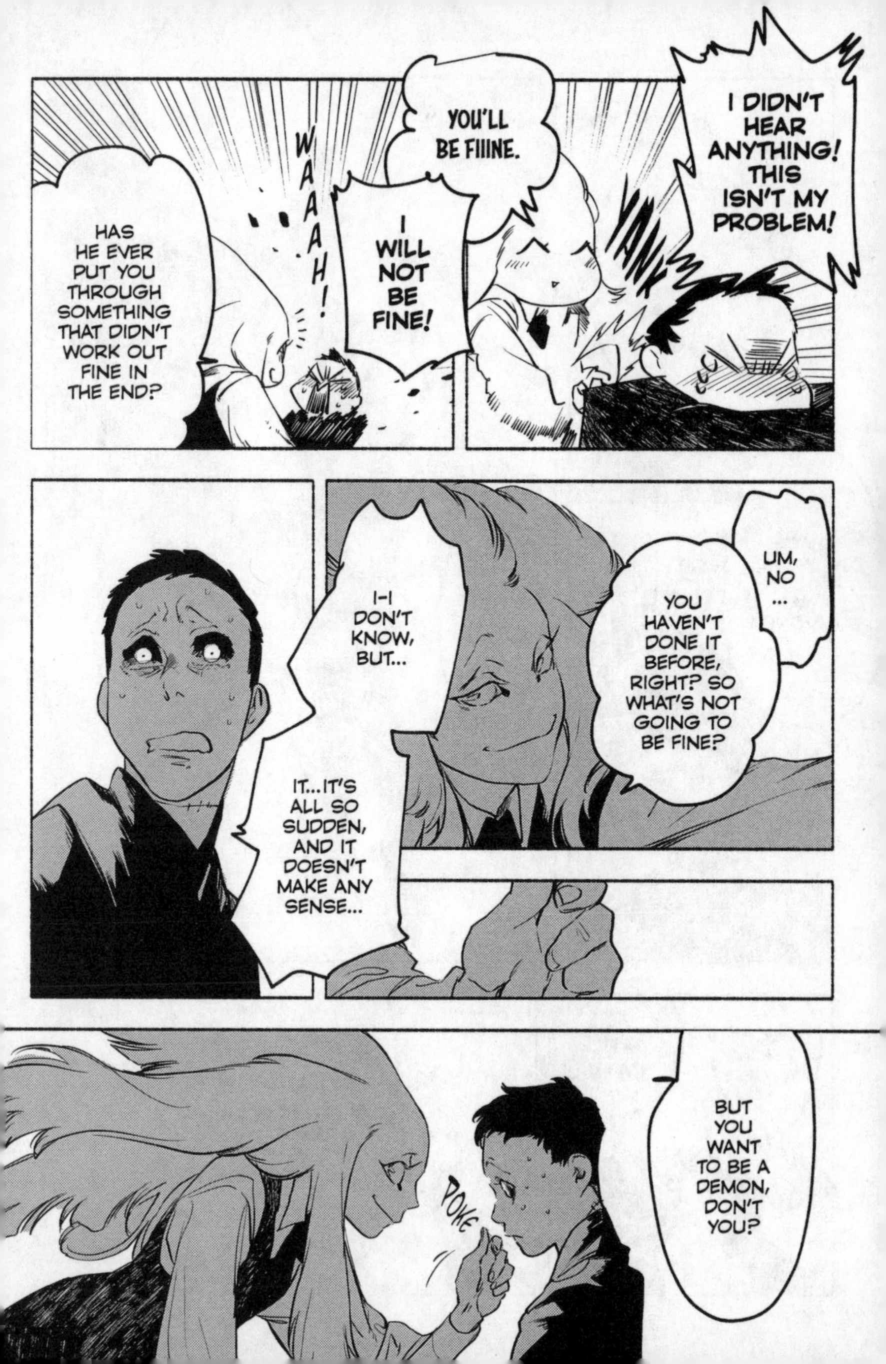
I DIDN'T HEAR ANYTHING! THIS ISN'T MY PROBLEM!
YOU'LL BE FIIINE.
YANK
I WILL NOT BE FINE!
WAAAH!
HAS HE EVER PUT YOU THROUGH SOMETHING THAT DIDN'T WORK OUT FINE IN THE END?
UM, NO ...
YOU HAVEN'T DONE IT BEFORE, RIGHT? SO WHAT'S NOT GOING TO BE FINE?
I-I DON'T KNOW, BUT...
IT...IT'S ALL SO SUDDEN, AND IT DOESN'T MAKE ANY SENSE...
BUT YOU WANT TO BE A DEMON, DON'T YOU?
POKE

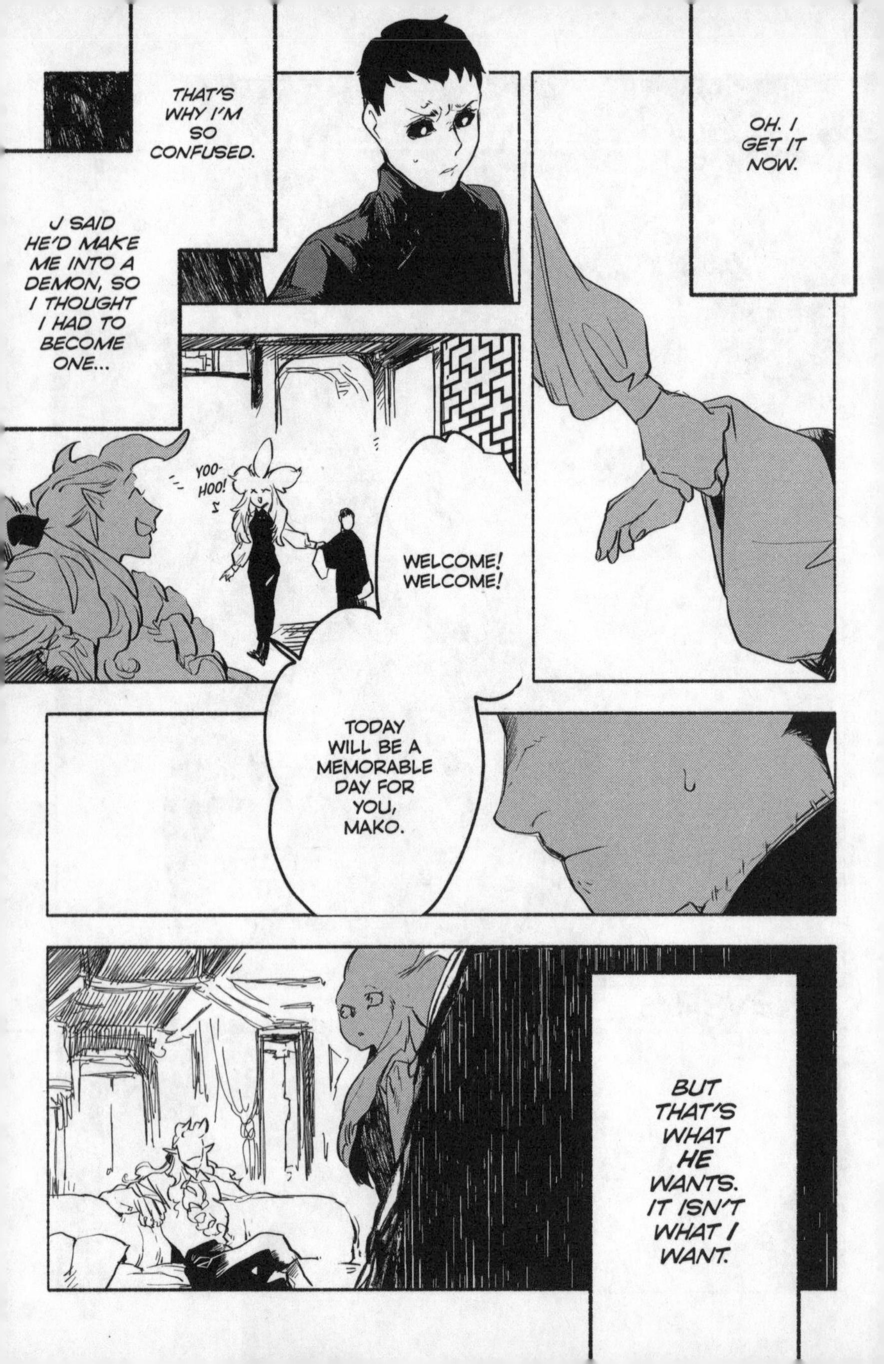
OH. I GET IT NOW.
THAT'S WHY I'M SO CONFUSED.
J SAID HE'D MAKE ME INTO A DEMON, SO I THOUGHT I HAD TO BECOME ONE...
WELCOME! WELCOME!
YOO-HOO!
TODAY WILL BE A MEMORABLE DAY FOR YOU, MAKO.
BUT THAT'S WHAT HE WANTS. IT ISN'T WHAT I WANT.

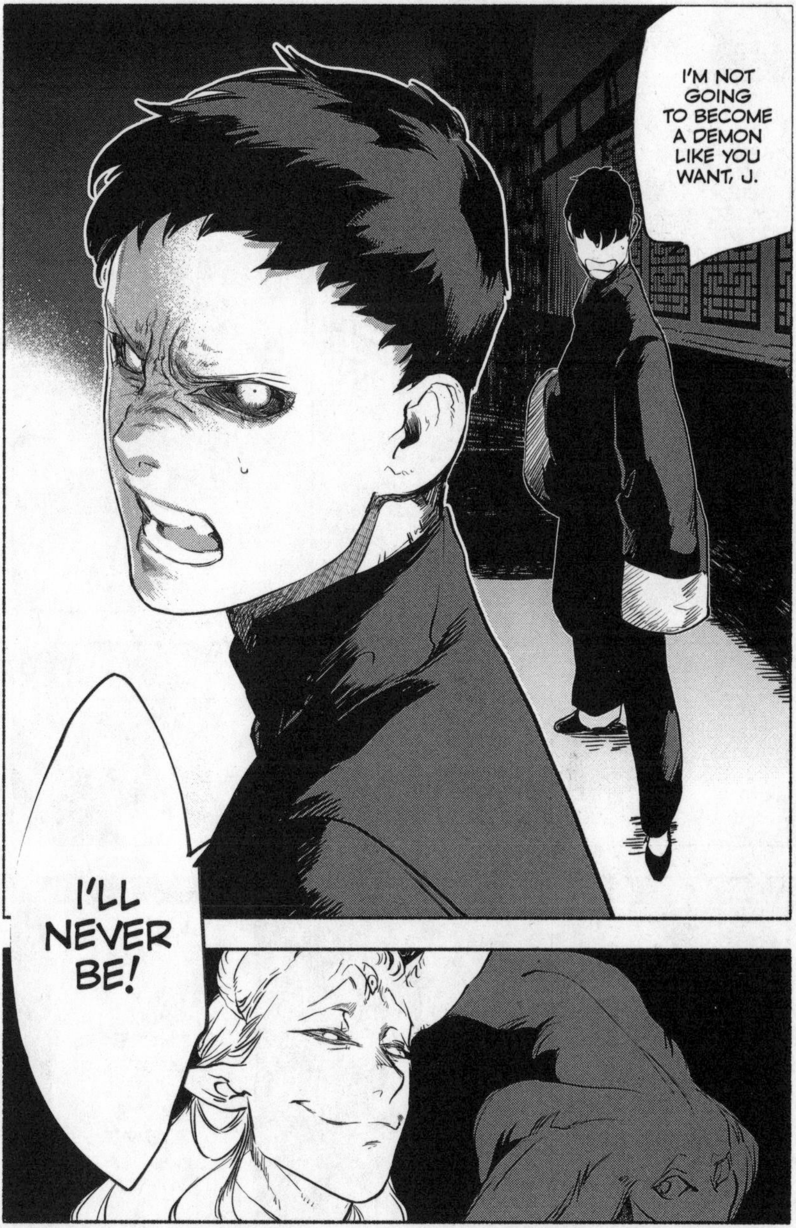
I'M NOT GOING TO BECOME A DEMON LIKE YOU WANT, J.
I'LL NEVER BE!

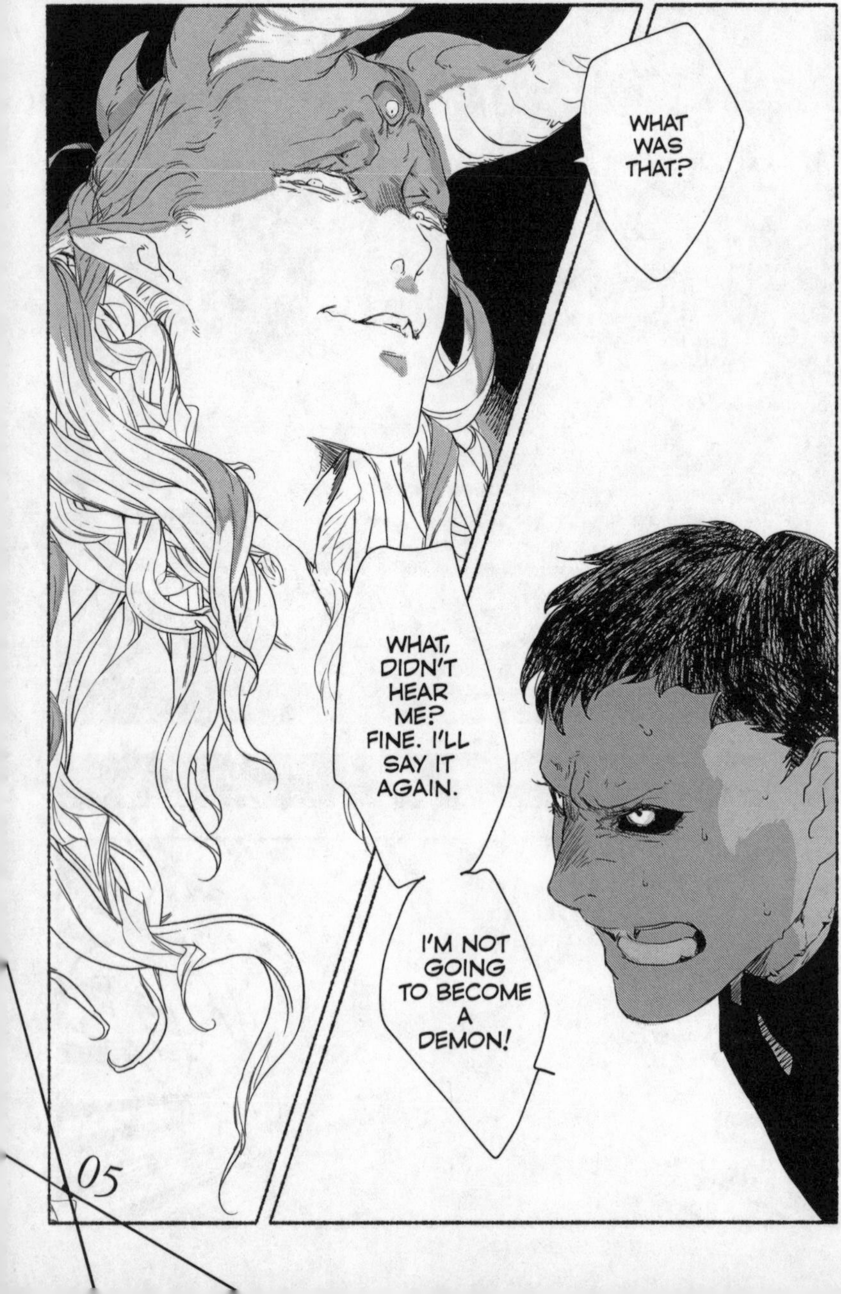
WHAT WAS THAT?
WHAT, DIDN'T HEAR ME? FINE. I'LL SAY IT AGAIN.
I'M NOT GOING TO BECOME A DEMON!
05

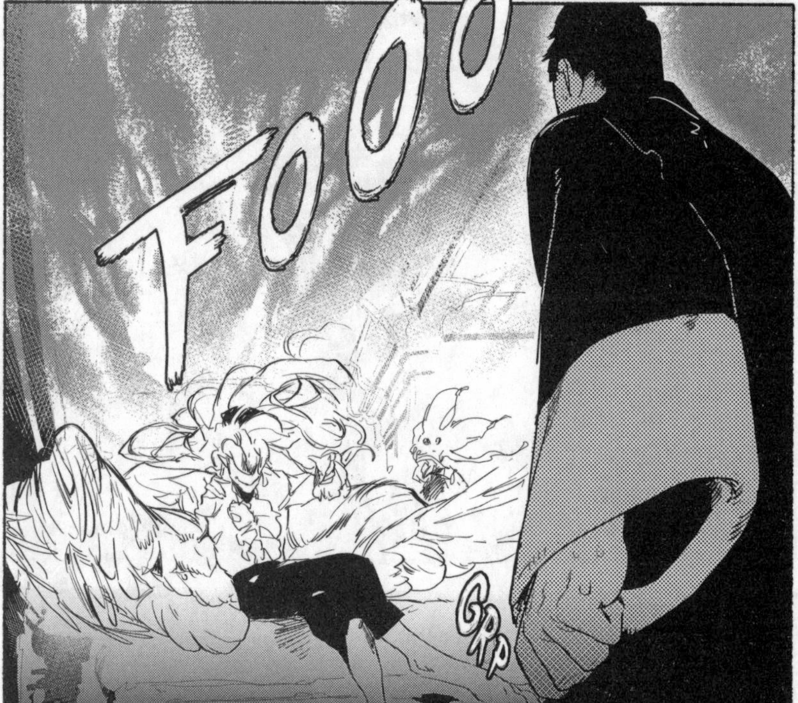
FOOOO
GRP
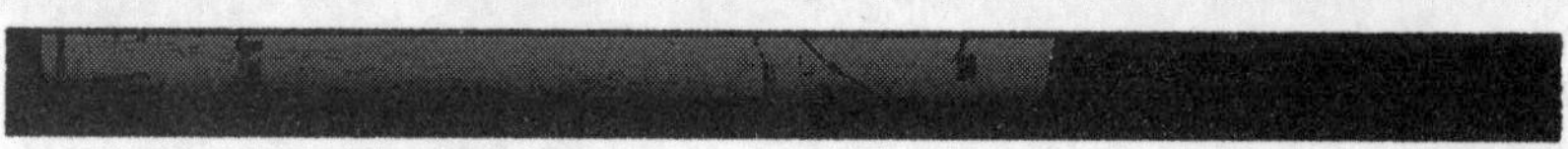
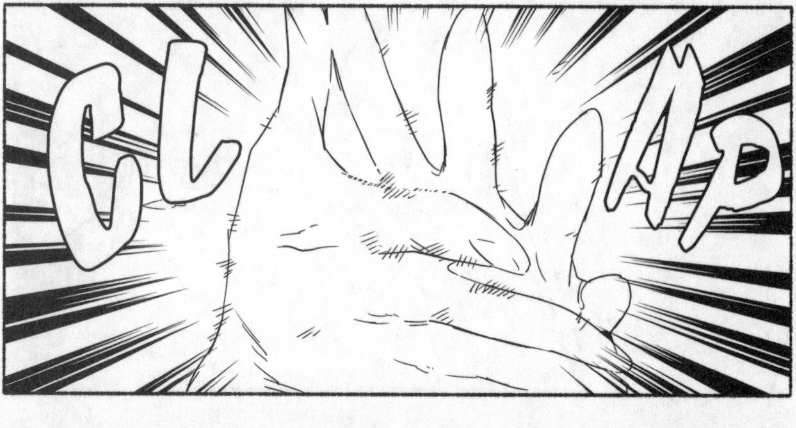
CLAP

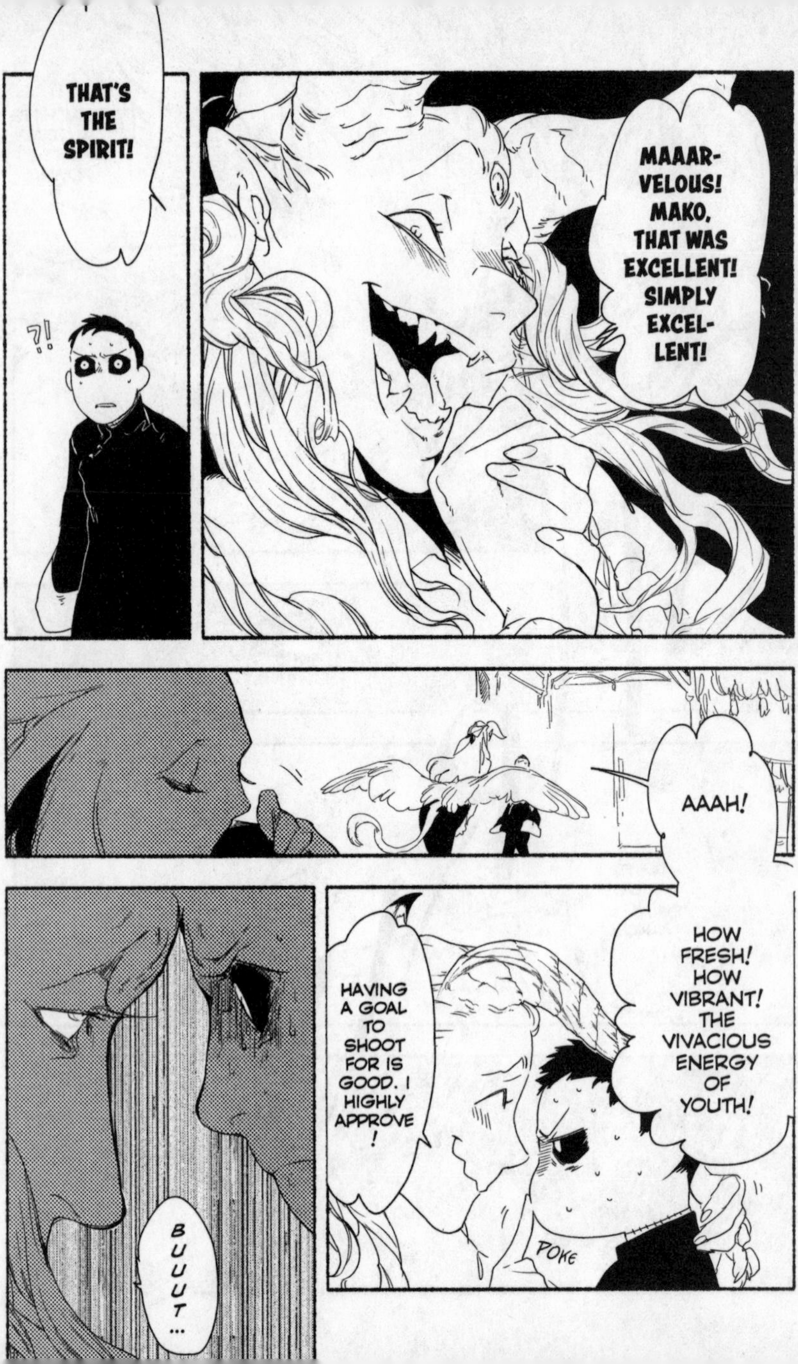
MAAAR-VELOUS! MAKO, THAT WAS EXCELLENT! SIMPLY EXCEL-LENT!
THAT'S THE SPIRIT!
?!
AAAH!
HOW FRESH! HOW VIBRANT! THE VIVACIOUS ENERGY OF YOUTH!
HAVING A GOAL TO SHOOT FOR IS GOOD. I HIGHLY APPROVE!
POKE
BUUUT...

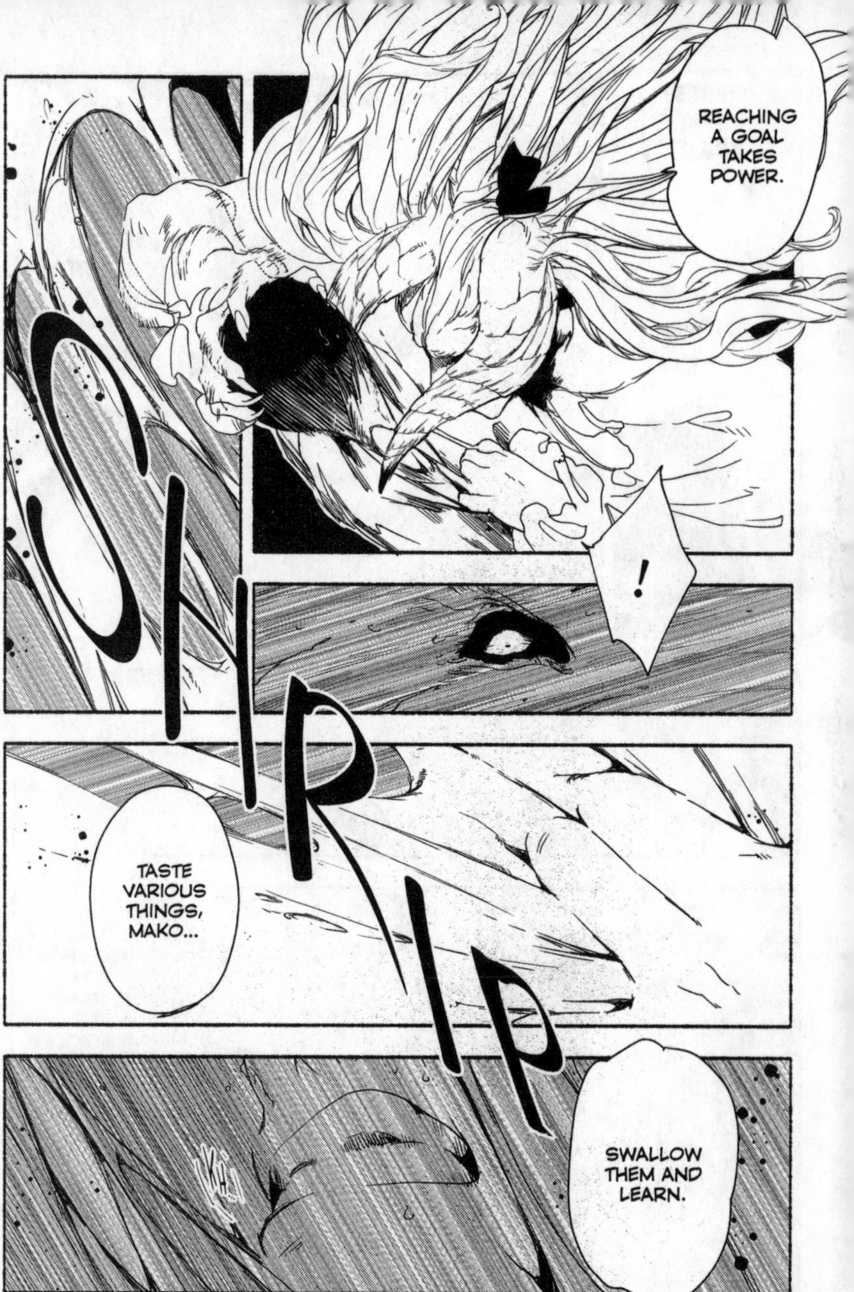
REACHING A GOAL TAKES POWER.
!
SHRIP
TASTE VARIOUS THINGS, MAKO...
SWALLOW THEM AND LEARN.

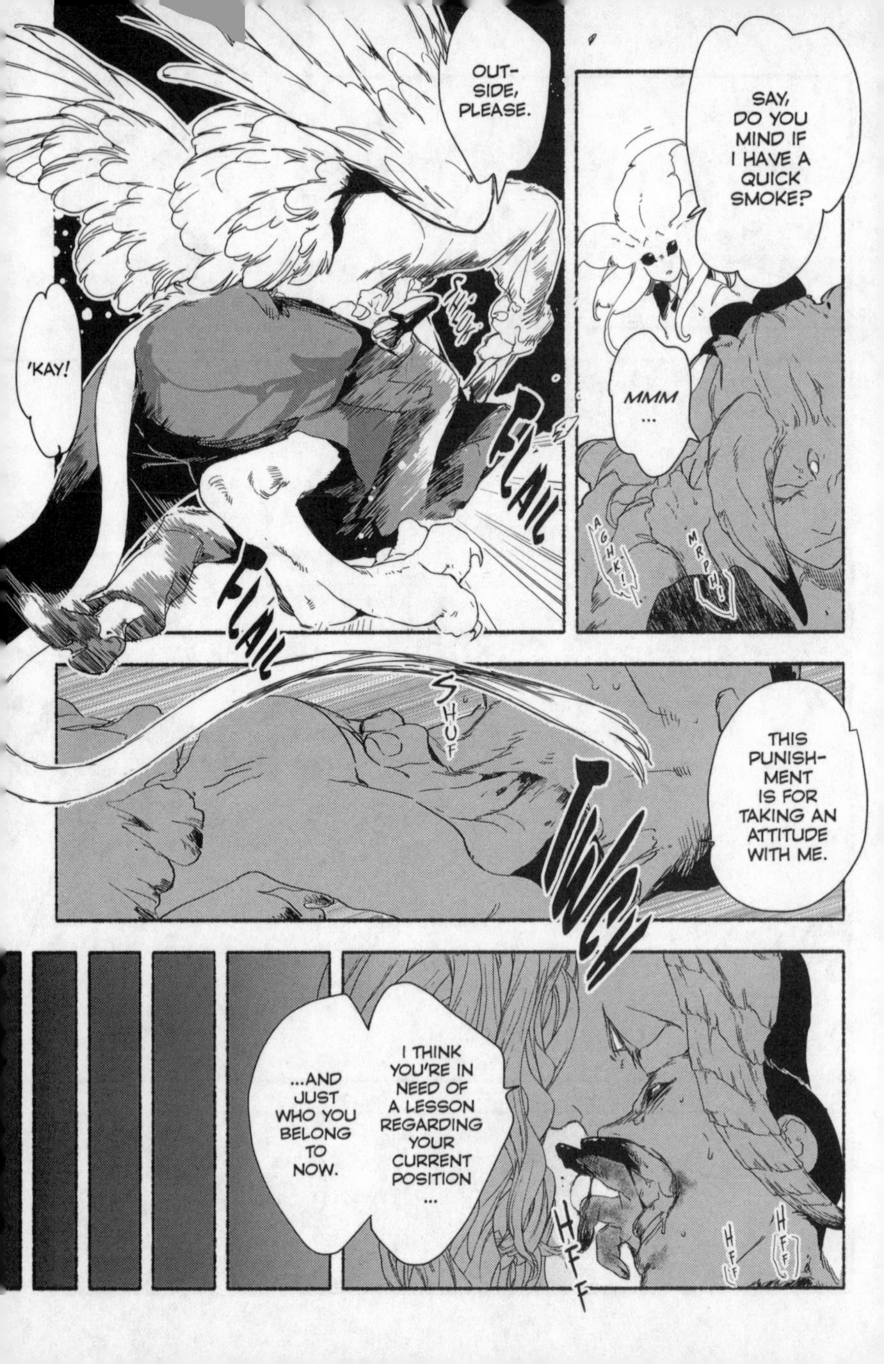
SAY, DO YOU MIND IF I HAVE A QUICK SMOKE?
MMM ...
MRPH!
AGHK!
OUT-SIDE, PLEASE.
'KAY!
FLAIL
FLAIL
THIS PUNISH-MENT IS FOR TAKING AN ATTITUDE WITH ME.
SHUF
TWITCH
I THINK YOU'RE IN NEED OF A LESSON REGARDING YOUR CURRENT POSITION ...
...AND JUST WHO YOU BELONG TO NOW.
HFF
HFF
HFF

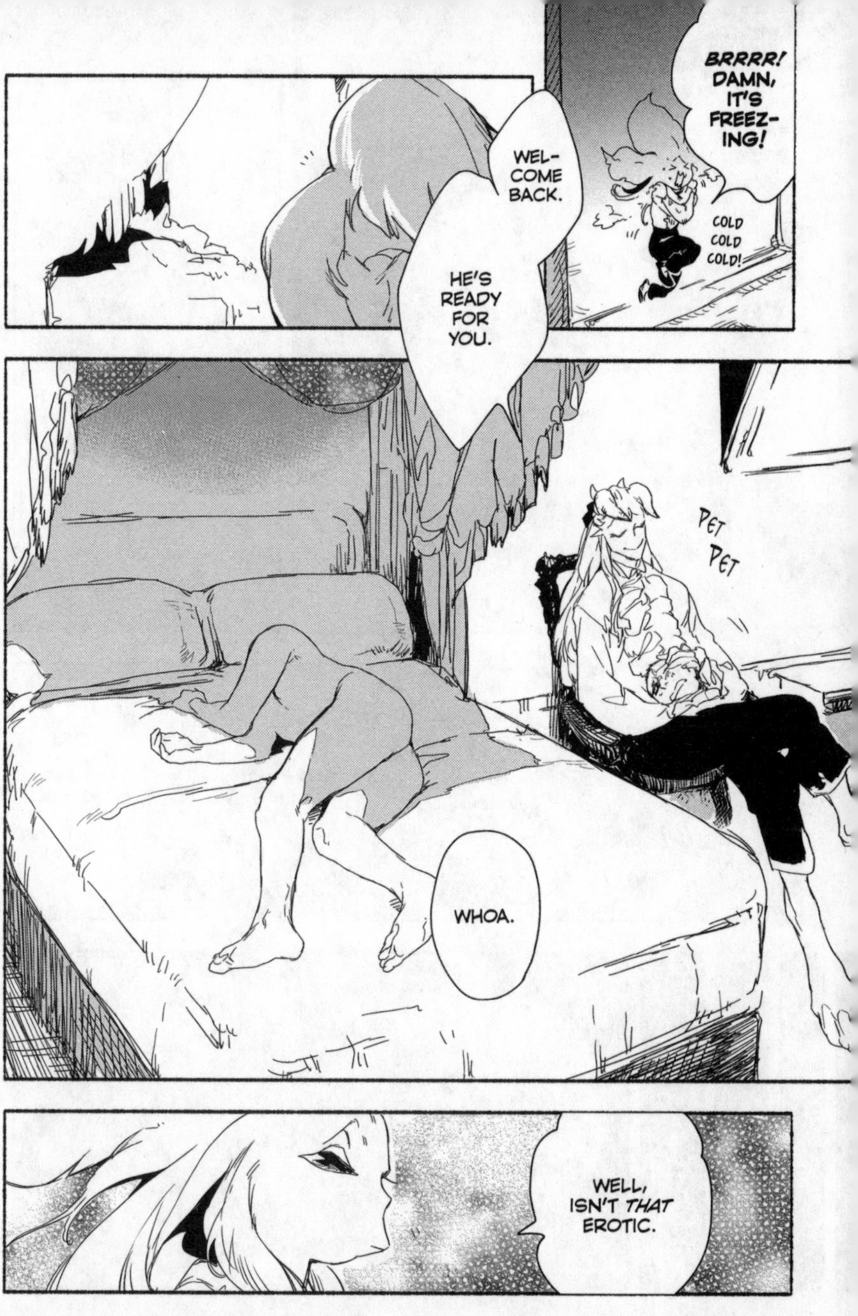
BRRRR! DAMN, IT'S FREEZ-ING!
COLD COLD COLD!
WEL-COME BACK.
HE'S READY FOR YOU.
PET PET
WHOA.
WELL, ISN'T *THAT* EROTIC.

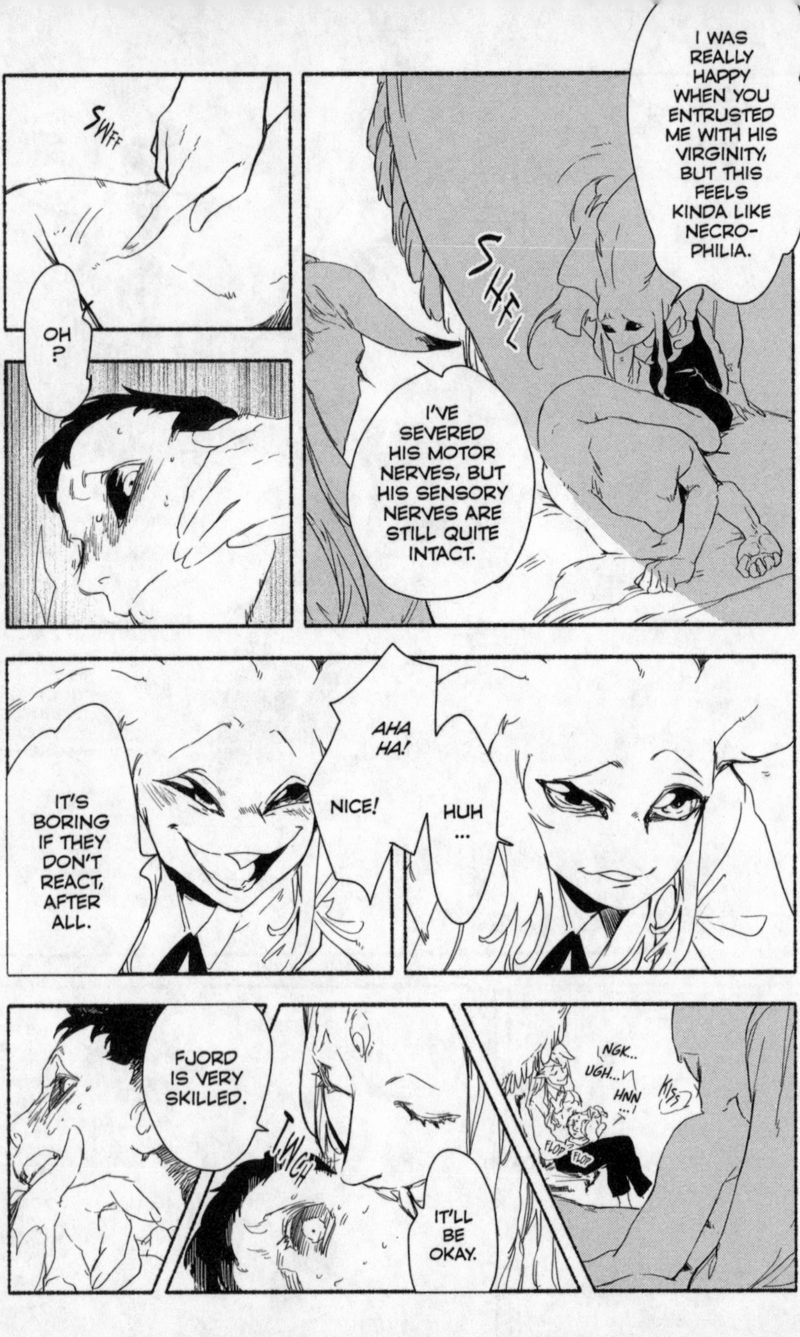
I WAS REALLY HAPPY WHEN YOU ENTRUSTED ME WITH HIS VIRGINITY, BUT THIS FEELS KINDA LIKE NECRO-PHILIA.
SHFL
I'VE SEVERED HIS MOTOR NERVES, BUT HIS SENSORY NERVES ARE STILL QUITE INTACT.
SWFF
OH?
HUH...
AHA HA!
NICE!
IT'S BORING IF THEY DON'T REACT, AFTER ALL.
NGK..
UGH...
HNN...!
KISS
FLOP FLOP
FJORD IS VERY SKILLED.
TWCH
IT'LL BE OKAY.

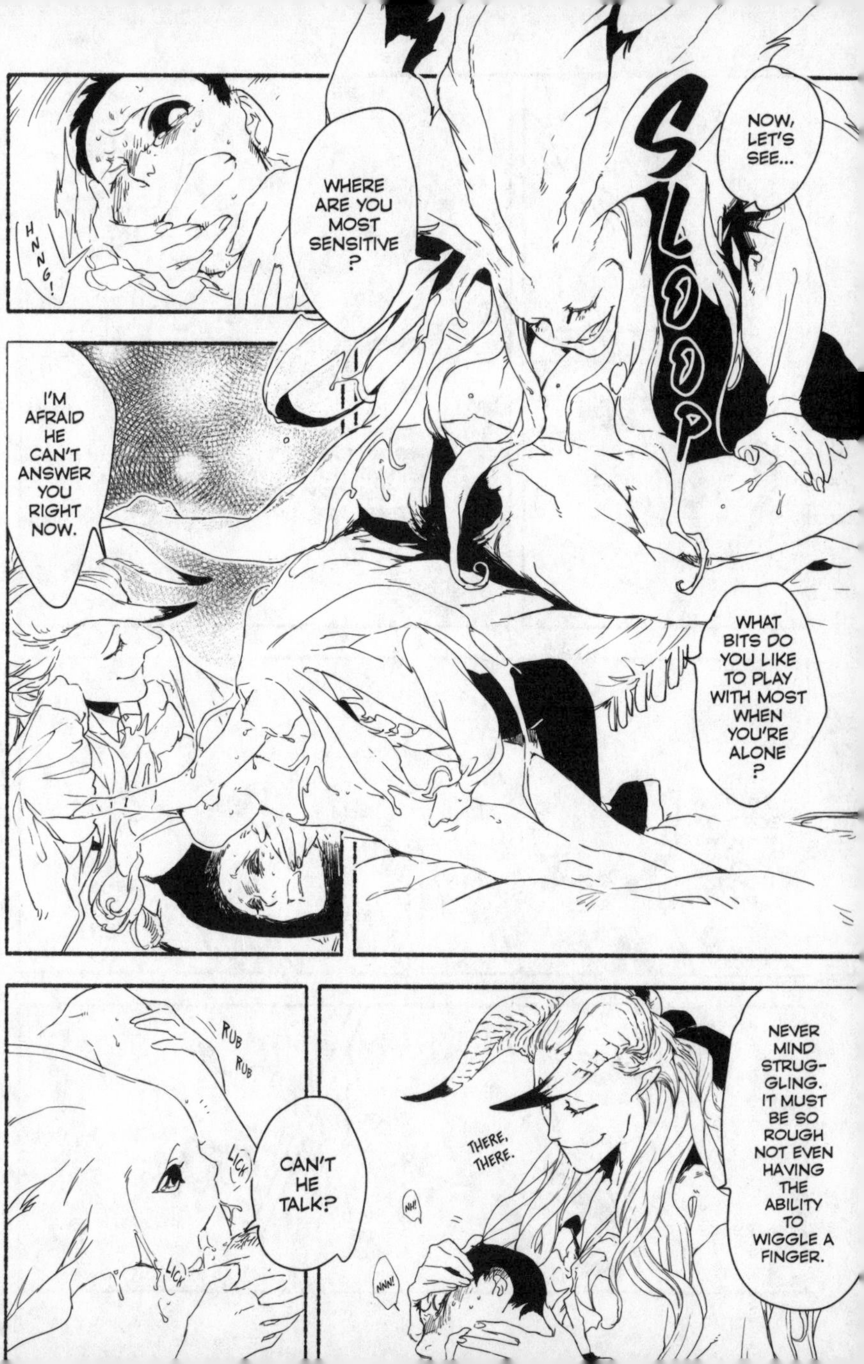
NOW, LET'S SEE...
SLOOP
WHERE ARE YOU MOST SENSITIVE?
WHAT BITS DO YOU LIKE TO PLAY WITH MOST WHEN YOU'RE ALONE?
HNNG!
I'M AFRAID HE CAN'T ANSWER YOU RIGHT NOW.
NEVER MIND STRUG-GLING. IT MUST BE SO ROUGH NOT EVEN HAVING THE ABILITY TO WIGGLE A FINGER.
THERE, THERE.
NH!
NNN!
RUB RUB
CAN'T HE TALK?
LICK
LICK

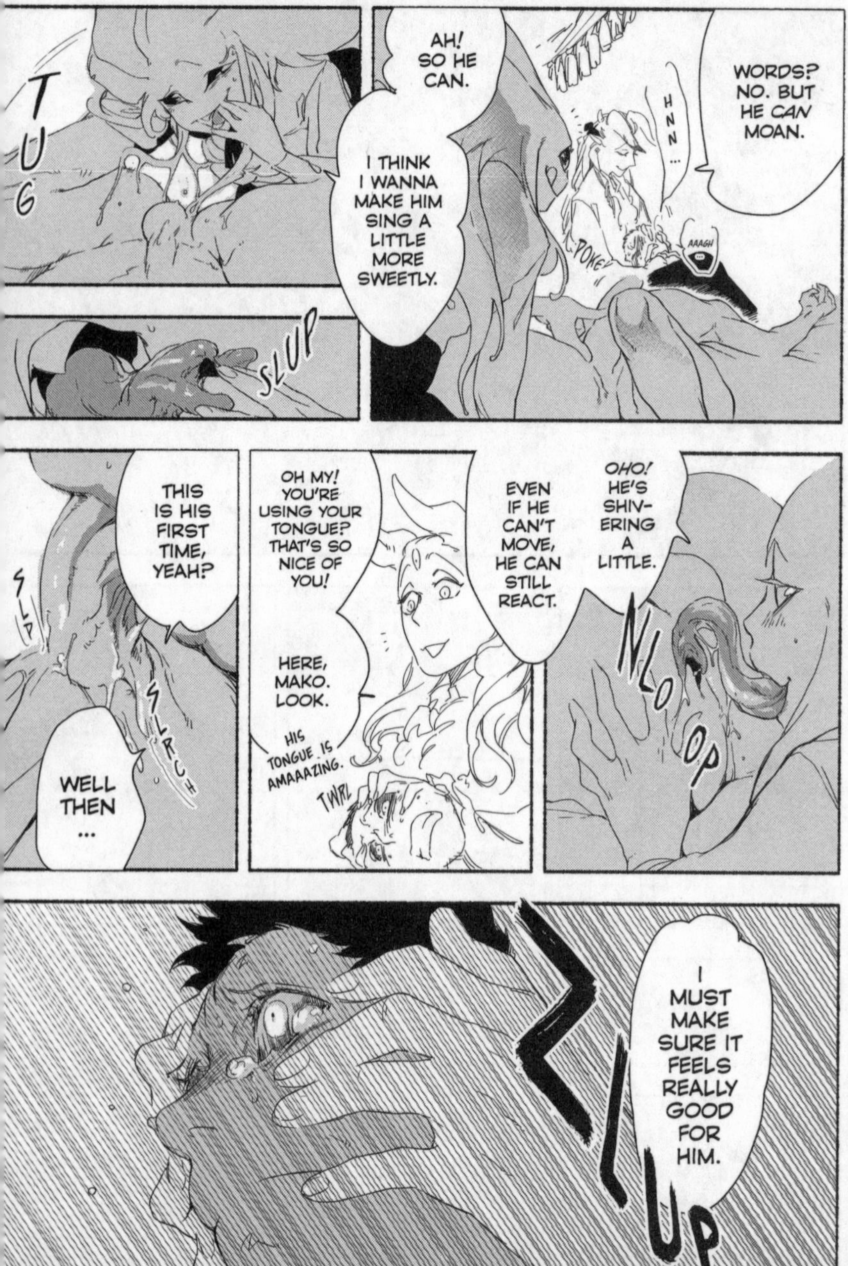
WORDS? NO. BUT HE CAN MOAN.
HNN...
AH! SO HE CAN.
I THINK I WANNA MAKE HIM SING A LITTLE MORE SWEETLY.
POKE
AAAGH
TUG
SLUP
OHO! HE'S SHIV- ERING A LITTLE.
NLOOP
EVEN IF HE CAN'T MOVE, HE CAN STILL REACT.
OH MY! YOU'RE USING YOUR TONGUE? THAT'S SO NICE OF YOU!
HERE, MAKO. LOOK.
HIS TONGUE IS AMAAAZING.
TWRL
THIS IS HIS FIRST TIME, YEAH?
SLP
SLRCH
WELL THEN ...
I MUST MAKE SURE IT FEELS REALLY GOOD FOR HIM.
CLUP

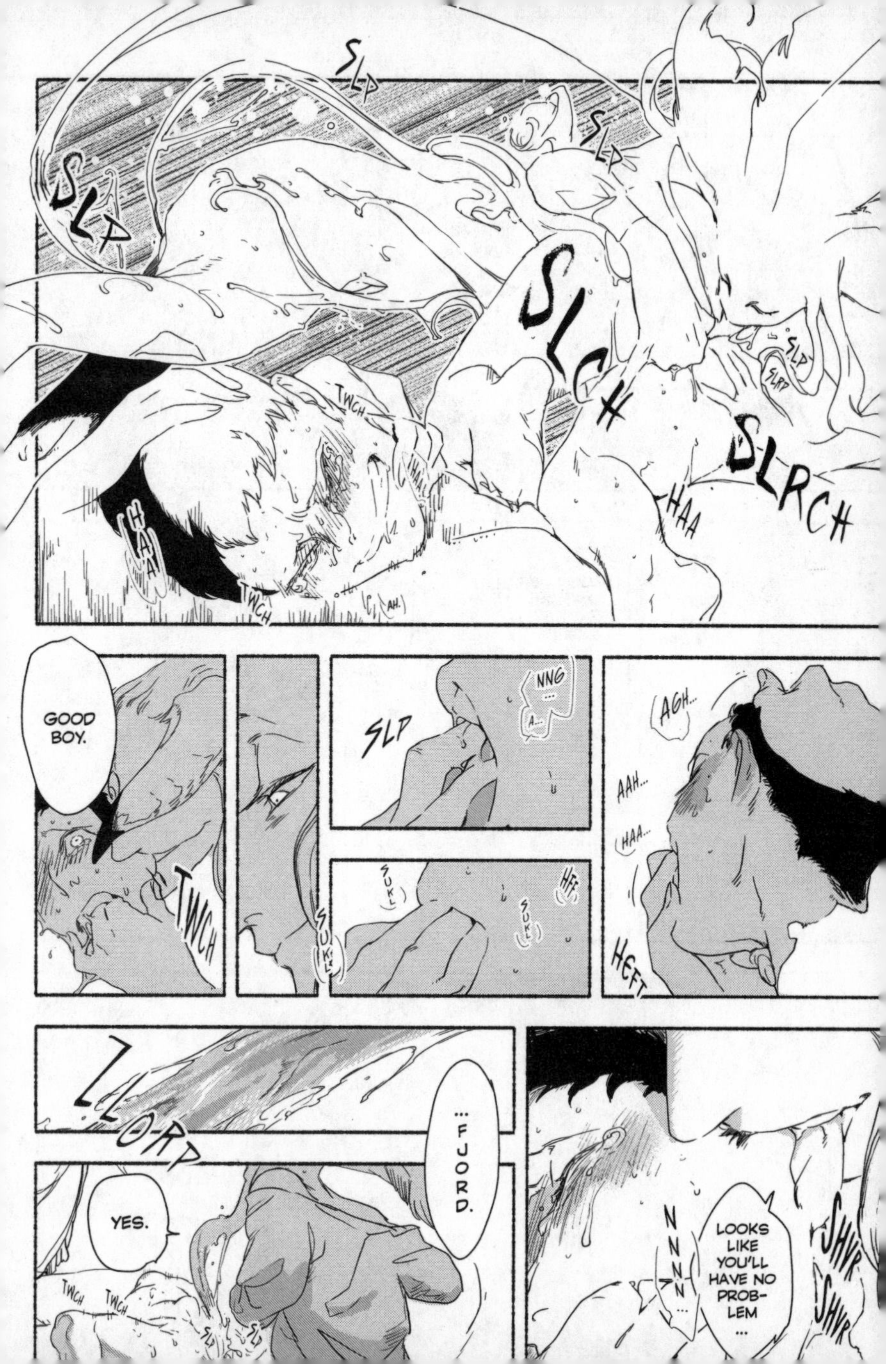
SLP
SLP
SLP
SLRP
SLCH
SLRCH
HAA
TWCH
HAA
HAAA
TWCH
AH.
AGH...
AAH...
HAA...
HEFT
NNG... A...
SLP
HFF
SUKL
SUKL
SUKL
TWCH
GOOD BOY.
SHVR
SHVR
LOOKS LIKE YOU'LL HAVE NO PROB-LEM...
NNNN...
ZLLORP
...FJORD.
YES.
TWCH
TWCH
SLP
SLP

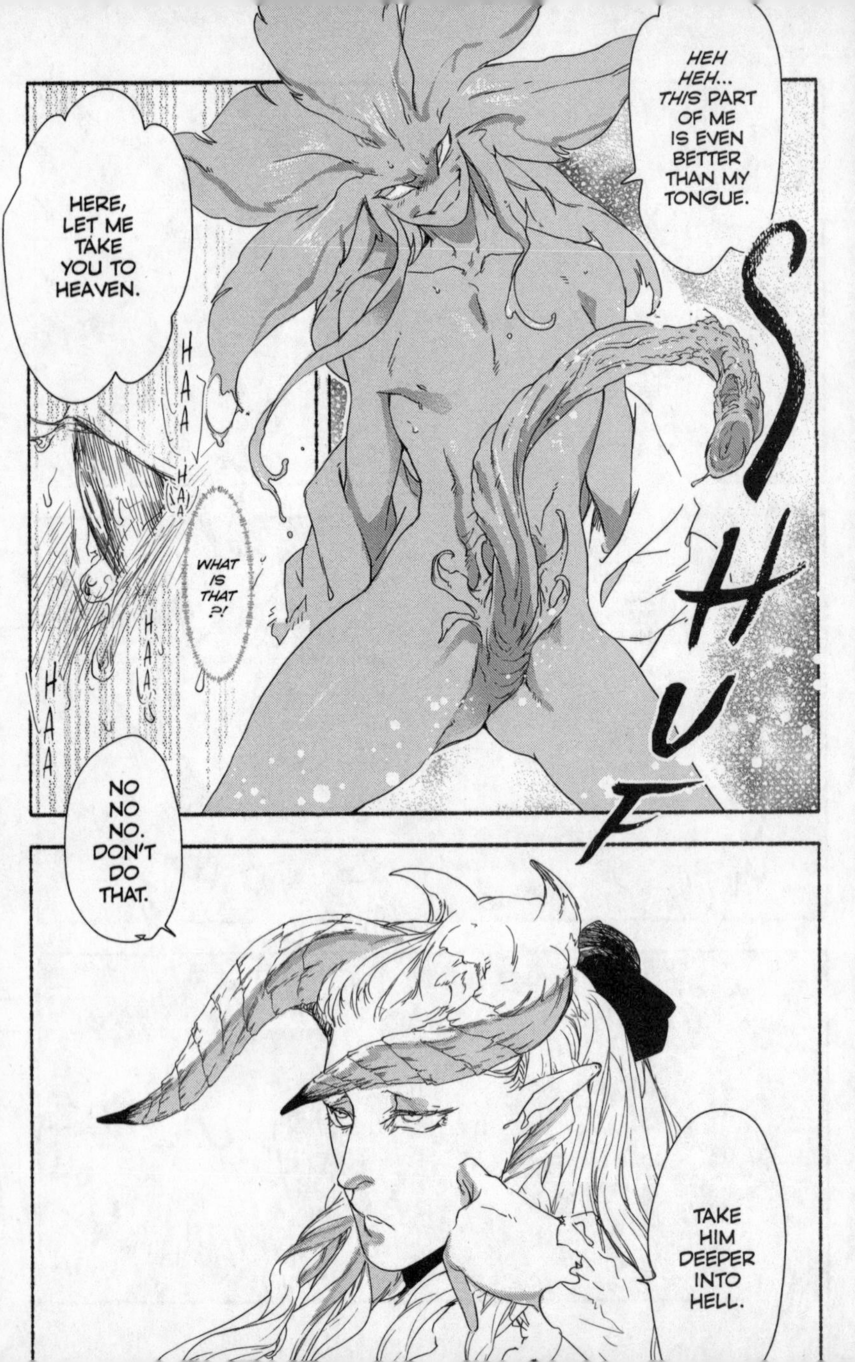
HEH HEH... THIS PART OF ME IS EVEN BETTER THAN MY TONGUE.
HERE, LET ME TAKE YOU TO HEAVEN.
SHUFF
HAA
HAA
WHAT IS THAT ?!
HAA
HAA
NO NO NO. DON'T DO THAT.
TAKE HIM DEEPER INTO HELL.

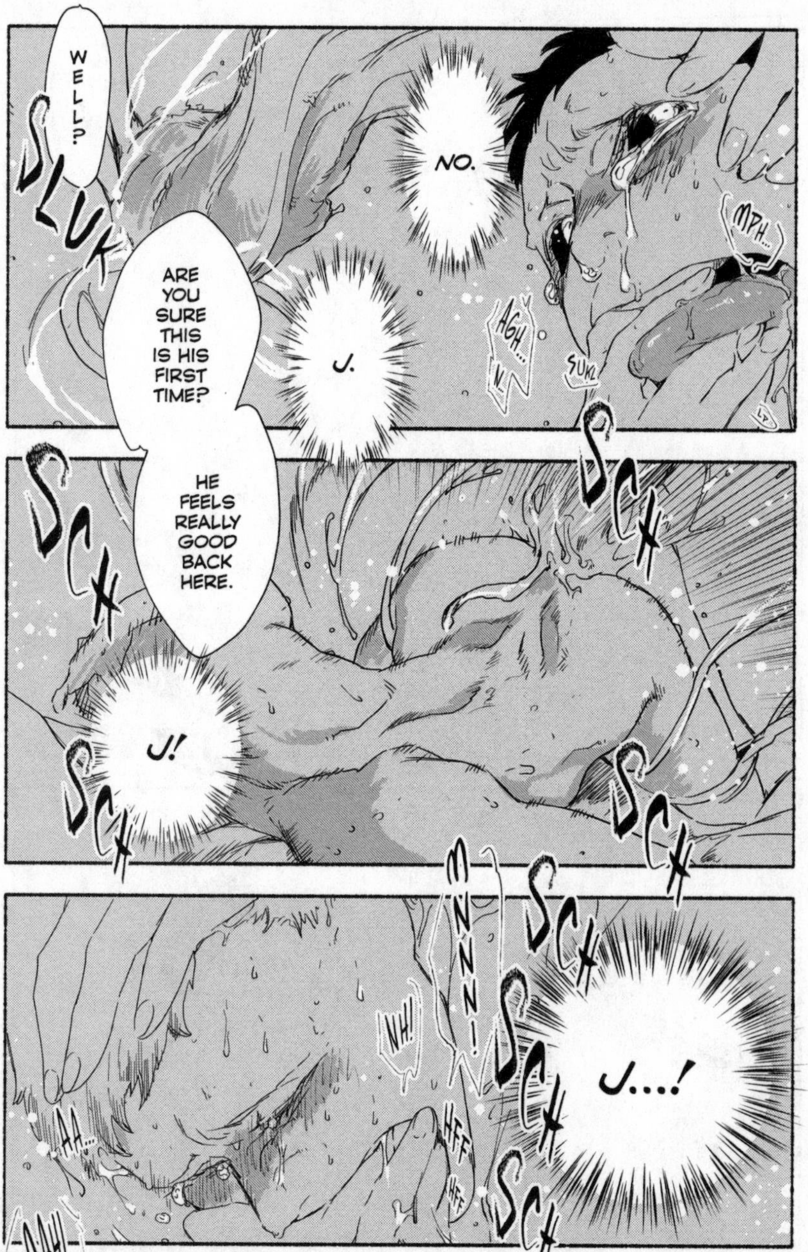

MPH...
NO.
AGH... N...
J.
WELL?
SLUK
ARE YOU SURE THIS IS HIS FIRST TIME?
SCH
SCH
HE FEELS REALLY GOOD BACK HERE.
J!
SCH
SCH
SCH
SCH
SCH
J...!
MNNN!
NH!
HFF HFF
AA...
AAH!

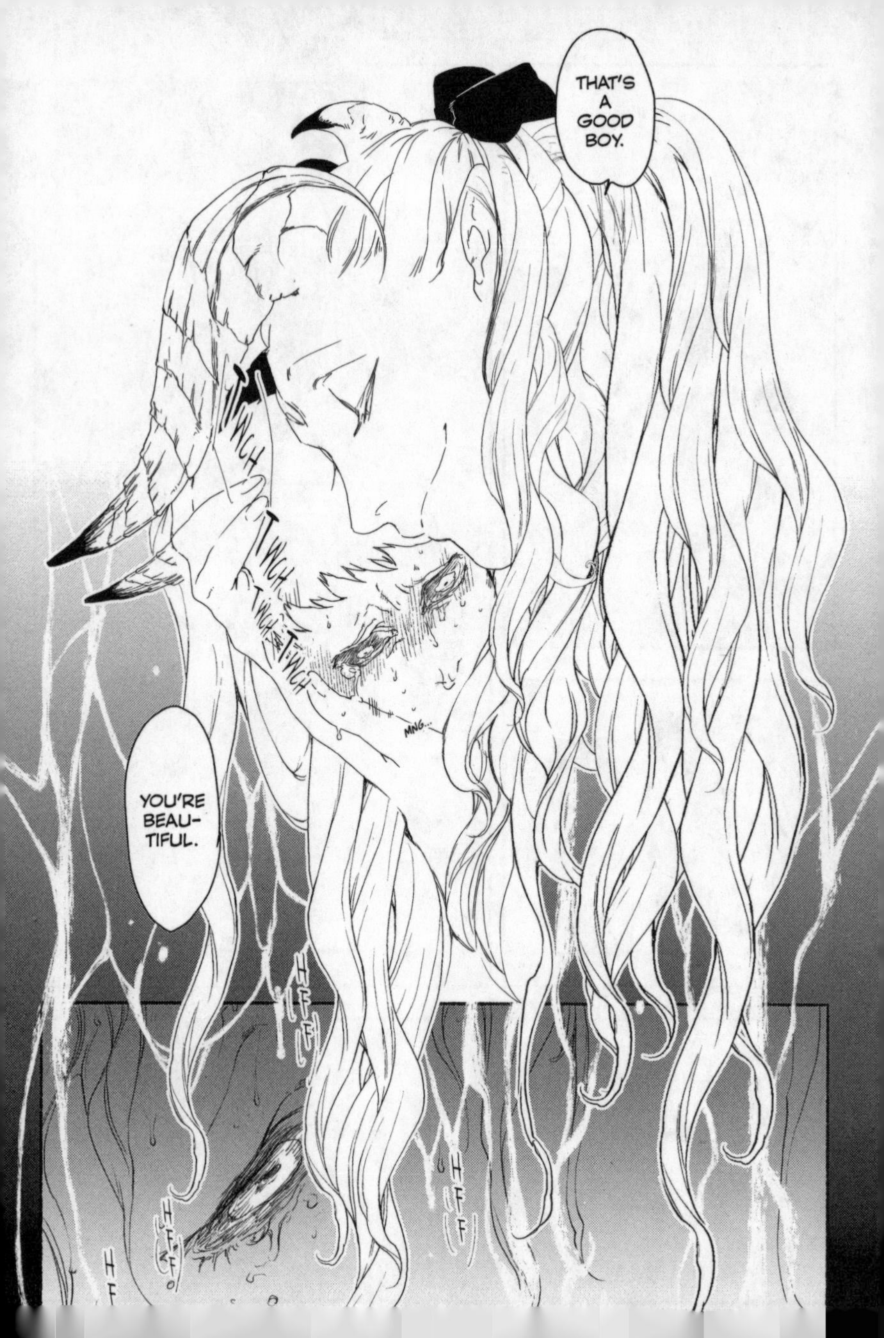
THAT'S A GOOD BOY.
TWITCH
TWITCH
TWITCH
TWITCH
MNG...
YOU'RE BEAU-TIFUL.
HFF
HFF
HFF
HF

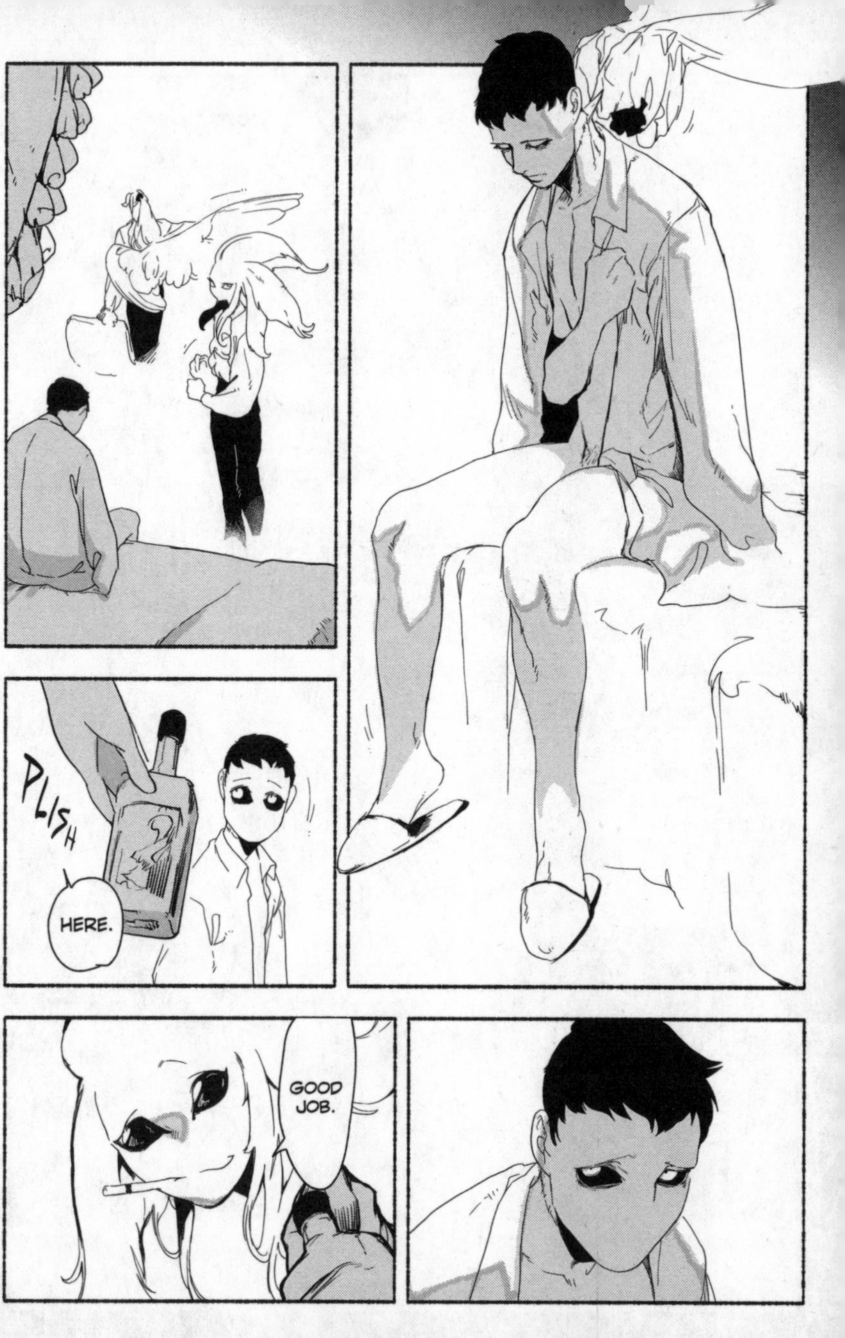
PLISH
HERE.
GOOD JOB.

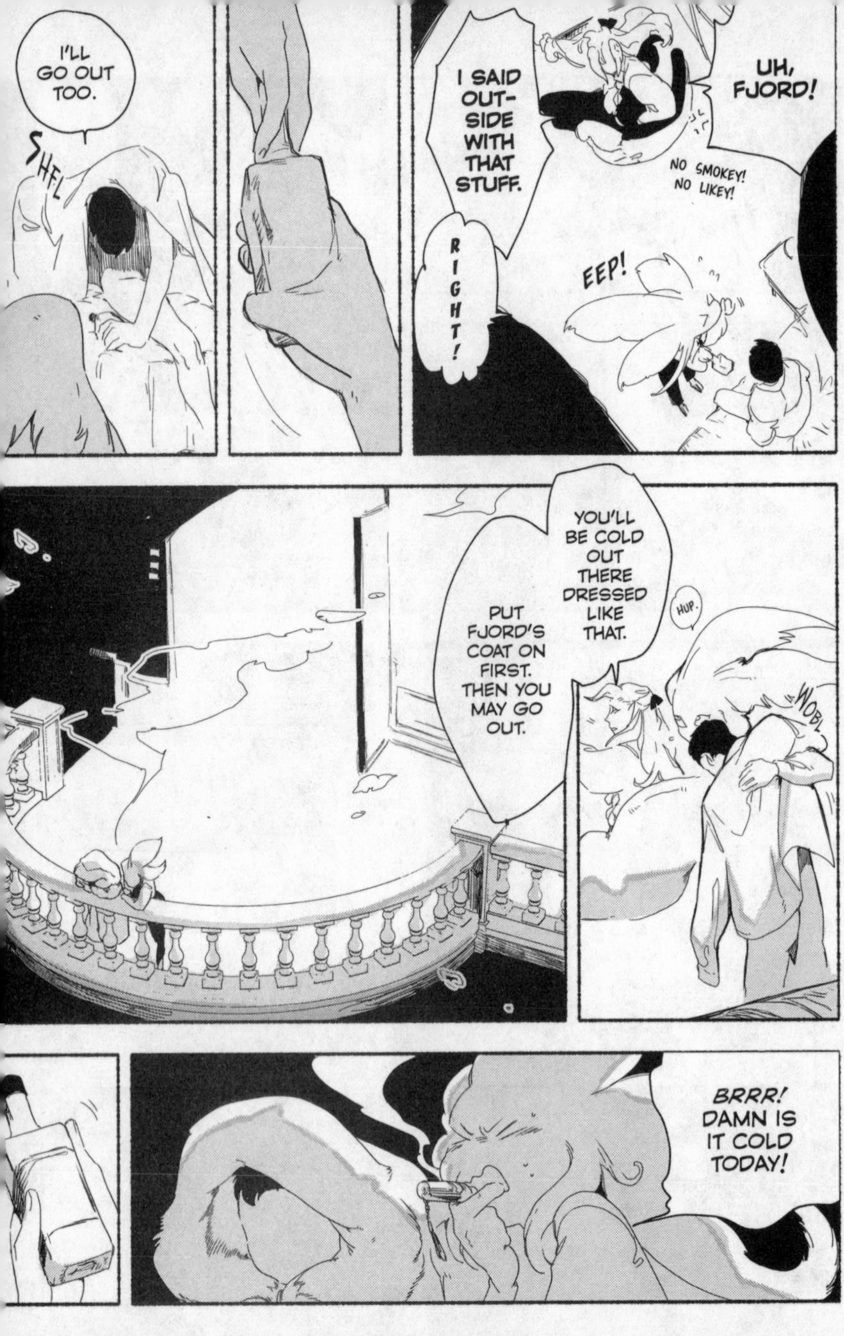
UH, FJORD!
I SAID OUT-SIDE WITH THAT STUFF.
NO SMOKEY! NO LIKEY!
RIGHT!
EEP!
I'LL GO OUT TOO.
SHFL
YOU'LL BE COLD OUT THERE DRESSED LIKE THAT.
HUP.
PUT FJORD'S COAT ON FIRST. THEN YOU MAY GO OUT.
WOBL
BRRR! DAMN IS IT COLD TODAY!

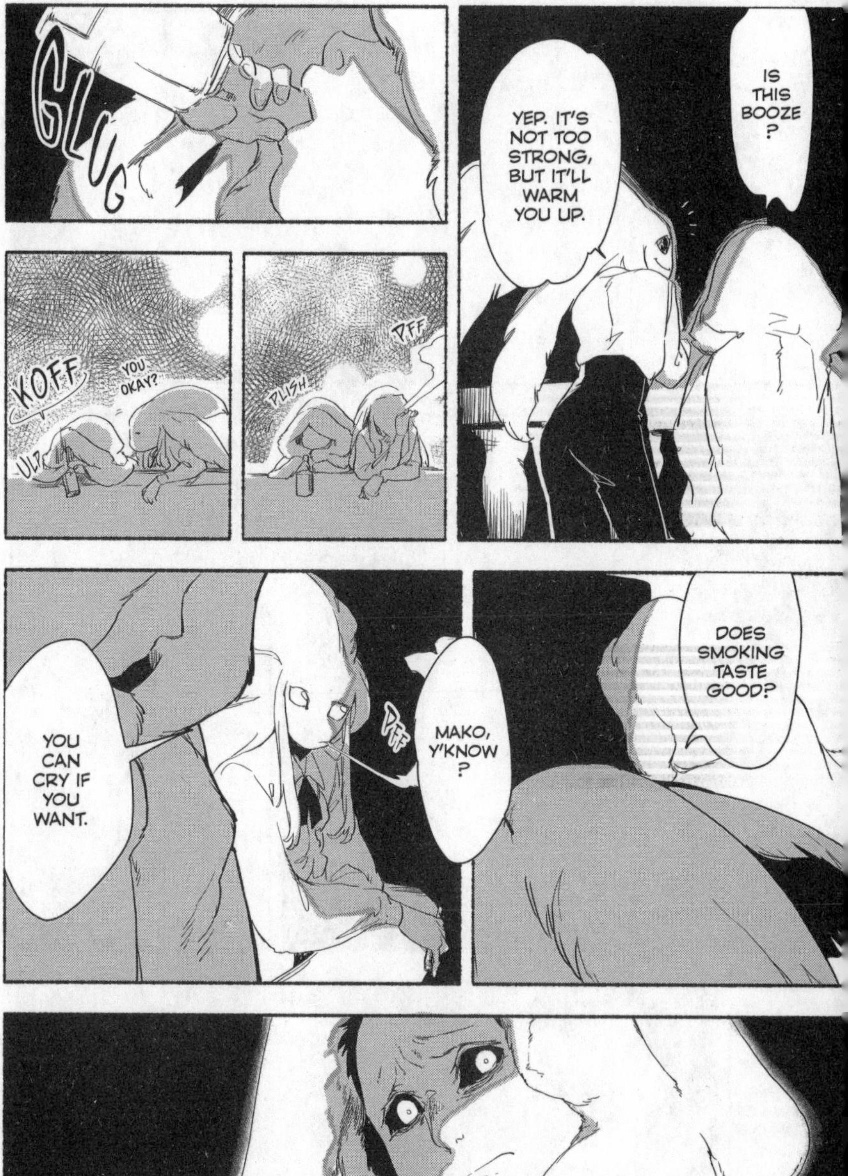
IS THIS BOOZE?
YEP. IT'S NOT TOO STRONG, BUT IT'LL WARM YOU UP.
GLUG
PFF
PLISH
YOU OKAY?
KOFF
ULP
DOES SMOKING TASTE GOOD?
MAKO, Y'KNOW?
PFF
YOU CAN CRY IF YOU WANT.

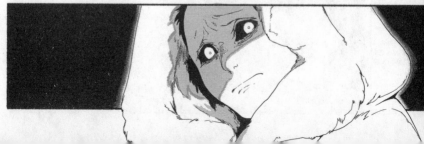

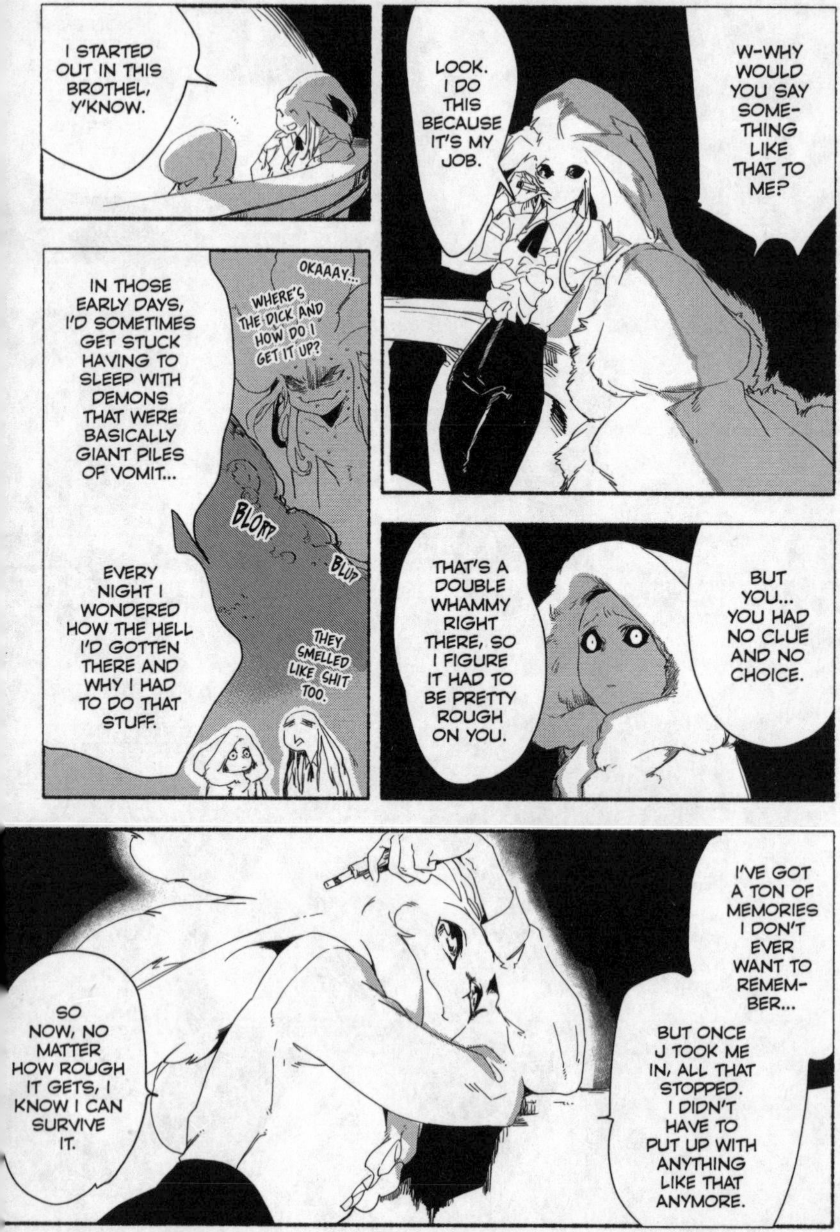
W-WHY WOULD YOU SAY SOME-THING LIKE THAT TO ME?
LOOK. I DO THIS BECAUSE IT'S MY JOB.
BUT YOU... YOU HAD NO CLUE AND NO CHOICE.
THAT'S A DOUBLE WHAMMY RIGHT THERE, SO I FIGURE IT HAD TO BE PRETTY ROUGH ON YOU.
I STARTED OUT IN THIS BROTHEL, Y'KNOW.
OKAAAY...
WHERE'S THE DICK AND HOW DO I GET IT UP?
IN THOSE EARLY DAYS, I'D SOMETIMES GET STUCK HAVING TO SLEEP WITH DEMONS THAT WERE BASICALLY GIANT PILES OF VOMIT...
BLORT
BLUP
THEY SMELLED LIKE SHIT TOO.
EVERY NIGHT I WONDERED HOW THE HELL I'D GOTTEN THERE AND WHY I HAD TO DO THAT STUFF.
I'VE GOT A TON OF MEMORIES I DON'T EVER WANT TO REMEM-BER...
BUT ONCE J TOOK ME IN, ALL THAT STOPPED. I DIDN'T HAVE TO PUT UP WITH ANYTHING LIKE THAT ANYMORE.
SO NOW, NO MATTER HOW ROUGH IT GETS, I KNOW I CAN SURVIVE IT.

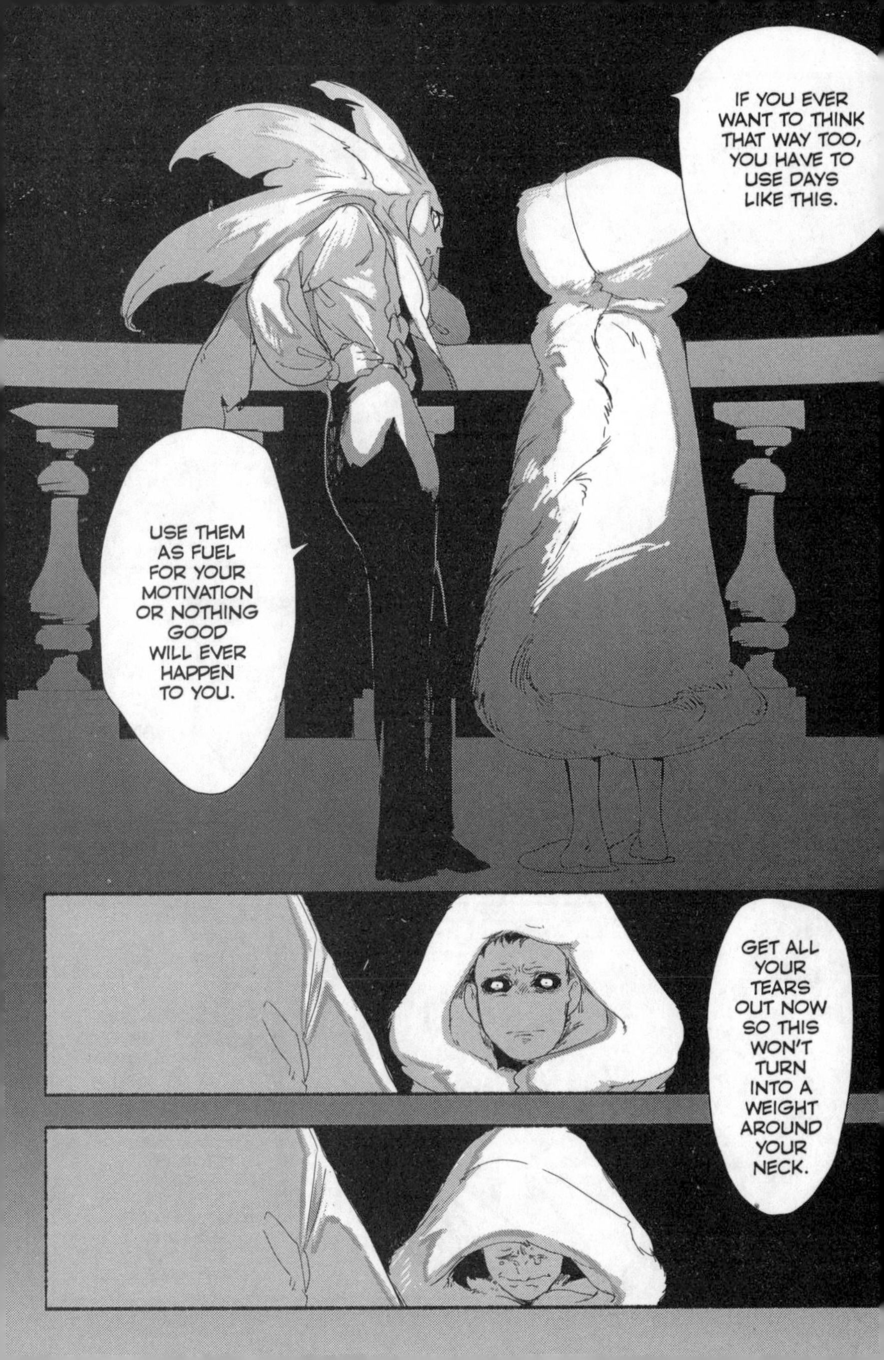
IF YOU EVER WANT TO THINK THAT WAY TOO, YOU HAVE TO USE DAYS LIKE THIS.
USE THEM AS FUEL FOR YOUR MOTIVATION OR NOTHING GOOD WILL EVER HAPPEN TO YOU.
GET ALL YOUR TEARS OUT NOW SO THIS WON'T TURN INTO A WEIGHT AROUND YOUR NECK.

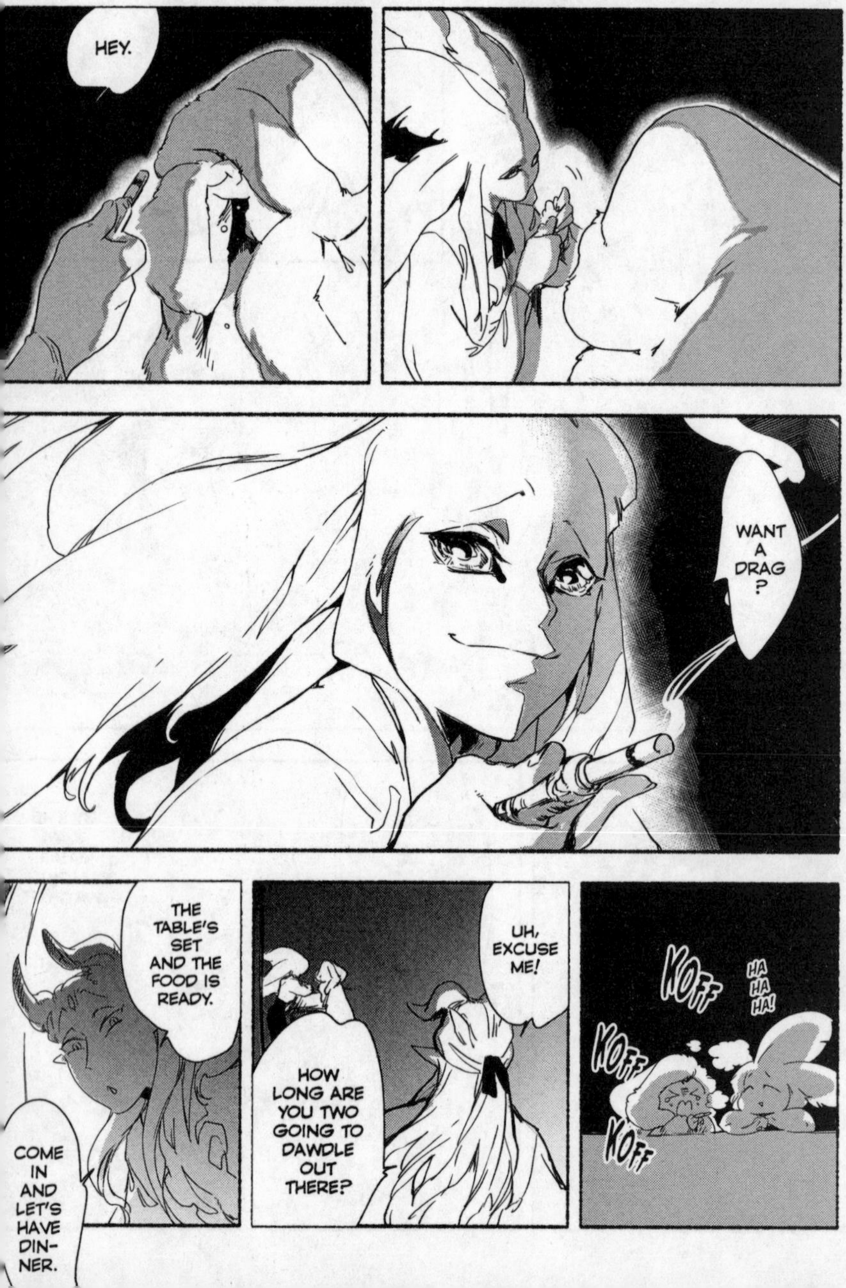
HEY.
WANT A DRAG?
HA HA HA!
KOFF
KOFF
KOFF
UH, EXCUSE ME!
HOW LONG ARE YOU TWO GOING TO DAWDLE OUT THERE?
THE TABLE'S SET AND THE FOOD IS READY.
COME IN AND LET'S HAVE DIN-NER.

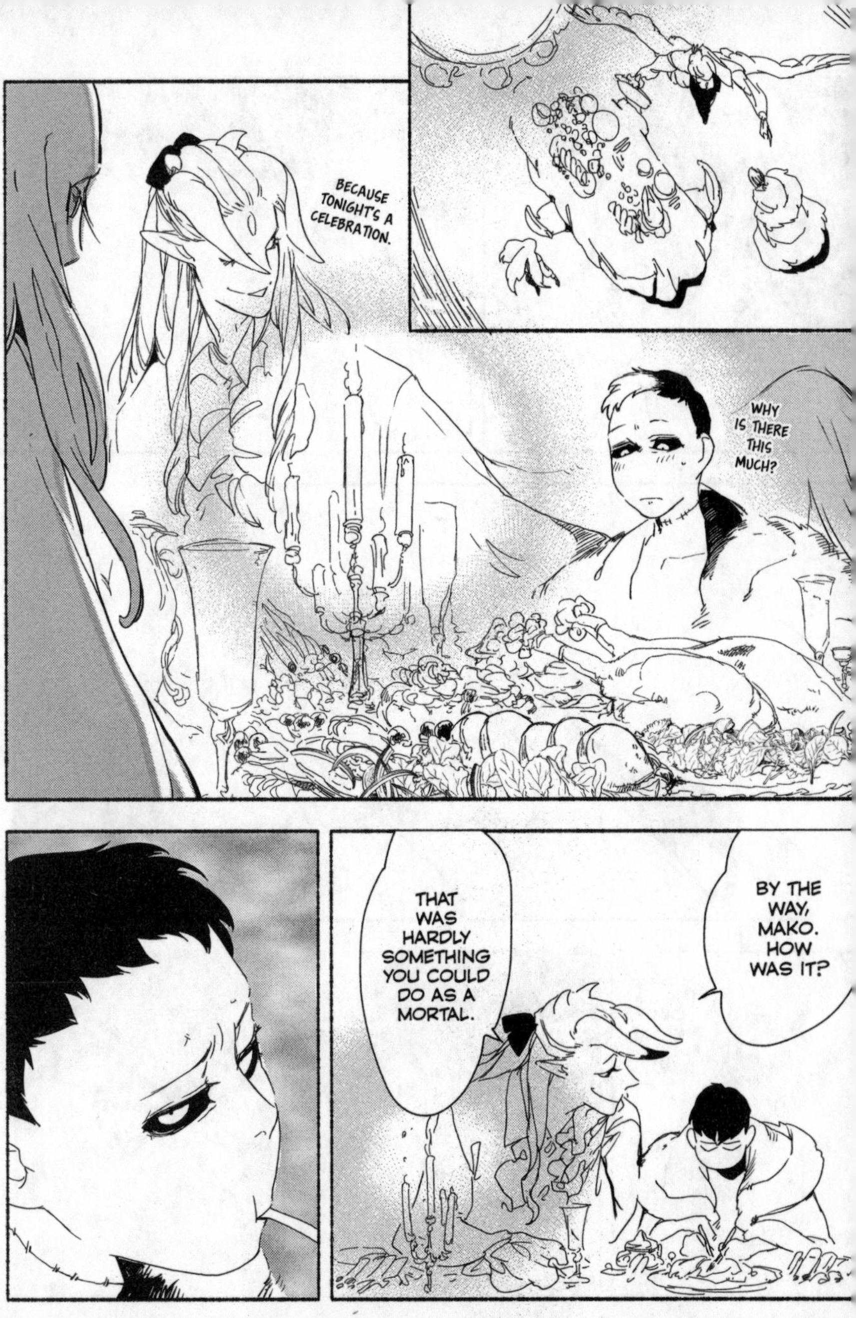
WHY IS THERE THIS MUCH?
BECAUSE TONIGHT'S A CELEBRATION.
BY THE WAY, MAKO. HOW WAS IT?
THAT WAS HARDLY SOMETHING YOU COULD DO AS A MORTAL.

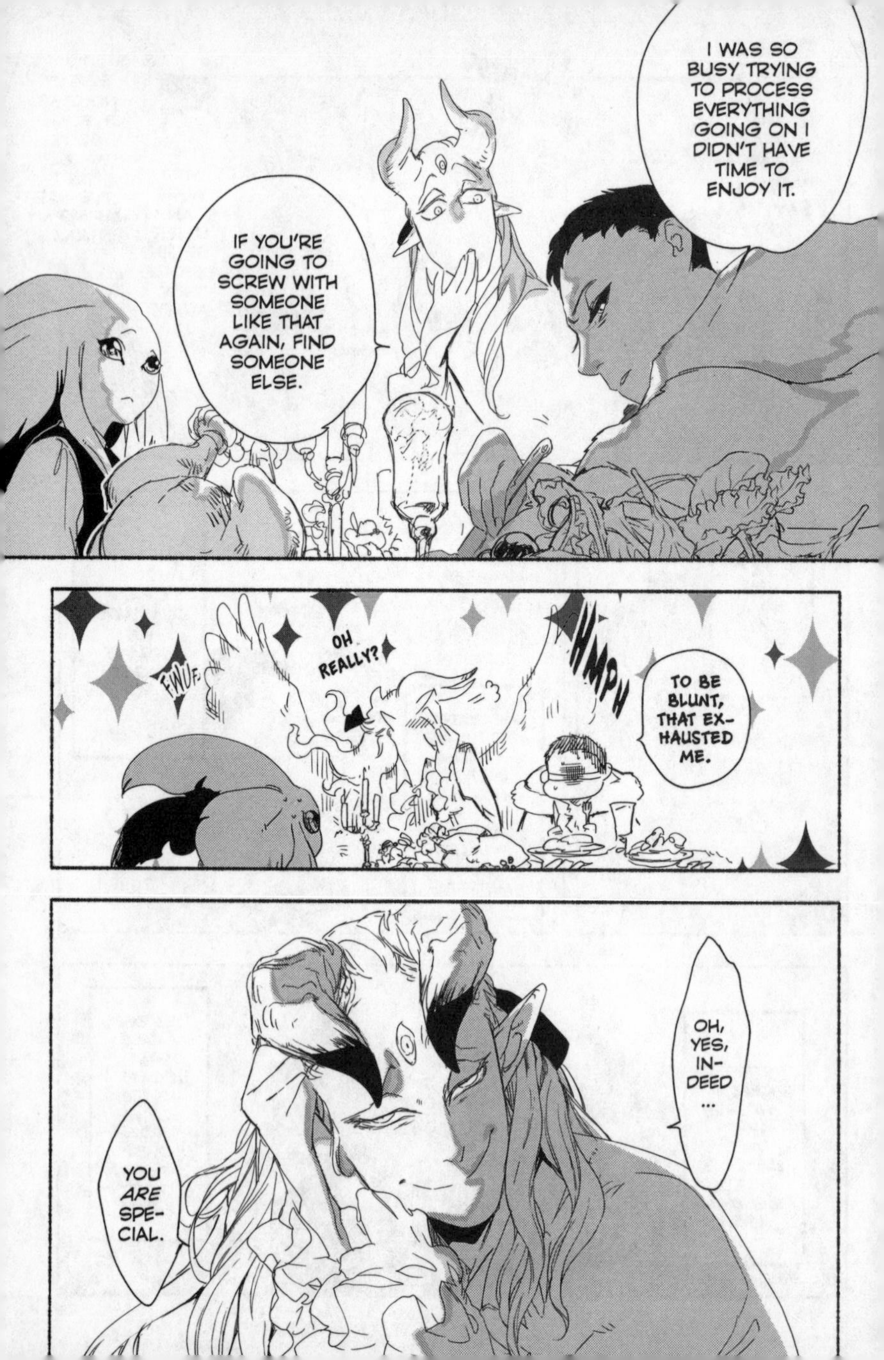
I WAS SO BUSY TRYING TO PROCESS EVERYTHING GOING ON I DIDN'T HAVE TIME TO ENJOY IT.
IF YOU'RE GOING TO SCREW WITH SOMEONE LIKE THAT AGAIN, FIND SOMEONE ELSE.
TO BE BLUNT, THAT EX-HAUSTED ME.
HMPH
OH REALLY?
FWUF
OH, YES, IN-DEED ...
YOU *ARE* SPE-CIAL.

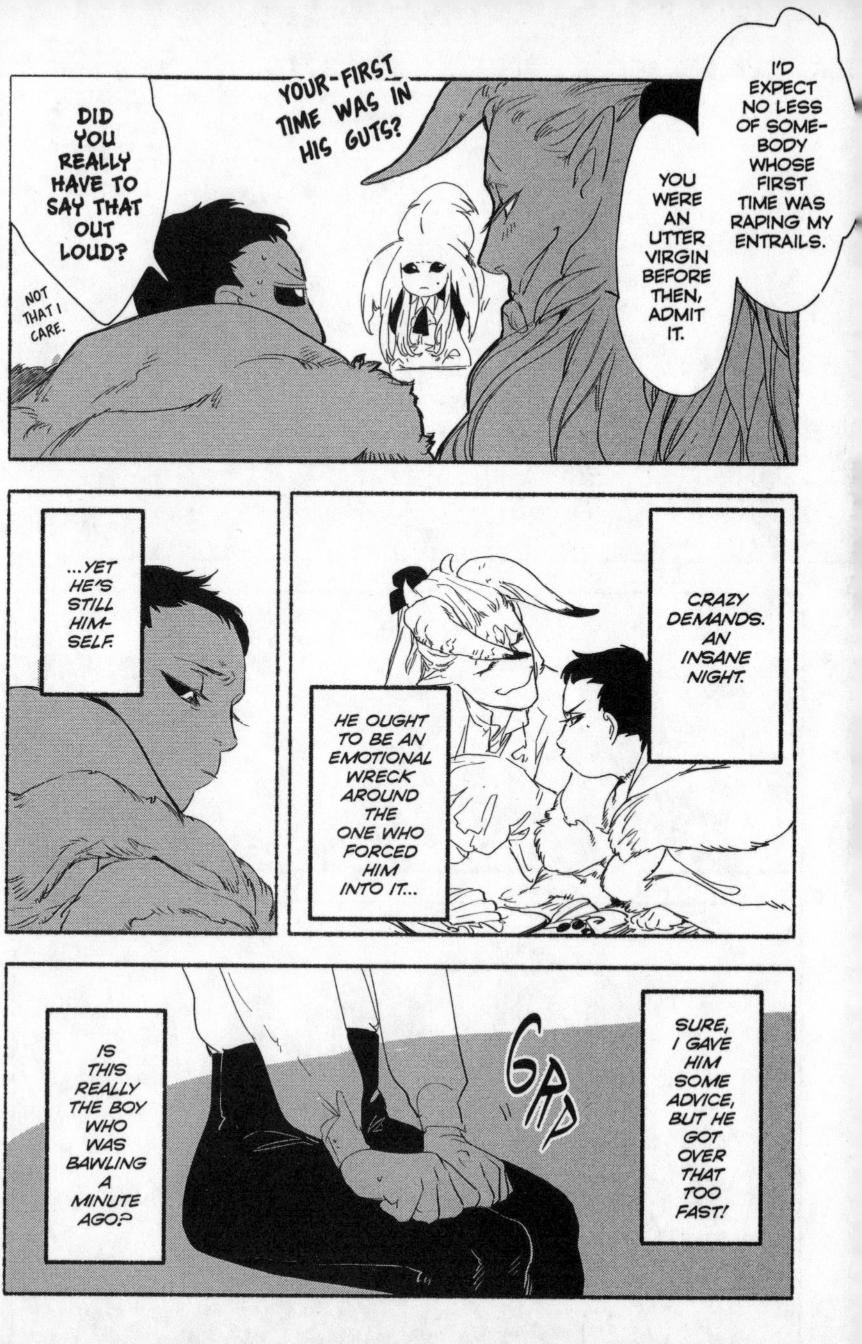
I'D EXPECT NO LESS OF SOME-BODY WHOSE FIRST TIME WAS RAPING MY ENTRAILS.
YOU WERE AN UTTER VIRGIN BEFORE THEN, ADMIT IT.
YOUR-FIRST TIME WAS IN HIS GUTS?
DID YOU REALLY HAVE TO SAY THAT OUT LOUD?
NOT THAT I CARE.
CRAZY DEMANDS. AN INSANE NIGHT.
HE OUGHT TO BE AN EMOTIONAL WRECK AROUND THE ONE WHO FORCED HIM INTO IT...
...YET HE'S STILL HIM-SELF.
SURE, I GAVE HIM SOME ADVICE, BUT HE GOT OVER THAT TOO FAST!
GRP
IS THIS REALLY THE BOY WHO WAS BAWLING A MINUTE AGO?

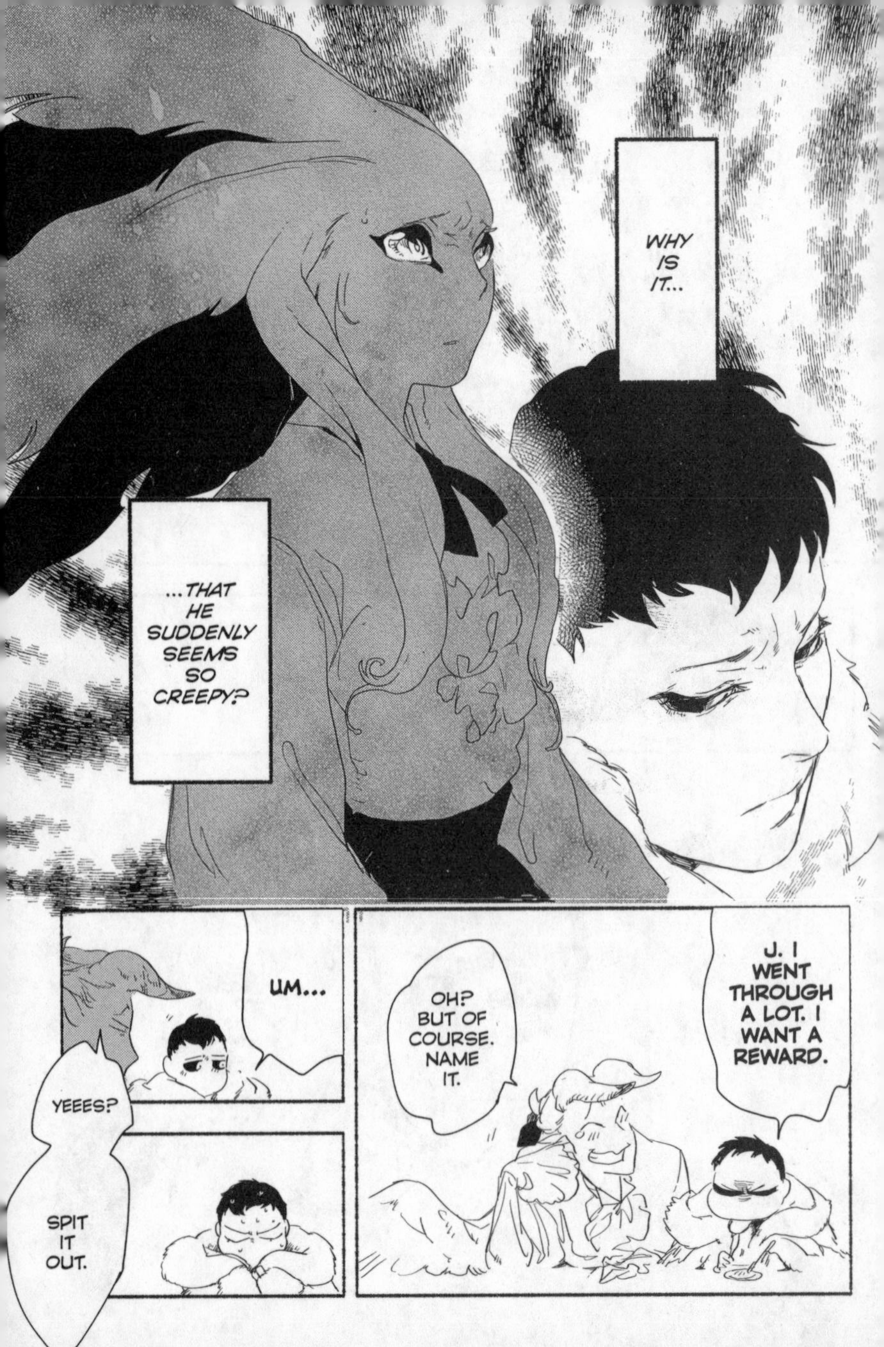
WHY IS IT...
...THAT HE SUDDENLY SEEMS SO CREEPY?
J. I WENT THROUGH A LOT. I WANT A REWARD.
OH? BUT OF COURSE. NAME IT.
UM...
YEEES?
SPIT IT OUT.

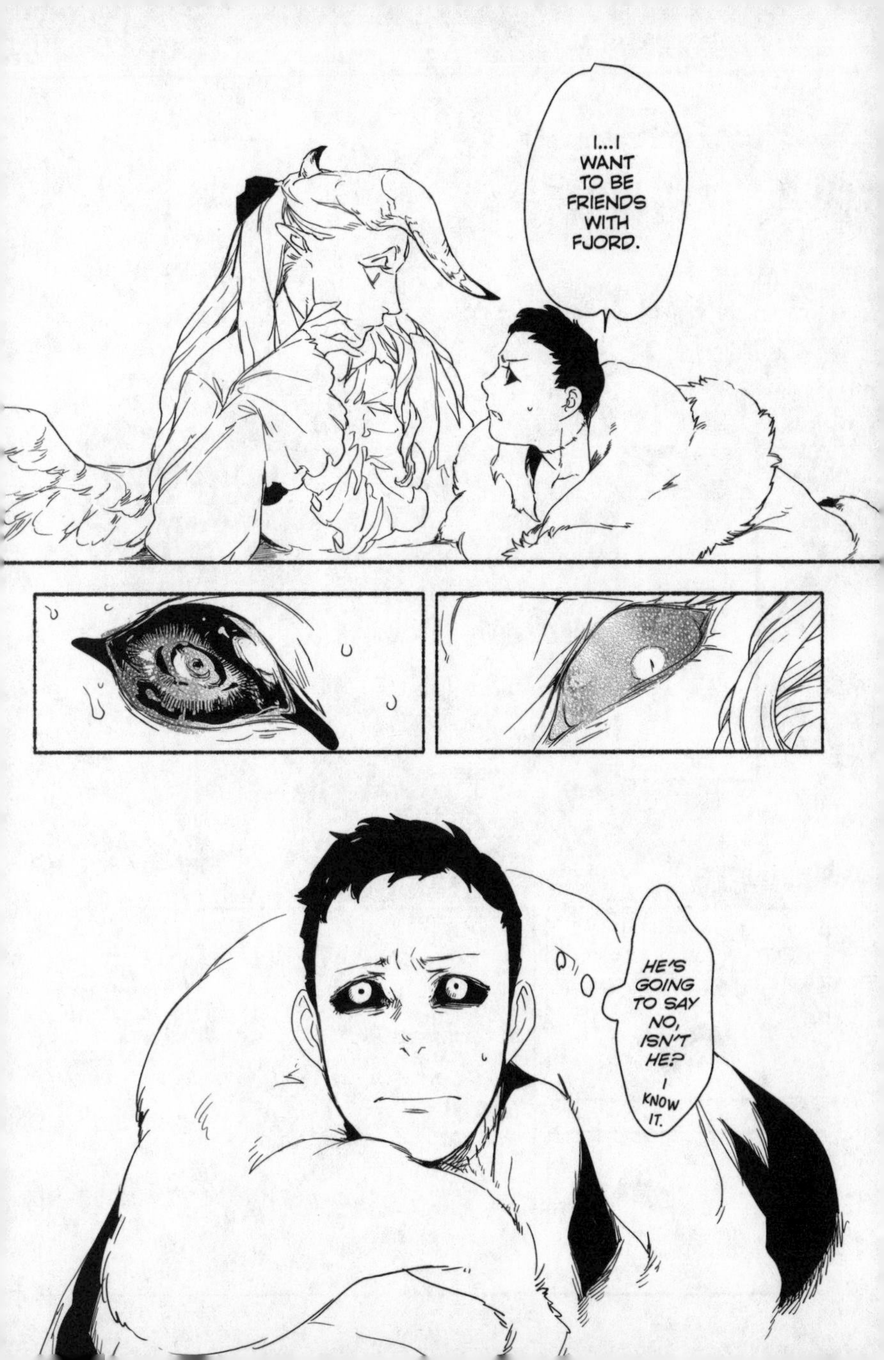
I...I WANT TO BE FRIENDS WITH FJORD.
HE'S GOING TO SAY NO, ISN'T HE?
I KNOW IT.

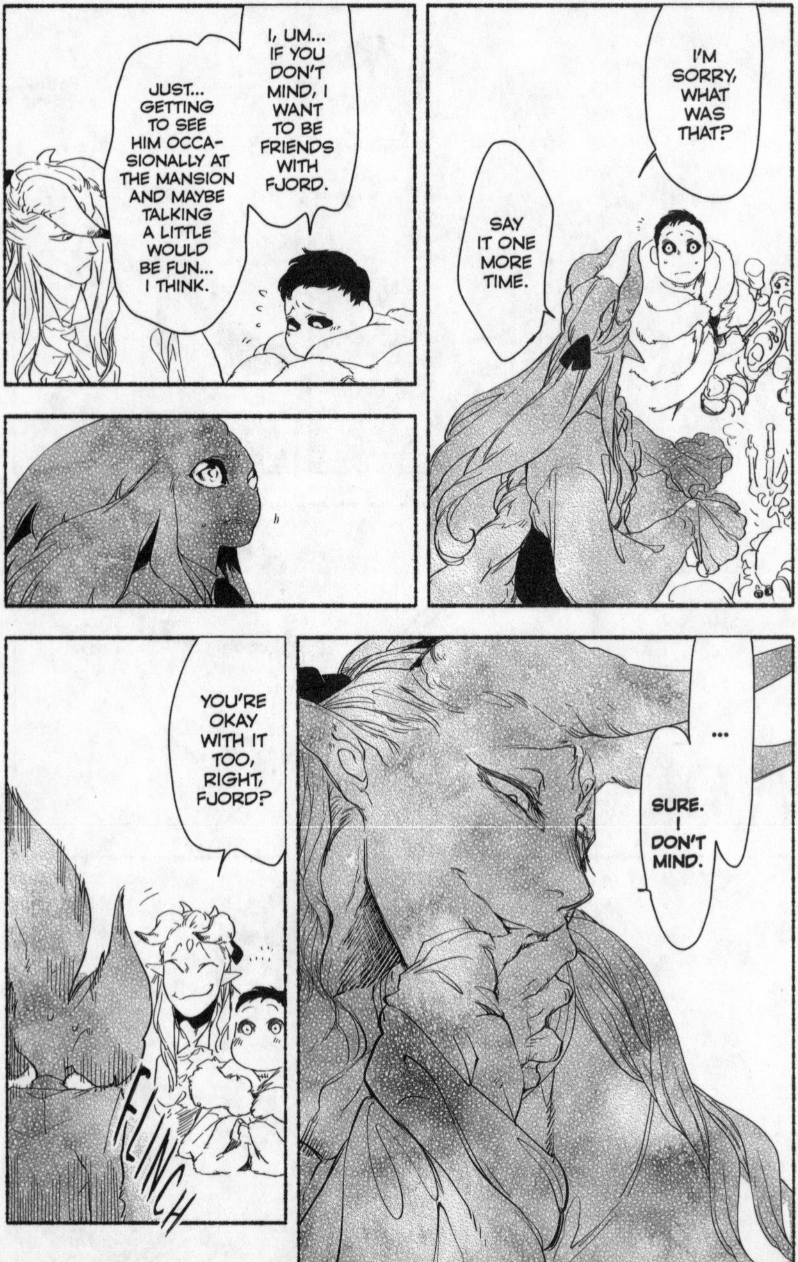
I'M SORRY, WHAT WAS THAT?
SAY IT ONE MORE TIME.
I, UM... IF YOU DON'T MIND, I WANT TO BE FRIENDS WITH FJORD.
JUST... GETTING TO SEE HIM OCCA-SIONALLY AT THE MANSION AND MAYBE TALKING A LITTLE WOULD BE FUN... I THINK.
...
SURE. I DON'T MIND.
YOU'RE OKAY WITH IT TOO, RIGHT, FJORD?
FLINCH

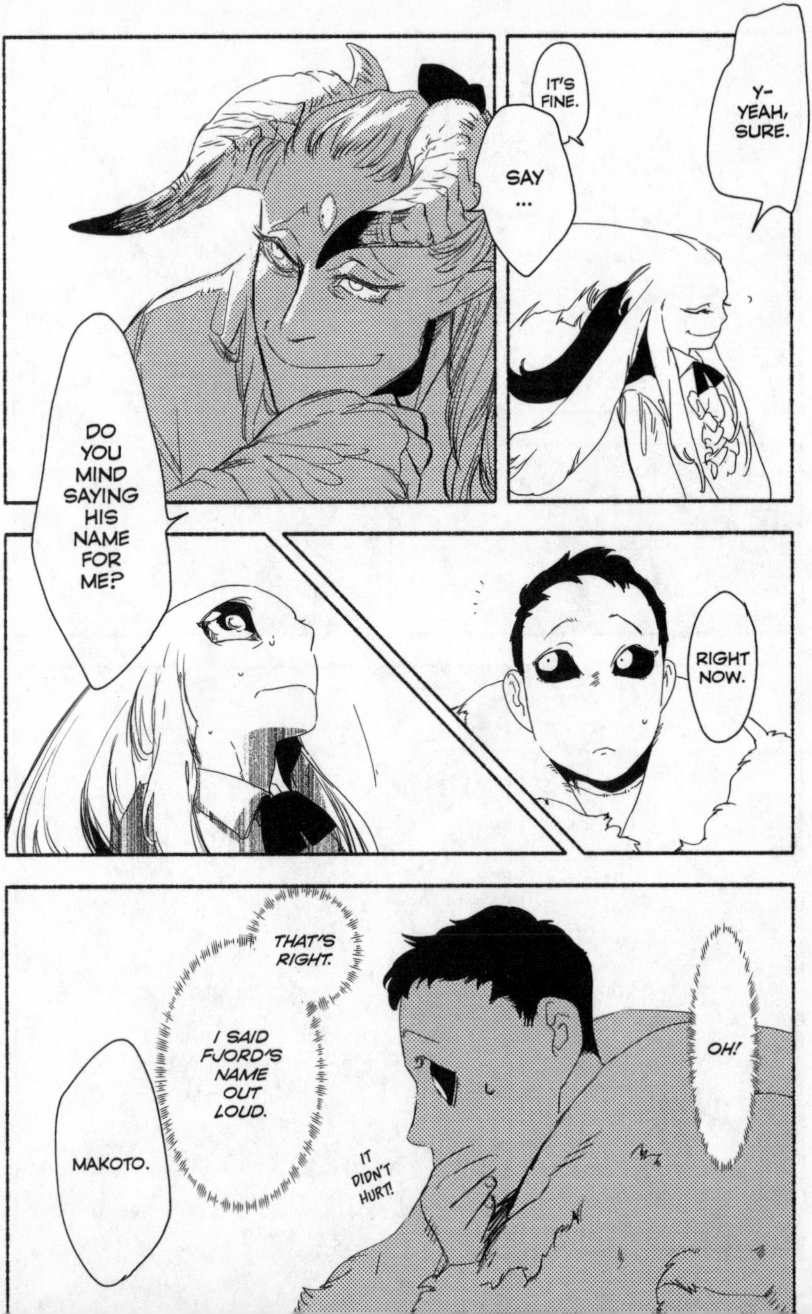
Y-YEAH, SURE.
IT'S FINE.
SAY ...
DO YOU MIND SAYING HIS NAME FOR ME?
RIGHT NOW.
OH!
THAT'S RIGHT.
I SAID FJORD'S NAME OUT LOUD.
IT DIDN'T HURT!
MAKOTO.

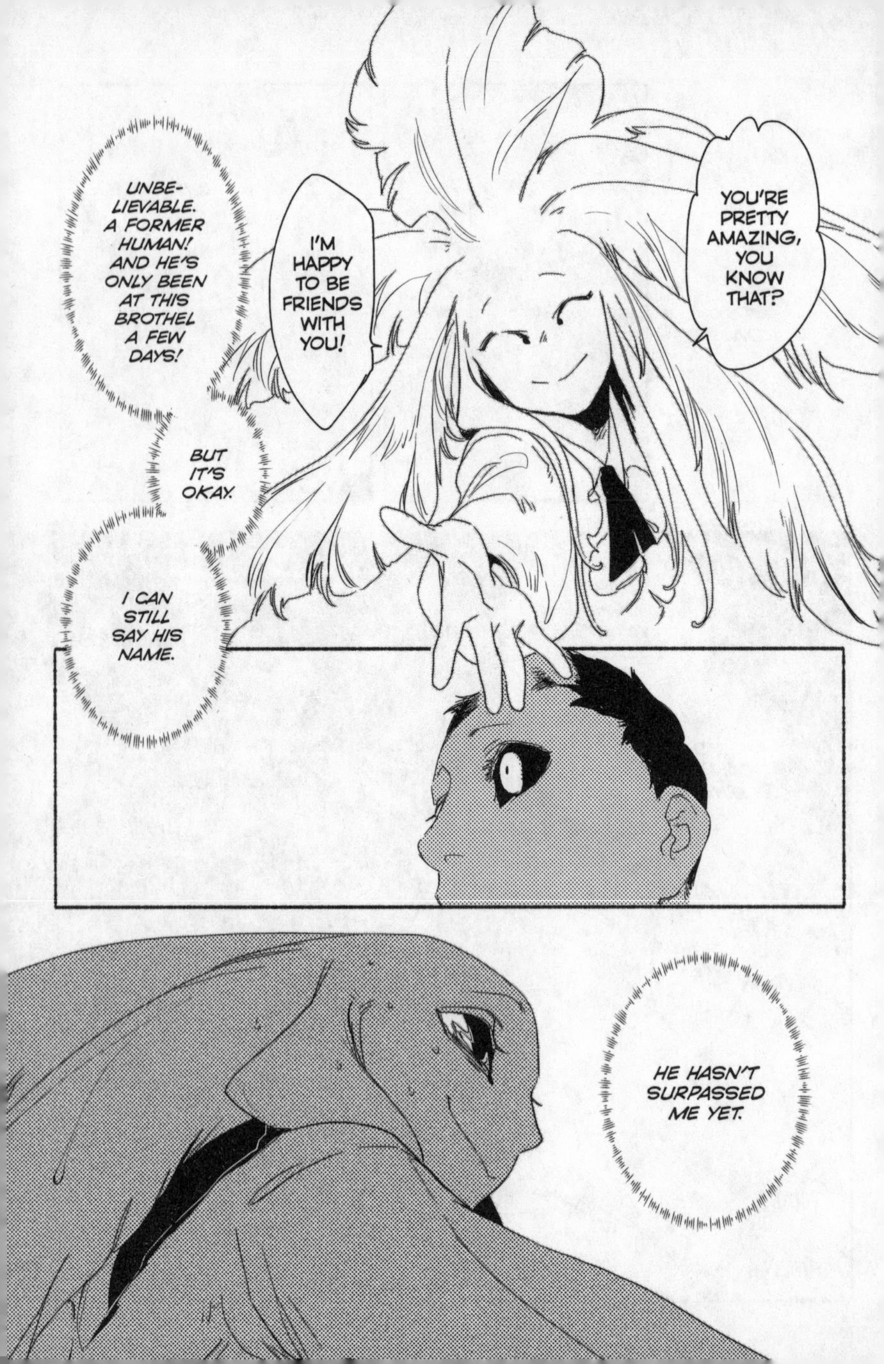
YOU'RE PRETTY AMAZING, YOU KNOW THAT?
I'M HAPPY TO BE FRIENDS WITH YOU!
UNBE-LIEVABLE. A FORMER HUMAN! AND HE'S ONLY BEEN AT THIS BROTHEL A FEW DAYS!
BUT IT'S OKAY.
I CAN STILL SAY HIS NAME.
HE HASN'T SURPASSED ME YET.

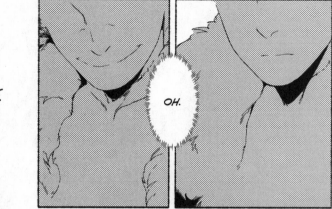

I THINK I GET IT NOW.

OH.

AS LONG AS IT'S SOMEONE WHO CAN'T UNNERVE YOU...

...YOU CAN SAY THEIR NAME.

SAME.

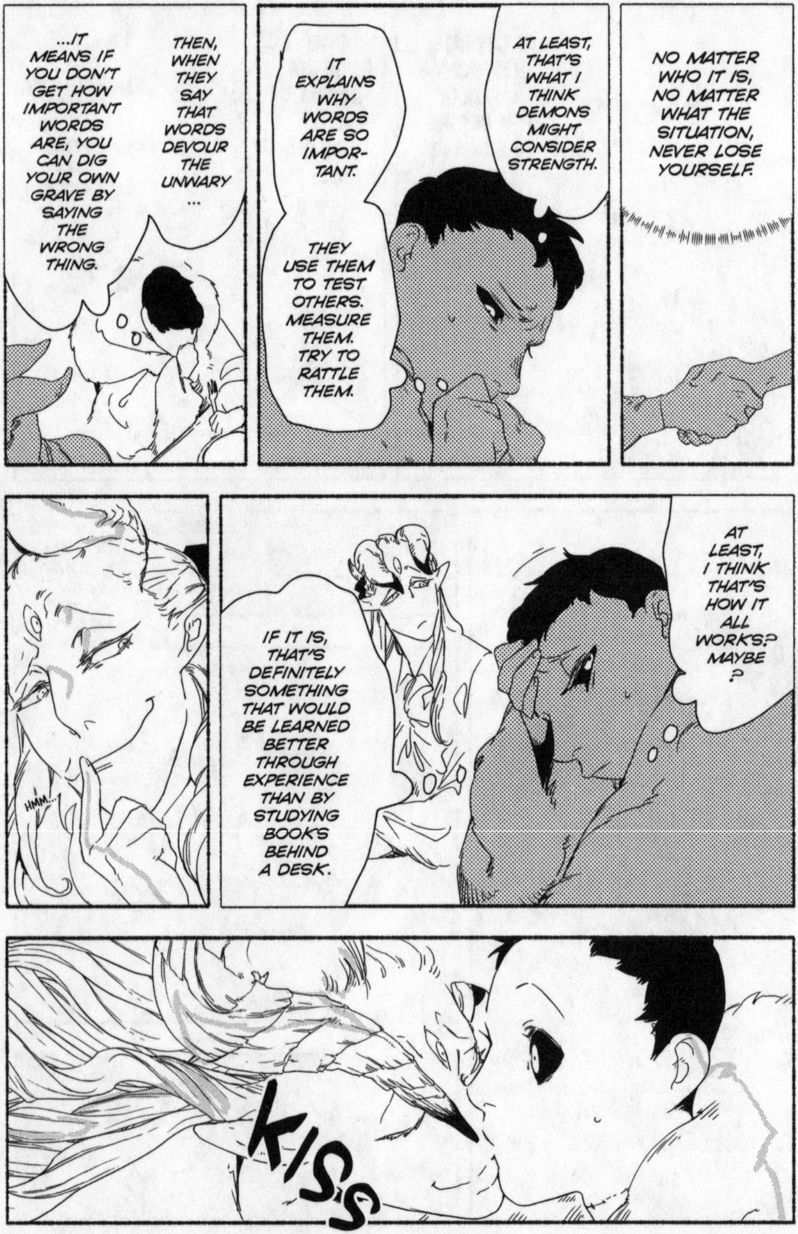
NO MATTER WHO IT IS, NO MATTER WHAT THE SITUATION, NEVER LOSE YOURSELF.
AT LEAST, THAT'S WHAT I THINK DEMONS MIGHT CONSIDER STRENGTH.
IT EXPLAINS WHY WORDS ARE SO IMPORTANT.
THEY USE THEM TO TEST OTHERS. MEASURE THEM. TRY TO RATTLE THEM.
THEN, WHEN THEY SAY THAT WORDS DEVOUR THE UNWARY...
...IT MEANS IF YOU DON'T GET HOW IMPORTANT WORDS ARE, YOU CAN DIG YOUR OWN GRAVE BY SAYING THE WRONG THING.
AT LEAST, I THINK THAT'S HOW IT ALL WORKS? MAYBE?
IF IT IS, THAT'S DEFINITELY SOMETHING THAT WOULD BE LEARNED BETTER THROUGH EXPERIENCE THAN BY STUDYING BOOKS BEHIND A DESK.
HMM...
KISS

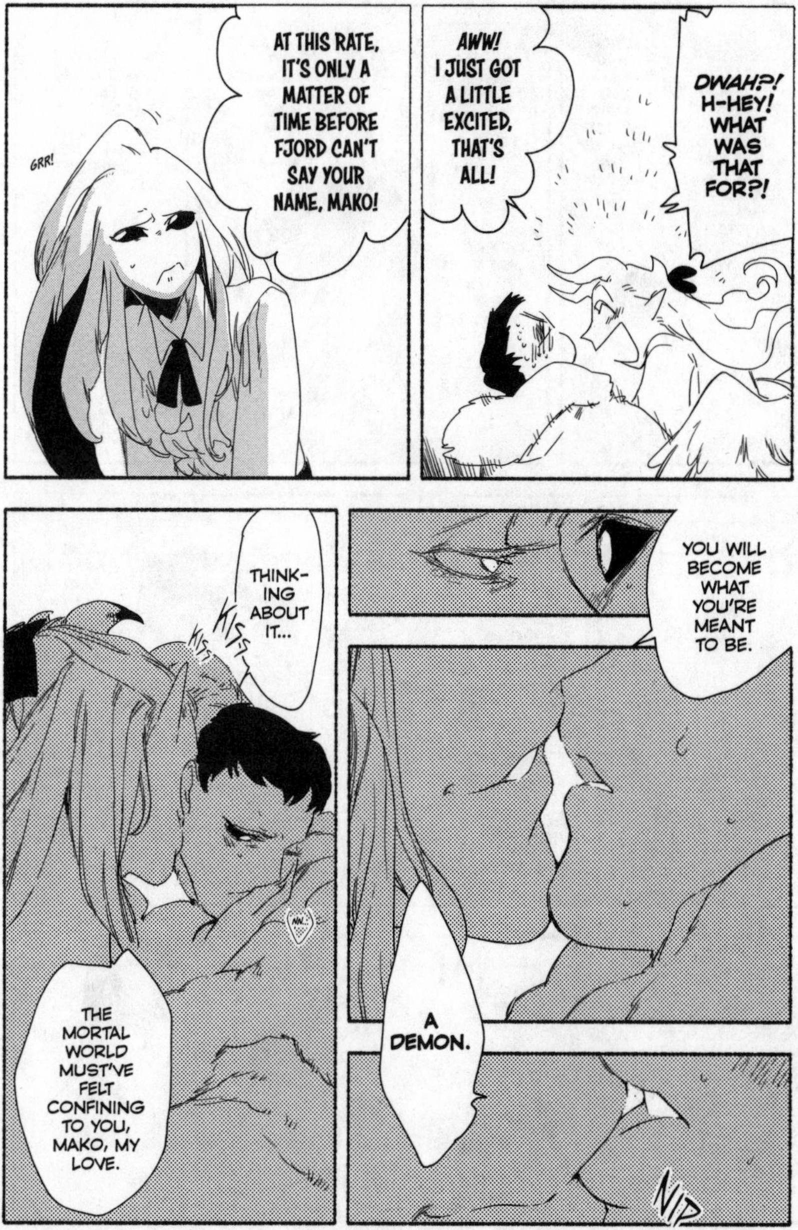
DWAH?! H-HEY! WHAT WAS THAT FOR?!
AWW! I JUST GOT A LITTLE EXCITED, THAT'S ALL!
AT THIS RATE, IT'S ONLY A MATTER OF TIME BEFORE FJORD CAN'T SAY YOUR NAME, MAKO!
GRR!
YOU WILL BECOME WHAT YOU'RE MEANT TO BE.
A DEMON.
NIP
THINKING-ING ABOUT IT...
KISS
KISS
NN.
THE MORTAL WORLD MUST'VE FELT CONFINING TO YOU, MAKO, MY LOVE.

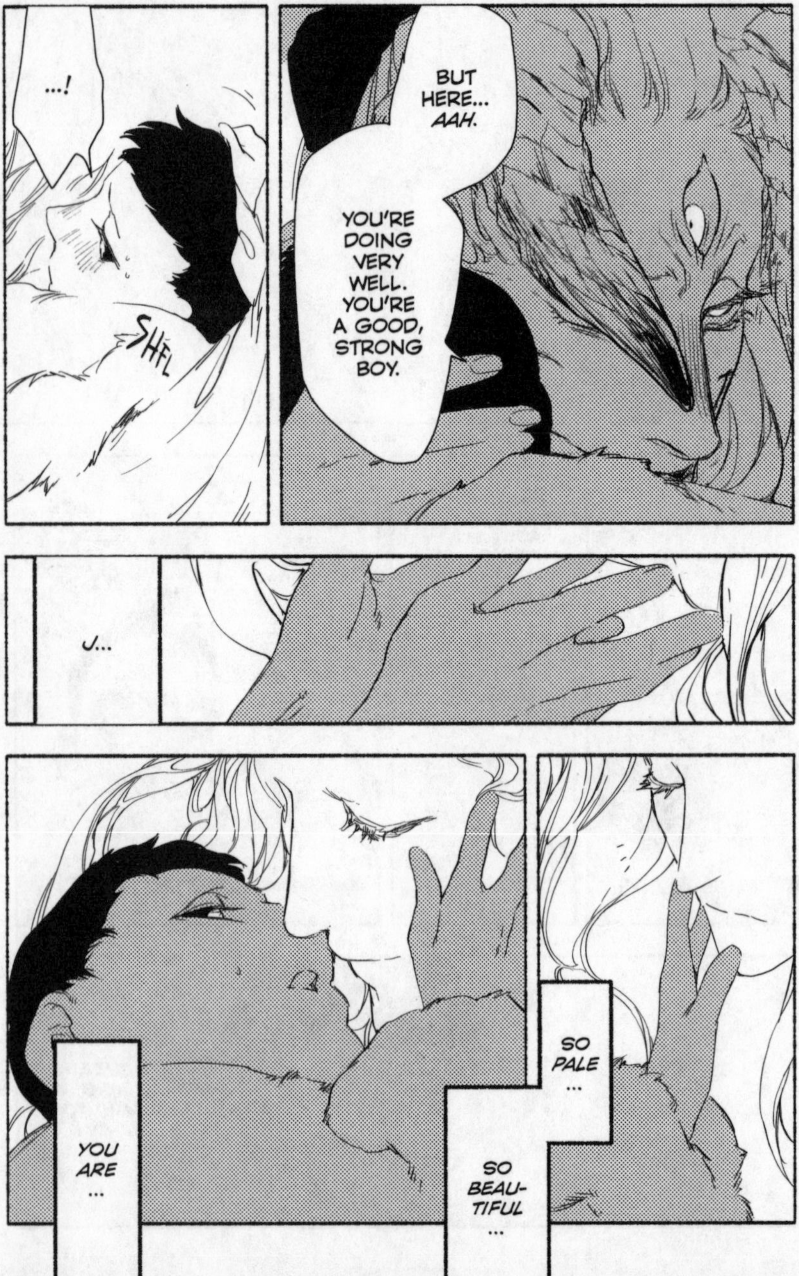
BUT HERE... AAH.
YOU'RE DOING VERY WELL. YOU'RE A GOOD, STRONG BOY.
...!
SHFL
J...
SO PALE...
SO BEAUTIFUL...
YOU ARE...

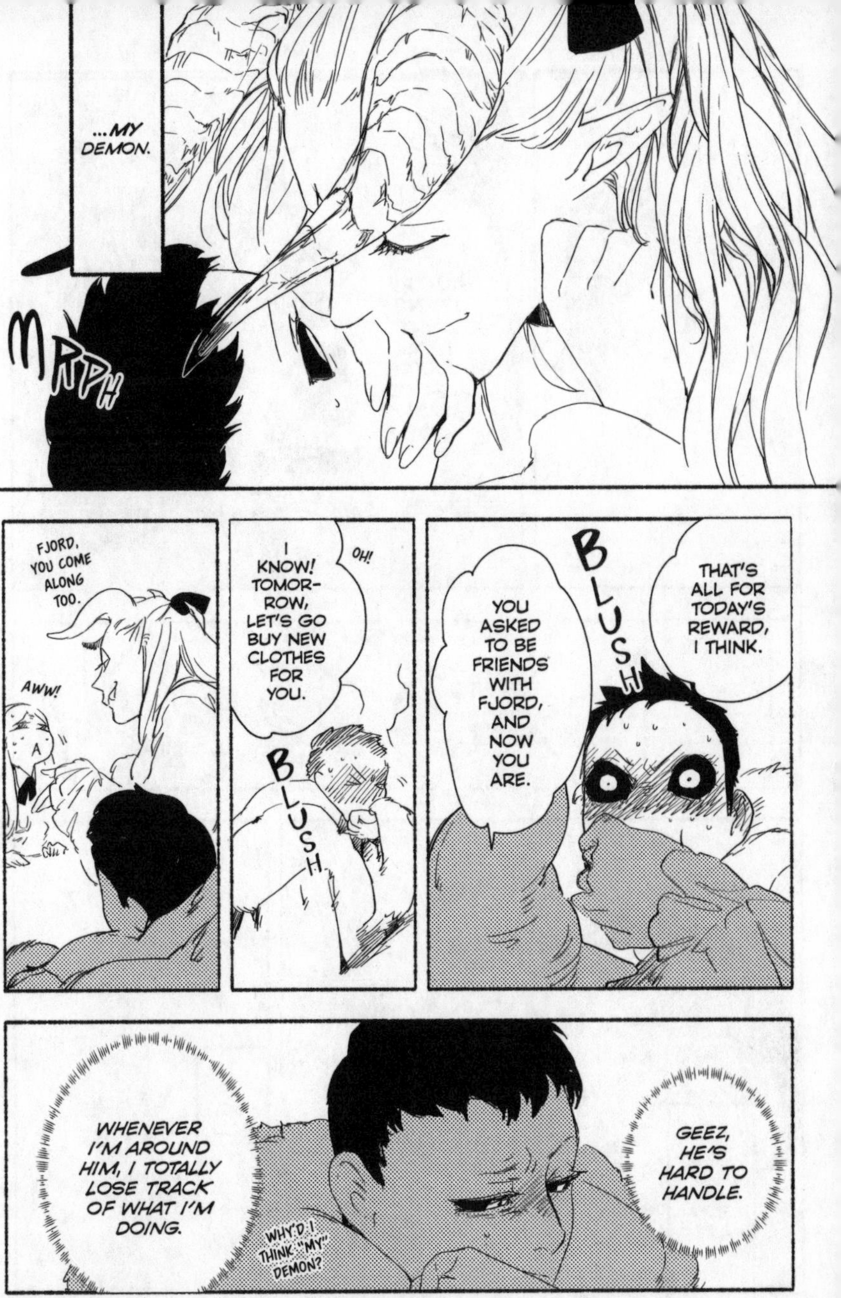
...MY DEMON.
MRPH
THAT'S ALL FOR TODAY'S REWARD, I THINK.
BLUSH
YOU ASKED TO BE FRIENDS WITH FJORD, AND NOW YOU ARE.
OH!
I KNOW! TOMORROW, LET'S GO BUY NEW CLOTHES FOR YOU.
BLUSH
FJORD, YOU COME ALONG TOO.
AWW!
GEEZ, HE'S HARD TO HANDLE.
WHENEVER I'M AROUND HIM, I TOTALLY LOSE TRACK OF WHAT I'M DOING.
WHY'D I THINK "MY" DEMON?

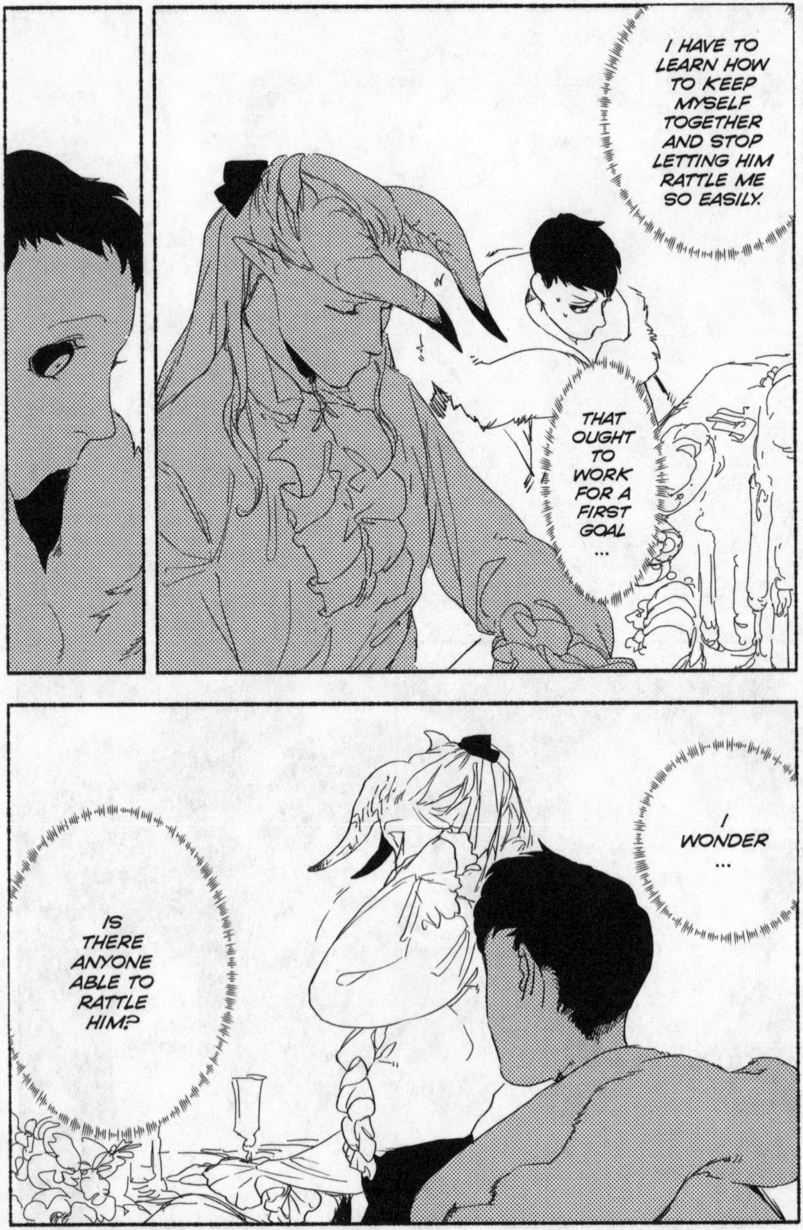
I HAVE TO LEARN HOW TO KEEP MYSELF TOGETHER AND STOP LETTING HIM RATTLE ME SO EASILY.
THAT OUGHT TO WORK FOR A FIRST GOAL...
I WONDER...
IS THERE ANYONE ABLE TO RATTLE HIM?

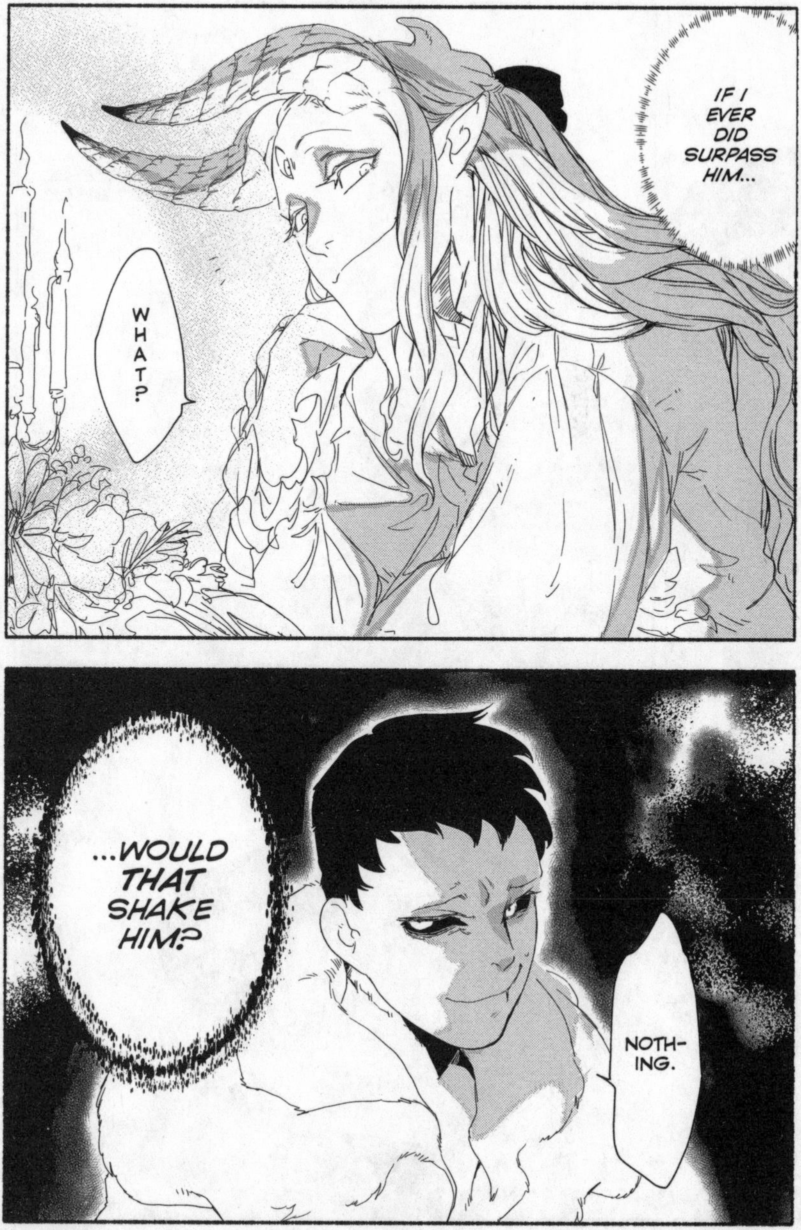
IF I EVER DID SURPASS HIM...
WHAT?
NOTH-ING.
...WOULD THAT SHAKE HIM?

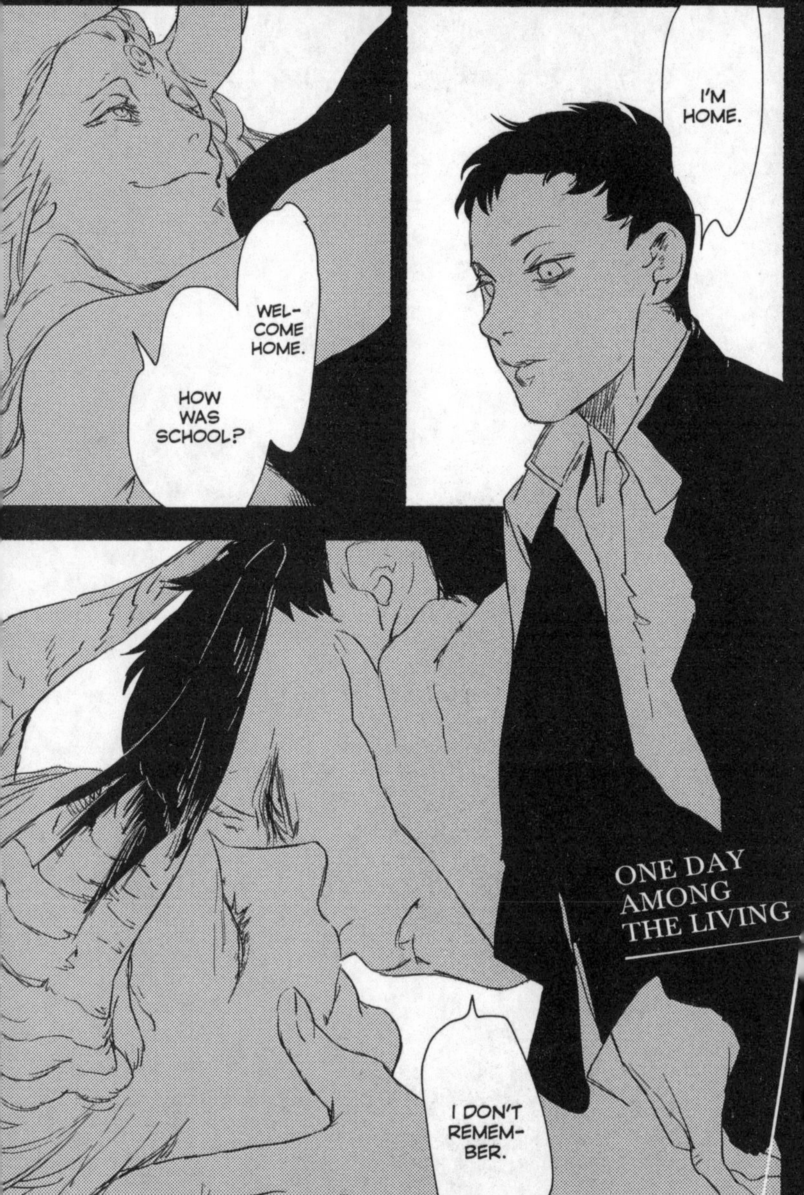
I'M HOME.
WEL-COME HOME.
HOW WAS SCHOOL?
ONE DAY AMONG THE LIVING
I DON'T REMEM-BER.

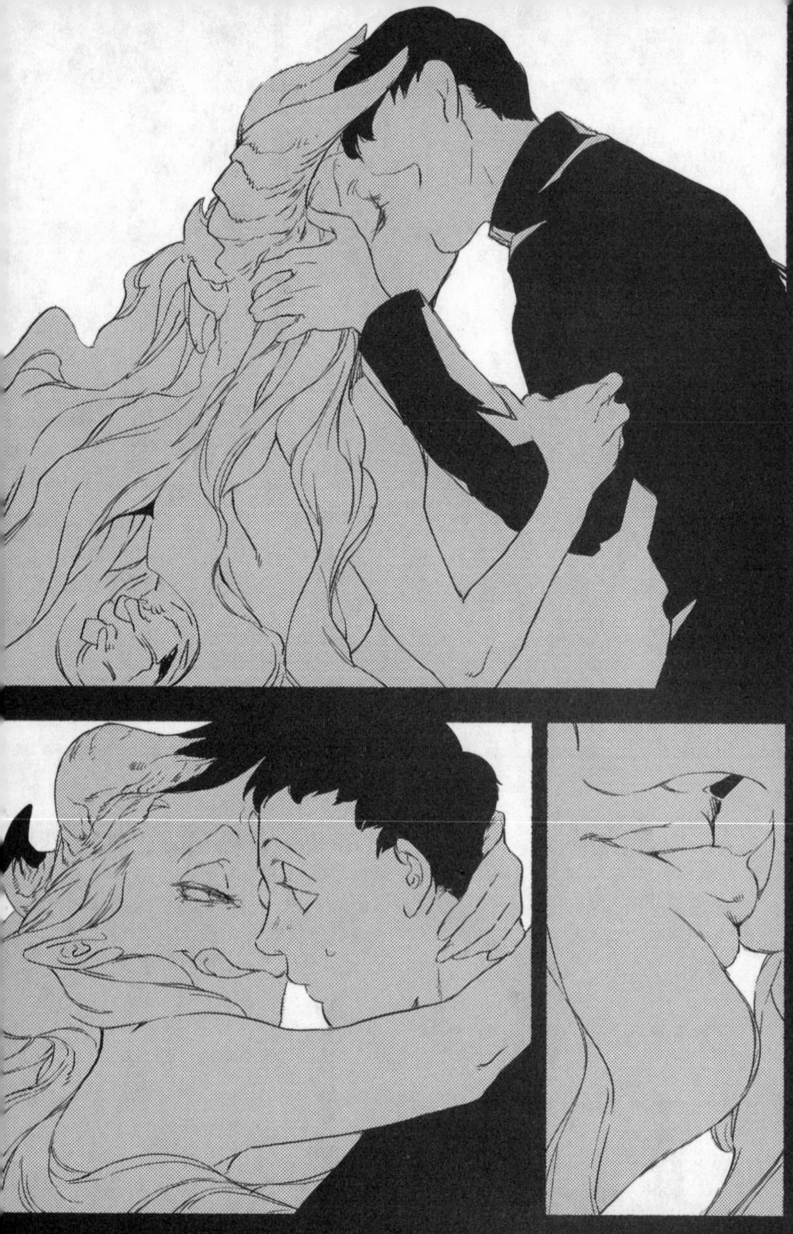

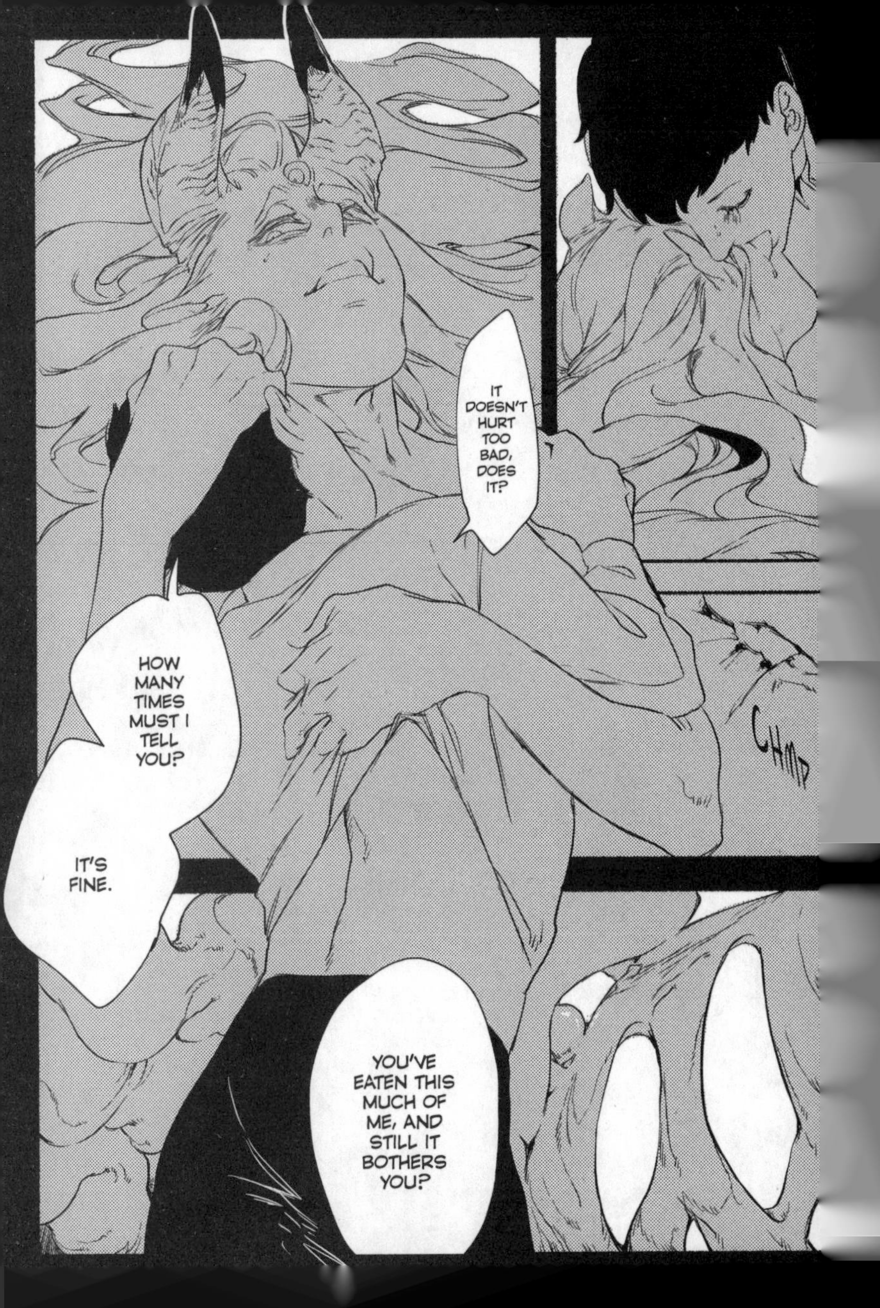
CHMP
IT DOESN'T HURT TOO BAD, DOES IT?
HOW MANY TIMES MUST I TELL YOU?
IT'S FINE.
YOU'VE EATEN THIS MUCH OF ME, AND STILL IT BOTHERS YOU?

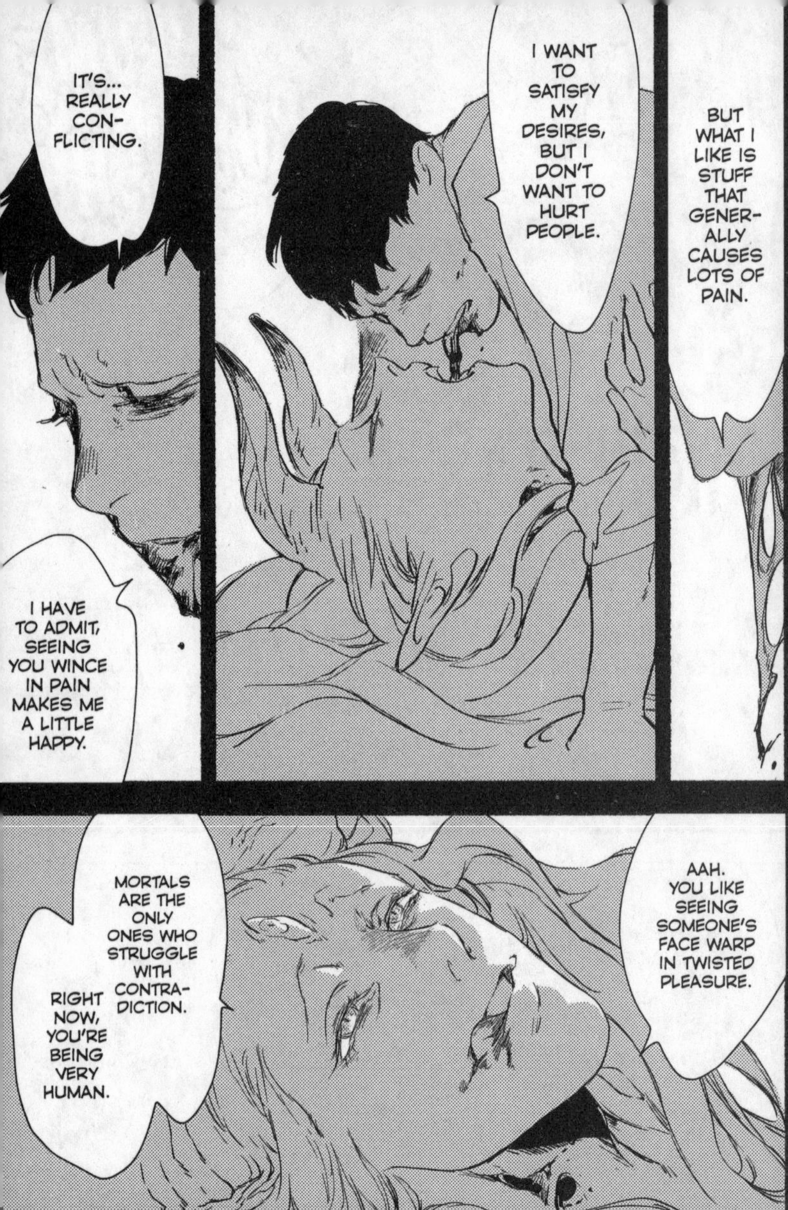
BUT WHAT I LIKE IS STUFF THAT GENERALLY CAUSES LOTS OF PAIN.
I WANT TO SATISFY MY DESIRES, BUT I DON'T WANT TO HURT PEOPLE.
IT'S... REALLY CONFLICTING.
I HAVE TO ADMIT, SEEING YOU WINCE IN PAIN MAKES ME A LITTLE HAPPY.
AAH. YOU LIKE SEEING SOMEONE'S FACE WARP IN TWISTED PLEASURE.
MORTALS ARE THE ONLY ONES WHO STRUGGLE WITH CONTRADICTION.
RIGHT NOW, YOU'RE BEING VERY HUMAN.

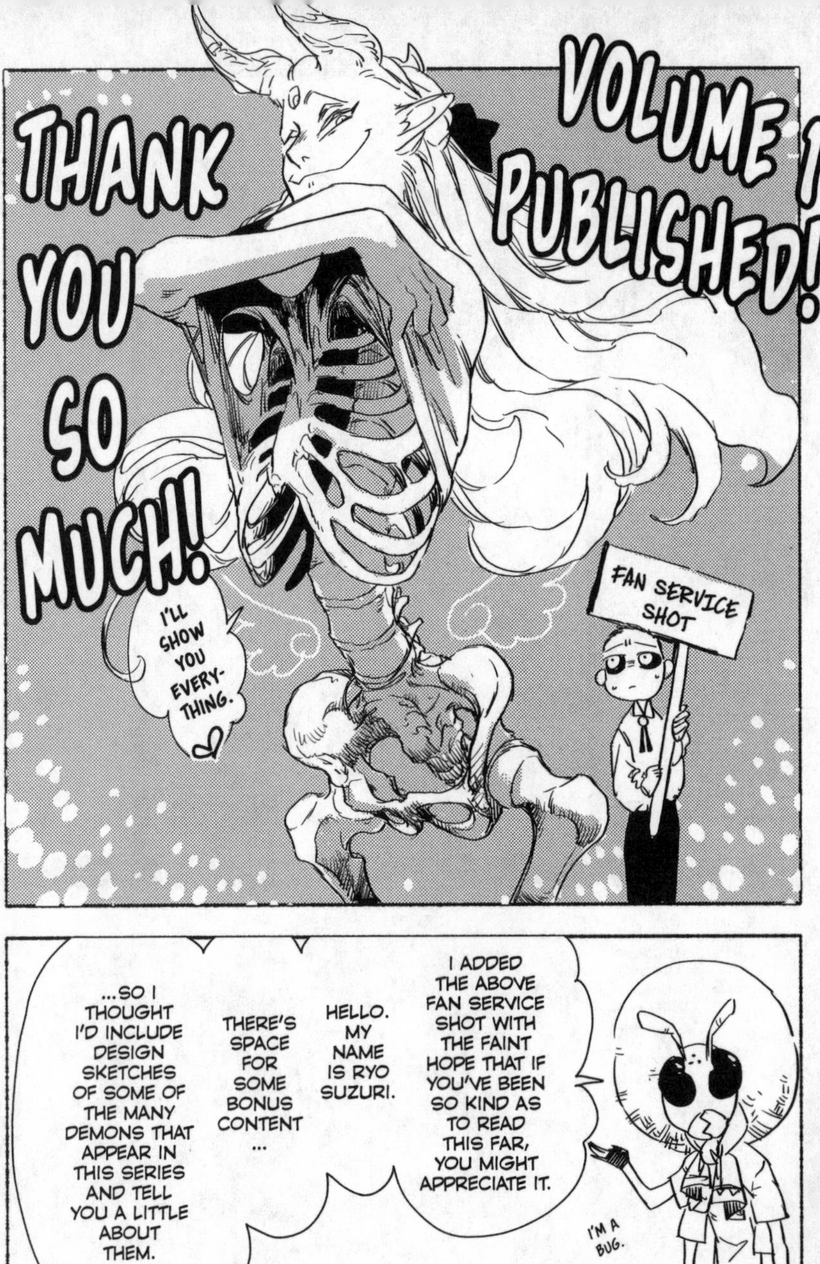
VOLUME 1 PUBLISHED!
THANK YOU SO MUCH!
FAN SERVICE SHOT
I'LL SHOW YOU EVERYTHING.
I ADDED THE ABOVE FAN SERVICE SHOT WITH THE FAINT HOPE THAT IF YOU'VE BEEN SO KIND AS TO READ THIS FAR, YOU MIGHT APPRECIATE IT.
HELLO. MY NAME IS RYO SUZURI.
THERE'S SPACE FOR SOME BONUS CONTENT...
...SO I THOUGHT I'D INCLUDE DESIGN SKETCHES OF SOME OF THE MANY DEMONS THAT APPEAR IN THIS SERIES AND TELL YOU A LITTLE ABOUT THEM.
I'M A BUG.

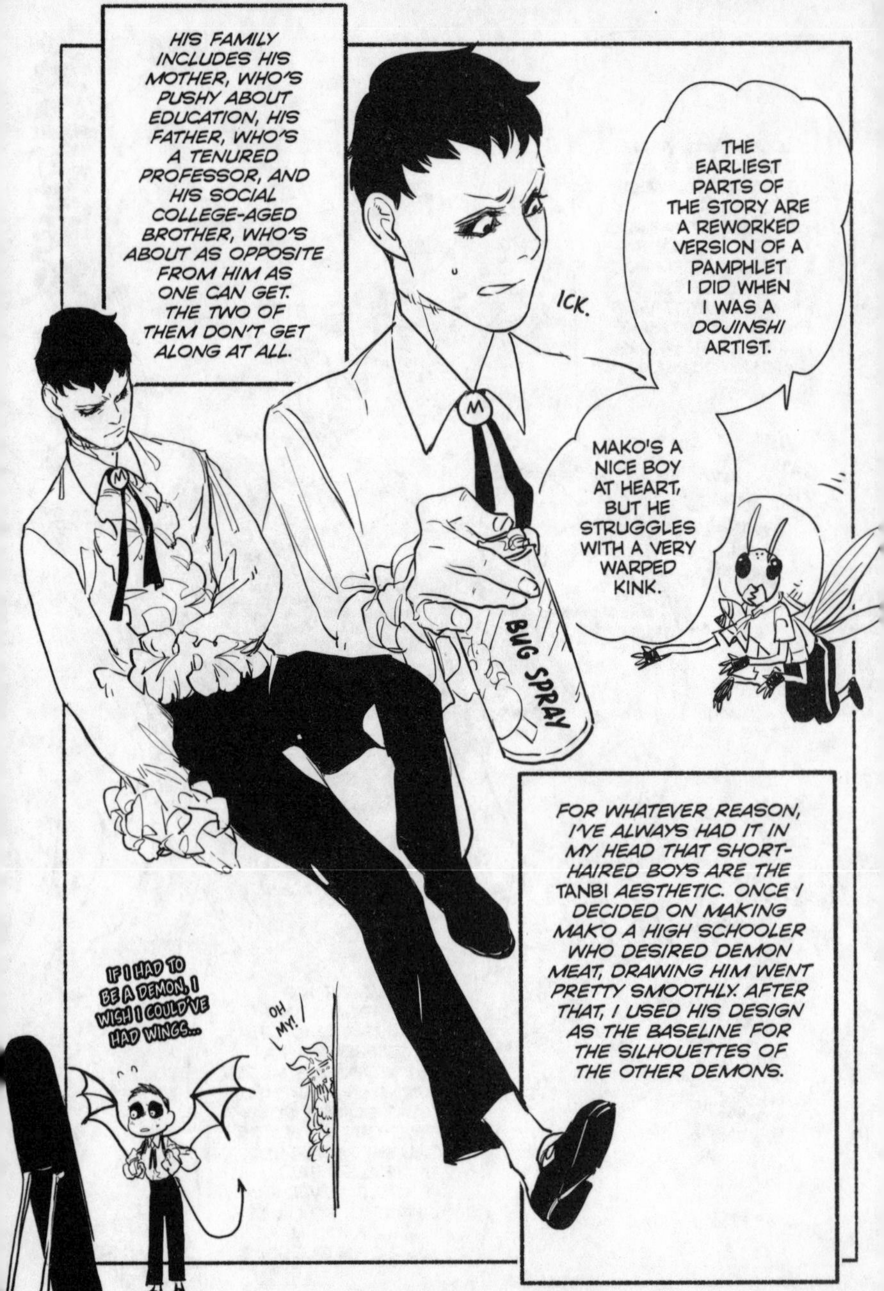
THE EARLIEST PARTS OF THE STORY ARE A REWORKED VERSION OF A PAMPHLET I DID WHEN I WAS A *DOJINSHI* ARTIST.
MAKO'S A NICE BOY AT HEART, BUT HE STRUGGLES WITH A VERY WARPED KINK.
ICK.
HIS FAMILY INCLUDES HIS MOTHER, WHO'S PUSHY ABOUT EDUCATION, HIS FATHER, WHO'S A TENURED PROFESSOR, AND HIS SOCIAL COLLEGE-AGED BROTHER, WHO'S ABOUT AS OPPOSITE FROM HIM AS ONE CAN GET. THE TWO OF THEM DON'T GET ALONG AT ALL.
BUG SPRAY
FOR WHATEVER REASON, I'VE ALWAYS HAD IT IN MY HEAD THAT SHORT-HAIRED BOYS ARE THE *TANBI* AESTHETIC. ONCE I DECIDED ON MAKING MAKO A HIGH SCHOOLER WHO DESIRED DEMON MEAT, DRAWING HIM WENT PRETTY SMOOTHLY. AFTER THAT, I USED HIS DESIGN AS THE BASELINE FOR THE SILHOUETTES OF THE OTHER DEMONS.
OH MY!
IF I HAD TO BE A DEMON, I WISH I COULD'VE HAD WINGS...

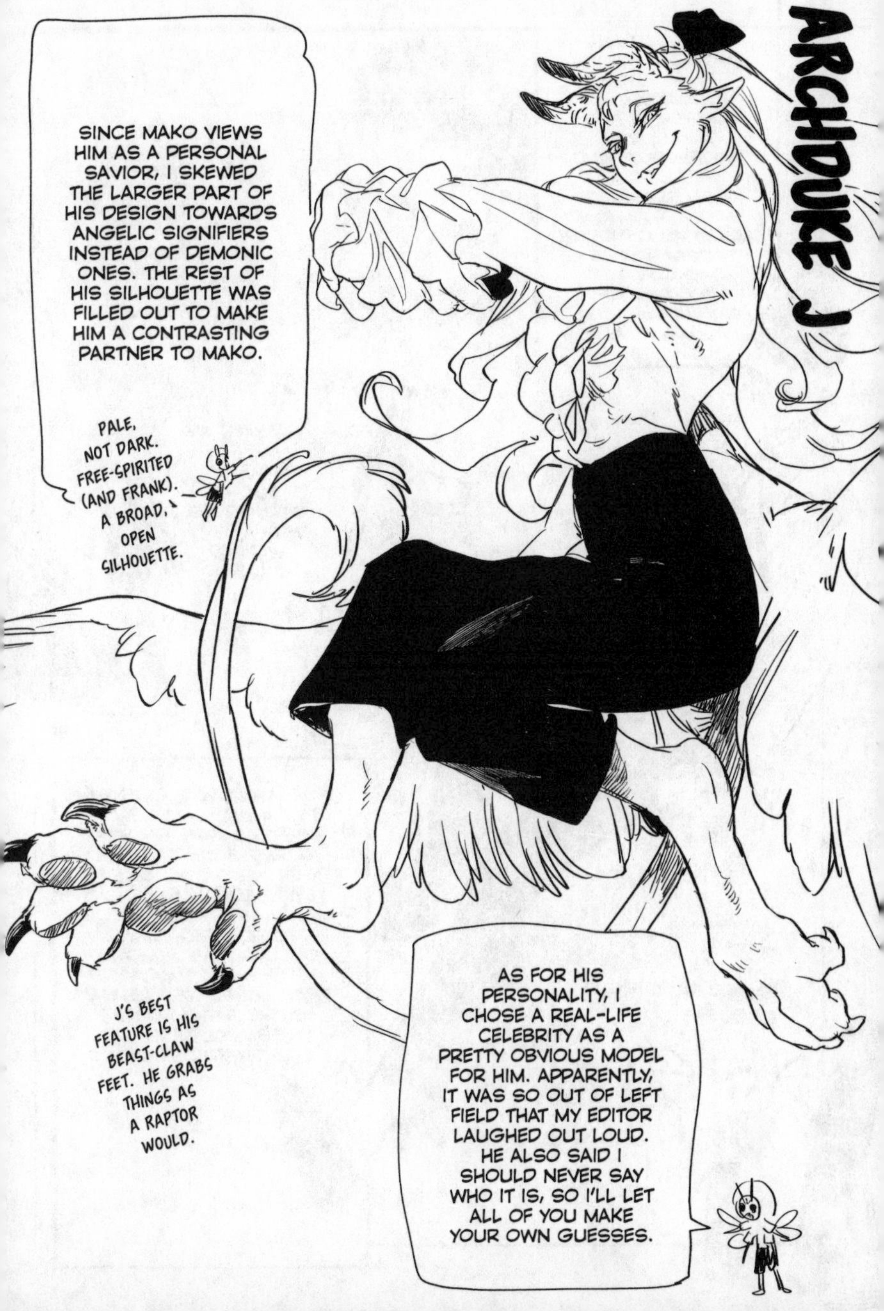
ARCHDUKE J
SINCE MAKO VIEWS HIM AS A PERSONAL SAVIOR, I SKEWED THE LARGER PART OF HIS DESIGN TOWARDS ANGELIC SIGNIFIERS INSTEAD OF DEMONIC ONES. THE REST OF HIS SILHOUETTE WAS FILLED OUT TO MAKE HIM A CONTRASTING PARTNER TO MAKO.
PALE, NOT DARK. FREE-SPIRITED (AND FRANK). A BROAD, OPEN SILHOUETTE.
AS FOR HIS PERSONALITY, I CHOSE A REAL-LIFE CELEBRITY AS A PRETTY OBVIOUS MODEL FOR HIM. APPARENTLY, IT WAS SO OUT OF LEFT FIELD THAT MY EDITOR LAUGHED OUT LOUD. HE ALSO SAID I SHOULD NEVER SAY WHO IT IS, SO I'LL LET ALL OF YOU MAKE YOUR OWN GUESSES.
J'S BEST FEATURE IS HIS BEAST-CLAW FEET. HE GRABS THINGS AS A RAPTOR WOULD.

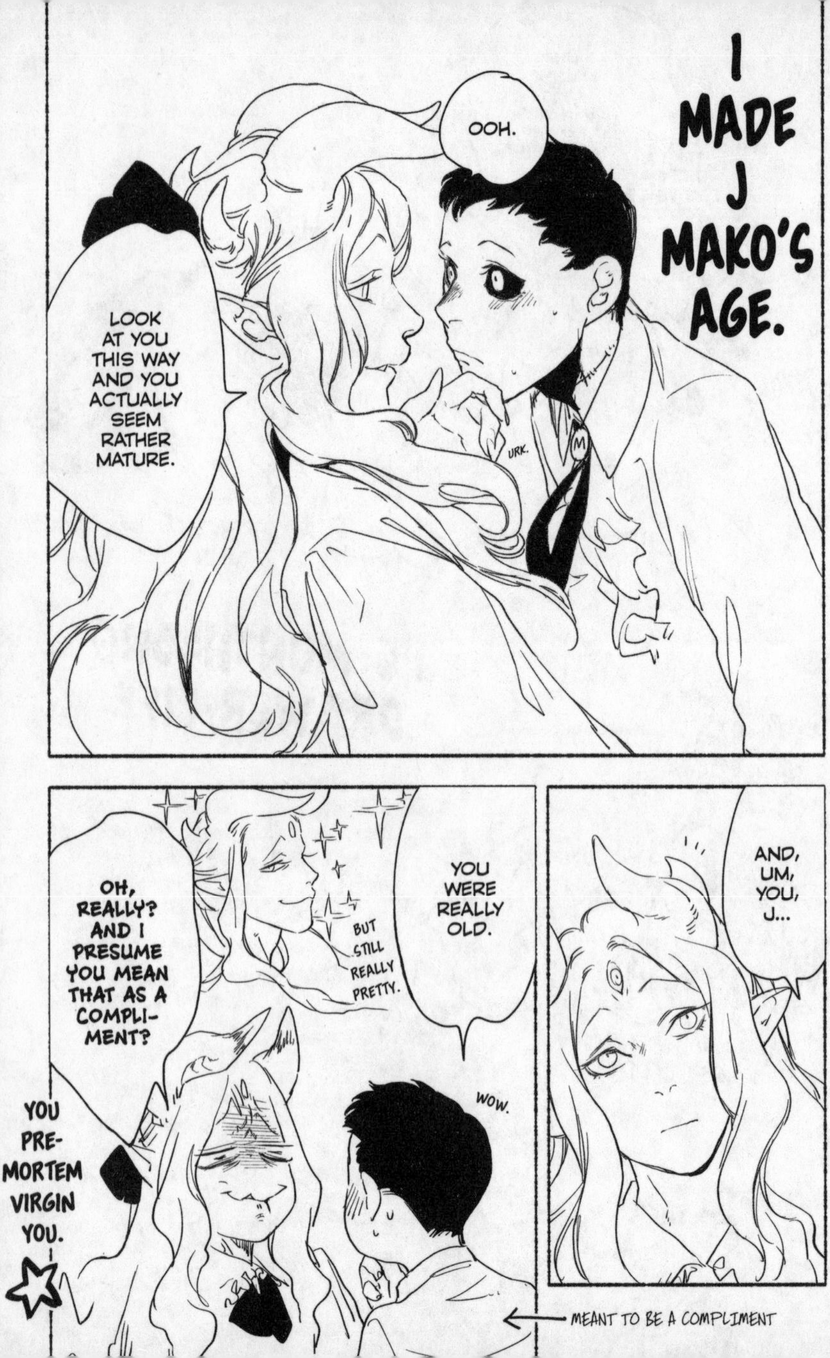
I MADE J MAKO'S AGE.
OOH.
LOOK AT YOU THIS WAY AND YOU ACTUALLY SEEM RATHER MATURE.
URK.
AND, UM, YOU, J...
YOU WERE REALLY OLD.
BUT STILL REALLY PRETTY.
OH, REALLY? AND I PRESUME YOU MEAN THAT AS A COMPLIMENT?
WOW.
YOU PRE-MORTEM VIRGIN YOU.
MEANT TO BE A COMPLIMENT

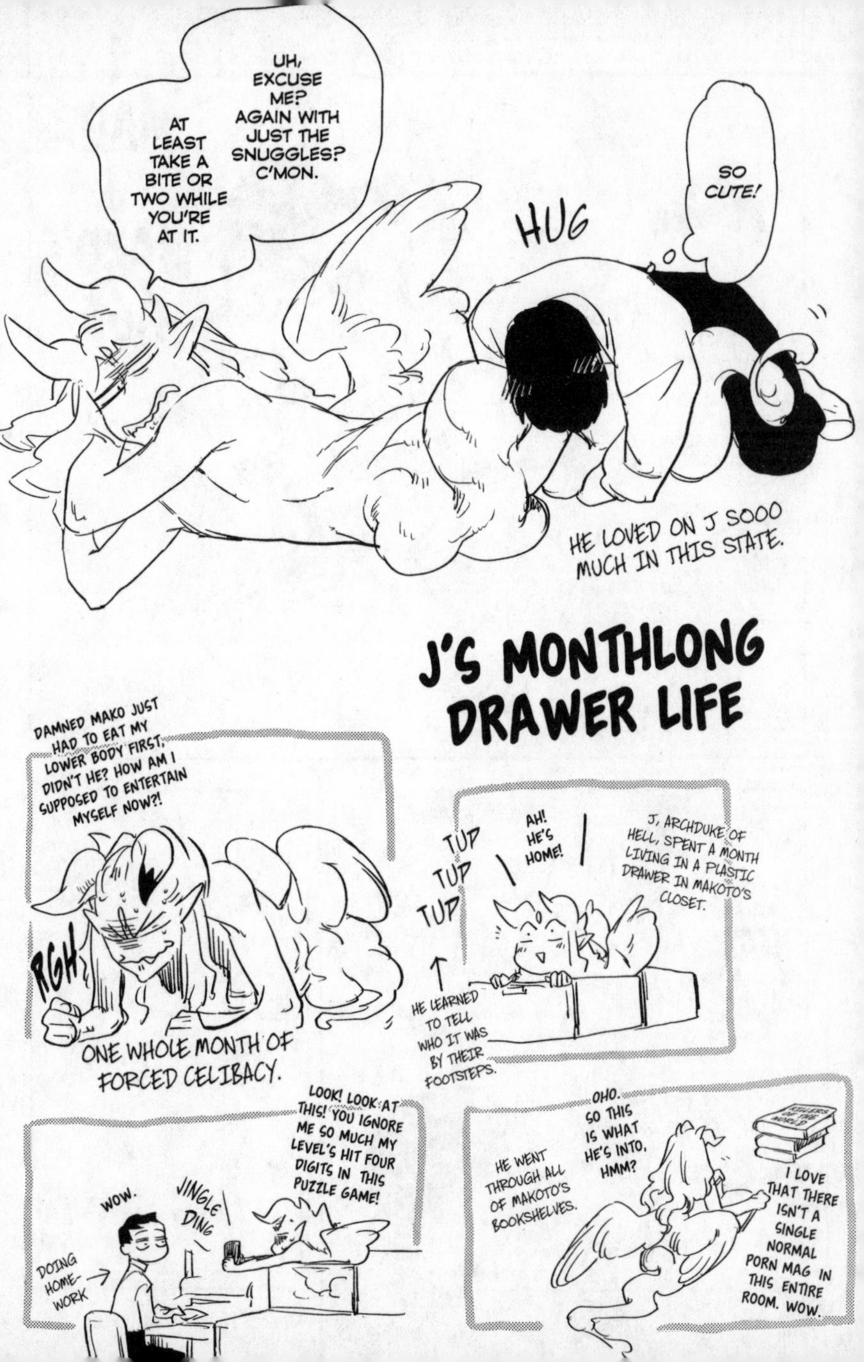
SO CUTE!
HUG
UH, EXCUSE ME? AGAIN WITH JUST THE SNUGGLES? C'MON.
AT LEAST TAKE A BITE OR TWO WHILE YOU'RE AT IT.
HE LOVED ON J SOOO MUCH IN THIS STATE.
J'S MONTHLONG DRAWER LIFE
J, ARCHDUKE OF HELL, SPENT A MONTH LIVING IN A PLASTIC DRAWER IN MAKOTO'S CLOSET.
AH! HE'S HOME!
TUP TUP TUP
HE LEARNED TO TELL WHO IT WAS BY THEIR FOOTSTEPS.
DAMNED MAKO JUST HAD TO EAT MY LOWER BODY FIRST, DIDN'T HE? HOW AM I SUPPOSED TO ENTERTAIN MYSELF NOW?!
RGH
ONE WHOLE MONTH OF FORCED CELIBACY.
I LOVE THAT THERE ISN'T A SINGLE NORMAL PORN MAG IN THIS ENTIRE ROOM. WOW.
OHO. SO THIS IS WHAT HE'S INTO, HMM?
HE WENT THROUGH ALL OF MAKOTO'S BOOKSHELVES.
LOOK! LOOK AT THIS! YOU IGNORE ME SO MUCH MY LEVEL'S HIT FOUR DIGITS IN THIS PUZZLE GAME!
JINGLE DING
WOW.
DOING HOME-WORK

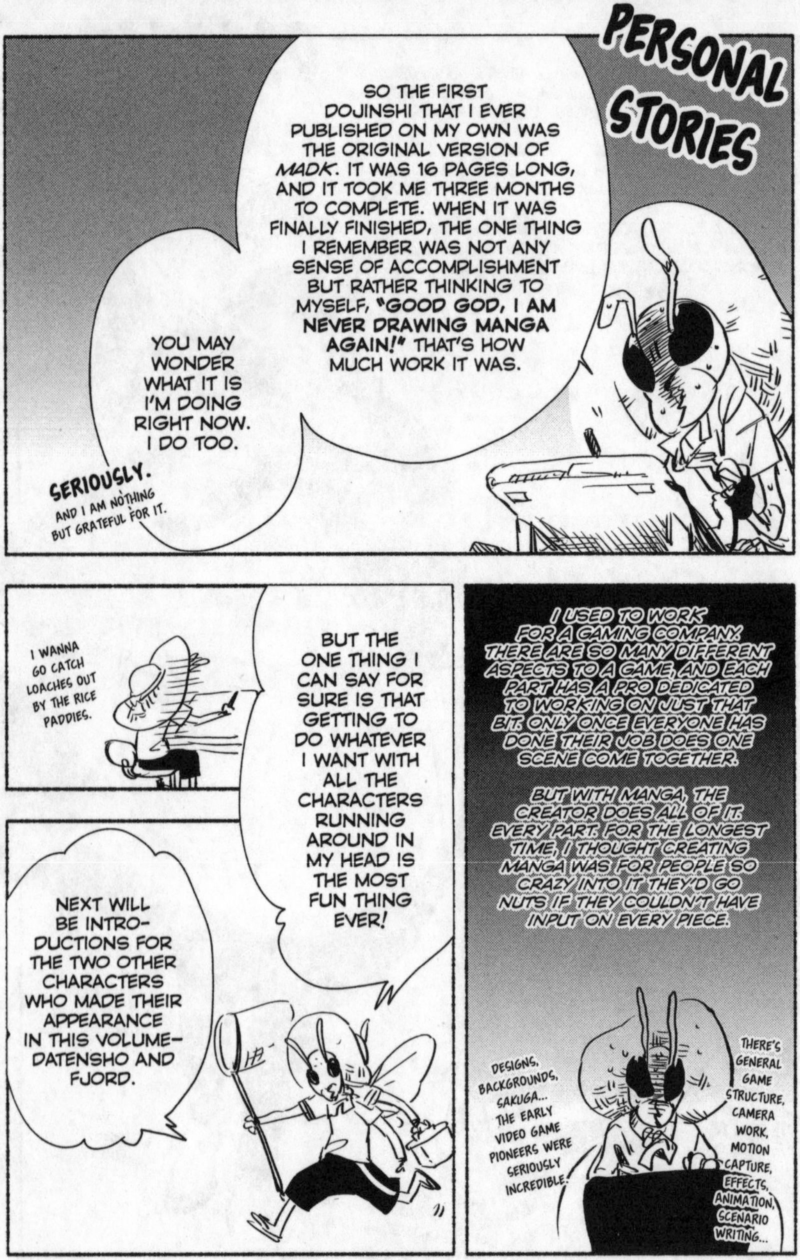
PERSONAL STORIES
SO THE FIRST DOJINSHI THAT I EVER PUBLISHED ON MY OWN WAS THE ORIGINAL VERSION OF *MADK*. IT WAS 16 PAGES LONG, AND IT TOOK ME THREE MONTHS TO COMPLETE. WHEN IT WAS FINALLY FINISHED, THE ONE THING I REMEMBER WAS NOT ANY SENSE OF ACCOMPLISHMENT BUT RATHER THINKING TO MYSELF, **"GOOD GOD, I AM NEVER DRAWING MANGA AGAIN!"** THAT'S HOW MUCH WORK IT WAS.
YOU MAY WONDER WHAT IT IS I'M DOING RIGHT NOW. I DO TOO.
SERIOUSLY.
AND I AM NOTHING BUT GRATEFUL FOR IT.
I USED TO WORK FOR A GAMING COMPANY. THERE ARE SO MANY DIFFERENT ASPECTS TO A GAME, AND EACH PART HAS A PRO DEDICATED TO WORKING ON JUST THAT BIT. ONLY ONCE EVERYONE HAS DONE THEIR JOB DOES ONE SCENE COME TOGETHER.
BUT WITH MANGA, THE CREATOR DOES ALL OF IT. EVERY PART. FOR THE LONGEST TIME, I THOUGHT CREATING MANGA WAS FOR PEOPLE SO CRAZY INTO IT THEY'D GO NUTS IF THEY COULDN'T HAVE INPUT ON EVERY PIECE.
THERE'S GENERAL GAME STRUCTURE, CAMERA WORK, MOTION CAPTURE, EFFECTS, ANIMATION, SCENARIO WRITING...
DESIGNS, BACKGROUNDS, SAKUGA... THE EARLY VIDEO GAME PIONEERS WERE SERIOUSLY INCREDIBLE.
I WANNA GO CATCH LOACHES OUT BY THE RICE PADDIES.
BUT THE ONE THING I CAN SAY FOR SURE IS THAT GETTING TO DO WHATEVER I WANT WITH ALL THE CHARACTERS RUNNING AROUND IN MY HEAD IS THE MOST FUN THING EVER!
NEXT WILL BE INTRO-DUCTIONS FOR THE TWO OTHER CHARACTERS WHO MADE THEIR APPEARANCE IN THIS VOLUME-DATENSHO AND FJORD.

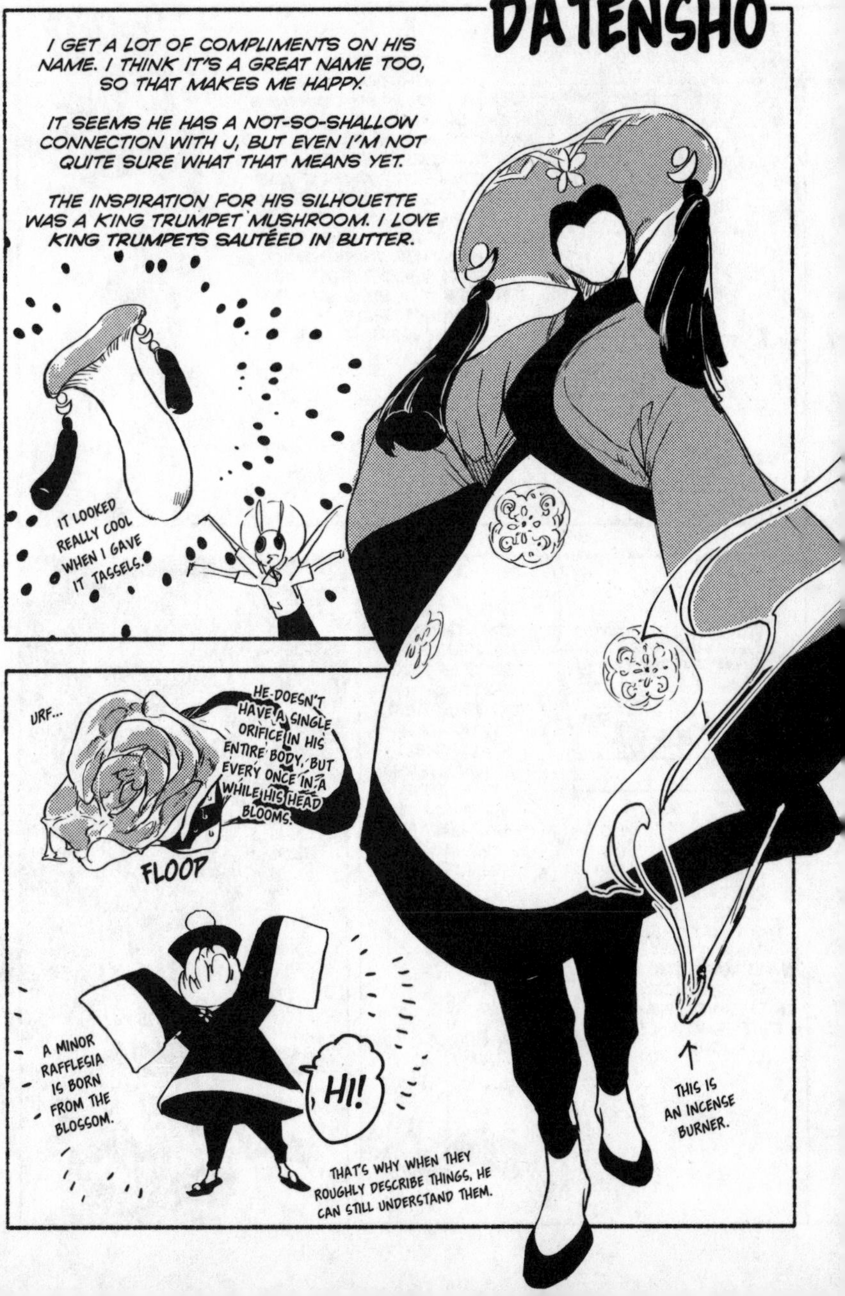
DATENSHO
I GET A LOT OF COMPLIMENTS ON HIS NAME. I THINK IT'S A GREAT NAME TOO, SO THAT MAKES ME HAPPY.
IT SEEMS HE HAS A NOT-SO-SHALLOW CONNECTION WITH J, BUT EVEN I'M NOT QUITE SURE WHAT THAT MEANS YET.
THE INSPIRATION FOR HIS SILHOUETTE WAS A KING TRUMPET MUSHROOM. I LOVE KING TRUMPETS SAUTÉED IN BUTTER.
IT LOOKED REALLY COOL WHEN I GAVE IT TASSELS.
↑ THIS IS AN INCENSE BURNER.
HE DOESN'T HAVE A SINGLE ORIFICE IN HIS ENTIRE BODY, BUT EVERY ONCE IN A WHILE HIS HEAD BLOOMS.
URF...
FLOOP
HI!
A MINOR RAFFLESIA IS BORN FROM THE BLOSSOM.
THAT'S WHY WHEN THEY ROUGHLY DESCRIBE THINGS, HE CAN STILL UNDERSTAND THEM.

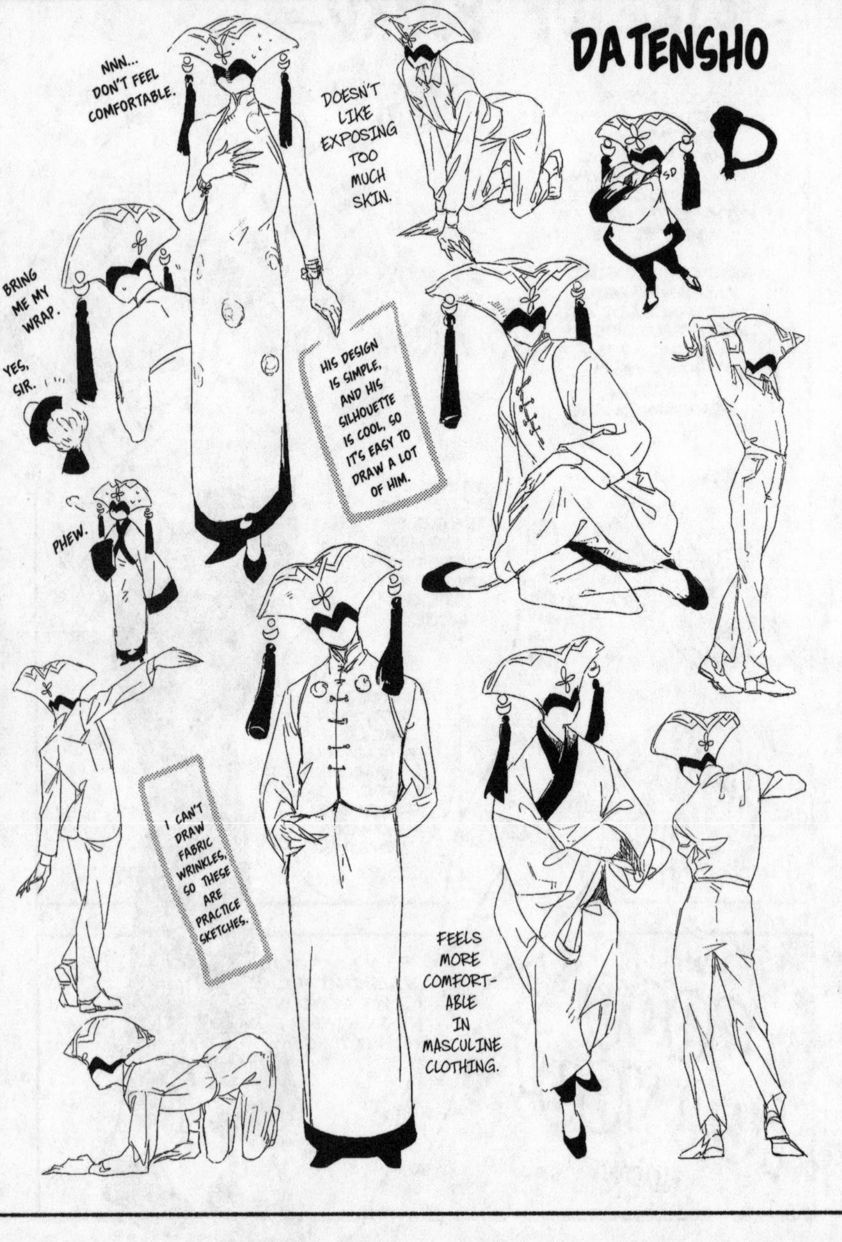
DATENSHO
D
SD
DOESN'T LIKE EXPOSING TOO MUCH SKIN.
NNN... DON'T FEEL COMFORTABLE.
HIS DESIGN IS SIMPLE, AND HIS SILHOUETTE IS COOL, SO IT'S EASY TO DRAW A LOT OF HIM.
BRING ME MY WRAP.
YES, SIR.
PHEW.
FEELS MORE COMFORT-ABLE IN MASCULINE CLOTHING.
I CAN'T DRAW FABRIC WRINKLES, SO THESE ARE PRACTICE SKETCHES.

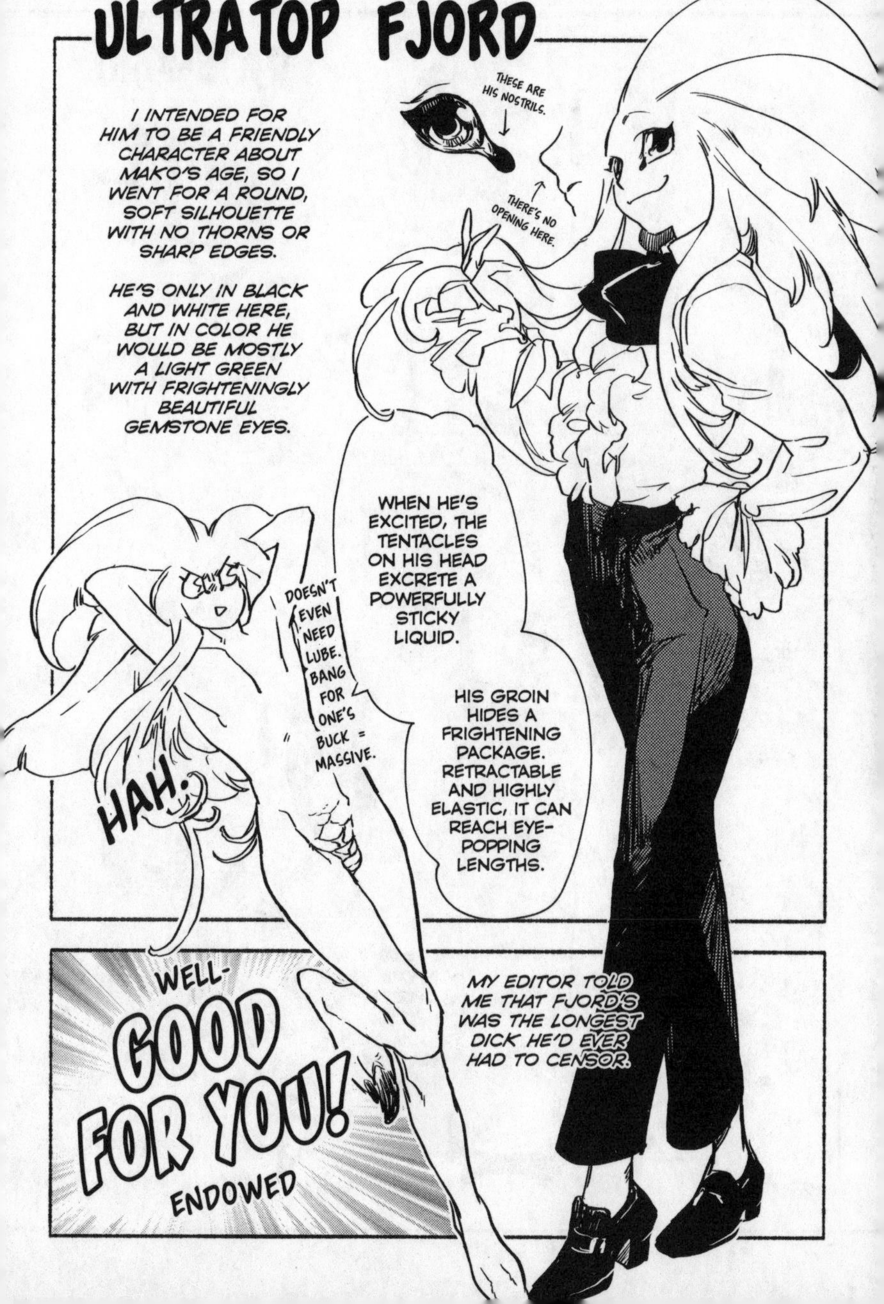
ULTRATOP FJORD
THESE ARE HIS NOSTRILS.
THERE'S NO OPENING HERE.
I INTENDED FOR HIM TO BE A FRIENDLY CHARACTER ABOUT MAKO'S AGE, SO I WENT FOR A ROUND, SOFT SILHOUETTE WITH NO THORNS OR SHARP EDGES.
HE'S ONLY IN BLACK AND WHITE HERE, BUT IN COLOR HE WOULD BE MOSTLY A LIGHT GREEN WITH FRIGHTENINGLY BEAUTIFUL GEMSTONE EYES.
WHEN HE'S EXCITED, THE TENTACLES ON HIS HEAD EXCRETE A POWERFULLY STICKY LIQUID.
HIS GROIN HIDES A FRIGHTENING PACKAGE. RETRACTABLE AND HIGHLY ELASTIC, IT CAN REACH EYE-POPPING LENGTHS.
DOESN'T EVEN NEED LUBE. BANG FOR ONE'S BUCK = MASSIVE.
HAH.
MY EDITOR TOLD ME THAT FJORD'S WAS THE LONGEST DICK HE'D EVER HAD TO CENSOR.
WELL-
GOOD FOR YOU!
ENDOWED

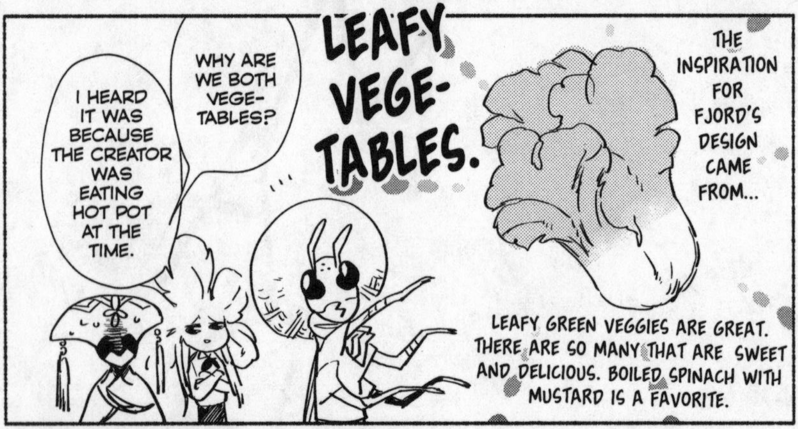
THE INSPIRATION FOR FJORD'S DESIGN CAME FROM...
LEAFY VEGE-TABLES.
WHY ARE WE BOTH VEGE-TABLES?
...
I HEARD IT WAS BECAUSE THE CREATOR WAS EATING HOT POT AT THE TIME.
LEAFY GREEN VEGGIES ARE GREAT. THERE ARE SO MANY THAT ARE SWEET AND DELICIOUS. BOILED SPINACH WITH MUSTARD IS A FAVORITE.

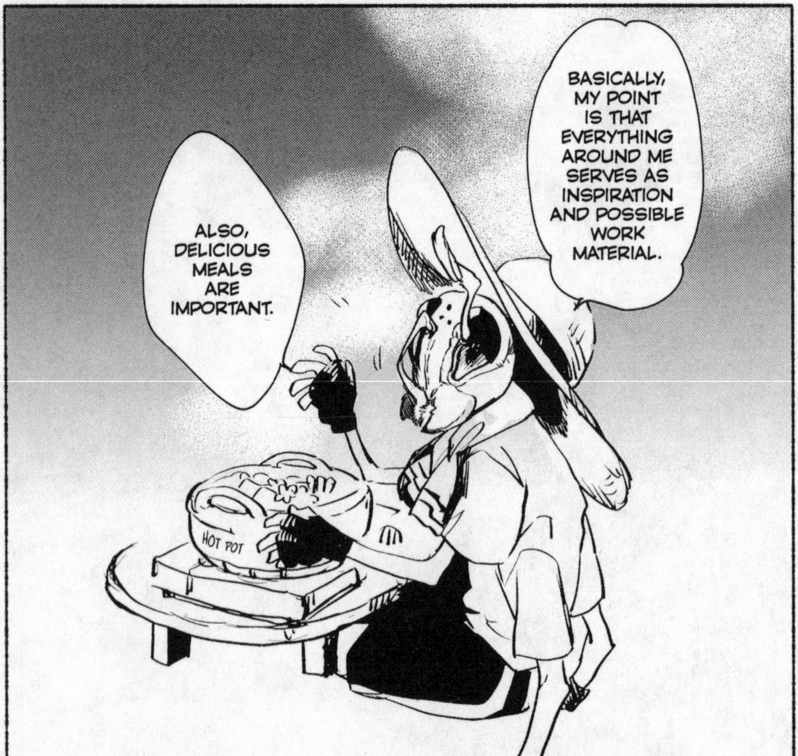
BASICALLY, MY POINT IS THAT EVERYTHING AROUND ME SERVES AS INSPIRATION AND POSSIBLE WORK MATERIAL.
ALSO, DELICIOUS MEALS ARE IMPORTANT.
HOT POT

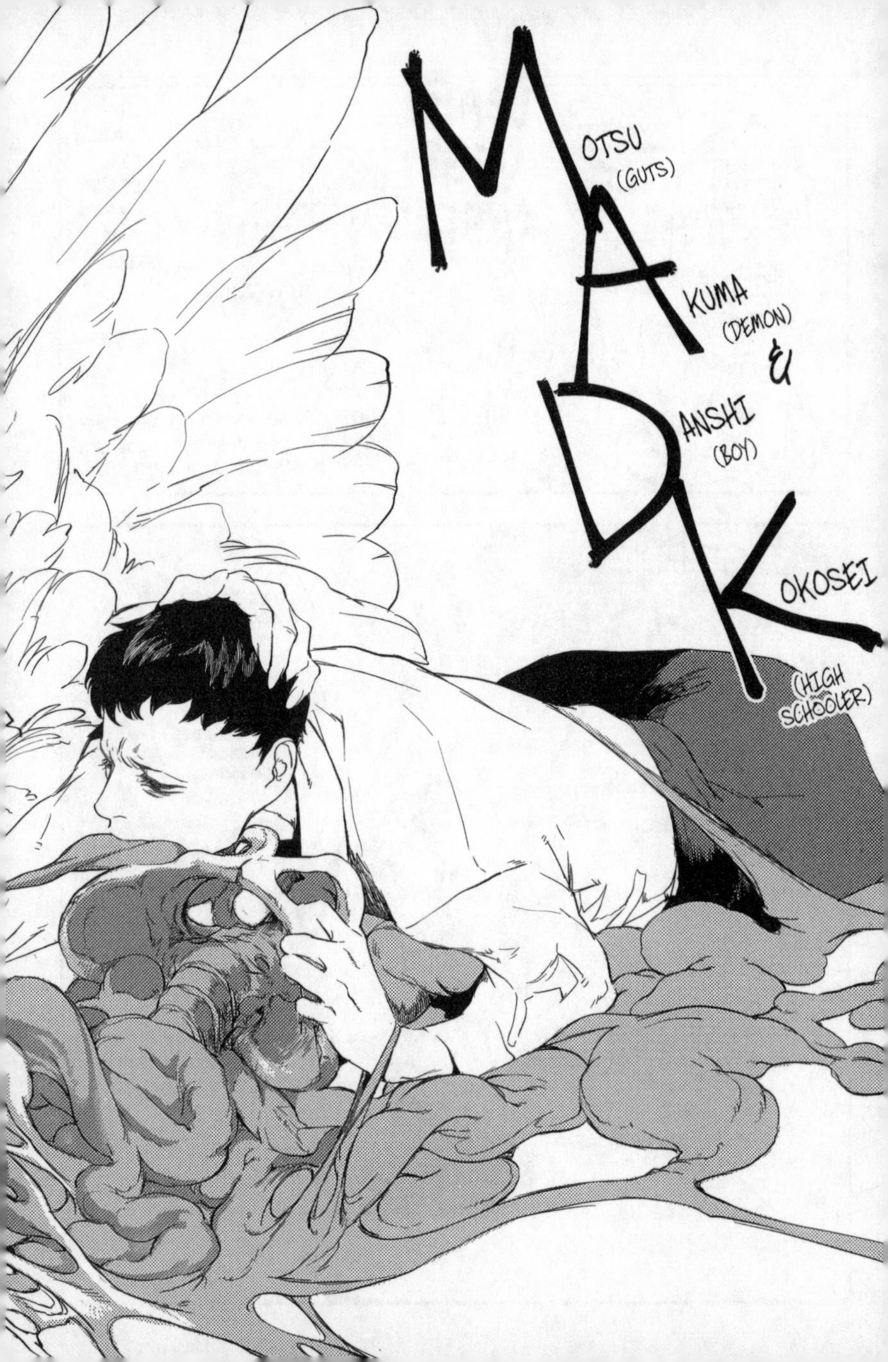

MOTSU (GUTS)
AKUMA (DEMON)
&
DANSHI (BOY)
KOKOSEI (HIGH SCHOOLER)

TALK ABOUT A SIMPLISTIC TITLE. HELLO AGAIN. I'M RYO SUZURI. IN 2017, THROUGH A MASSIVE TWIST OF FATE, I SUDDENLY BECAME A MANGA CREATOR. IT WAS LIKE A CYCLONE HAD SOMEHOW HIT MY LIFE. IT WAS THIS STORY, *MADK*, THAT KICKED IT OFF.

TO EVERYONE WHO HAS KNOWN OF IT SINCE ITS DOJINSHI DAYS, THANK YOU FOR STAYING WITH US FOR SO LONG.

TO EVERYONE JUST DISCOVERING IT, THANK YOU FOR PICKING UP A BOOK THAT IS PROBABLY A LITTLE TOO WEIRD AND A LITTLE TOO CRAZY TO EVEN BE CONSIDERED NICHE.

AND THANK YOU VERY, VERY MUCH TO MY EDITOR, WHO SAW THIS STORY ABOUT A BONKERS SEX KINK RUN WILD AND SUGGESTED WE PUBLISH IT FOR THE WORLD.

I FULLY INTEND TO DO MY BEST TO LET THEIR STORY RUN ITS FULL COURSE. I HOPE YOU WILL HONOR ME BY COMING ALONG.

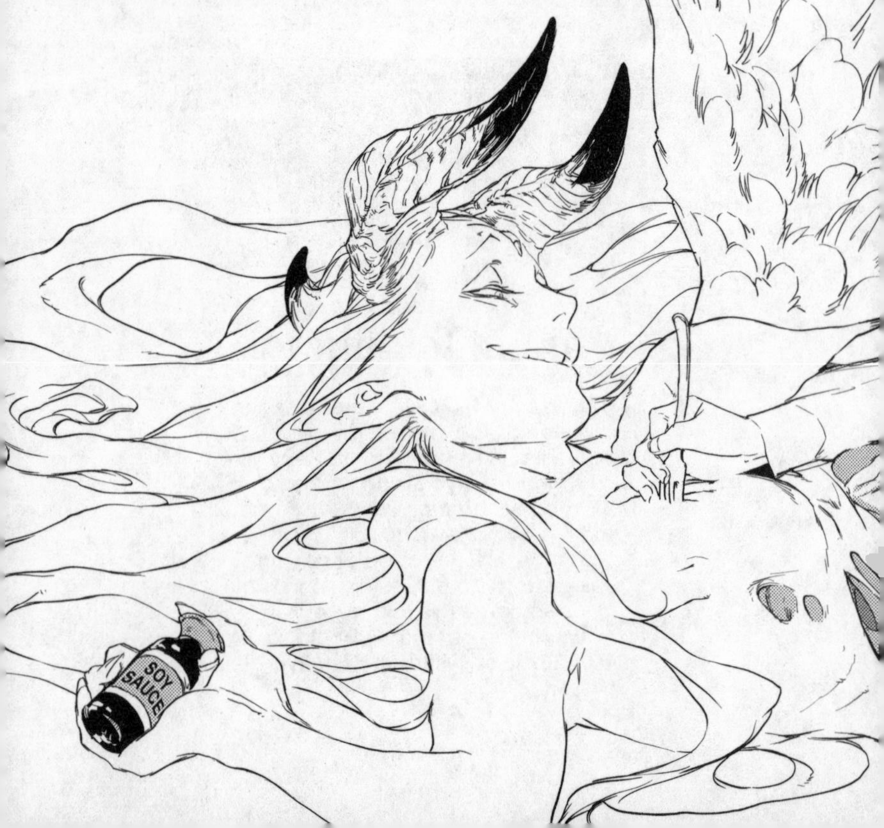
SOY SAUCE

Thank you for picking
up this volume. I hope
that this story will be an
interesting one for you.

About the Author

Although *MADK* is the creator's first
English-language release, it was previously
published in French. Prior to becoming
a mangaka, **Ryo Suzuri** worked as a
3D modeler on *Monster Hunter* for the
gaming company Capcom. In addition
to boys' love, the creator has also
released shojo and seinen under the
pen name Ryo Sumiyoshi. You
can find out more about Ryo
Suzuri on Twitter at **@szr_Ryo**.

MADK
Volume 1
SuBLime Manga Edition

Story and Art by **Ryo Suzuri**

Translation—**Adrienne Beck**
Touch-Up Art and Lettering—**Deborah Fisher**
Cover and Graphic Design—**Yukiko Whitley**
Editor—**Jennifer LeBlanc**

Original Japanese edition published by FRANCE SHOIN

This English edition is published by arrangement with FRANCE SHOIN Inc., Tokyo
in care of Tuttle-Mori Agency, Inc., Tokyo.

Canna Comics

Printed in the U.S.A.

Published by SuBLime Manga
P.O. Box 77010
San Francisco, CA 94107

10 9 8 7 6 5 4 3 2
First printing, February 2021
Second printing, September 2021

M MATURE **PARENTAL ADVISORY**
MADK is rated M for Mature and is recommended for mature readers. This volume contains graphic imagery and mature themes.

SUBLIME
www.SuBLimeManga.com

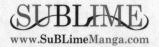

For more information

on all our products, along with the most up-to-date news on releases, series announcements, and contests, please visit us at:

 SuBLimeManga.com

 twitter.com/**SuBLimeManga**

 facebook.com/**SuBLimeManga**

 instagram.com/**SuBLimeManga**

 SuBLimeManga.tumblr.com